House Full

Fieldwork Encounters and Discoveries

A series edited by Robert Emerson and Jack Katz

House Full

INDIAN CINEMA AND
THE ACTIVE AUDIENCE

Lakshmi Srinivas

The University of Chicago Press CHICAGO & LONDON

LAKSHMI SRINIVAS is associate professor of sociology at the University of
Massachusetts, Boston.

The University of Chicago Press, Chicago 60637
The University of Chicago Press, Ltd., London
© 2016 by The University of Chicago
All rights reserved. Published 2016.
Printed in the United States of America

25 24 23 22 21 20 19 18 17 16 1 2 3 4 5

ISBN-13: 978-0-226-36142-0 (cloth)
ISBN-13: 978-0-226-36156-7 (paper)
ISBN-13: 978-0-226-36173-4 (e-book)
DOI: 10.7208/chicago/9780226361734.001.0001

Library of Congress Cataloging-in-Publication Data
Names: Srinivas, Lakshmi, author.
Title: House full : Indian cinema and the active audience / Lakshmi Srinivas.
Other titles: Fieldwork encounters and discoveries.
Description: Chicago ; London : University of Chicago Press, 2016. | Series: Fieldwork
encounters and discoveries | Includes bibliographical references and index.
Identifiers: LCCN 2015047974| ISBN 9780226361420 (cloth : alkaline paper) | ISBN
9780226361567 (paperback : alkaline paper) | ISBN 9780226361734 (e-book)
Subjects: LCSH: Motion picture audiences—India—Bangalore. | Motion pictures—
Appreciation—India—Bangalore. | Motion picture theaters—India—Bangalore. | Motion
pictures—Social aspects—India.
Classification: LCC PN1993.5.I8 S674 2016 | DDC 791.430954—dc23 LC record available at
http://lccn.loc.gov/2015047974

♾ This paper meets the requirements of ANSI/NISO Z39.48-1992 (Permanence of Paper).

For my parents

TABLE OF CONTENTS

A C K N O W L E D G M E N T S

I am deeply grateful to Bangaloreans for their hospitality and many kindnesses without which this book could not have been written. I would like to thank filmgoers, fans, families whom I accompanied to the cinema, and others who took the time to share their experiences and views. They must remain name-less for confidentiality reasons and also because some I never got to know by name. Thanks are also due to all those in the film business—theater managers and staff, distributors, filmmakers, and members of the cast and crew who taught me so much. My special thanks to (in alphabetical order) Nagathihalli Chandrashekar, Puneet Rajkumar, Ramesh Aravind, Shivarajkumar, S. V. Ra-jendra Singh Babu and Mrs. Rajendra Singh Babu, and T. S. Nagabharana, who gave me time and access to their sets, some even granting me permission to film and photograph on set. I would also like to acknowledge the officials at the Karnataka Film Chamber of Commerce.

A number of people in Bangalore and in the United States helped with intro-ductions and connections, facilitated the research in other ways, and extended their friendship. While I am unable to acknowledge them all individually here, I wish to express my sincere thanks to M. Bhaktavatsala of Sharada Movies, Ashok Kashyap, Mr. Raman, Mr. Shinde, Richard Louis, Rajagopal Kadambi, Shama Bhat, G. K. Karanth, B. G. Kulkarni, V. N. Lakshminarayana, Sundar Sarukkai and Dhanu Nayak, Hamsa Kalyani, Aparna Rao, and Ram Kumar; to Navroze Contractor, Sharath Srinivasan, and Nandith Jaisimha for taking photographs at my request; and to B. S. Srivani, S. Shailaja, Mrs. Kavitha Jamakhandi, and the friendly staff at the *Deccan Herald*, E. Raghavan, Vrushali Haldipur, and P. Nataraj. Paul Fernandes of aPaulogy, Bangalore, granted me permission to reprint his delightful watercolor cartoons of Bangalore theaters and graciously agreed to draw maps of Bangalore Cantonment and City expressly for the book. It is a privilege to be able to have his artwork illustrate the book.

This book has benefited from the scholarly advice of a number of people along the way. I wish to thank Steven Clayman, Robert Emerson, and Vivian Sobchack at the University of California, Los Angeles, for their intellectual support. I am indebted to Jack Katz in particular for his critical interest and guidance, for sharing his unique insights, and for his unfailing support over the years. Most recently Jack undertook to translate sections of Emmanuel Grimaud's ethnography of Bombay filmmaking to allow me to access it as per the recommendations of the anonymous reviewers at the University of Chicago Press. I can never adequately express my gratitude.

House Full is a somewhat different book from the one I set out to write. Its present form and organization are the result of unforeseen circumstances, accidents, and delays, as well as feedback and critical interest from friends and colleagues. My sincere thanks to Freddy Bailey, Sara Dickey, Wimal Dissanayake, Jyoti Puri, Bandana Purkayastha, and Arvind Shah who gave generously of their time and read draft chapters, some the entire manuscript. Howard Becker offered thoughtful comments and practical advice on an earlier draft of the manuscript. Paul Hockings drew on his wealth of knowledge about South India to offer suggestions for reworking sections of the book and patiently fielded my queries regarding photographs. I am grateful to the anonymous reviewers at the University of Chicago Press for their insightful and incisive assessment of the manuscript and their constructive recommendations, which were of enormous help in revising the manuscript and sharpening its focus and argument.

The book has developed through multiple visits to the field and through articles published in journals, papers I presented at conferences, seminars, and workshops. I am grateful to Eli Anderson, Sara Dickey, Wimal Dissanayake, Rajinder Dudrah, Moti Gokulsing, Preminda Jacob, and Paul Hockings for their valuable feedback on articles I had submitted to *Visual Anthropology* (1998, 2009), *South Asian Popular Culture* (2005, 2010), *Ethnography* (2010), *Media, Culture and Society* (2002), and Routledge (2013). Thanks are also due to participants at conferences and workshops for their contributions. While the contributions of many have improved the book, adding to whatever merits it may have, the errors and faults are mine alone.

Research was supported by the Leroy Nieman Center for the Study of Arts and Society at the University of California, Los Angeles; the Joseph P. Healey grant; the dean's research and travel awards and the Endowed Faculty Career

Development Fund at the University of Massachusetts, Boston, each of which carried modest funding for travel and fieldwork and reduced my teaching responsibilities. A faculty fellowship at the Newhouse Center for the Humanities at Wellesley College allowed me to write part-time. I was also fortunate to receive a fellowship from the National Endowment for the Humanities, which supported the crucial last stage of fieldwork and writing.

My warm thanks to Claire Thomlinson and Helen Snively for their careful copyediting, encouragement, and friendship. At the University of Chicago Press, Doug Mitchell gave his enthusiastic and friendly support through the many delays in the completion of the manuscript. Kyle Wagner was equally helpful in bringing the manuscript to its final form. I would also like to thank Erik Carlson, Steve LaRue, Ashley Pierce, and Martin White.

Many friends and colleagues expressed an interest and offered moral, intellectual, and other kinds of support. My sincere and heartfelt thanks to colleagues and friends at the University of Massachusetts, Boston, in Cambridge, Massachusetts, and the University of California, and especially to Veena Das, Sara Dickey, Wimal Dissanayake, Rajinder Dudrah, Rachel Dwyer, Brian Halley, Preminda Jacob, Moti Gokulsing, Susan Gore, Kirin Narayan, Bandana Purkayastha, Vinod Tewari, and Mridula Udayagiri. Freddy Bailey offered me the loan of his study and peace and quiet to write. Had I accepted his kind offer, the book might have been completed earlier.

I cannot thank Krishna and Aruna Chidambi enough for their warmth and enormous generosity, for opening their home to me, for taking an interest in my research, and for their help. My deep thanks to Anuradha Rao for her kindness when we were both students, and to Bharati Mandapati, Kalpana Asok, and Kishore Seshadri. Popsi Narasimhan, my brother-in-law and a movie enthusiast, helped in countless ways both in Bangalore and in Boston, not least with his computer expertise. There are no words to thank my sister, Tulasi Srinivas, who put up with me throughout and affectionately extended all manner of help, including taking photographs and offering advice. My parents have been a constant source of support and inspiration; theirs and my sister's affection kept me going at times when I despaired of completing the book. My father shared in my excitement with fieldwork, and I am still discovering what I have to learn from him. Some of my most poignant memories are of introducing the social world of cinema I became acquainted with to him and to my mother, who patiently read multiple drafts of chapters, gave me detailed and invaluable feedback, and shared stories of her cinemagoing. This book is dedicated to them.

CHAPTER 1

Introduction

It's not—we have done something. We've made only a film, but the audience has made it history.

BOMBAY FILMMAKER YASH CHOPRA[1]

The popular Indian film is recognized the world over as the "Bollywood" song-and-dance extravaganza, a variable mix of melodrama, spectacle, travelogue, action, romance, and comedy. Less well known is the culture surrounding film reception in India, yet anyone familiar with India's cinema halls will have encountered to varying degrees the social and participatory aesthetic that shapes film viewing. People talk throughout the film; piercing whistles, yells and cheers from boisterous "front benchers" punctuate the screening. Cinema halls are sites of performance and spectacle both on and off the screen. Young men shout out improvised dialogue, make "catcalls" and lewd comments, people sing or hum along with the songs, and some may even dance. Audiences are known to import ritual practices of (Hindu) worship to the cinema hall as they propitiate the stars on-screen with incense and lighted camphor and throw coins and flowers at the screen in appreciation. If the film fails to live up to expectations, or if the electricity goes off, viewers take out their frustration on their surroundings, ripping the upholstery with razor blades and knives. Audiences also wreak havoc on seating, "pull the stuffing out" in carnivalesque exuberance when, for example, they respond to on-screen spectacle such as the heroine's charms.[2]

Cinema's roots in a performance tradition and in "folk culture"[3] are evident in the elaborations outside the theater. Newly released films are celebrated as festivals with processions, bands, and fireworks. Theaters decorated with marigolds, jasmine, roses, mango leaves, and banana fronds present an auspicious face. "Cutouts" of the stars in costume, fifty to eighty feet tall, loom above the street, fixed to the theater facade and garlanded on the occasion of the premiere. This is a cinema that "overwhelms the senses"[4] and that Euro-centric film theory, with its focus on film texts and narratives, seems to have overlooked.

"House Full" signs outside theaters not only alert audiences that a show is sold out but also serve as publicity for the film and the theater even as they mark an auspicious start to a film's run at the exhibition setting. House Full is also shorthand for the excitement of crowds. It conjures images of an auditorium packed with enthusiasts: people spilling into the aisles, the deafening ovations that greet the arrival of the star on-screen, the frenzy that can accompany ticket purchase, and the excesses of fans; in short, the effervescent spectacle that constitutes "film experience." Film reviews refer to it, and a film's life in the theater depends on the number of days it is "House Full." As is true for "House Full" signs, understanding film's significance calls for an embedded perspective, one informed by cinema's lived social realities.

Drawing on ethnographic research in the southern Indian city of Bangalore, in this book I take film studies "off the couch" and into the field toward an "experience-near" understanding that is grounded in cinema's expressive culture and in its social world as well as in audiences' cinemagoing practices and experiences rather than in the analysis of film texts.[5] I came to the study as a moviegoer. While a student at the University of California, far away from home in India, the cinema provided one of my few diversions from the pressures of student life. Watching Hollywood movies in West Los Angeles and Santa Monica and elsewhere in the United States, I was struck by the anonymity of the experience and the individualized and silent absorption that characterized in-theater experience at these venues. In comparison, watching Bombay films screened to South Asian audiences in and around Los Angeles, I felt I was in another world. Here families chatted loudly, children screamed and ran around, people loudly "passed comments" on the film and applauded favorite stars and "dialogue delivery"—recreating, though in muted fashion, the cinema hall experience in India. Traveling to and from Bangalore to visit my parents, I happened to watch the same Hollywood film in the United States and in a cinema hall there on a couple of occasions and found the experience of the film itself to be vastly different. Implicit comparison of these different social worlds of cinema framed my interest from the start.

The subtitle of the book refers to the overtly participatory reception aesthetic that shapes the experience of watching films in India's cinema halls. The *active audience*, a key theme in the study of media reception, gained prominence with British cultural studies,[6] which highlighted audience agency in the interpretation or "decoding" of media texts; it was a response both to

European theories of media domination and functionalist studies of media "effects" in which media were seen to *act on* passive audiences who were seen as recipients of ideological messages and subject to the power of the medium. The term has since become highly contested, attracting its share of critics.[7] It has led to questions of what *active* or *passive* mean when one is considering audience behavior and engagement with media even though selective audiences, such as those for early cinema in America, are described as "vibrant," "riotous," and "raucous."[8] I use *active* to describe the voluble cinema hall audience and an in-theater experience marked by spontaneity, improvisation, and performance that is far removed from the silent absorption of film associated with mainstream audiences in Anglo-American and Western European exhibition (multiplex) settings. I am not arguing that *all* Indian cinemagoers necessarily engage with films overtly and with an interactive and participatory aesthetic to the same degree or that such an aesthetic is to be found *only* among Indian audiences. Anthropologists Elizabeth Hahn and before her Hortense Powdermaker, for example, have described interactive and voluble audiences in Tonga and in (what was then) Rhodesia. Historically, film audiences in the West were loud and participatory, while present-day participatory audiences of film are associated with cult films and "midnight movies" such as the *Rocky Horror Picture Show*. However, what I have described as an active aesthetic, or an active audience, is part of a mainstream aesthetic of engaging with cinema that can be found to varying degrees in cinema halls in India and with Indian moviegoers watching Indian films outside India.

Writing about cinema in Egypt, anthropologist Walter Armbrust asks, "what happens in other societies when the lights go down?" Similarly, one may ask, what is "film reception" in India where an aesthetic of "active viewing" shapes in-theater experience? What can the "less familiar" setting of cinema in India tell us about film,[9] its nature, and the audiences' experience and about cinema more broadly and its social existence? When I next returned to Bangalore in 1996, I carried out an exploratory study with these questions in mind. I interviewed moviegoers and distributed a survey to school and college students. I spoke to old Bangaloreans and journalists who reported on cinema, met officials at the local Karnataka Film Chamber of Commerce, and watched movies in theaters. This pilot study of sorts led to an intensive period of field research that started in 1998 when I spent about four months in Bangalore. I continued fieldwork through return visits there over the years, the most recent in 2009–2010 and in 2012. Between visits I kept in touch with filmgoers, film-business insiders, journalists, film commentators, and others in Bangalore and continued watching the films on DVDs. What emerged was a study situated in the dispersed sites and spaces in which audiences encounter films, in film-going rituals, and in the social relations and negotiations that "produce" and refashion film and its collective experience.

My association with the field over several years, at a time when both the Indian film business and Bangalore were undergoing rapid change, added to the challenges of fieldwork. But the period I had inadvertently focused on—the late 1990s, after India had enacted its economic liberalization policies—turned out to be significant in the context of the changes that followed and that were evident each time I returned to India. I revised my "sense" of cinema in Bangalore, taking into account some of the changes underway as well as things that had stayed the same with a view to "render[ing] my accounts more faithful to the realities of the field."[10] However, the focus of this book largely remains on cinema in Bangalore in the late 1990s.

My decision to examine cinema "in the field," in Bangalore, brought my study closer to some of the urban ethnographies of the Chicago School and to sociology and social anthropology in India, where ethnographers studied societies they had lived in and were familiar with, rather than traditional anthropological field studies. I had lived in Bangalore since the early 1970s and attended both school and college there. My familiarity with the city, its spaces and way of life, afforded me the advantages of "opportunistic research."[11] However, growing up in Bangalore I rarely visited the cinema. Ours was not a family that saw many movies, and it was only in college that I ventured to Hindi (Bollywood) films with classmates. I was therefore not all that familiar with the terrain or "landscape" of cinema in Bangalore, which thus proved to be a new field site.[12]

In this chapter I provide background for the research and describe the field setting, briefly identifying some of the limitations, both theoretical and methodological, that have shaped the study of film and its reception and the resultant gaps in understanding that have arisen as a result. I draw on multidisciplinary research and studies of cinema both within and outside India to examine what an immersive ethnography of film reception would be. In addition, I note some of the challenges for a grounded perspective on cinema that addresses actual audiences and the social realities of cinema. Finally, I outline my research strategy and comment on fieldwork.

THE SETTING AND THE FIELD

Bangalore, the capital of the South Indian state of Karnataka, is now recognized internationally for its information technology industry and business process outsourcing. This is a fairly new identity for the city, which has cycled through many avatars: once a sleepy "pensioner's paradise," India's "garden city" and later "pub city," it has also been known for its public-sector industries and as a "science city" for its many research institutions, some world renowned.

Demographically, Bangalore is diverse, home to many ethnic and linguistic groups: Kannada speakers local to the state make up roughly 33 percent of the city's residents, but there are also sizeable numbers of Urdu, Hindi, Tamil, Telugu Konkani, and Tulu speakers and Keralites, Marathis, Gujarathis, Punjabis, and other in-migrants from other states. In the 1990s Bangalore was recognized as the second fastest-growing city in India after New Delhi. The city's population grew from nearly five million in the late 1990s to 8.3 million in 2010 even as its name was changed from the anglicized Bangalore to Bengaluru, the result of proregionalist movements in the face of increasing in-migration.

Leisure and entertainment in Bangalore has for decades revolved around cricket, horse racing, the city's parks and gardens, its many clubs and associations, and festivals and holiday outings. Classical music and dance recitals as well as popular music concerts, fashion shows, visiting ballet troupes, theater productions—including a lively English-language theater as well as folk theater and dance-drama performances such as *Yakshagana* indigenous to the region—and agricultural fairs (*sande*) on the outskirts of the city have long presented residents with a cultural mix of activities and events. The annual dog and flower shows and the Nilgiris cake exhibition around Christmas are attended by middle-class residents and by those who participate in the city's anglicized Cantonment lifestyle. Several nightclubs, restaurants, pubs, ice-cream parlors, coffee shops, *darshinis* (local fast-food style eateries for those who want to eat on the go), and small hotels attest to Bangaloreans' fondness for eating out. Recently, luxury hotels, resorts, and upscale malls have multiplied.

Cinema has been a constant in the city since the early 1900s. Some of the earliest movie theaters doubled as dance halls when British troops were stationed in Bangalore. The Elgin, the city's oldest movie theater, which screened films until 2011, dated back to 1896, only a year after the cinema was invented in Paris. Filmgoing in Bangalore and in India transcends social differences of class, regional culture, and ethnicity and is a popular pastime for people from almost all walks of life. A filmmaker informed me that in the 1950s and 1960s Bangalore was "Asia's number one city" for its cinemas.[13] According to a resident cinematographer, the area in and around Kempegowda Road alone had 50 to 60 theaters.[14] The city presented another advantage for ethnographic study of cinema, one I did not consider initially, as I expected to focus solely on audiences and their film-viewing experiences. It is also the site of the Kannada-language film business, known irrepressibly as Sandalwood.[15] The logic of naming was explained to me by a filmmaker: "Hollywood, Bollywood, Sandalwood!" (after all, sandalwood was a local product). The city potentially offered access to filmmakers and producers as well.

The study of cinema in any city or "place" will have its particularities that evoke the place. More recently, film scholars who have pursued situated studies of cinema have made a case for the "ordinariness" of their choice of locale. According to Mark Jancovich, studying cinema in Nottingham makes sense precisely because it is not a "metropolitan centre" or world city like London, New York, or Los Angeles.[16] Therefore, a note on Bangalore's "exceptionalism" is in order.

Some have argued that Bangalore cannot provide an example for other cities in India, given its distinctiveness on many fronts. Even before the information technology industry was established there, the city was described as "middle-class" and "cosmopolitan," more Westernized or anglicized in many ways than other cities in India. In fact, Bangalore's cinema audiences may not be as boisterous as those elsewhere in India. Within South India, it is widely believed that film audiences in the states of Tamil Nadu and Andhra Pradesh can be really rowdy; one moviegoer remarked that they are "nothing compared to audiences in Madras or Andhra [in the neighboring states of Tamil Nadu and Andhra Pradesh]. Man, those guys are crazy!" Yet based on my experiences, I argue that Bangalore does provide a suitable setting to study the reception aesthetic I identify as "active" and that is to be found elsewhere in India perhaps in a more heightened form.

The broader context or "field" is also India's mammoth film business. Both in terms of the number of films produced each year and viewers reached, the Indian film industry is the largest in the world, annually producing eight hundred to one thousand films, approximately twice as many as Hollywood and selling between three and four billion tickets, roughly a billion more than Hollywood.[17] Yet the power and influence of Indian cinema cannot be gleaned simply from statistics on the number of films made or from ticket sales. Ashis Nandy describes the Indian film as "society's most influential myth-maker."[18] Along with cricket, popular cinema is a national passion dominating not only entertainment but public life. Film music is heard everywhere—in shops, restaurants, taxicabs, on the street, even at festival celebrations and political rallies, and more recently as cell phone ringtones. Films supply content for television programs, and a large number of film magazines in a variety of languages address the public appetite for celebrity news and gossip. The visual culture of popular cinema influences fashion and provides a template for weddings and honeymoons. *Filmi* dialogue inserts itself into conversations. Cinema has shaped political life; several film stars have become politicians, and fan clubs double as campaign centers for stars turned politicians.

Thus, cinema exists in the interstices of everyday life in India. Its power is evident in its ability to mobilize people, in the spectacle created by the massing of crowds and the outpouring of public emotion. The funerals of stars, for example, draw millions of mourners, and funeral processions can bring entire cities to a halt. In 1987, when the Tamil film icon and chief minister of the state, M. G. Ramachandran (MGR) died, "People were crying in the streets; shops closed." Madras city "witnessed one of the world's largest funerals," with over two million mourners, many of whom had traveled long distances to walk in the funeral procession. Mock funerals were organized by those who could not attend; in them, "images of MGR were taken in procession and buried with full ritual. Countless young men tonsured their heads, a Hindu ritual performed when a family member dies.[19] Thirty-one followers, unable to contain their grief, committed suicide."[20] In July 2000, the bizarre kidnapping of Dr. Rajkumar, screen legend beloved by the Kannada masses, by the elephant poacher K. M. Veerappan, brought Bangalore to a standstill. The city shutdown, or *bandh*, lasted for three days amid fears of angry fans going on the rampage. Streets and public places were empty, public transportation ground to a halt; schools were closed for fifteen days and cinemas for nearly two months. Even the "virtual city" was paralyzed, as many homes lost their cable connections.[21] Cell phone services were reportedly suspended after being overwhelmed with calls.

The "field," then, includes Indian cinema's "public culture," defined by Arjun Appadurai and Carol Breckenridge as a "zone" or "arena" of "cultural debate," a "partially organized space" where various cultural forms encounter and contest one another.[22] Included are "producers of culture, audiences and the mass media . . . in relationship with one another."[23] Building on these understandings, I shift the locus of inquiry from the film as aesthetic object to the social practice of cinema, its articulation with place and local traditions, to explore cinema at the "reception-exhibition interface,"[24] its lived culture, one of the most under-studied aspects of film in India and elsewhere.

The anthropologist Ulf Hannerz has argued that "diversity is anthropology's business" and that the study of "the variety of human life" is what anthropology has always been about.[25] My objective is also to bring greater diversity to current understandings of film and its reception that are dominated by "Westerncentric" film studies. As a local study that addresses cinema's "indigenous qualities," this ethnography of cinema in Bangalore provides a concrete case to question the transcultural relevance of theories of film and its reception that have rested on a "Western tradition" of mass communication that focuses on texts and on the content of communication messages[26] and on ideas of the mass audience. In film theory, ideas of hypothetical and imagined spectators are derived from the conventions of Hollywood narrative film[27] and the monolingual Hollywood model. Even phenomenological studies of reception take for granted a normative "Western" reception setting and culture.[28]

Hindi-language cinema made in Bombay is the most visible of India's many cinemas worldwide and is viewed across India and South Asia and the Middle East. However, given India's decentralized film production, several states have their own film industries that produce feature films in a variety of vernacular languages. Cinema in India is thus an expression of the country's mind-boggling diversity. There are twenty-two official languages recognized, but many more are identified, each with "their own scripts, grammatical structures and cultural assumptions."[29] Linguistic plurality is only one dimension of India's diversity that has an effect on cinema. Commercial cinema has evolved in the context of the need to appeal to audiences differentiated by religion, class, a number of regional cultures, caste, rural-urban differences, and varying levels of education and literacy.[30]

The plurality and heterogeneity that characterizes cinema's public culture, its institutions, and its audiences is reflected in Bangalore. A filmmaker described the city as a place where "a person can watch at least 3 to 4 languages [regional-language films] and go from one culture to another: world cultures, local cultures, you have so much choice!" Apart from Bombay films, cinema halls and now multiplexes screen locally produced Kannada (language) films as well as films made in the neighboring states of Tamil Nadu, Andhra Pradesh, and Kerala, each in the language spoken in the state, in addition to Hollywood films in English. This diversity of film offerings was observable even in the 1950s.[31] This multilingual and multicultural cinema field together with its heterogeneous audiences leads to varying forms of aesthetic engagement and constructions of cinema and its experience. The very experience of the cinema hall is shaped by social difference as moviegoers' practices of engaging with the film or of simply occupying public space draw attention to and heighten differences between them. People from various walks of life, bringing their different sensibilities, worldviews, and styles of aesthetic engagement, even clash over *how* to watch or engage with a film and each other. Cinema becomes a battleground; skirmishes break out in the auditorium as groups of moviegoers fight over the film and theater space, seeking to appropriate and recast the reception experience.

The tensions between heterogeneity and the need for a broad appeal affect all branches of making and delivering films to audiences. Take exhibition, for example: until the arrival of the multiplex in India, urban audiences saw films exclusively in cinema halls: single-screen theaters that seat over a thousand people, where seating is stratified by ticket price. Yet even this arrangement does not accommodate all moviegoers from all walks of life. Located on the outskirts of cities or near slum settlements and in rural areas, "tent" theaters cater to low-income viewers and the urban poor. At the other end of the scale, the introduction of multiplex cinemas, intended as an upmarket experience for the urban middle- and upper-income classes, has hastened the demise of older cinema halls. But a century after films were first screened in India, cinema halls and tents continue to contribute to the mix of exhibition spaces available.

Empirical study of Indian cinema therefore brings much-needed variation to film studies.[32] The cinema-hall experience, for example, throws into relief the mainstream reception aesthetic of niche-marketed Hollywood films in Anglo-American settings and the (Eurocentric) model of film and spectatorship that is based on idealized settings where individuals go into darkened rooms to gaze silently at a screen. This ideal of reception has been normalized and generalized as a "universal" film experience thought to rest in film's "mode of address." Study of the active audience complicates such understandings, revealing them to be conventions of public reception that are historically and culturally specific.[33] Apart from reception practices, the "obdurate" nature of the films themselves[34] is not to be overlooked: the traditional Indian song-and-dance "mass entertainer" film, with a screening time of over three hours, points to the need to locate cinema in different "disciplines of time and space,"[35] which have consequences for exhibition and for filmgoing. Where film posters may line a street like wallpaper for the city (see fig. 1) and where film music blaring from shops, restaurants, and autorickshaws becomes a "soundtrack for everyday life," simply moving around the city constitutes "reception."

The distinctive plurality and heterogeneity of Indian cinema and its audiences raises further questions about certain received understandings or "truths" about film as mass medium. The very premise of mass media and assumptions about its homogenizing influences, its uniformity of address and experience, which drive theories of mass society and the Frankfurt School,[36] rest on the presumed "equivalence" and "anonymity" of individual audience members, their "interchangeability" or "sameness." Karin Barber traces these assumptions to social transformations in Western Europe,[37] calling for more "local and historically specific" studies of performance and reception that are sensitive to the various ways in which "a text or performance addresses a pub-

FIGURE 1. Film posters line a street. Photograph by the author, Bangalore, 2012.

lic and the ways in which people out there take up that address, selectively and for their own purposes."[38] What happens when film encounters heterogeneous audiences as it does in India? How do audiences differentiated by religion, language, regional culture, education, and literacy, by rural or urban background, and by "popular philosophies of irreducible human difference"[39] shape film? How do they "receive" or appropriate it?

Cinema in India then becomes a fertile site to reimagine and reformulate ideas about contemporary film and its experience.[40] Very simply, one can ask, what is a film? And how can its meaning and nature be determined? What do "active" and heterogeneous audiences mean for our understanding of cinema and for the intersubjectivity of film experience, and what is the relevance of local traditions for film's social existence? These questions once again shift inquiry to the contexts and practices that situate cinema and away from understandings centered on the medium and on texts.

By focusing on a non-Western cinema and culture industry and a distinctive public culture of reception and localized production, I also seek in this book to move the study of popular film beyond the framework of media imperialism and the export of Western media and culture as well as local audience response to Western (largely American) popular media, what has been described as the "first" and "most obvious layer of theorizing about culture" in media studies.[41] At the same time, I do not wish to "exotify" Indian cinema; rather, in keeping with the ethnographic project, my aim is to understand Indian cinema "on its own terms."[42] I ask how a situated study can inform our understandings of cinema more broadly and what it means for a possible comparative and cross-cultural perspective on cinema and its lived experience.

CINEMA STUDIES IN INDIA

Over the past two decades, the study of Indian cinema has exploded with research spanning film analysis, the study of celebrity, and production and producers. Yet scholarly work on Indian cinema continues to be dominated by a film-centered approach. There are numerous informative film retrospectives and studies of directors and stars in existence.[43] While there have been calls for understanding films "in relation to their social and cultural traditions,"[44] culture has been addressed mostly through the analysis of the films and their content, meaning, narratives, and representations of Indian society.[45] A number of studies have pursued ideological analyses of films as sociopolitical narratives exploring themes such as nationalism, modernity, cultural and identity politics, postcoloniality, and more recently, globalization.[46]

Scattered studies of Indian cinema's visual and public culture and its institutions are beginning to make inroads into the earlier dominance of textual approaches.[47] A few excellent ethnographic and qualitative studies of film production are recent additions to this expanding field.[48] While studies of spectatorship have emerged, the majority of studies have "read" spectatorship by focusing on viewer identities through the films and their stories and representations[49] and have mostly explored audience response to film themes and content or fans' relationships to films and to their favorite stars.[50] Significant gaps remain. For anthropologist Stephen Hughes, film exhibition is "one of the most under-studied, under-theorized, and unappreciated areas in the study of cinema in India."[51] Empirical studies of audiences and reception also continue to be marginalized.

The Indian film industry is currently in a period of expansive growth and transformation.[52] Both domestically and internationally there is a great deal of interest in the Indian media and film market. Within India, reports on film entertainment are focused on the potential for market expansion that rests on reaching various "underserved" sections of the population; at the same time, international production houses are seeking to collaborate with Indian film producers, and Hollywood stars are traveling to India to promote their films and seek Indian audiences. Thus, the "whole world is interested" in India's billion-plus audience,[53] and yet apart from recent marketing reports, audiences and reception are the most understudied areas of cinema in India. As yet we know little about cinema's lived culture and its social life and the phenomenology of filmgoing and film experience in India.

RETHINKING RECEPTION

In focusing on the film as an object of inquiry, film studies in and of India have merely followed the Western "tradition." In literary and poststructuralist film studies, theory-driven analyses of films and their texts, genres, medium, and directors and producers outnumber studies of audiences and reception. Film studies' spectators are hypothetical and ideal constructs, "positioned by the text" and inferred in armchair analyses of film "effects."[54] The idea of disembodied spectator-subjects is taken to an extreme in "gaze theory" for example, where the spectator is reduced to "a giant disembodied set of eyes."[55]

Poststructuralist film studies with roots in literary and psychoanalytic theory has dislodged spectatorship from the sociocultural and historical contexts, even the immediate local settings that locate its reception. The absence of a tradition of empirical research[56] has meant that received understandings of spectatorship are largely speculative and rest on the personal views, tastes, politics, and ideological leanings of analysts rather than on the perspectives and experiences of actual audiences and their social reality. Experts speak for audiences and tell audiences what they are seeing, feeling, or thinking or how they are, or should be, "reading" or interpreting films[57] in what has been described as a "top-down" approach and "condescending attitude" toward audiences.[58] Apart from marketing research and studies of extreme audiences and fans and (post-1980s) historical studies of exhibition and cinema going, empirical research on actual, socially situated audiences and their filmgoing practices remains one of the most underexamined areas of film.[59] The anthropologist Sara Dickey observes that in the mid-1980s, when she began her study of popular film and its significance in South India, the idea of talking to audiences about their responses to a film was not common.[60]

Preoccupation with the film and its texts and messages has meant that current studies of film reception are conceptualized narrowly as how "film audiences" engage with specific texts: how they "read," "make sense of," or "respond to" them.[61] From a phenomenological perspective, such understandings assume that the film text and its meanings are always at the forefront of the audience's experience.[62] Yet many audiences hardly care about closely following the intended or "encoded" meanings of a film or even the narrative. According to industry executives, in the United States, teenage boys, audiences for *Godzilla* (1998), were "not concerned with the quality of the film, or even whether it was in focus, as long as there was action and popcorn."[63] For audiences who routinely watch films in languages they do not speak or fully understand and who cannot rely on subtitles or dubbing, the practice of closely following the film, its dialogue and story, is optional.[64] Given that a significant percentage of the moviegoing audience worldwide lacks formal education and is illiterate or semiliterate and that a variety of aesthetics and sensibilities govern audiences engagement with film, it is unclear how relevant the term *reading*—used as a default for *reception*—is, even as a metaphor.

Various explanations are offered for the film and text centeredness of film studies; these range from its literary roots to the study of film as art to institutional explanations having to do with the industry's very positioning of film. From an industry perspective, the standardization and homogenization of film experience and the move to delocalize it that has accompanied the development of the Hollywood entertainment complex may be seen to have encouraged a focus on the film and its "text," which is reflected in studies of film and its experience. Elizabeth Hahn has argued that the preoccupation with texts and their meaning is rooted in a "Western tradition" or "ideology" of mass communication where "meaning is contained primarily in the message or text itself," this being "the heart of the concept of 'mass media.'" Where the focus is on transmitting a stand-alone message that can be "understood anywhere, by anyone,"[65] audiences are conceptualized in terms of their relationship to the message and as "receivers of information."[66] These assumptions are accompanied by understandings of audience behavior grounded in "a normative Western conception of how to absorb information" where reception is an "*individual* act" of understanding.[67] Film plays to an audience of "solitary individuals" who are engaged in "a private act of interiorizing the story."[68] Even phenomenological studies of film experience address generalized individuals who are asocial and acultural.[69]

Again, such understandings of reception, which neglect the group character of the audience[70] and the social and interactive audience capable of collective action,[71] are at odds with how real audiences experience film. Psychoanalyst and social theorist Sudhir Kakar's recollections of his childhood cinemagoing in northern India are illustrative:

As a five-year-old boy, I sat in the cool, darkened cinema hall in the afternoons . . . surrounded by dauntingly grown up students who were giving their

studies and teachers a temporary breather, tonga-drivers taking a break from
the afternoon heat, domestic servants prolonging their shopping errands and
others who had no urgent matters to attend to. . . . In the anonymity of the
darkness, pierced by a flickering light which gave birth to a magical yet familiar world on the screen, I was no longer a small boy but a part of the envied
world of adulthood though I sensed its rituals and mysteries but dimly. I always
joined in the appreciative laughter that followed a raucous comment, even if
the exact meaning escaped me. I too, would hold my breath in the hushed
silence that followed a particularly well-acted love scene, and surreptitiously
tried to whistle, with the "O" of the thumb and the index finger under the
tongue, in imitation of the expert whistles that greeted the obligatory scene in
which the heroine fell into the water or was otherwise drenched.[72]

Kakar's vivid account draws attention to the limitations of reception analysis
that frames reception as merely "understanding" film and its meanings, an
interpretive exercise focused on a text. It substantiates the notion that film
is a "creative good," consumed in a "social context, not by isolated hermits,"
where its "satisfaction is subjective."[73] The source of "magic" of the cinema,
as Kakar so evocatively illustrates, is its social and collective experience. What
is significant is not so much "how [film] addresses audiences" as how "audiences constitute themselves around [cinema]" and construct shared experience.[74] Audiences may in fact engage with a film ideologically and politically,
as media scholars have shown, but the average moviegoer mostly goes to be
entertained, to pass the time with friends and family.[75] Thus, studies that rest
on an "artificially marked-off encounter between spectator and film as object"[76] offer an incomplete if not distorted sense of reception.

Cinema may be understood to be a "play-form";[77] people watch with ir-
reverence and humor, and mood and atmosphere are often more important
to collective experience than the film alone. Yet these pleasures—often at the
forefront of the moviegoers' experiences—are frequently overlooked in intel-
lectualized debates that privilege the interests and agendas of researchers.[78] A
focus on message and the medium (or technology) presumes that film experience is placeless, that film *contains* the audience and its experience. Along with
studies that focus on media power or that examine film consumption within a
critical and political economy perspective, these approaches frequently miss
the immediate contexts and institutional settings that situate entertainment
that is social and embodied, a leisure activity.

This book, then, positions itself partly as a response to the predominance
of theories and approaches that are centered on the film, its text. Cinema as

an "experience good" calls for a phenomenological understanding that addresses social practices and their role in shaping film experience. Yet there is currently no "sociology of film reception." As sociologist Rajinder Dudrah has observed, while there are sociological approaches to the study of mass media and communication, sociology's attention to cinema has been sporadic.[79] Early sociological studies of film consumption carried out by Chicago School sociologists and social psychologists stemmed from public concern about popular film's negative effects on children and youth;[80] later on, social science perspectives were brought into research on media reception through studies of mass communication and statistical research in the 1940s and 1950s and then in the 1970s and 1980s via cultural studies.[81] Yet apart from scattered studies of the interpretation of film content or analysis of film within cultural stratification theory, the investigations of "high" and "low" culture forms, taste and consumption, fan culture and media in domestic and semipublic spaces that follow the cultural studies tradition,[82] sociology has been largely peripheral to the study of film audiences and the public reception of film.

PLACING CINEMA

A growing awareness of the limitations in the study of (film) reception and the neglect of on the ground complexities have led to calls to broaden reception analysis, its analytic frame.[83] Some anthropologists and film historians have underscored the importance of place and context for cinema and its experience along with the practices that construct and produce such experience and that are place based.[84] Historical studies of film exhibition in the United States, for example, have shown that the social construction of cinema and its experience cannot be separated from the spaces of exhibition.[85] Early exhibitors, the legendary Balaban and Katz, for example, when faced with both a variable supply and indifferent quality of films, constructed the theater as "attraction" focusing on the "staging" of film.[86] Theater location, decor, the comforts and services offered to moviegoers, as well as orchestras and live acts all served to draw audiences to the cinema.[87] Indeed, historical studies of film exhibition and reception underscore the considerable local and regional variation in exhibition and reception, further illustrating the importance of place and of audience makeup.[88] However, the assumption that film is homogenizing and universalizing, that its experience transcends context, has tended to favor explanations of film experience that are dislodged from context. Where the consumption of popular film is even thought to "*threaten* the local construction of place"[89] and to "erode . . . cultural distinctiveness,"[90] relatively few studies exist that examine the significance of place (and culture) for contemporary cinema experience.[91]

Contemporary studies of cinema that recognize the importance of understanding film experience as a sited and social experience are emerging, but they are scattered and remain at the periphery of film studies.[92] For example, research like Phil Hubbard's, which examines cinemagoing while taking into consideration the materiality and location of exhibition sites and demonstrates that cinema is as much about "bodily and social" pleasures as it is about engaging with the story and its meanings, serves as a "corrective to those accounts of cinemagoing preoccupied with visuality and gaze."[93] Yet once again, studies that address local contexts of exhibition and filmgoing practices are located mostly in Western (Anglo-American and Western European) settings and tend to focus on media produced in the West (mostly in the United States).[94] Rarely does the examination of film reception in cultural studies and mass communications research address "culture as a whole."[95] Variation in reception that is sociocultural or civilizational has been underexplored.[96]

There is also a great unevenness in the treatment of context and in its definition.[97] Mark Jancovich has observed, for example, that so-called studies of cultural contexts are actually focused on institutional settings.[98] Further, popular media has been framed in terms of a "dichotomy between high and low culture" and as "taste cultures," or as "ordinary culture" and "popular pastimes" that exist *within* Western capitalist societies.[99] Aggregate categories of social class, gender, sexuality, race, or ethnicity are treated as "subcultures" and have become stand-ins for social context or culture and primary identifiers of audiences.[100] Understandings of cinema and film experience therefore suffer from too narrow or "thin" a cultural substrate for the generalizations attempted. Few studies recognize that reception, its constitution and experience, "is deeply connected to the nature of social life of the age and place."[101] We know little about cinema's relationship to local customs and ways of life and the "different ways of being an audience."[102]

FILM AS COLLECTIVE ACT AND PERFORMANCE

Descriptions of film viewing such as Sudhir Kakar's draw attention to audiences' overt and collective construction of film experience and anticipate Howard Becker's insight that cinema film, like other "artworks," is the product of the efforts of many people, a "collective act." This fact is evident, Becker points out simply, in the lengthy list of credits at the end of any film.[103] Looking at film as a "collective act" implies examining *all* aspects of film's negotiated character, including the making and delivery of films to audiences and film's social life at the reception interface, which together shape its multiple realities and which, unlike textual analysis, is embedded in institutional realities and a social and cultural context. It answers the call to broaden the analysis to include the "networks of interaction and organization within which works are made by some people, remade by others as they view them."[104] In this "long view" of film's "career,"[105] filmmakers' practices, the organization of distribution and exhibition, the materiality and institutional workings of exhibition spaces, audiences' filmgoing rituals, and the social and sensual experience of engaging with film in public settings together with the film itself, and the constraints it imposes, all are seen to have bearing for a "holistic" understanding of film.

As a 'total' approach,[106] the collective act draws attention to cinema as performance, an "immersive experience"[107] that "takes stock of the whole, attending to audiences, performers and creators as well as the place, style and text of the performance."[108] It allows reception analysis to move beyond linear formulations of text-viewer engagement to address the "constellation of processes,"[109] the nexus of place, audience composition, and reception aesthetics that contribute to the audience's experience.

METHODOLOGICAL CHALLENGES

Part of the challenge in studying film reception has been practical and methodological. Movie audiences are "transient," "dispersed," and "unstructured collectivities,"[110] and therefore they are difficult to access and make sense of. In the West, where silent viewing is the norm in public settings, atomized audiences are invisible as a social collectivity. These settings, described as "phenomenologically impoverished,"[111] pose additional obstacles to the study of reception in situ. However, the normalization and generalization of mainstream reception settings and audience aesthetics in the West has meant there is little discussion of their opacity and the obstacles they present for empirical study. Significantly, in film studies rooted in literary and psychoanalytic theory, there is no discussion of method.[112]

Given the many difficulties involved in the study of actual audiences, it is not surprising that textual studies of film outnumber empirical studies of reception.[113] Where audiences are dispersed and shifting, placing the text or cultural product at the center of analysis also serves to bound or frame the inquiry. Film-centered studies have focused on the reception of a particular genre, a single film, or a film phenomenon. Media ethnographers have also turned to settings that are bounded and more manageable. This has often meant a retreat from public sites of consumption to the "radically circumscribed" spaces of the household;[114] thus, the domestic consumption of television is far better studied than the public reception of cinema.[115] Following cultural studies, a popular approach has been to selectively examine a subgroup or audience "subculture,'" such as fans, cult film audiences, or a demographic such as children or teens who are less likely to be socialized into silent viewing and so offer access to reception practices that are otherwise opaque. With their extreme behaviors, fans are also often easier to access; they are more easily identifiable than dispersed and unstructured cinema audiences—and therefore, they have been overstudied.[116]

Conventional social science research preoccupied with macrotheoretical constructs or with measurement, variable analysis, and "truth claims," has found it difficult to access the sociality and sensualities of engagement with media in public settings and so has missed the locus of media experience.[117] Rigid coding and analytic schemes interfere with "a more ethnographic or emic attempt to investigate audience reception."[118] Large sample surveys and focus-group studies that aggregate the audience by social class, gender, age, ethnicity, or distinctions such as "domestic" versus "international," "decompose groups and social networks."[119] Background factors are made into identities and motivations,[120] while audiences' routine practices and experiences are ignored, as are interactions in the foreground and at the reception interface.

*

Difficulties in accessing reception and its affective experience have meant that empirical studies of real audiences have resorted to experimental methods, surveys and focus groups, all of which establish artificial settings. Viewers have been video- and audiotaped while watching a screen, and their responses to particular on-screen sequences have been recorded by asking them to press buttons when signaled by beepers.[121] Even more intrusive are psychological studies such as the GSR (galvanic skin response) and ERIS (Emotional Response Index Systems),[122] designed to predict a movie's success by analyzing its script as measured by galvanic skin responses. Individuals are wired to monitor their body temperature, pulse rate, pupil dilation, and perspiration, indicators of their emotions and therefore their "response" to the "text." These methods entirely miss the social and subjective aspects of media engagement. As the cultural and social dimensions of viewing are idiosyncratic and difficult—if not impossible—to measure, they are not considered significant.

While ethnography is most suited for a grounded and local study of cinema, the practicalities of conducting ethnography of media have made it a difficult method to adopt. It is recognized as being "inordinately time-consuming and labor-intensive";[123] and some question whether a lone researcher can even attempt media ethnography.[124] The "ethnographic turn" in media studies is more a "qualitative turn"; studies that rely on interviews, focus groups, surveys, even secondhand reports on the audience in newspaper articles, film reviews, and advertisements are described as ethnographies.[125] Researchers spend little time in the field or in settings where media are consumed. Further, the research is not immersed in the daily lives of audiences, nor does it thickly describe their practices of engagement with media.[126] Together with research based exclusively on interviews with individual respondents, such studies also miss the collective and social activity in public reception settings.[127] Culture, too, is examined "at a remove, . . . not as 'lived' but as 'told' or 'represented in the interview situation.'"[128] Not surprisingly, anthropologists have found so-called media ethnographies in the cultural studies vein to be "thin."

The aesthetics of (active) reception in India suggest that rather than alienated consumers "receiving" a film, active audiences participate in the process of crafting a film and are involved at various "nodes" in the construction of film experience. "Spectator-participants" in cinema halls make visible what has been invisible in text and film-centered approaches and in studies of mainstream settings of film reception in the West, making the ethnography of cinema in India an ethnography of a strategic site. With active audiences it becomes possible to study reception in situ, opening up what has been a black box in media reception studies and allowing for engaged observation of what is otherwise only implied: the "hidden" operations that constitute reception and the unique interactions and negotiations, embodied practices of meaning making, cultural appropriation, and elaboration[129] that "produce" film at the reception threshold and recast it as localized entertainment.[130]

FIELD RESEARCH AND ORGANIZATION OF THE STUDY

In her landmark ethnography of television in Egypt, Lila Abu-Lughod asks how one might conduct an ethnography of a nation and of national television.[131] A similar question confronted me: when the "significance of popular media," its ethnography, to paraphrase Abu-Lughod, "is still being worked out,"[132] how does one conduct a field study of cinema, a mass phenomenon, and examine its social practice and lived culture? With few models for a field study when I began the research, I turned to a select few studies of film reception in India that have adopted ethnographic and qualitative methods. Among them, Beatrix Pfleiderer's and Lothar Lutz's work on urban, small-town, and rural moviegoers that explored audiences' views on films and on society seems to have functioned as an early model for research that followed.[133] One of the earliest anthropological studies of cinema reception in India is Sara Dickey's ethnography in which she investigates the popularity and significance of Tamil cinema for its audiences.[134] Her study is situated in the broader context of the everyday lives of the urban poor as well as the relationship between film-makers, films, and audiences. Steve Derne's "cultural analysis" of filmgoing in Dehra Dhun and Benares uses popular film and its consumption as a lens for understanding masculinity, family relations, and modernity in India.[135] These works draw on participant observation, interviews and informal conversation, surveys, and film analysis. In addition, interdisciplinary studies of fans and the fan-star relationship provided insights on reception and public culture.[136] Studies of cinema in other societies that adopt a sociological or anthropo-logical approach and that locate cinema in practices of leisure, as well as his-torical studies of exhibition and audiences,[137] also helped me to think about and frame the study, as did works on "active" audiences for theater and music performances and popular entertainment.[138]

Situating reception in the complexities of public settings, I sought to selec-tively map the "negotiation field" of cinema and the social landscape[139] of au-dience experience to locate cinema in the interactions that produce film and its experience and in the dispersed sites and contexts where film is elaborated.[140] Given I was carrying out a study that addressed cinema's lived experience and social existence at the reception threshold,[141] my aim was to privilege "ordi-nary people's knowledge" or value their "everyday competencies"[142] rather than the "worldviews" and abstract theoretical formulations of scholars that characterizes "high theory."

The "total approach" that the collective act and cinema as performance offers is clearly beyond the scope of any single study. Further, as "artworlds do not have sharp boundaries,"[143] it becomes necessary to bound the study. I faced the immediate question of how to study cinema in a city with a population of about five million. Also, in the late 1990s, over one hundred movie theaters were scattered across Bangalore's metro area and its outskirts, presumably screening hundreds of films to millions of moviegoers.[144] An exhaustive study of cinema in Bangalore being clearly beyond the scope of this ethnography, I offer a selective exploration of cinema that is focused on certain areas in the city, a snapshot of cinema in Bangalore. Participant observation and the im-mersive nature of fieldwork itself placed boundaries on the study.[145]

I started out watching films at cinema halls in different parts of the city, hoping to get a sense of reception at these different venues with audiences that may be hyperlocal in their filmgoing habits. As fieldwork progressed I concentrated on two areas along the east–west axis of the city where clusters of cinema halls were located at the time: the cantonment in the northeastern part of Bangalore, and "Majestic" or Gandhinagar to the southwest of the cantonment, recognized locally as the nerve center for Kannada film. These areas, associated with distinct cultures of cinema going together offered access to a heterogeneity of audiences, films, and classes of theaters. With time in the field, I came to focus on particular cinema halls in these localities, though I would occasionally watch films in theaters in other parts of the city. In chapters 3 and 4, I explore the cultural geography of cinema in Bangalore and the consequences of location for exhibition, for the market, and for audience's filmgoing practices.

I attended a total of 143 film screenings, mostly at select cinema halls. As my objective was to locate the study in the distinctive heterogeneity that characterizes cinema in India, I did not restrict my film viewing to Hindi (Bollywood) films, the study of which has dominated writings on Indian cinema. Instead, I watched a mix of films that arrived in theaters: Kannada and Tamil cinema, with the odd Telugu film, and Hollywood films screened in the original American English, as well as Hindi-language Bombay films. I watched both "superhits" and "flops" and sometimes attended multiple screenings of the same film. Thus, fieldwork involved hundreds of hours watching films. The films themselves constituted a field site. To get a sense of film culture and immerse myself in the world of the commercial Indian film, I also watched films on DVDs. Altogether, I watched a total of about 312 films for the study.

I also draw on 137 open-ended and conversational interviews in Bangalore, ninety-eight of which were with moviegoers and the remainder with film-business insiders including stars, various members of the cast and crew, distributors, exhibitors, and theater staff. I spent time with film society organizers, journalists writing on cinema, and other affiliates of the cinema world as well as Bangalore residents who were observers of cinema. Countless informal exchanges in the field shaped my understanding. Seeking to immerse myself in the public culture of cinema and in the social world of habitués—my term for those who had grown up watching films and were insiders to the culture of cinema in India—I accompanied them to the movies whenever I could and spent time with them outside the movie event.

Fieldwork may be better described as "polymorphous."[146] I read film magazines, news articles, and film reviews; listened to film music; visited stores

FIGURE 2. Theater exterior on Kempegowda Road presents a festive air with flower garlands, mango leaves and pennants. Photograph by the author, Bangalore, 2012.

that sold music and DVDs or LCDs; and talked with store personnel and customers. Telephone conversations, e-mail exchanges, blogs, and online forums also inform the study. I draw marginally on fieldwork I conducted in the United States that involved watching Indian films screened in theaters in Los Angeles, Boston, and suburbs of these cities and with audiences who were almost exclusively Indian or South Asian, and on conversational interviews with moviegoers and exhibitors at these screenings. Over the years, I conducted roughly forty interviews with filmgoers in the United States and attended about fifty-five screenings of commercial Indian films.

While I watched films at a few multiplexes when they first appeared post-2003, the study largely concentrates on single-screen cinema halls, the dominant exhibition setting in the 1990s and into the new millennium.[147] I spent a lot of time hanging around cinema halls in attempts to "tune my senses" to the sights, sounds, and smells that attend cinema in public space and the filmgoing event:[148] the calls of footpath vendors, the fragrance of jasmine and roses from the garlands and flower-draped theater awnings (see fig. 2), which mingled with the smell of boiled peanuts from vendors' carts and other street odors ubiquitous in India, the noisy overhead fans inside the auditorium, which competed with the soundtrack, the smells from the toilets, the complaints from filmgoers about nails in the seats and the mosquitos that claimed attention over the film ("how we were bitten!").

A sense of the routines of exhibition and filmgoing and the rhythms of life outside the theater gradually emerged: the gathering and dispersal of crowds, the groups of middle-class youth outside theaters in the cantonment leaning on motorbikes and two-wheelers (mopeds or scooters), queues that formed on the pavement and suddenly vanished, the attendant movement of footpath vendors, scalpers navigating the terrain of risk and opportunity, the sudden appearance of the police, which signaled more than the usual skirmishes in ticket queues, and perhaps the arrival of a star or director. I began to recognize fans and movie obsessives outside theaters, and they began to recognize me, as did the ushers who whiled away time between screenings, and sometimes during them, at cigarette stalls on the street. These activities and encounters shaped the "frequencies" and the "sensibilities" of the field.[149]

I spread out my film viewing and observations at different times, on different days, and at different stages in a film's life at the theater to get a sense of the variation and patterns in filmgoing, reception, and exhibition. Taking an autorickshaw to the theater in the morning around 9:30 before the morning show, which typically began between 10:30 and noon, I would hang around chatting with theater staff and moviegoers. I watched matinees and first shows in the early evening and late shows that ended well past midnight. I also sat in different sections of the stratified theater.

While at first I stayed on at a theater for multiple shows to get a sense of an entire day there, I found I was unable to write detailed field notes after these long hours of observation, even using my jottings in the theater. Then I attempted to restrict my observations to four to five hours, but this was not always possible if I found moviegoers or theater staff who were willing to talk and be interviewed. On days when I accompanied moviegoers to the cinema, I spent time with them before and after the film whenever the opportunity arose. These were long hours to document, and again I had to find ways to write notes as I went along. I took breaks from watching the film and jotted notes in the theater lobby or went to a nearby café. If it was feasible and people permitted, I used a tape recorder, which helped somewhat.

After repeated visits to some theaters, the staff and security guards let me in free; they wanted to know how many movies I had seen, talked about the film being screened, and offered their observations on its reception. Theater managers sometimes invited me to their air-conditioned offices where we would chat over tea or cool drinks. I sat in on conversations with distributors' representatives and the managers' friends, some of them staff at neighboring theaters. The police would occasionally drop in on their beat, as would inspectors from the electricity board. I also met producers, sound engineers, fans, and the hangers-on who seemed to spend all their time in the vicinity of cinema halls. I was sometimes introduced as a writer on film, at other times as a student. These encounters were invaluable: I learned about some of the inside workings of film exhibition, the troubles exhibitors faced, and occasionally even film's "collections" and audiences. They also helped me to refine my questions in subsequent exchanges and interviews.[150]

Through observations at theaters and conversational interviews before and after the film, I tried to get a measure of the theatrical experience and audience aesthetics that shape film experience and that I elaborate on in chapter 6. Every day in the field it was brought home to me that for audiences, the experience and significance of cinema is more than merely watching a film on-screen, a point that cinema and media scholars have sought to address.[151] When I asked people about the films, they spoke at length about the difficulty of getting tickets, the merits of one theater over another, of being duped by scalpers, or of chance meetings with friends at the theater. As fieldwork progressed I tried to get people to elaborate on their routines and practices of filmgoing. With a view to tracing the "natural history"[152] of the movie event from "start" to "finish" and gaining firsthand appreciation of practices of filmgoing—including filmgoers' navigation of the city, their negotiation of the contingencies of the movie outing, and its sensualities and rhythms—I accompanied habitués on their movie outings, as I describe in chapters 3–5.

With time, the importance of interconnections, the web of relationships, the innumerable interactions and negotiations that embed cinema and that "produce" it and shape its social existence[153]—and that are invisible in linear spectator-text explications of reception—became evident. The "sense"[154] of cinema as a collective act then emerged only after I had spent some time in the field, and it is the "ethnographic surprise" of the study.[155] Thus, while my efforts were focused on imposing some boundaries on the study, I also found that I needed to expand these boundaries.

The frame of the collective act and of performance gave new meaning to my study. The relationship between actors who are situated at various social nodes in the process, the preparations for the cinema event, its staging, the site, the audience, the period following the screening—all these assumed new significance. Key players at exhibition and reception sites and their role in producing the institutional and social context for the audiences' experience became visible. For example, theater managers and projectionists routinely participate in the collective constitution of film experience, as do ushers, theater security guards, and employees at concessions counters. Hindu priests officiate at film *muhurats*. Their services are also called on to offer film reels ritually to the gods before the first-day screening of a film; thus, priests and astrologers are involved in film production and distribution and at both the beginning and end of the social process of constructing cinema, if such beginnings and endings can be so identified.[156] Unofficial participants include scalpers, footpath-stall vendors who sell snacks and drinks to moviegoers queuing outside theaters, and street urchins who play film songs on bamboo flutes. Those who craft decorations on theater awnings and fashion the forty-foot garlands that decorate the cutouts; fans who take out processions to celebrate a newly released film—all are involved in "producing" film as local spectacle and in shaping its collective public experience and sensual environment. Studying cinema as collective act made visible this broader, richer, more complex and chaotic process that contributes to the production of film experience and that is overlooked in narrow filmcentric conceptualizations of reception.

As fieldwork evolved into an examination of cinema's social relationships and of film as an ongoing "assemblage,"[157] the location of the Kannada film industry in Bangalore proved a boon. After repeated effort, I was able to contact film-business insiders and gain access to film sets at the Kanteerava Studios. I also observed film shootings in the city, which lasted anywhere from a few hours to 12–14 hours, a typical workday for film crews. Through observations at these sites and interviews and conversations with filmmakers and members of the cast and crew, I explored filmmakers' anticipations of audiences and the practices and traditions of filmmaking in Bangalore in the late 1990s, which became significant as part of the "collective act" of cinema film and that I elaborate on in chapter 2.

As I sought to address cinema and its reception in public settings, I encountered the challenges associated with access in these settings. The problems posed by mobile and dispersed audiences, their shifting terrain, and the transience of film screenings contributed in no small measure. Crowded public spaces and the volatility of fans and movie enthusiasts affected fieldwork. I address the flavor of doing fieldwork in these public spaces in chapters 4 and 7.

Rather than a "sitting" exercise in front of a screen, mine was a "mobile ethnography";[158] I roamed around the streets in the cantonment and in the Gandhinagar-Kempegowda Road area where theaters were clustered. I also traveled across the city to interview people, attend a film shooting, or go to any one of the many sites at which cinema was elaborated in the city. During a screening I would sometimes wander around inside the theater to get a sense of the audience seated in different sections or to see what theater staff were doing or how the screening was proceeding. And this let me seek out the opinions of other theater staff, including ushers, workers at concessions counters, and "sweepers."

As with other media ethnographies, my fieldwork was "incommensurate" and "uneven," spread across a variety of spaces and settings.[159] In addition to cinema halls and film sets, I hung around places in the city where I met moviegoers and film-business insiders and attended film music recording sessions, story and dialogue sessions, and meetings of the cast and crew where film footage was previewed. Whenever I knew about them, I went to the ritual inaugurations of a film's shooting schedule, the *muhurat*, at which the film is launched at an astrologically auspicious moment, an occasion for the cast and crew and their families to celebrate. I also attended first show celebrations of new releases at select cinema halls, as I describe in chapter 7.

The settings where I conducted interviews varied from highly informal and impromptu—such as ticket queues on the street—to the offices of directors and producers. I met with moviegoers wherever they would agree to talk: in their homes, in restaurants and cafés, or at their places of work. Informal conversations at stores, banks, doctors' offices, beauty parlors where women consumed film magazines, college campuses, and bus stops inform the study. I met with members of local fan associations at theaters, at their hangouts in the city, and on film sets. Many autorickshaw drivers were fans and self-appointed commentators on the film world, and on long rides in autos I was informed by their views and their considerable behind-the-scenes knowledge, gossip, and insights.[160] Often these informal conversations successfully captured the spirit and mood that attended filmgoing events. In all these exchanges, my ability to speak Tamil and understand Hindi and make myself understood in it as well as my ability to understand conversational Kannada and manage simple conversation facilitated rapport and connections in the field.

The study is situated in the many companionable pre- and postmovie chats over coffee or at lunches and dinners with moviegoers, family get-togethers, shopping trips, and birthday, anniversary, and festival celebrations—the broader sociality that embeds film experience. It is also located in the camaraderie of fans whose acquaintance I made and in informal conversations with many strangers. Among filmgoers and enthusiasts, "movie talk" is a way to pass the time, to connect with one another; the question "Seen any movies lately?" is a common conversational opener. Conversations about filmgoing and film experience that blurred the boundaries between movie talk and interviews also helped me to establish rapport. After exchanges about films and filmgoing—which at times started out as a conversational interview—I was on occasion invited to go on a group movie outing.

However, the sociability that embedded movie events that at times facilitated my participation at other times proved a frustrating constraint. Social circles delimited by class and gender made it easier for me to spend time with and accompany middle-class moviegoers, families, women, college students, and professionals on their movie outings. Though I went to the movies a few times with women belonging to the lower socioeconomic classes whom I met in queues and at theaters or through my social networks in Bangalore, it was more difficult to participate in cinema events with men belonging to lower socioeconomic groups, except for some fans whom I accompanied to films starring their idols.[161] They included autorickshaw drivers, low-level workers in offices, shop assistants, and a few who did contract work for agencies. A couple of these men looked after footpath stalls; some were unemployed. I went to one screening with a hanger-on at a theater who also managed the autorickshaw stand opposite it and with whom I had chatted about the films screened in the theater. I attended a couple of screenings with the men who ply taxis in the city and accompanied fans to first shows. By electing to sit in the cheaper seats in front of the screen, a space exclusively occupied by men belonging to the lower classes, I gained proximity to some of the viewing activities and aesthetic involvement of this section of the audience.

Unevenness rather than uniformity also characterized interviews in terms of the people, the routines that led to interviews, and the interviews themselves. While I did not carry out any systematic or random sampling of moviegoers, I spoke with people from varying socioeconomic, ethnolinguistic, and cultural backgrounds and ages. I also sought out people who lived in different parts of Bangalore. It became my strategy to "talk movies" with practically anyone I could get to speak with me: vegetable vendors, domestic servants, waiters in cafés, teachers and students, the manager of the local photocopy shop, and people I met at the dry cleaners, the post office, and at dinner parties. People sometimes volunteered their friends and relatives for interviews. This gave me a mix of habitués and regular attendees at the cinema as well as occasional and infrequent moviegoers. I conducted "follow-up interviews," which were more extended conversations over time whenever I got the opportunity. I approached filmmakers, directors, producers, stars, members of the cast and crew, and distributors and exhibitors for interviews. Those whom I spoke with and observed on set were mostly in the Kannada film business, though some had also worked in regional film industries, and a few had worked in Bombay.

I also drew on media interviews with directors and stars in the newspapers, magazines, and television, which I treated differently.

The broader participatory culture that I was examining in connection with film viewing shaped fieldwork as well. As moviegoing is a group activity, interviews, too, became an activity for the group. Very public interviews,[162] which often took place on the street, drew a crowd of onlookers who at times would join in, contribute their views, or answer in place of the "interviewee" or "correct" him. Thus, while I never conducted focus groups or sought out group discussions of films, sometimes groups became involved simply because people wanted to participate. Interviews were rarely one-sided; people were curious about me and what I was doing, and they would ask questions in return. Seeing me jotting notes in the darkened theater, they would sometimes ask me what I was writing. (I then started leaving the theater to jot notes.) Some explained to one another that I "must be press." In late 2009 and after marketing surveys became more common, I was asked if I was conducting a survey. Many were keen to know what I would do with the information.

In the early days of fieldwork I explained I was a student and was doing a project on cinema. This sometimes led to further questions of where I was a student and what I was studying. To some I described my activities simply as writing about cinema in Bangalore. Seeing me show up at multiple screenings of their favorite films, fans assumed I was writing about the star. Exhibitors in theaters that screened a particular type of film, say Kannada films, introduced me as a writer on Kannada cinema. In all encounters I was seen as middle class or "well off." People would address me as "madam" and use respectful forms of address in Kannada or Tamil but also referred to me as a "girl." Interactions in the field meant fielding personal questions: what language did I speak at home? where did I live? what did my parents do? was I married? was I a relative of the star or director? why had I decided to study cinema in Bangalore? and so on.

Many Bangaloreans I encountered, some with postgraduate degrees, were interested enough to discuss my study with me and offered helpful suggestions. They drew my attention to newspaper and magazine articles, books, film reviews, and other such materials and put me in touch with people who could be of help, and I was grateful for their interest and support. I was also given advice on how to conduct my study by people I encountered in the film business, moviegoers, and others. They suggested theaters to go to and films to watch, stars and directors to interview, and questions to pose. On film sets, members of the crew and sometimes the cast would instruct me about some aspect of what they were engaged in. As I got to know fans, they kept me up-to-date on the new releases of their idols. Along with curiosity about my project, I encountered skepticism. Some did not hesitate to tell me that it was pointless to study cinema in Bangalore. Kannada filmmakers seemed hard pressed to understand why someone living in Los Angeles would come to Bangalore to study cinema. They encouraged me to go to Bombay or, better yet, Hollywood. One filmmaker suggested I interview Stephen Spielberg. More than one person advised me to abandon the study and go back to Los Angeles; and more than once, I was tempted to take their advice.

The spontaneity and improvisation that infused all areas of cinema in Bangalore also shaped my fieldwork. At first, I spent a lot of time attempting to do things "by the book." I tried to impose structure on my routines and on interviews. I also had preconceived notions about the problems of access I would encounter. Only with time in the field did I learn to recognize what would work or be appropriate in a particular setting and accept the spontaneity and informality that guided the field research. The more time I spent in Bangalore, the more I recognized the importance of "going with the flow," of "letting the field take over," and "following the grain of the society."[163]

In retrospect, many key moments in the field appeared governed by chance, something M. N. Srinivas alerted me to when fieldwork proved frustrating. Theater managers I became acquainted with introduced me to producers and distributors simply because I happened to be on the spot. Routine moviegoing with families led me to witness a procession at a new-release event. After trying for weeks to contact people in the Kannada film industry, I bumped into a fan at a theater who was able to put me in touch with stars and producers. Following a chance meeting with a Kannada superstar at one of the theaters screening his film, I was granted access to his film sets and to the cast and crew of his film. These turned out to be big breaks.

Fieldwork was also subject to cultural rhythms and the patterning of local events. Films were often released to coincide with festivals and holidays: Varamahalakshmi Puja, Ganesh Chaturti, Deepavali, Eid, Christmas holidays, and school and college vacations. Other significant and auspicious if less public days also affected fieldwork as the films of some stars were released on their birthdays or the birthdays of their spouses, their fathers, or an auspicious day for the director. The same held true for film *muhurats* (inaugural ceremonies) whose timings were often set by astrologers. Similarly, moviegoing with habitués was subject to the rhythms of the setting and events in their lives.

Thus, flexibility, if not uncertainty, shaped my fieldwork, which depended on the routines, availability, and moods of countless others. Filmmakers and stars would travel a lot,[164] and I might suddenly learn they were "in station" and could grant me a meeting. I would receive last-minute information about a film shoot in the city, the venue often unspecified until half an hour before filming began. I sought the help of friends and relatives when I had to dash across the city sometimes past midnight. The duration of a film shoot was also open ended, introducing further unpredictability. Similarly, it was difficult to get advance information about fan celebrations on the occasion of a film's theatrical release. Moviegoers I sought to accompany to the cinema would frequently inform me of their plans at the last minute. Unforeseen happenings in their lives would mean postponed or canceled movie outings. At times I had to decide between going to the movies, interviewing a moviegoer, or meeting a filmmaker. Refusing such opportunities in order to stay home and write up my field notes sometimes led to a lull of a few days.

As per fieldwork conventions, I have used pseudonyms to preserve respondents' anonymity. In a few instances I have removed or altered details regarding their families and areas where they lived that would identify them. I also identify individuals by their occupational roles for the same reason; for example, using broad terms such as filmmaker or producer to encompass directors, producers, or other major occupational roles as long as it did not affect the data. I have, however, identified a few in the film business by their real names because they are well-known public figures or they offered expert opinions and information. However, if I felt information imparted during an interview would compromise or embarrass an individual, I preserved his or her anonymity.

Chapters trace the social life of cinema as it is elaborated in the course of moviegoing and present the fragmented form of film experience, its in-process constitution. The selective nature of ethnographic research and participant observation together with the unevenness of fieldwork has also shaped chapters that may appear more like separate essays than a neatly integrated whole. Chapter 2 selectively describes filmmakers' practices and their anticipations of their market and potential audiences, all of which shape the collaborative process of making a film. Chapters 3–7 are organized around the natural history of the filmgoing event and focus on audiences' routines and practices, in-theater experiences, and postmovie sociality. In chapter 3 I investigate the significance of urban geography and spatial cultures for exhibition and audiences' filmgoing experiences. Chapters 4 and 5 explore filmgoers' negotiation of the mundanities of cinemagoing along with related interactions in public. Chapter 5 focuses on families and groups at the cinema and the hospitality customs and sociality that construct the experience. Chapters 6 and 7 most directly address the phenomenology of film reception and audiences' experience both inside and outside the theater. In chapter 6 I provide a descriptive analysis of participatory and interactive reception culture, highlighting the performative aspects of engagement with film and the collective experience in the cinema hall. Chapter 7 introduces the phenomenon of the new release, "film in transition," and the celebratory activities that situate film at the threshold space and that elaborate it as festival, spectacle, and performance. The study therefore gives a justifiably fragmented view of the whole, an assembly of heterogeneous practices and experiences that exists in parts that are themselves changing and evolving.

CHAPTER 2

Participatory Filmmaking and the Anticipation of the Audience

Every story has to have poetic justice; otherwise the auditorium will slap you!
DIALOGUE WRITER, Bangalore

Indian cinema celebrated its centenary in 2013, the first feature film made in India being recognized as Dadasaheb Phalke's *Raja Harishchandra* in 1913. In the 1920s and 1930s filmmaking in India grew rapidly.[1] Major studios scattered all over the country were crucial to the early development of Indian cinema and established it as one of the oldest non-European cinematic traditions in the world.[2] By the 1980s cinema was India's sixth largest industry, grossing roughly $600 million annually and employing three thousand workers.[3] Yet commercial filmmaking continued to operate like a small business rather than a mature capitalist industry, and it was characterized by informality and ad hocism. Only in 1998 was the film business officially granted industry status by the Indian government,[4] after which it has seen rapid though uneven corporatization and growth.

This chapter explores filmmaking in Bangalore with reference to filmmaking in India in the late 1990s. While an ethnography of the Kannada film industry, "Sandalwood," located in Bangalore is beyond the scope of this study, I examine shared aspects of filmmaking between Sandalwood as a regional film business and the Bombay film industry with a view to identifying a set of distinctive practices that shape a culture of filmmaking in India and that are consequential for the films produced and the way they are received and appropriated. Some of my respondents worked in Sandalwood as well as in Bombay; many had collaborated with production teams in the neighboring Tamil film industry. Some of the findings in this chapter correspond with observations that scholars have made about Bollywood and Tamil cinema.[5] Where I have noticed discrepancies, I have discussed them here. However, I do not comment on the differences in modes of operation of various studios and production companies, which is beyond the scope of this chapter.

I investigate filmmaking as a "collective act" involving a number of individuals, including audiences who are part of the "complexity of cooperative networks" responsible for constructing a film and shaping its experience[6]—an idea I explore further in subsequent chapters. The chapter addresses filmmaking conventions and considerations and examines how filmmakers think about and anticipate their audiences and the ways in which they address risk and unknowns, all of which crafts the film. In selectively describing the strategies and practices of filmmaking that I encountered, and that contribute to what I describe as an interactional or relational model of cinema, and placing them within a comparative framework, my objective is not to pass judgment on what is a better or more effective way to make films. I seek to understand filmmaking that is rooted in an expressive culture and that is characterized by spontaneity, improvisation, and performance. While the chapter addresses filmmaking in the late 1990s, I have attempted to point to continuity in certain practices after 2000.

HETEROGENEITY AND INFORMALITY

Filmmaking in India developed as a decentralized and multinodal enterprise[7] and in the absence of a unified national market.[8] Hindi-language Bombay cinema, the best known and most widely viewed both in India and internationally, is just one of several indigenous film industries scattered across the country. India's plurality and its multiplicity of languages and cultures has shaped all aspects of making films and their appropriation. For example, those who work in the film business come from a variety of social and cultural backgrounds, from across India and the subcontinent (from Sri Lanka, Bangladesh, Pakistan, and Nepal), from what was Burma, and more recently from the United Kingdom. Hindus of various castes, along with Muslims, Parsis, Sikhs, Jews, Christians, and Anglo-Indians, have starred in Bombay films. Regional film businesses are also very diverse in terms of the ethnolinguistic and regional identities of directors, producers and members of the cast and crew.

Film and media professionals are typically identified as a group with social power that, along with the power of the medium, allows them to dictate to and manipulate audiences, an idea that animates mass culture theory. Today's Hollywood entertainment professionals are described as "members of the knowledge classes" who are "highly educated" and have grown up in comfortable middle- or upper-middle-class families with "material or cultural capital or both."[9] In India, it is difficult to make such general claims. While some younger filmmakers may have college degrees and belong to the middle or upper-middle classes, many do not fit this description. The older generation, who established the film business and who continue to make films, had little formal training. Their education in film was through experience. Not unlike the pre-Hollywood film entrepreneurs who shared a common background with their immigrant and working-class audiences,[10] many commercial filmmakers, dialogue writers, dance choreographers, and musicians may be closer to their lower-middle-class and lower-class audiences and so share their tastes and sensibilities.

Filmmaking also attracts people from small towns and rural areas. Anthropologist Sara Dickey observes that while successful (Tamil) filmmakers belong to the middle and upper-middle classes, many have grown up among the urban and rural poor.[11] Director Bharatiraja, for example, comes from a rural, lower-class background; the Tamil film icon and politician M. G. Ramachandran (MGR), grew up in an "impoverished family."[12] The currently reigning superstar and producer of Tamil films Rajinikanth also comes from a similar background and worked as a coolie and bus conductor in Bangalore as well as doing odd jobs before taking acting classes and achieving megastar status. In a news interview, the Kannada director and star Upendra talked about his father being a cook and his humble beginnings growing up in a "very small room in Chamarajpet."[13]

The description of being "middle class" itself needs qualification. While director Yash Chopra describes himself as middle class and talks about his school and college days, he recollects a childhood where he had to walk everywhere because the family did not own a car, and borrowing a bicycle was a luxury. He did not have shoes to wear, only *chappals* (inexpensive sandals), and he had no money even to go to the movies.[14] Ram Gopal Verma, one of Bombay's most successful directors, is described as having been "a shy, young video-parlor salesperson from Hyderabad."[15] Many film-business insiders are not professionally educated. A few have college degrees in unrelated fields, but many seem to have grown up in lower-middle-class or lower-class families and learned their craft by apprenticeship—through hanging around sets and trying their hand at various skills. Some join a family business. Members of film production crews were also from similar backgrounds, though some even lacked a high school education.

In the late 1990s exhibitors and theater owners in Bangalore were typically longtime residents of the city and were an ethnolinguistically diverse group.[16] One theater manager, a movie enthusiast, had spent much of his youth hanging around cinema halls in Majestic. He was given odd jobs at the theater by his friend, who was an exhibitor and gradually advanced to a managerial position. Another owner of multiple theaters, also an old Bangalorean, was known in the city as a film buff and wrote frequently in newspapers and magazines about cinema. Actors and other members of the cast and crew were also highly heterogeneous in terms of their social, linguistic, and educational backgrounds. Some had drifted into cinema through friends and family connections. Many theater artistes and directors worked in Kannada cinema, bringing with them the sensibilities of folk theater. Gubbi Veeranna, doyen of Kannada cinema in the 1940s, was a stage artist who moved into cinema through his Gubbi Veeranna Theater. He formed Gubbi Karnataka Productions, which was responsible for many famous movies.[17] Kannada film icon Dr. Rajkumar came from a family of traveling theater artistes. Directors such as T. S. Nagabharana also bring a theatrical tradition to their films and have routinely cast theater artists in their productions.

INFORMALITY AND IMPROVISATION

In an interview in the mid-1990s, Bombay star Sunil Shetty commented on the inefficiencies stemming from the lack of planning and organization that characterizes commercial filmmaking. He was critical of what he saw as an absence of professionalism, where, "no one cares about film economics and nearly 25 percent of the budget is wasted. . . . Producers are in a hurry to start a film without planning the details.[18] Given the size and productivity of India's film industry, the degree of informality that characterizes various aspects of the film business is quite striking. While recent corporatization of Indian cinema is reported to have brought about significant change, there is great variation within the film business between Bombay and Madras or Bangalore, for example, and even among different directors and film crews within the industry.

Informality in the functioning of the film business is seen in the lack of scripts. In his impressive ethnography of Bollywood, Emmanuel Grimaud comments on the absence of scripts and observes that a film's title, needed to launch the project, is often independent of the script or theme.[19] He tells the story of a Bombay film set in France that had "no developed story; however, the star [Govinda] improvised, suggesting that they make up the story as they travel through Europe on a bus. The director then instructed the scriptwriter to write from that point of view, i.e., of traveling on a bus."[20] The anecdote reveals both the lack of control of the film by a script and the improvisational culture that filmmaking draws on. After commenting that "nine times out of ten, the script is non-existent" Sunil Shetty remarks on how for the film *Bhai* (1997) filmmaker Kader Khan had "narrated the story, complete with dialogue, on an audio cassette."[21]

Rather than reviewing scripts, then, the initial stages of filmmaking involve story-narration sessions where the director, actors, producer, and others gather to discuss key elements of the story or to narrate stories to one another.[22] This "oral" and improvisational culture of filmmaking has shaped both Bollywood and regional film businesses for decades.

A similar improvisational aesthetic (and informality) was at work in Bangalore where scripts typically seemed either nonexistent or evolved alongside the film, as did scenes and dialogue.[23] Often when filmmakers talked about a "script," they were referring to the documentation of dialogue that appeared to be a last-minute effort and at times even took place *after* the scene had been shot. On one set the dialogue writer worked on the script (written by hand) in collaboration with the director and the cinematographer as filming progressed. Seated in a circle in a room with smudged windowpanes and over cups of tea, members of the cast and crew would conversationally discuss scenes, comedic interludes, and suggest lines of repartee that might capture the audience's attention. Dialogue for the afternoon's shoot would be finalized the previous day or even the morning when filming began.

These practices appeared to be continuing a decade later in Bombay. In a television interview, Bollywood superstar Madhuri Dixit also described dialogue written on the set a few lines at a time, and actors learning their lines minutes before cameras rolled.[24] Bollywood superstar Akshay Kumar said he decided to sign onto the film project *Chandni Chowk to China* (2009) when he saw the poster for the film, which inspired him, and when he *heard* the story.[25] Reports that some of the larger production houses "insist" on written scripts are indications that others continue to operate as before.[26]

Criticizing the "huge amount of wastage in the film industry," Bollywood's Sunil Shetty described filmmaking where "usually just one production manager and his two subordinates handle all the various aspects of a film" even for a film with a substantial budget.[27] While one hears of actors, cinematographers, and writers becoming directors in Hollywood, the extent to which there is overlap and a blurring of the boundaries between tasks and roles in the film business in Bangalore (and in other film businesses in India) appears extreme in comparison.[28] I met directors and distributors who produced movies, theater actors who had turned their hand to film directing, and still photographers turned cameramen who seemed to be directing scenes on the set. On one set, the director had written the story and the dialogues and was also the chief cameraman. The role of producer is very loosely defined, if at all. On some sets "producer-directors" were directing scenes, and an "executive producer" who had started off as a costume consultant on her husband's films told me that she was responsible for all the arrangements on set—even providing tea at regular intervals to the cast and crew. Other "producers" were financiers who were dabbling in filmmaking.

Where filmmaking is not controlled by a script, various individuals can influence and shape the film and its scenes. On one set the cameraman in consultation with the art director and dance choreographer altered scenes, props, and even dialogue as the shot was being readied, while the director, seated in the shade of a tree, looked on from a distance. Costumes for dancers were debated on set and often at the last minute by a group of individuals including the director, the choreographer, the cinematographer, and the chief tailor. The cinematographer even appeared to be involved in the casting of minor roles. I found stars instructing the cameramen; in between setting up the shots, a star took the cameraman aside to discuss more favorable lighting and camera angles for himself. MGR, who was believed to "know the audiences' likes and dislikes," influenced writers, even changed dialogue.[29] Bollywood star Govinda "had a reputation for liking young producers because he could easily impose his views."[30]

Stars have also been known to refuse to film certain scenes or wear certain costumes. Even supporting actors and dancers seem to have veto power. On set, a group of male dancers refused to shave off their moustaches for a scene, which resulted in a standoff that delayed filming for several hours. Not only members of the cast and crew, but even relatives of stars, producers, and directors give advice and suggestions that shape the film. Younger actresses are chaperoned by their mothers on set, and mothers often have a say in costuming and roles. On another day when I happened to be on set, filming stalled when the heroine objected to an outfit she deemed too revealing, which then had to be adjusted after protracted deliberations and in phone consultation with her mother. Stars' mothers as well as fans have objected to the star's "death scene," believing it to be inauspicious for the star and prompting directors to present an "invincible and deathless" hero.[31]

Fans and friends of the cast and crew regularly appeared on the sets and suggested "improvements" to scenes. At Shopper's Stop, in Bangalore, the shooting of a Kannada film that went on into the early hours of the morning drew a growing crowd of enthusiastic onlookers and fans who gleefully shouted out suggestions for the scene, a couple of which were implemented on the spot. Such last-minute improvisation was standard practice. In the suburb of Jayanagar, a group of elderly men sitting on the pavement and enjoying the morning sun were included in a scene when it became difficult to move them in time for the shot. Dance steps and action sequences were finalized minutes before cameras rolled, and improvisation continued as filming proceeded. Similarly, locations were often decided at the eleventh hour. I accompanied film units as they wandered around the city navigating traffic and gathering crowds while attempting to lock down locations amid last-minute negotiations and confusion over the scores of permissions they needed for "street shooting" (to film in the street).

The extent of informality in arrangements was brought home to me early in my fieldwork while I was watching filming late into the night. A scene in the film *Bhoomi Taayi Chochchala Magaa* (1998) required the two male stars of the film to jump from a sixty-foot tall scaffolding to the ground, where there was a safety net. The stars had not received any training for the shot. The director standing below with a megaphone encouraged them to take the leap, assuring them that it was safe and that "nothing would happen." After much delay they nervously did a few practice "takes." Later, chatting with the directors and stars, I asked about insurance, realizing too late how out of place my question was. They looked surprised and a bit annoyed and informed me there was no insurance. It seemed a new concept. Stars routinely do stunts and fight scenes taking enormous risks, and some gain a reputation for their fearlessness. While filmmaking everywhere has elements of such informal and ad hoc practices, the extent of informality and improvisation differ. In Hollywood much is made of a director, such as Robert Altman, who encourages improvisation, while on film sets in India, improvisation is routine, part of the culture.

This style of operating involving what may be described as a participatory aesthetic rather than a strict division of labor, displays similarities to indigenous performance genres in India. The Ram Lila festival is one example. Described as an amateur and popular institution,[32] annual performances may involve an entire village or small-town community who are participants as well as spectators.[33] The actors are largely "unskilled artistes," many recruited locally. Performances range "from 3–5 day affairs staged by a handful of village enthusiasts who double and triple up on major roles to a month-long extravaganza involving hundreds of actors and 'extras.'"[34] They are improvised and are described as "mov[ing] on amidst a degree of confusion."[35]

RISK AND UNCERTAINTY

In his study of the Eastern European Jewish immigrants responsible for the creation of Hollywood, Neal Gabler describes a world of risk and opportunity.

The individuals who inhabited this world seemed similar to the filmmakers I encountered in Bangalore—pioneers who made up their own rules and operated on speculation and hunches. A Bangalore-based distributor, Mr. Gupta, who had worked in both regional Kannada cinema and in Bollywood, commented on the risk-ridden nature of the business: "[it's] . . . a crazy business. People who are involved in movie business, they have to be mentally mad! Not the audience—people who are connected to the movies . . . even after thirty-two years I never feel myself secure. Some element of risk is there." [36] Fickle audiences are central to the uncertainty; a Tamil star is quoted as saying, "You never know how long you will be popular. The audience can drop you as soon as they take you up."[37] Filmmakers become so used to living in this world of risk (and spectacle) that they may seek out similar atmospheres even when on holiday: an Indian filmmaker visiting the United States for a month made two visits to Las Vegas.

Commercial filmmaking in India is described as a "heterogeneous production,"[38] where thousands of small independent producers work with money raised by individual entrepreneurs.[39] Just as in Hollywood, where six to seven out of every ten movies fail,[40] filmmakers in India function in an environment where failures outweigh successes by over 70 percent;[41] each year, only fifteen to twenty films enter the top bidding range,[42] and a large percentage of film projects are never completed.[43] India's regional cinemas may operate in a climate of even greater risk. In the late 1990s, eighty to ninety Kannada films were made (or completed) on average each year and distributed. Kannada film-business insiders acknowledged that in a given year only ten percent of the annual releases are viable, the rest being failures that do not even recoup their costs. In some years the films that succeeded were far fewer than this ten percent.[44]

The absence of industry status and uncertain financing amplified risks for filmmakers. Into the late 1990s and even beyond, producers, unable to secure loans from banks, worked with uncertain private financing, or "merchant capital";[45] money was borrowed at "usurious rate(s),"[46] and stars were often paid "in black."[47] It has been customary for distributors to finance films by bidding for screening territories in advance of films being completed. Even music companies and record makers finance films.[48] The disaggregated nature of filmmaking in India has meant that the business has been a magnet for anyone with "unaccounted for" money who wished to invest or launder it, from "bucket manufacturers and horse-breeders [to] real estate developers, failed politicians and underworld dons,"[49] and for entrepreneurs who "arrived with suitcases filled with currency notes to launch a [Bollywood] film."[50] A cameraman in Bangalore told me that even "those who sell bananas wholesale in the market . . . will put up some money to make a movie."

Rarely have films been assured of complete financing from their inception. Instead, financing acquired in stages was patched together, and many films remained unfinished because of lack of funds. The lack of financial guarantees and security has bankrupted producers and financiers when their films flopped.[51] In interviews, more than one Kannada filmmaker spoke about the high-stakes gamble filmmaking was and revealed that they had had to resort to drastic measures, including pawning or selling their belongings; one filmmaker said he had sold his wife's jewelry to make a film,[52] all of which speaks to the informality of filmmaking, which functions like a family business.

Unsurprisingly, the film business has gained a reputation for scams and speculative ventures. A Bangalore distributor who had close contacts in Bombay described a great deal of "cheating" on deals. Starting in the late 1990s, news reports highlighted the involvement of criminal elements in the industry amid growing concern over the involvement of the Bombay underworld with connections to financiers in the Middle East.[53] Recently, film conglomerates have appeared on the scene and are changing the way films are financed and produced. Yet in 2012 when I visited Bangalore, stories of scams and scandals in the film business were the subject of local gossip.

The changes brought about by India's liberalization reforms enacted in the 1990s created a shifting terrain for the film business in terms of markets and audiences.[54] Economic liberalization increased competition from Hollywood as more of the films were screened in India and soon after their release in the United States. The reforms had an effect on the middle classes, setting off a consumer revolution. Indians witnessed a sudden boom in television and in satellite television,[55] differential exposure to which was seen as responsible for bringing about shifting tastes in film. Audiences and their filmgoing practices were also changing in other ways: the middle classes, estimated at between 190 and 300 million,[56] were returning to theaters they had abandoned in the 1970s.[57] Audiences under the age of thirty continued to grow,[58] and the international or nonresident Indian (NRI) audience was emerging as an influential market segment.[59]

These factors, taken together, meant that filmmakers were forced to deal with increasing unpredictability and competition as the market appeared to be differentiating in several ways: by region, by rural-urban distinctions, and by the social class of the viewer.[60] While earlier filmmakers could count on "all-India hits," the segmenting market made this less likely. In 1999 no single Hindi/Bollywood movie achieved the status of a universal hit.[61] The industry was described as being in crisis. Filmmakers were aware that both their practices and their assumptions about audiences were outdated. In interviews, filmmakers admitted that they had been "playing catch up" with audiences, who were frequently ahead of them in their sophistication and appreciation of quality filmmaking.

FILMMAKERS ADDRESS UNCERTAINTIES AND UNKNOWNS

Forecasting the box office for a film that is newly released, or one yet to be, remains a challenge even in Hollywood, where in spite of the significant resources devoted to market research and audience testing, the unknowns in film reception continue to perplex producers. Only a minority of films make a profit, and both hits and flops continually provide surprises, leading to a constant questioning of received wisdom.[62] As so-called scientific box-office predictions leave something to be desired, there is constant searching for ways to determine how a film will fare upon its release.[63]

The ways that film-business insiders deal with risk and uncertainty offers insights into traditions and cultures of filmmaking. In Hollywood, where the selling of a film is serious business, the millions of dollars spent on marketing and audience testing often exceed a film's production costs.[64] Indeed, the marketing of a film may begin even before production, and marketing departments have a say in the selection of scripts.[65] Selling a movie to the first-weekend audience is a highly systematized and orchestrated operation, rather like a military campaign, and it involves publicity events, the coordination of merchandising with the film's release, and saturation advertising, all to create a "buzz."[66] Hollywood studios have for decades tested titles, stories, characters, and star casts before production and have surveyed audiences postproduction and held preview screenings.[67] Although audience research is acknowledged to be underdeveloped and full of flaws, such methods continue to be used and refined.[68]

Rosie Thomas has commented on the absence of market research in Bollywood in the 1980s, and this appeared to be true a decade later.[69] Sociologist Patricia Uberoi refers to the "canny marketing and distribution strategy" for *Hum Aapke Hain Kaun* (Who am I to you? [1994]), where "for the first time in India the producers made use of cable TV" to publicize the film and banned the release of video rights, releasing the film only in "a few select movie halls."[70] The strategy of film marketing described as "new" by Uberoi is quite basic in its use of television and attempts to prevent video piracy. This together with the absence of a separate budget for marketing a film is evidence that the high-intensity marketing and audience testing taken for granted in Hollywood was relatively unknown in India despite the enormous productivity and global reach of its film business.[71]

Films are publicized variously in India: through newspaper advertisements, film magazines, and television programs. The informality and spontaneity that characterizes filmmaking and production extends to publicizing films as well. Traditionally, word of mouth has played a central role in India, where people, especially the mass audience, many of whom are illiterate, do not read film reviews in newspapers or film magazines (though greater access to television has brought about some changes in communication). In small towns and villages "film advertising" used to mean a man on a bicycle with sandwich boards or in an auto-rickshaw with a megaphone riding around shouting "goppa action chitram!" (big action picture!) while providing information on who was starring,[72] a practice similar to hawkers wandering the streets shouting their wares. Cinema's visual presence in the city is itself a form of spectacular publicity that generates word of mouth. Giant hoardings or billboards, towering cutouts that loom above the street, and brightly colored movie posters all generate awareness about the films while bringing a surreal quality to everyday spaces. Any discussion of marketing and publicity is incomplete without mentioning film music, which is released before a film and effectively creates awareness about it. Months before a film is in theaters, its songs are heard everywhere. Audiences frequently select a film based on its soundtrack and wish to "see the songs" ("picturized" song sequences).

I found that many filmmakers in Bangalore were wary of releasing too much information to the media before a film's release. More than one filmmaker I spoke with insisted that it was "dangerous" to provide information and details about the film too early. Kannada producer and former child star Puneet Rajkumar said that he did not believe in excessive, saturation advertising of the kind known in Hollywood, as it gave away too much information: "you see the trailers of movies coming out and the interviews with stars; you know everything before the movie! That's not for us." Instead, secrecy was important. Filmmakers preferred to "[make] the film quietly," and they explained, "We don't let the press inside the film. When we're making the film, we don't let much of video advertising. . . . Because what's the use? At the end of it all you watch *Jurassic Park* and come out, you know what they've done; they've given such kind of special effect, they've given this. Not for this industry! This is too small."[73]

I asked Puneet about the success of *Om*, made by his family owned production company, which featured gangster types or "rowdies"; fans had flocked to the film because they had heard that "real rowdies" had acted in it. He replied, "It was basically word-of-mouth publicity, see, like, how you got to know—go and talk to others. See, I generally don't believe in marketing much." Instead, loyal fans are used as a resource for spreading positive word of mouth in advance of a film's release. A star acknowledged, "We'll call them and tell them about the film, tell them to come to shootings." Fans who identified themselves as friends of stars would show up at filming sites at the studios and in the city, which were otherwise a well-kept secret, and would be given backstage information on the film. They would relay the same to a larger group and thereby generate a buzz. On multiple occasions when I dropped by the offices of a producer, I found him sipping tea and chatting with fans about movies that were either in the theater or in production. He would supply them with select bits of information on the progress of a film, inform them of the date of the "music launch" or informally question them about what they had heard people say or the scenes they had watched being filmed, and so on, a "focus group" tactic also used by theater managers. This personalized style of interaction continues today, facilitated by Twitter, Facebook, and other social media.

Rather than quantify variables and risk, film-business insiders in India in the late 1990s appeared to operate within a meaning system that embraced unknowns. Their ways of talking and thinking about their work and their audiences expressed the difficulty, even futility, of forecasting outcomes. They frequently spoke of "risk," "chance," "unknown outcomes," "gambles," "miracles," and of films "clicking" or not with audiences, a serendipitous outcome, something that cannot be predicted, replicated, or in any way controlled. A film that turns out to be "good" or that is well received by audiences (a distinction that is not always made and that some see as irrelevant for a commercial film enterprise), is understood to be a chance outcome. One director said he could never take full credit for making a film, because "films just happen . . . so many things have to come together, they may not come together." Rather than "fixing" a film using audience feedback, filmmakers in Bangalore hoped for a serendipitous outcome: "sometimes we do this kind of mistake, but we take a chance! We have to. Sometimes it (the film) may click (with audiences) also."

Despite the increasing volatility in the market, the larger sums of money at stake, differentiating audiences, rapidly segmenting markets, and the complications of a globalized media, filmmakers expressed skepticism about audience research and product testing.[74] In conversation with a Kannada director, I mentioned that women I had spoken with at a theater screening a popular Kannada film had objected to the film's ending when the hero was not reunited with the heroine. The director felt it was pointless to ask audiences *after* the fact—that is, after the film had reached the theater: "People have liked it, no?

Ultimately, judgment is theirs. Once they like it . . . we can't probe them—*why* they liked it or not. . . . And it's an *ultimate*. Once they give a judgment, yes, this film is good, and their verdict is final." On further discussion it became evident that he was not familiar with preview screening, used routinely in Hollywood at the time. He explained the futility of attempting to "repair" a film or of dissecting a film after its release: "See what happens, by the time we repair this film, the film is over! So the whole context of the next film, the content, everything will be different."

A filmmaker who had been in the business long enough to have had his share of hits and flops also subscribed to the view that tinkering with a film after it was made was neither feasible nor productive. He argued that given the element of chance and the degree of subjectivity in filmmaking compounded by the vagaries of audiences' tastes, producers can only wait until the film is "judged" by the audience. "You may argue in different actor, I may argue in a different actor [that a different star should have been cast] but ultimately people have to judge. Till that time we have to pull [till the film is screened in the theater and audiences respond, filmmakers have to work with uncertainty and make their efforts]. There on the auditorium [floor] only that will take place." Filmmakers felt that even if a particular film was replicated as per formula (made with the same ingredients as another film that was successful) and released, there would be no guarantee that the audience would approve of it: "Only *we* can assess and dissect the thing. *Why* it happened? See, same thing if you repeat, it may not run. . . . Even if [director of a hit film] repeats himself, people may not like. These kind of things go on."

Such views, produced as truths, while they express the difficulties of gauging the audience's tastes, make little allowance for Hollywood-style assessment of a film's reception involving systematic methods of garnering feedback and with the purpose of altering a film after its completion.[75] One filmmaker explained patiently that moviemaking is not a transparent or logical exercise with a predictable outcome: "Because we don't have any definite proposition for this, it's not mathematics or science. In mathematics 2 plus 2 is equal to? *You* have to say 4, *I* have to say 4! It's not like that here." Compare this to the search for precision in minimizing unknowns in the United States, where computers are being used to assess scripts and scenes for maximizing the box office.[76]

MAGIC, LUCK, RITUAL

Filmmakers everywhere are a superstitious lot. Hollywood from its inception has been rife with superstition.[77] In India, belief in luck, chance, good and bad times, lucky and unlucky numbers, dates, and places shapes filmmaking. Robert Hardgrave quotes a character actor in Tamil films: "In cinema it's all luck. . . . You have to be lucky to get in, to become known and to stay in."[78]

While filmmakers did not subscribe to known methods of market research and product testing, they did tap into cultural practices that traditionally seek an auspicious outcome. For example, a film project, or the music for a film, is "launched" at an inaugural ceremony, the *muhurat* or *muhurtam*—a ritual and auspicious beginning for any major event or ritual occasion. The *muhurtam* for a Hindu wedding, for example, is an auspicious sliver of time during which the actual marriage ritual is scheduled. The film *muhurat* brings together astrologers and priests with filmmakers, producers, actors, distributors, their families, and well-wishers as well as members of the film crew. On an auspicious date set by astrologers, a *pooja* (ritual worship) is conducted by Hindu priests either at a temple or at the home of the director or producer to ensure the film's smooth progress. Lord Ganesha, remover of obstacles, is propitiated, as is Goddess Saraswati, whose portfolio is learning and the arts. A family deity may also be worshipped. Frequently, the first scene (the *muhurat* shot) is set in a temple and filmed on the auspicious inaugural day. The scene then finds its way into the film—which in part explains what used to be mandatory scenes of temples and worship in Indian films.[79] To ensure success at the box office, a prayer for Lord Ganesha or Goddess Lakshmi (the goddess of fortune) is often placed at the beginning of the film, even before the opening credits. Parents, grandparents, and kin who have passed on may be remembered and thanked, their blessings sought.

Astrologers as well as numerologists and other soothsayers may be consulted at various stages in the making of a film or in the careers of film-business insiders. Websites list lucky numbers for a number of Bollywood and regional cinema stars along with their birthdays and other astrological details. Films are often released on an auspicious day based on the horoscope of the star, the producer, or the director, evident in this news report on the release of the superhit *Sivaji, The Boss* (2007): "Moreover Rajini's lucky day is Thursday. Director Shankar's lucky number is 8. Both believe in astrology. Both would like to release the film on their lucky date." Similarly, films starring Kannada cinema's Shivarajkumar are released on particular dates considered lucky for him. His fans informed me that his wife and *her* horoscope were thought to have brought him luck, so his wife's birthday was one such auspicious date; another was his father's birthday. Waiting for a lucky day to release a film may affect other films. The delay in the release of *Sivaji* was reported to have in-

F I G U R E 3 . Chilies and lemons hung outside the box office at the Everest theater remove the
evil eye. Photograph by the author, Bangalore, 2012.

terfered with the plans of "about 15 producers who (are) in a quandary about
when to release their own films."[80]

In regional cinema communities, which include its audiences and media
covering the film world, the stars' lucky numbers, birthdays, and wedding
anniversaries are part of film lore. Shivarajkumar's lucky numbers are widely
known in the Kannada film community to be nine and one. According to
newspaper reports for his recent film, *Mylari* (2010), his remuneration was
rumored to be ninety-one lakhs, neatly bringing together his two lucky numbers. According to another report, the star "demanded the producers to pay
that amount."[81] In an interview, Shivarajkumar confirmed that these were his
lucky numbers but denied he was being paid that amount.[82] Stars may also
wear certain protective amulets and rings, and many continue to wear them
while filming irrespective of the character they portray.

Certain theaters are considered lucky for the release of a film, and stars and
directors may visit theaters that they believe to be auspicious for them, rather
like visiting shrines. The Pramod Theater is thought to be lucky for Kannada
film superstar Puneet Rajkumar, who is reported to watch his films at this

theater on the first day of their release.[83] Superstition is also rampant among Bollywood's elite; they point to flops made or released at an inauspicious time or those that did not have a lucky title. For some time Bombay producer Karan Johar selected film titles with words that started with the letter K, thought to bring him luck.[84] A news item focusing on astrological predictions for the new Bollywood film *We Are Family* (2010) gives fairly detailed predictions for the fate of the film, its stars, and director Karan Johar:

1. The name of the film adds up to 37, a number considered fortunate in love, sex, and partnerships.
2. The film is being released on Thursday the 2nd; a combination of Neptune and the sun adds up to number 5, which is Mercury, which augurs well for Karan "Gemini" Johar. From his point of view, he is playing safe.
3. Kajol [a heroine] is likely to get maximum applauds [sic] but Kareena [another heroine] too is going through her best phase (astrologically) and will serve a commendable performance.
4. Arjun Ramphal [a hero] is also going to benefit from the film since he falls into the brackets of numbers 3, 6, 8 and 9.
5. However the year 2010 (number 3) clashes bitterly with the number 1 (the Sun) and this may stall the film in the long run. Therefore the film would do a decent business initially but wouldn't quite rattle the box office. Not to run for weeks, that is.[85]

FILMMAKERS STUDY AUDIENCES AND RECEPTION SETTINGS

The more accurately a film's audience is forecast, the better its chances at the box office. Anticipating the audience becomes an important way to lower risk. Yet given the informality in the functioning of the film business and the lack of audience studies and market research, how do Indian filmmakers get a sense of their audience and the potential reception of their films? While filmmakers expressed their skepticism about preview screenings, audience testing, and marketing and maintained that all they could do was wait for audiences to either accept or reject a film, they nevertheless used informal means to get a sense of how their films were received. More than one director informed me that he gets a sense of how a film is doing by tapping his social circle, "talking with people at parties," and asking family members what they think of the film. Another emphasized his "different" approach. He claimed that he never asked his family or friends for their opinion; instead, he relied on his household help or the film's tea boy, whose opinions he believed more closely approximated the mass audience, a tactic apparently followed by Bombay filmmakers as well.[86]

The personalization and lack of specialization that characterizes filmmaking extends to anticipations of audiences at cinemas. Both the star and the director of *America! America!* told me they visited the theater where the film was playing and talked with the parking lot attendant to get a sense of the audience reaction. The attendant's daily income became an indicator of the film's success. Ramesh, the star of the film, reported, "And that . . . parking lot guy who used to be selling parking tickets told me, 'Sir, I'm making 500 to 600 rupees a day. I've never made this money before!' See, that's the feedback you get!" These practices are again similar to those of pre-Hollywood movie entrepreneurs. At a time when filmmaking was run more like a small business, a good businessman would be on-site to get the consumer's response. Adolph Zukor, who later built Paramount Pictures, traveled through Europe and America and personally observed audiences at theaters.[87] In the 1920s, Carl Laemmle, founder of Universal Pictures, began his film career carrying out informal field studies of audiences.[88]

Although Rosie Thomas observed that those in the Bombay film business rarely watch films in theaters with audiences,[89] I found that film-business insiders in Bangalore routinely did so. Once a film is released, the exhibition site becomes the focus of attention. In what amounts to "participant observation," stars and directors often attend screenings to get a firsthand glimpse of audience response and to absorb the mood in the theater.[90] On multiple occasions I encountered filmmakers, stars, producers, cinematographers, and dialogue writers at theaters, where they chatted with theater managers, ushers, ticket clerks, and audiences. On the weekend when the Kannada film *Kurubana Raani* (Shepherd's queen [1998]) was released, its star, Shivarajkumar, arrived at the Sagar Theater amid a frenzy of excited fans. Once inside, he watched the film "with" the audience and, in a leisurely fashion, engaged theater staff about the film's reception. Soon after this encounter, I went to the matinee of another newly released film, *Megha Bantu Megha* (The clouds are gathering [1998]). Arriving at the theater I found a group of excited moviegoers standing outside the gates, eagerly waiting for them to open. They told me that "Ramesh" (Aravind), star of the film, was inside watching his movie. People pressed against the gate and climbed on the walls of the theater trying to get a glimpse of him. They interrogated the security guard, asking for confirmation of the star's whereabouts. Later on, when I asked Ramesh about his visit, he replied, "I go once in a way, just to know the straight audience reaction. If most of the time you thought there's going to be a laugh here, and there is a laugh here, you feel good, your judgment is right. Sometimes in a place where you never expected a reaction, there's a reaction!" When I asked Shivarajkumar about his theater visits, he, too, indicated that he had gone several times, sometimes with his cinematographer friend, at other times with the director or family members. The practice appears to be in place years later. The stars of the Kannada film *Raam* (2010) were reported to have watched the movie in theaters on the first day of its release. The lead actress Priyamani is quoted as saying, "I wanted to see *Raam* with the audience. . . . A few people noticed me during the interval and I exchanged pleasantries with them."[91] Puneet Rajkumar, the hero of the film, was also reported to have seen the film with the first-day audience.

Recently, stars and well-known directors are known to visit theaters in what has become a promotional event. Their possible presence at theaters is enough to generate word of mouth and draw enthusiasts to first-day or first-weekend screenings. Director-producer Karan Johar was reported to be touring multiplexes in Bombay for his film *My Name Is Khan* (2009),[92] while Bollywood star Abhishek Bachchan reportedly went around the city with an entourage of six dancers, stopping at "multiple locations," including movie theaters, to promote his upcoming film *Raavan* (2010).[93]

HETEROGENEOUS AUDIENCES AND THE SOCIOLOGY OF UNIVERSAL APPEAL

Identifying what the audience wants has always been—and continues to be—the biggest challenge for filmmakers. Sam (Roxy) Rothafel, the son of a German immigrant and entrepreneur who transformed film exhibition in the United States between 1913 and 1934, complained that "the audience always knows what it wants after it has seen it."[94] This after-the-fact knowledge has plagued the movie business and has reduced movie executives to "reading box office tea leaves."[95] Film's uniqueness as a product, the nature of the moviegoing experience, competition from other films and various types of entertainment and leisure activities, and the "intangible and experiential nature of movie consumption" all contribute to the uncertainties of a film's reception.[96] Screenwriter William Goldman summed up the unknowns in filmmaking when he remarked, "Nobody knows anything."[97]

Rather than the question of how films have an effect on audiences—the question that preoccupies textual analysis and media effects research—it is important to ask instead how audiences shape films. Filmmakers in India use a combination of "background factors"—aggregates of class, social background, and culture as well as informal observations of the foreground, such as audience practices, habits of filmgoing, show timings and patterns of attendance at theaters, and filmgoers' lifestyles to anticipate their market and reception. A thorough discussion of such classifications and anticipations being impossible here, I will focus selectively on some of the aggregate categories that film-makers use to anticipate and identify audience groups and publics and that guide their thinking about filmmaking and audience expectations.[98]

Broad social categories are used to place both films and audiences in a hierarchy.[99] Films are classified into A, B, and C, a ranking that signals both the quality of the film and the terrain where it plays well. A-ranked films are popular in A centers: metropolises such as Delhi, Bombay, Madras, or Bangalore, as well as with NRI audiences overseas. B and C films play in small towns and villages as well as with lower-class viewers in cities and in tent theaters that cater to the urban poor. Based on these rankings, producers and distributors "intuitively" carve up the market into distribution territories, each with its own demographic characteristics.[100]

Implicit in this ranking are ideas of "class" and "mass." Class films are believed to appeal to the middle and upper-middle classes, the urban educated, and "ladies." A Kannada actress talked about "A class" comprising "family audiences and royal people (elites)," while a theater manager identified mass viewers at the bottom of this social hierarchy as "coolies, all types of poor people" or "front benchers," those who sit in the cheapest seats in the stratified theater. A film that appeals to the "class" audience is considered a very different animal from a "mass" film. Class (or A-ranked) films have big budgets and high production values, and they feature top-ranked stars in romances, light comedies, and dramas considered wholesome fare suitable for a family audience. In comparison, films that appeal to the mass audience are low-budget entertainment that deliver thrills in the form of risqué scenes, earthy comedy, action, and violence. The stars in these films may be favorites of C-class and rural audiences. Complicating the mass-class distinction is the rural-urban classification. These categories overlap and may be applied contextually; *rural* has connotations of lower class, uneducated or illiterate, and unsophisticated. Like mass audiences in urban areas, rural audiences are thought to favor mindless entertainment and thrills.

The social categories assigned to films also rest on their linguistic styles. An actress explained that mass audiences understand a form of Kannada that is considered low and rough (by educated urbanites). Therefore, to address the lower-class viewer or "front bencher," characters speak in a rural style of Kannada, which is recognized as impure. This "village language," its coarseness of expression and vulgar humor, is also thought to appeal to the uneducated.

Kannada star Jaggesh, known for his "explosive language," appealed to village folk who could understand him. At the same time, his coarse speech turned off "A-class" viewers, that is, family and elite audiences who prefer a "pure," "high," and "literary" form of the language: "*uppata* Kannada." Stars therefore carve out a niche for themselves with a particular audience base by film dialogue and its delivery.[101]

"Mass" and "rural" audiences are often conflated into a "C-class" category of uneducated hooligans, or "rowdies," who revel in crudity and foul language. A television entertainer explained, "They want entertainment, *that sort of language*, 'Your mother!' that sort of thing. They are that sort of people, so they go [for such films]." A distributor confirmed that in Kannada films that increasingly targeted the mass audience, characters "started talking like the *goondas*" (thugs and lowlifes).

Filmmakers and stars emphasized the importance of making "clean" and "decent" movies that would draw middle-class audiences with fare that families could watch together in theaters. Looking ahead to the viewing setting and the social aesthetic that frames filmgoing, filmmaker Yash Chopra is quoted as saying, "We must make clean and decent entertainers. I shouldn't feel embarrassed to sit with members of my family in a movie theater."[102] Discussions of decency and vulgarity surfaced frequently in conversations with film-business insiders and audiences and may be understood as another way to assign a hierarchy to films and audiences. Ramesh, whose films appealed to middle-class women, told me that he felt proud to have gained a reputation for making "decent" films to which parents could send their daughters. Stars presented themselves as catering to a "decent," "class" audience even if they appeared in films that appealed to "mass" audiences. Another Kannada star, known for his violent and, from a middle-class perspective, tasteless films that were popular with lower-class male audiences, told me that he liked his movies to be "clean, entertaining, something the whole family can see."

Discussions of "decent" films and audiences are part of a broader discourse about cinema that combines moral concerns and aesthetic judgments.[103] The class versus mass distinction informs such understandings; people link decency to taste and class. The widespread prejudice that exists against the mass audience, their tastes and powers of comprehension or lack thereof, is shared by many moviegoers who themselves belong to the lower socioeconomic orders. Filmmakers' preoccupation with making "decent" films reveal pressures similar to those encountered by pre-Hollywood movie entrepreneurs whose main objective once they had popularized movies was to capture wealthier middle-class patrons and to elevate and legitimize the movie business through gentrification.[104] Indeed, descriptions of films and images as being "clean" and "decent" may also have something to do with "interview bias" as filmmakers and audiences engage in a presentation of self that is moral, thus elevating their status.

Overall, filmmakers and film commentators apply the discourse of modernization to their categorization or ranking of audience groups. Bollywood's Shahrukh Khan is quoted as saying, "I've always felt films should be slick and modern . . . and have a modern sensibility."[105] The distinctions filmmakers make between rural and urban viewers, the educated and uneducated, and categories of class, mass, and NRI (diasporic) audiences speak to this modernization discourse. Different sites are placed on a continuum of modernization: "cosmopolitan" cities, where middle-class audiences are appreciative of more sophisticated fare, are contrasted with poorer, uneducated, and rural audiences, seen as undiscriminating consumers of spectacle. More recently, there has been a differentiation by region and also based on audiences' varied exposure to globalizing forces such as Hollywood films and international programs via satellite television as well as English-language education. Therefore, filmmakers have had to rethink audience classifications and how to appeal to audiences in the context of emerging and segmenting markets. Talk of "niche audiences" and "urban" and "multiplex" films are all evidence of the ongoing changes in audience groupings and markets.

AVOIDING REJECTION: FILMMAKING CONVENTIONS AND CONSTRAINTS

I met two kinds of filmmaker: a minority who felt they had to "to control the taste of the mass audience" and a larger group who believed they could not afford to impose their tastes and views on the audience. This second group of filmmakers believed that a film that was a box-office success could not be criticized because it had stood the acid test. They defended the popular aesthetic even as they displayed ambivalence about it. One director felt his taste in films was irrelevant, that he did not need to like a film he made: "Sometimes *we* may not like it—I didn't like —— film so much. . . . Ultimately the collection [box office], the people, *they* are going. See the film is made for *them*, and if *they* have accepted, then we should keep silent." Even filmmakers who preferred to make "thinking films," such as the Kannada novelist Nagathihalli Chandrashekar, emphasized the importance of appealing to "the mass": "*Unless* you reach the mass it becomes a problem. Because film is a commercial product—I *have* to get common audiences. I *have* to relate to the masses! Otherwise, if I just make a documentary on Brain Drain [an underlying theme of his latest feature film], a few medicos or engineering students may go to the film, but what about the front bench?"

In the late 1990s and into the 2000s, reaching a broad audience was seen as necessary for a film's survival at the box office. The selection of film themes and content, the casting of the film are all done with this aim. Where cinema going remains a family and group outing, and where 50 percent of "any filmgoing crowd" are minors,[106] fragmenting the market by age and gender is not necessarily good business practice. A director explained the rationale for selecting the theme for a film, "See the whole family—the youngster, the older, the ladies, *all* they should come in one category. That kind of subject they should pick because that's more paying. . . . So even if we make a teenager's story, there will be a story of elders. It is not out-and-out teenagers." Even if films are given restricted ratings, theaters rarely enforce them. The ideal film is a blockbuster that will sweep all others off the board; Kannada filmmakers pointed to the success of *Titanic*, in theaters at the time, to justify this approach.

In interview conversations, film-business insiders frequently elaborated on the challenges of bridging the vast social differences among audiences. Dialogue writer Richard Louis expressed the difficulties of writing for a "villager" in the audience and a "fellow from the city. . . . If you tell [the story] in more detail, this fellow says why is he trying to tell it so many times? And that fellow doesn't understand it." Women in small towns and rural areas are seen as especially conservative in their tastes and likely to reject films that have modern or edgy themes. *Amruthavarshini* (1996), a Kannada film that told the story of an extramarital affair, failed to find an audience in territories other than big cities (A centers). A Kannada director explained, "See, Bangalore is a cosmopolitan city where people have grown a little."

Stars also worried that they would be unable to bridge the rural-urban divide and achieve the broad appeal across "class" and "mass" necessary for superstardom. I asked a director whether movies of a given star play mostly in metropolitan and urban areas, not small towns. He replied: "Exactly! Exactly! He has not reached the small towns where superstars like Ravichandra and Shivarajkumar they have reached there." Stars who are associated with "class" movies may not have the viability of "mass" heroes, and "urban stars" may find it difficult to enter the rural market. Consequently, stars develop constituencies in much the same way that politicians do. A filmmaker explained: "Jaggesh movies in villages, it goes very well. Only in villages, not here." Meanwhile an "urban" star said, "They claim that my films run only in cities. That's OK! Better than if it doesn't run anywhere!"

The tastes of the NRI audience are perceived to overlap with the urban middle classes in India. Both these groups enjoy big-budget movies and feel-good romances that are situated in urban settings in India or abroad. Stars who appealed to urbanites in India felt confident they would be popular with NRI audiences. However, because NRI audiences are removed from the everyday reality of India, they are seen to crave "a sugarcoated pill about India." That is, they "need to feel more Indian than Indians themselves and their notions of a mythical Indian family have to be kept alive."[107] Remarking that NRIs "reject action," distributor Mr. Gupta explained that "soft movies" and musicals, with their attendant themes of feel-good romance, provide a pleasing fantasy for "Asians, Pakistanis living in foreign countries such as England or America," and such films become big hits there.

Regional film businesses with smaller markets determined by linguistic boundaries are especially challenged by having to straddle the expectations of a heterogeneous audience while satisfying the requirements of making films that will appeal to "a decent crowd." The Kannada film business, for example, cannot afford to ignore the mass viewer. Following the "retirement" and later demise (in 2006) of megastar and film legend Dr. Rajkumar, whose films had wide appeal and were considered "clean," "family-oriented" entertainment, Kannada films were believed to have marginalized themselves with vulgar entertainers catering exclusively to the "mass," or the lower rungs of the social strata described in interviews as "revenue site owners,"[108] slum dwellers, and poor people. Film-business insiders bemoaned the fact that films increasingly exploited sexual innuendo and cheap thrills and used, as Richard Louis put it, "double-meaning dialogues, filthy comedy and all that . . . to hold the auditorium. So obviously, the educated and the class people slowly drifted away." According to a cinematographer, "a lot of films were made about antiheros in the eighties, [and] even now." The tastes of this audience were seen increasingly to shape the films, which further alienated the educated middle classes:

> When the taste was so specified to one group of people, such people started coming—they [the films] started catering to their feelings—[such as] highlighting and honoring *goondaism* (vandalism and crime) that was also a frustration of the lower class. . . . So [if a] fellow from the slum will become a hero [in the film], the people started talking like *goondas*.

Kannada films that appeared to cater exclusively to young, lower-class men are regarded as being at the bottom of the hierarchy or "caste system" of films.[109] An entire film business has found itself stigmatized by such films. Filmmakers expressed their concern over the loss of the middle-class audience who, they said, had been lured away by Hollywood and Bollywood films. Some directors were annoyed that the middle classes had abandoned them and that they had to go out of their way to woo them back as viewers: "Now the Mountain has to go to Mohammed. Why can't they come to the theater? They will go for foreign film, art film." This has changed somewhat with a new clutch of stars and directors who make "class" films and with the "Bollywoodisation" of regional cinema, which has popularized the middle-class family entertainer.

Filmmakers function with taken-for-granted understandings of the likes and dislikes of various audience groups even as they aimed for a wide appeal for their films. A distributor voiced a commonly held view at the time: "Indian audiences, they can't be satisfied with just one type of movie. Give them just a comedy movie for three hours, they will not like it." The multigenre film that provides spectacle, travelogue, comedy, melodrama, and favorite stars in favorite roles and where narrative is subordinate to these formulaic ingredients is seen to satisfy audience expectations for variety rather than a narrative with a single storyline or homogeneity of emotion. The traditional masala film and its "omnibus" form may itself be understood to have evolved to address risk and uncertainty in the context of a heterogeneous audience and absence of market research.

Rules of thumb become useful fallbacks for filmmakers: having the hero play a double role, casting two heros (or heroines), casting currently popular "star-*jodis*" (romantic pairs), or inserting an "item-number" (a dance extravaganza with an attractive performer). According to one filmmaker, "whenever there is a rebel woman (character), the film clicks." He used the example of recent Kannada films such as *Janumada Jodi* (1996) and *O Mallige* (1997), which had "clicked" with women and with the "class" audience because of their progressive themes.

Incorporating a requisite number of song-and-dance sequences is seen as a way to satisfy audience expectations, extend a film's market, and reduce risk. Films have been known to survive on the strength of their "songs." For example, the films *Dil Se* (1998) and *Major Saab* (1998), which were flops in terms of their success across India, did well in certain regions because of one particular song in each movie. Talking about his foray into making commercial films, a cameraman-turned-director expressed confidence in the song sequences for his soon-to-be-released film even while he acknowledged that he was unsure about the plot. Consequently, the budget for picturized song sequences can form a significant proportion of the film's total budget. A single song sequence for *Endhiran* (Robot [2010]) was rumored to have cost Rs. 30 crore, when the film's total cost was Rs. 200 crore.[110]

Music appeals through emotion, and "emotional themes" are expected to reach across social differences.[111] A dialogue writer had clear ideas about what constituted this universal language.

> See, the theme should be a universal truth. And here visual is the only communicating factor. And emotion. The emotion is the only common thing between these two fellows [viewers of different social backgrounds—one urban and one rural]. However great he is, he is also prone to the same emotion, and however poor he is, he is also prone to the same emotion. The drama in the situation brings the two together. . . . It touches you, it touches me, it touches that person also.

In discussions of films, past and prospective, filmmakers would highlight emotion and "sentiment." On the set of a romantic comedy, a director contemplating his next film said that he wanted to make a film about "fathers and sons" because it was an "emotional relationship." Indeed, "sentiment" and "universal themes" play a part in the selection of Hollywood films that are the inspiration for indigenous remakes. The popularity of the Kannada remake of *A Walk in the Clouds* (1995) was attributed to its "typical Indian sentiment," and a director recommended it to me enthusiastically: "You see that film! It has an Indian sentiment! . . . It has been made into ——. It clicked! . . . Ultimately the film that remains (lasts), that clicks, is the film of sentiment. Love."

Scholars of Indian cinema have described filmmakers' fears of disappointing audiences, audiences "walking out of theaters" or "stoning theaters," concerns that shape content. Rosie Thomas notes that filmmakers "operate with an explicit concept of their audiences' imposing constraints on their filmmaking" and that "a central preoccupation . . . is whether or not the audience will accept certain representations or narrative outcomes." In sessions where the script or story is discussed, she notes, "considerable time and energy are spent in discussing what is or is not acceptable, and devising screenplay ideas that will please their audience. It is common to hear in script-development sessions phrases such as 'our audiences will not accept' . . . and 'they'll burn the theaters down if we show.'"[112] Audiences, then, are understood to wield considerable power over a film and its reception. Tamil film icon Shivaji Ganesan acknowledged the power of the audience when he said he had to "take into due consideration the likes and dislikes of the patrons of the cinema," even "shape (his) performance . . . to their requirements."[113]

This understanding of the power of the mass audience is sometimes portrayed in the films themselves. In a scene in the Bollywood film *Rangeela*

(1995), the central character, Munna, a lower-class youth, goes to the movies with his girlfriend. Munna saunters into the theater after the film has begun, talks throughout the film, and creates a ruckus when he puts his feet up on the seats, kicking the person in front of him. Later, fully aware that as the "public," his comfort and amusement is of the utmost importance, he defends his behavior, demonstrating a self-consciousness about the power of his patronage: "I have a right to my opinion [of the film]. If I don't get value for my money, the picture is finished!"

Munna represents the audience that social anthropologist M. N. Srinivas recalls from his childhood experiences of watching movies in Mysore city, about 130 kilometers southwest of Bangalore. The boisterous viewers who occupied the cheapest seats close to the screen were forthright and vocal in their reactions to films even then. Filmmakers were fearful of the reactions of these "four anna rajahs" who sat in the cheapest seats yet determined the fate of the film.[114] Indeed the relationship between filmmaker and audience displays shades of a patron-client relationship; filmmakers are dependent on the audiences' patronage and are willing to compromise and craft the film to appeal to audience expectations.[115]

Over coffee at the Coffee Board café, Mr. Louis linked storytelling rules to the need to anticipate and avoid rejection from the audience. After defending a film on which he had worked on the grounds that it had many "clapworthy dialogues,"[116] he described how films were crafted specifically to speak to the audience's desire to see the hero vanquish the villain: "Every story has to have poetic justice, otherwise the auditorium will slap you!" Many films are "morality plays in which good inevitably triumphs over evil" and the heroes are expected to be virtuous: "Whatever the role it is always the same. The audience expects and demands it." [117] Audiences watch films with preconceived ideas about the roles certain stars should play. Therefore, casting a film predetermines its storyline and ending. A popular hero carries the story and its outcome in himself and therefore cannot be defeated by the villain. When filmmakers want to tell a different story, they cannot employ well-known stars who have a particular relationship with the audience that is their "brand." Mr. Louis explained how (Tamil) director Balachander had to bring in new star-heroes to tell a "new type of story which cannot be told through MGR or Shivaji Ganesan" because audience expectations of the roles these iconic stars should play would not permit it. "Imagine MGR going away singing a song, a disappointed lover! [A viewer] would simply catch Balachander [the director] and shake him. And MGR himself would not do such a role."

There is a strong economic incentive to make films that appeal to the middle-classes and the family audience. Not only does multigenerational appeal broaden the prospective audience, the family audience is thought to extend a film's life at the theater; as one director put it, "film runs only if families come." Additionally, as the 'ladies audience' is thought to bring in the family audience, catering to female moviegoers, especially middle-class women, is good strategy. Another director insisted, "Only when there are ladies in the audience, the film will run constantly." Film-business insiders held onto this "truth" in spite of the runaway success of *A*, which was then mostly drawing men, and which was dismissed as an anomaly or as evidence of the director's "Midas touch."

Filmmakers would become very nervous, therefore, if they thought their movies included scenes that would put off women and the family audience. This may be surprising to the cultural outsider, who may see storylines based on romance and dance moves and costumes that may appear suggestive, and wonder about their suitability for children, as some of my American friends did. Insiders, however, recognize distinct conventions that define what appropriate family fare is. A director who breaks the rules of filmmaking or is unaware of the culture and local context in which films are viewed risks offending viewer sensibilities. Hollywood films, for example, are subject to censorship in India, but viewers can still find them offensive if they violate the conventions of suitable family fare. Over the course of a lengthy conversational interview, I asked a middle-class career woman in Bangalore whether she had ever walked out of a film because she did not like it, or was upset by the content. She was very Westernized in many ways and had lived in the West, yet she subscribed to cultural conventions of what is appropriate for a family or "class" film, immediately responding, "Yes. *Ace Ventura*. It was awful! Awful! We had taken the kids so we just walked out. It was gross and vulgar at the same time. It was just gross! Snot and all that—it was vulgar, a lot of underlying things, (sexual) undercurrents, which I just don't want the kids to watch."

The need to follow filmmaking conventions places constraints on both filmmakers and stars and can lead to aesthetic conflicts.[118] A director complained, "How do you tackle a serious subject when every half hour the actors have to break into song and dance?"[119] In the typical commercial film, the hero and heroine are featured singing duets. Stars are usually enthusiastic about song interludes or at least recognize their importance. They may insist on having them in the film. Refusal to conform to this formula is seen as a radical departure, "breaking the rules" as Ramesh described it as he went on to explain, "I don't insist on songs in my films. Generally the hero insists on five songs, five duets. That's the way the hero is portrayed, no? If there are two heroes, main songs considered the hero. That's what I've been breaking here. . . . I don't believe in the hero going and dancing every time."

An extreme case of audience power is seen when fans object vociferously to a star's role or the ending meted out to his character. Fans may identify so strongly with the actor who plays the hero that they may turn against a film and a director for portraying the hero in a poor light. According to M. S. S. Pandian, directors of films starring Tamil film icon MGR have altered roles to appease angry fans: "Again the story of Pallandu Vazgha [1975] . . . required the hero to die at the end. Hearing of MGR's impeding death on the screen, his fans became restive and the director of the film had to change the end to present an invincible and deathless MGR."[120] In this way fans and enthusiasts become unwitting collaborators or writers and directors in making the film.[121] Tamil films starring MGR, for instance, have to have fight sequences where the star-hero remains invincible if the film is to be accepted by the star's fan base.

Filmmakers and stars who attempt new themes and roles run the risk of turning away their audience base. For Ramesh, the challenge of pleasing the audience yet doing films that interested him was "tightrope walking." His image of respectability or "decency" imposed very real constraints on the roles he could play. When he deviated from this image to play the husband in a troubled marriage, he received irate letters from female viewers who berated him for doing "bedroom scenes" and demanded to know "why are you taking off your shirt and doing scenes like this?" He elaborated on these reactions from his audiences:

> Not that I have a set image—but overall I have a basic decency in all my films. So I crossed the limits of decency in that film, according to [the audience]. I didn't! Personally I didn't feel that way. They didn't like it. They said "please don't do it." . . . The film was about the night life of a couple where the woman was refusing to sleep with a man. So it had to be in the bedroom, with all decency. Even now there is nothing vulgar in that film, but the very concept they didn't like. "No! You shouldn't bare your chest and do things like this on screen!" That's the reaction they give you immediately!

Such reports of audience reaction illustrate the personal and emotional relationship between audiences and stars. Ramesh felt his role had "hurt" his audience: "Of course, after that you want to try different kind of roles. You want to be a killer, you want to be a sex maniac, and so you do—it hurts them [the audience]! I tell you, I've tried!"

Stars who are cast in the mold of all-round entertainers feel the pressure of having to satisfy audience (and filmmaker) expectations. Shivarajkumar, Kannada cinema's "hat-trick hero,"[122] described his job as "very tough" compared with his Hollywood counterparts, as he had to be "everything" in a given film—"a husband, lover, son, and brother"—as well as having to dance and do fight scenes and comedy. His description of his role fits with the storytelling and entertainment forms of high emotionality that are characteristic of traditional Hindu epics,[123] where the central characters are able to evoke a range of emotions from the audience.[124] The popularity of the "double" or even "multiple" role in Indian cinema may be traced to this aesthetic style. Thus, Tamil superhero Shivaji Ganesan played nine roles in one film.[125]

In the need to satisfy audience expectations, even the logic of the narrative may be compromised. According to one director, well-known Kannada writers Beeji and Puttappa not only had a perfect understanding of their audience but also appreciated the absurdities involved in satisfying these audiences: "There is a saying in Kannada—Beeji used to say 'for our audience, even if they [the film's characters] are dying, we should write they were living happily ever after. Even after death.' That kind of ending they like."

In conversations with Kannada filmmakers, the view that most frequently came across was that filmmakers propose and the audience disposes. The audience is regarded as the judge and arbiter rather than as consumers whose tastes and preferences may be manipulated. The release of a film is less like putting a product on the market and more like a performance that may be accepted or rejected—a view that has parallels in live theater. As one director put it, "ultimately people have to judge. There on the auditorium only that will take place." The film itself becomes a space in which the relationship between audiences and stars is expressed and constructed, making the audience very much a participant in the making of the film, which is both a performance and a contract with the audience.

PARTICIPATORY FILMMAKING AND AUDIENCE AS COLLABORATOR

Filmmaking in India in the mid- to late 1990s and even into the first five years or so of the twenty-first century shares certain characteristics with the pre-Hollywood filmmaking of the Nickelodeon era, an important transitional period in cinema where "mom and pop entrepreneurs . . . gave way to mass merchandising."[126] Rather than the division of labor and impersonality often associated with mass consumer culture seen in making and selling films in contemporary Hollywood, this stage in the film business saw a great deal of overlap between the various functions of producing, directing, distributing, and exhibiting movies. The relationships between directors, producers, exhibitors, distributors, stars, and audiences were close, not having developed the anomic quality that accompanies the mature, commercialized industry. Similarly, filmmaking in India involves a high degree of personalization and informality. The multiplicity of producers and financiers and the lack of control by a script brings a variety of influences into the production of a film, making for a distinctive model of filmmaking far removed from the hierarchical studio system in Hollywood. [127] In the absence of formal market research, filmmakers' understanding of audiences is gained through on-site observation, face-to-face interaction, and personal networking. I have described this as an ethnographic perspective. The period since the mid-1990s has been a critical period of growth and change affecting production, distribution, and exhibition for both national and regional film businesses.

Scholars of Indian cinema have identified the roots of commercial film in classical and folk entertainment forms.[128] Indeed, cinema in India has been regarded as part of folk culture,[129] and the influence of folk theater[130] and religious mythology (seen in themes and story types as well as in narrative structure, format, and aesthetics[131]) is often used to explain film content. The argument can be made that not only the films but filmmaking practices, too, are grounded in a culture of folk and traditional performance such as dance drama and oral storytelling, which are characterized by spontaneity and improvisation as well as by community participation.[132] Many of the individuals attracted to regional cinema started out in traditional performance, folk theater, and so on, and some move between regional theater and cinema, thus continuing the influence of indigenous performance traditions on cinema.

The way filmmakers talk and think about their work is evocative of performance. Talk of film that has to "come together on the auditorium floor," for instance, acknowledges the part played by the audience as collectivity and the interactive nature of reception. This sense of performance is also reflected in the comment made by dialogue writer Richard Louis that the "audience will slap you" if it is not happy with the story, suggesting a face-to-face and interactive relationship.

Much has been written about the film business's recent corporatization and professionalization, and some see little similarity between filmmaking today and the way things were even ten years ago.[133] However, as a great deal of variation exists in regional film businesses—and among different production houses and directors within the Bombay industry itself—it may be argued that old ways of filmmaking continue alongside the new. Thus, many eras of filmmaking, exhibition, and audience engagement coexist.

It is far from clear that the audience's involvement is diminishing over time as the industry becomes professionalized. For example, Bollywood director Karan Johar is reported to have solicited ideas for his film's title (2010) on Twitter.[134] If making a film and delivering it to the audience is a collaborative activity or "collective act"[135]—and in the context of Indian film, such collaboration extends to the audience—it follows that audiences should be included in the list of credits—and filmmakers in India may have already taken this next step. According to one report, the audience has been recruited to finance *I Am* (2010). The director, faced with financial difficulties, is reported to have used his Facebook page to appeal for contributions.[136] People were able to become "co-owners" of the film and were promised credits at the end of the film. Those who made larger contributions were made partners and shared in the profits. The film drew nearly 70 owners and 350 co-owners and successfully raised Rs. 85 lakhs ($191,334). Since then, crowdsourcing has taken off in the United States with sites such as Kickstarter.

CHAPTER 3

Cinema Halls, Audiences, and the Importance of Place

The reputation of theater also builds up the reputation of the picture show. People will think, "Oh, picture coming to Santosh? It must be a big movie!"

DISTRIBUTOR, BANGALORE

When I asked Nandini, an upper-middle-class woman in her thirties, whether she was interested in seeing *Titanic*, she responded with, "Where is it showing?" The *Titanic* was being screened in two theaters, the Sangam in the City near the bus stand, and the Galaxy on Residency Road in the cantonment. Nandini preferred the "Galaxy in Town," which she said would be easier for her to get to. In interviews, Bangaloreans confirmed the rather narrow range of theaters they frequented. Nandini explained, "We usually end up going to a few theaters—Rex, very often, then Plaza, also Galaxy, very rarely go to Cityside—Majestic and all that."

Moviegoers choose the films they wish to see by the theaters they are screened in. Those in the film business have always recognized the importance of exhibition sites for the cinema experience.[1] Marcus Loew, one of the earliest Hollywood moguls and one of the first to own and operate a theater chain in the United States, is reported to have said, "We sell tickets to theaters, not movies."[2] However, as "film experience" is presumed to be based on the film alone, a universal and placeless experience, such "nonfilm" aspects of moviegoing have taken a back seat both in scholarly work on film and its spectatorship and in the way film is presented to audiences.

In this chapter I investigate the significance of place and locality for cinema. I examine cinema's location in the cultural geography of the city, spatial cultures that shape cinema's social existence, and the idea that cinema, its experience, is not only locally situated but is produced by the "spatial practices"[3] of exhibitors and distributors and by audiences and their practices of cinema going. The public culture and experience of cinema is then shaped by the complex set of relationships that exist between urban space cultures, individual cinemas and their reputations, films, and heterogeneous audiences.[4] Consequently, a phenomenology of the cinema experience is incomplete without an understanding of the meaning and significance of place.

THE SPACE CULTURES OF CINEMA IN THE CITY

Heterogeneity and Locality

Bangalore has long been a magnet not only for migrants from small towns and rural areas within Karnataka state but from neighboring states and from other parts of India. A variety of Hindu groups make up roughly 79 percent of the population, while Muslims make up 13 percent. The city has smaller numbers of Sikhs, Jains, and Parsis as well as Christians of various denominations, including Anglo-Indians of mixed British and Indian ancestry. Even with the homogenizing effects of modernization, regional, ethnic, and religious identities are expressed in the clothes people wear—in the way women drape their saris for example—or their jewelry, in the burkas worn by Muslim women, in various types of caps and turbans worn by men, and, in a multilingual setting such as Bangalore, in languages spoken and the way people speak. Even autorickshaw drivers, waiters in restaurants, shopkeepers, and others can converse in 2–3 languages. Wearing Western clothing, eating food that is not Indian or South Indian, and speaking fluent English (or Hindi) or demonstrating incompetence in Kannada all mark a more "cosmopolitan" upper-middle or middle-class identity. Nonresident Indians (NRIs) who visit Bangalore may find that they are addressed in English or Hindi even when they speak in Kannada.

Cinema reflects this plurality. A young cinematographer and filmmaker elaborated on the many choices of film available that shape moviegoers' habits: "People are very diverse. My next-door neighbor may tell *A* film [let's go see the Kannada film *A*]; his neighbor may see Malayalam movies, then they start talking about *Titanic*. Finally, someone says 'Let's go see a Hindi film'; they go for a Hindi film!" In summer 2012, films screened in theaters expressed this linguistic and culturally plural cinematic landscape, including *Adhuri*, *Dandupalya*, and *Godfather*, all in Kannada; *Billa 2* (Tamil); *Eega* (Telugu); *Cocktail* (Hindi); *The Dark Knight Rises* (English/Hollywood); and more. This multiplicity of films jostles for space in cinema halls and multiplexes and in filmgoer's consciousness, just as their posters and billboards compete for space on the streets (fig. 4).

FIGURE 4. Wall of posters for Hindi, Kannada, Telugu, and Tamil films, evidence of a multilingual and multicultural public sphere. Against the backdrop of posters, commerce continues at a footwear repair service. Photograph by Tulasi Srinivas, Bangalore.

Movie enthusiasts may wander from one theater to another, taking in multiple shows in a day. One moviegoer in his late thirties reported that at one point in his life he would watch three films a day: "morning Kannada, then in the afternoon I watched Tamil or Hindi, and in the evening English [Hollywood]." Typically, social class, education, and cultural background shapes moviegoers' habits and preferences. The English-speaking and Westernized middle classes are more likely to choose Hollywood and "art" films or on occasion the latest Bollywood extravaganza. Regional, southern Indian cinema caters to speakers of Tamil, Telugu, Malayalam, or Kannada, including fans largely belonging to the lower socioeconomic orders. Diversity in the audience is reflected in heterogeneity in exhibition, where cinema halls coexist with "tent" theaters for the urban poor and more recently with multiplexes.

The Cantonment and the City

Bangalore has been described as a dual or twin city. For centuries the cantonment in the northeast and the (old) city in the west, established during different periods in the city's history, developed separately, each with its own population mix and culture. A cantonment was a British military installation in India. In Bangalore, the Cantonment, referred to as "Town" or "Cantt" or in terms of its main commercial areas—Commercial Street, Mahatma Gandhi Road (M. G. Road), and Brigade Road—forms one node or hub. The City is the other node, where the old market area or *pettai* is located. When Bangalore residents talk of the City or refer to City-side, they include the area around Krishnarajendra, or City Market, Avenue Road, and Kempegowda Road (K. G. Road). The area known as "Majestic," perhaps derived from the old Majestic cinema hall and known for its many movie theaters, several situated along K. G. Road, together with the adjacent localities of Gandhinagar and Sheshadripuram, is distinguished from the Cantonment.

The Cantonment and the City are recognized as cultural spaces that have long organized urban life.[5] The Cantonment started out as a station for British troops in the early 1800s and was then settled by the British and by Tamil-speaking migrants from the Madras presidency. Officially designated a Civil and Military Station in 1868, it was an independent area under the control of the Government of India. This anglicized part of the city was known for its treelined avenues, churches, and bungalows with gardens. As a young army officer, Winston Churchill lived in the Cantonment, played polo, grew roses, and collected butterflies. When he left Bangalore he also left an unsettled account at the exclusive Bangalore Club. The club proudly displays this connection to Churchill to this day. Like the Bangalore Club, markers of the city's colonial past are everywhere in the Cantonment: a statue of Queen Victoria stands at the Cubbon Park end of M. G. Road, a spot for street vendors to gather and a favorite perch for pigeons. The British Council library was on St. Mark's Road (named after the church); the Victoria Hotel[6] was another Cantonment institution.

In contrast, the old city was established as a "fortified settlement" and capital in the sixteenth century by Kempegowda, a feudatory ruler of the Vijayanagar empire, and belonged to the princely state of Mysore. A walled town with four main gates, it developed into a dense and vibrant area of mixed residential and commercial, manufacturing, and religious activities.[7] Old Bangalore families came from localities of the City such as Chickpet, Doddapet, and Chamarajpet and then gradually moved out to the newer residential areas.[8] The old fort and temple, a major railway station, and the interstate (Kalasipalayam) bus terminus are located here, as are several banks and old business houses. Cubbon Park separated the Cantonment from the old city, as the British were concerned about the populations from these two sections mixing.[9]

Cultural differences between the Cantonment and the City persisted long after the formation of Karnataka as a linguistic state in 1956 and even after the two cities were brought together under the administration of the Bangalore

City Corporation in 1969. While the Cantonment was the site for English-speaking elites and Tamil immigrants who settled there as well as Telugu and Urdu speakers, the linguistic culture of the old city has been described as "Kannada centered," with some Urdu.[10] However, here, too, there is linguistic and cultural plurality as immigrants from North and South India brought with them a mixture of languages and cultures.[11]

The Cantonment and the City shape the social imagination of Bangalore. Long associated with Western ways and with the English-speaking population, the Cantonment for Bangalore residents was another world where they went to learn how to use a knife and fork and to try out their English-language skills on waiters who themselves were not fluent in English.[12] Going to the Cantonment was seen as practice for going abroad—that is how Westernized it appeared.[13] For some older residents, the Cantonment and its alien culture "meant the den of sin."[14] Yet the City, with its crowded streets and vibrant markets, is an equally alien space for many Cantonment residents.[15] The City and the area around K. G. Road and Gandhinagar is "densely settled" with a mix of commercial establishments and residences.[16] "Military" hotels and inexpensive lodges cater to out-of-town visitors. There are textile and sari showrooms, stores for luggage and household appliances, and small bazaars. Burma Bazaar was located in this area, as were "smuggler's markets." Film producers and distributor's offices are tucked away unobtrusively among shops and restaurants. Moviegoers have their favorite hangouts here. There are any number of eateries, snack joints, and *darshinis*.[17] Sukh Sagar and the Kamat hotel are well-known restaurants. People watching is a favorite pastime here, too.

Many belonging to the upper-middle and middle classes are prejudiced against the City and perceive it as a place where dangers lurk in the form of pickpockets and eve teasers (fig. 5).[18] Crowded streets provide opportunities for "rowdies" and "loafers"[19] to make lewd comments, brush up against women, and even pinch them. Middle-class women, especially younger women, avoid the City as much as possible, and I was always warned by friends and respondents not to go to Majestic and other crowded areas "City-side."

This cultural geography and spatially located linguistic, ethnic, regional, and class cultures organize and shape cinema and its experience. Rather than the film, its text alone constituting the audience, locality creates and establishes an audience. The drawing power of movies in the Cantonment has as much to do with the area and with certain theaters as with the film. "People will say, 'we've come all the way to M. G. Road,' they won't want to go back without seeing a movie," Mr. Kashyap, a cinematographer, explained. A young man in his twenties with eclectic tastes that span Bollywood, Hollywood, Kannada, and Tamil movies, said he goes to watch movies in the Cantonment because "M. G.

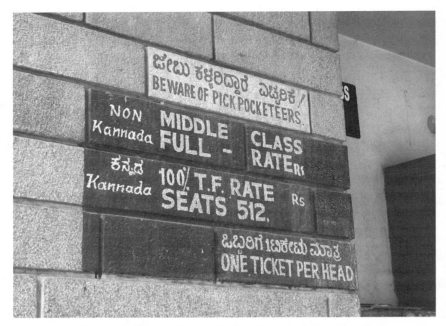

FIGURE 5. Sign outside Menaka theater. Photograph by the author, Bangalore, 2010.

Road is fun at night." With its high-rises, glass-fronted buildings, trendy boutiques, department stores, five-star hotels, and restaurants, the Cantonment has for decades been a place for the middle classes to people watch, shop, and spend an evening out. One saw groups of college students and young professionals at the cafés, ice-cream parlors, pubs, and restaurants on M. G. Road and Brigade Road.[20] A schoolteacher at a boy's school in the Cantonment reported that when she asked her tenth standard class to write an essay about what they did at weekends, one student responded, "I hang around outside Rex or Plaza (theaters) or on Commercial Street looking at beautiful girls." In the late 1990s a trip to a theater on M. G. Road meant the chance to browse in Higginbothams' bookstore and have an ice cream at Lake View parlor nearby or coffee at the India Coffee House. Families and couples would stroll along the treelined walkway next to the Parade Grounds, sit on the benches, and buy snacks from street vendors. Today the Cantonment continues to be a major hub for retail and leisure, but the pace has picked up, and many such activities have moved into the shopping malls or other localities. Yet even in 2013, a young professional in one of Bangalore's many technology start-ups described M. G. Road and Brigade Road as places where young Bangaloreans like to hang out, though many of the Cantonment's single-screen theaters have disappeared.

*

In the K. G. Road area, cinema halls are in the midst of a bustling market. "Footpath stalls" have their goods spread out on the sidewalk: piles of clothing, plasticware for households, mosquito nets, flyswatters, and plastic *dubbas* (boxes) as well as wallets, footwear, caps, and handbags with names of movie stars on them. Vendors outside cinemas sell savory snacks, sweets, tender coconut, freshly squeezed sugarcane juice, and cigarettes or *beedis*. Movie stars and cricketers look out from posters propped up against a low wall. People throng the pavement, and vendors call out to them, quick to follow a person's gaze. Picking up a violently colored poster of the Bollywood superstar, a vendor asks me, "Madam, you want Shah Rukh Khan?"

*

Between the 1940s and the 1970s, many of the movies that came to Bangalore would not make it to smaller towns in the region. A bus system and the railways linked villages and smaller towns such as Mandya, Mysore, or Hubli to Bangalore. Those who visited the city would make a point of taking in a "picture" or two. Theaters in the City near the interstate bus stand and railway station facilitated moviegoing for out-of-town visitors who could stay in the many inexpensive little hotels or "lodges." For middle-class residents of smaller towns, the English pictures in the Cantonment were a draw. For about four decades, starting in the 1940s, an English teacher living in Mysore, 130 kilometers to the southwest, would visit family in Bangalore several times a year, attend cricket matches, go to the club with friends, and watch English-language movies in the Cantonment. Mysore had only one theater, Gayathri Talkies, that screened Hollywood movies (see figs. 6, 7).[21]

THEATERS AND THE CINEMATIC LANDSCAPE

The Meaning of Theaters

Cinema has been around in Bangalore from the earliest days of motion pictures. Among the oldest theaters in Bangalore, the Elgin in Shivajinagar in the Cantonment, built in 1896, screened the first "talkie" in the city in 1931.[22] In a recent essay on the history of cinema halls in the city, K. N. Venkatasubba Rao recalls the Doddana Hall in Kalasipalyam, which was converted to Paramount Talkies in 1905 and which screened the first Kannada talkie in 1934. This was followed by a mushrooming of theaters, such as the Select, Shivananda

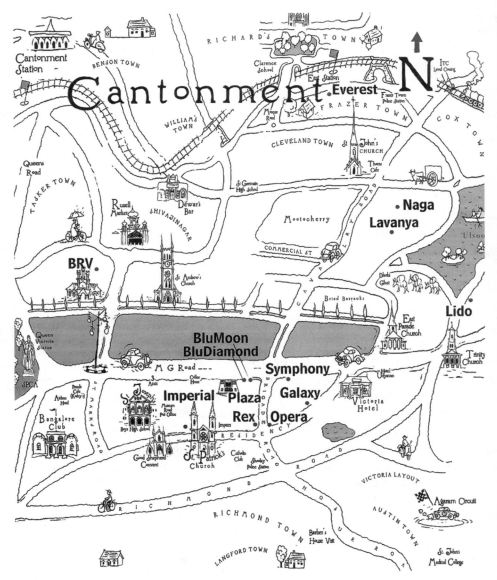

FIGURE 6. Map of Bangalore Cantonment showing movie theaters, by Paul Fernandes. Reprinted with permission.

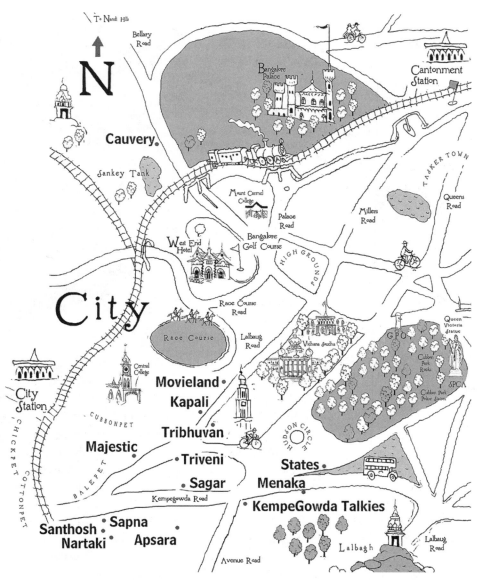

FIGURE 7. Map of Bangalore "City" showing movie theaters, by Paul Fernandes. Reprinted with permission.

F I G U R E 8 . BRV theater in its heyday by Paul Fernandes. Reprinted with permission.

Theatre, and Super Talkies in Majestic.[23] Between the 1960s and the 1990s, there was a sharp rise in the number of cinemas in the city.[24] According to some, the number peaked at approximately 120 and over 20 of these were in Majestic.[25] The names of theaters are illustrative of the social worlds of which they were a part. Clusters of theaters in the vicinity of Kempegowda Road with names such as Prabhat, States, Sagar, Kempegowda, Himalaya, Geetha, and Majestic screened Kannada and regional films,[26] while "English pictures" in the Cantonment were screened in theaters such as the Liberty (earlier the Globe) and Imperial, which along with the Plaza and Rex were among the earlier wave of theaters in the Cantonment.[27] Among them, the BRV (Bangalore Reserve Volunteers) theater (see fig. 8) was the "Defence Cinema," which "screened films only when there were no military-related activities on its premises."[28] The BluMoon, BluDiamond, and Symphony, all on M. G. Road, and the Lido in Ulsoor were later additions to Cantonment theaters.

Theaters that screen a particular linguistic genre of film are clustered together and set up economies of scale. Mr. Kashyap pointed out that the current James Bond film in theaters was "not a great film, it's a mediocre film compared to a Hindi film now. But it will run because of the current James Bond wave," and since the James Bond film and *Titanic* were running in theaters near one another, "overflow from *Titanic* goes to James Bond." In this way, in many parts of the city, theaters adjacent to one another brought about a "multiplex effect" long before the advent of multiplexes.

The cultural niches of cinema in the city have exhibitors and distributors engaging in an exercise of matching films and theaters with audiences' geographies of filmgoing. Early in my fieldwork I asked exhibitors, distributors, filmmakers, and audiences why Kannada or Hollywood movies were not screened outside the designated areas they were known for. When I asked a distributor why he did not screen a Kannada movie in a Cantonment theater such as the Lido, he responded exasperatedly, "What is the audience in that area?! See, we have tried, people have tried, but what is the use of showing if you don't get the audience?!" Because the distance between theaters in the Cantonment and the City is not more than a few kilometers, the audience for particular films and theaters is seen to be highly local. Most Kannada (film) theaters are in Majestic, while Tamil films are screened in pockets in the Cantonment and in specific theaters in Majestic devoted to Tamil films. A filmmaker explained how it was difficult for a film to survive outside its geographical and cultural niche or recognized terrain: "Kannada films will run only in Kannada-speaking areas. We don't have alternative theaters in the same area. The majority of Kannada speakers are not in east Bangalore. There is also no Kannada theater in north Bangalore. The south and west are the money-pulling areas for Kannada. In Rajajinagar there's only Navarang and another B-grade theater far away." A distributor confirmed that "theaters were pretty much reserved by language," as there were theaters for Hindi, Tamil, Telugu, and Kannada films.[29] This understanding is shared by audiences. One viewer is reported to have described the "intersection between [the localities of] Sheshadripuram and Malleswaram" as an area for theaters screening Tamil movies. The expectation is that, "Any Tamil-speaking guy from the Northern part of Bangalore will know Nataraj, Sampige, Central, and Kino talkies. [Though] Sampige primarily catered to Kannada cinegoers."[30] Moviegoers also recognize the Lavanya, Ajantha, Lakshmi, and Sri Balaji as Tamil film theaters, while Pallavi, Movieland, and Nataraj (which also screens Tamil films) are known to screen Telugu films.

Hollywood, too, is embedded in localities of the city, evidence of the significance of local distinctions and their global reach. When I asked Mr. Raman, a migrant from the neighboring state of Tamil Nadu and the manager of the Nartaki theater in Majestic, why the James Bond film was not screened in his theater, he referred to the spatial ordering of cinema, whereby a movie that was screened at the Rex in the Cantonment could not be screened at Nartaki as per agreement with local distributors and "MGM people."[31] I asked, "If you put James Bond here (at Nartaki) it won't run?" He responded that he had not tried, because MGM would not allow it. "They got some agreement with the company. Rex [a theater] people and MGM people—some agreement [according to which] if you put it in Rex, you can't put it in Nartaki." The Hollywood films that are screened in the Majestic or City area for the most part are either B films, old and scratched prints, or dubbed into Hindi.[32] I watched a dubbed (Hindi) print of *Jumanji* at the Triveni cinema, for example.

*

Moviegoers' decisions about which films to see then involve decisions about how to navigate and experience the city. People are reluctant to move out of their comfort zone and prefer to frequent theaters they are accustomed to.[33] They manage the risks and inconveniences of navigating the city by choosing films screened in theaters close to where they live. Nandini's preference for Hollywood movies screened in the Cantonment, where she lives, is shared by many middle-class moviegoers. Only an art film, a film made by a "quality" filmmaker, or a Bollywood film that has received unusually good reviews will draw this audience to theaters in the City or anywhere outside their stomping ground.

Moviegoers recalled childhood experiences of being allowed to only see films that were in "nearby theaters," which meant watching any movie that came to the theaters in question.[34] Some enthusiasts see every movie that comes to a theater near their home, it being convenient to "just walk down." A housewife in her forties said she "sees almost all the movies that come to Cauvery [a theater]. It's just here, and all the new releases come here." A long-time resident of Bangalore remembered frequenting the Minerva theater near his house, which screened Telugu, Tamil, and Kannada films, and walking back home at one in the morning after a "night show." He also saw movies in "Bharat and Shivaji theaters" and in theaters in Gandhinagar as well as the Paramount in City Market square, all close to where he lived. However, Swastik and Sampige in Malleswaram were "outside our beat."[35] Manjunath, an administrative assistant in his twenties, confirmed that he only goes to theaters "within our area limits"; M. G. Road, for example, and to a couple of theaters near Ulsoor in the Cantonment where he lives, the Ajantha theater being one of them, along with the "Galaxy and Naga which is close by." When a film moves from one theater to another in the city, moviegoers may feel they have "missed" the opportunity to see it. A viewer I spoke with at the Sagar theater was upset she had been unable to "catch" a film when it was in a theater near her home. Seeking out a theater one does not typically frequent is a huge effort.

At a screening of a Kannada film in Majestic, a woman who had come to watch the movie with her husband and sister-in-law explained, "we came all the way from R. T. Nagar! The movie was playing at Navarang theater, close to our house, but yesterday there was a new release there, so we came here." Another middle-class woman who had taken her children to the movies at the newly opened multiplex on Airport Road complained about how far it was and the petrol cost in getting there.[36] Even those who frequent multiplexes have their preferences and may choose to go to those nearer their homes or in an area of the city they prefer to visit.[37] This highly localized cinema, which has endured for the past seventy-odd years,[38] is frequently overlooked in analyses that focus on a distant mass culture industry and the supposedly universalizing effects of films. In Bangalore the increasing sprawl, congestion, and traffic problems have meant a further fragmentation of audiences. The arrival of the mall multiplex in localities such Koramangala, Indiranagar, or Malleswaram, means that those who live in Indiranagar rarely visit the by-lanes of Malleswaram.

Space, Place, and Hierarchy

As discussed in the previous chapter, films are ranked and placed in a hierarchy. The space cultures of cinema in the city also express a hierarchy that is reflected in print media as well. English-language news magazines such as *India Today* routinely have articles on Bollywood but feature regional cinema less often. Bangalore's English-language newspapers have daily and weekly write-ups about Hollywood and Bollywood movies and stars, but reviews of Kannada and other regional cinema, their stars and filmmakers, are given less prominence outside vernacular publications. For those who do not read Kannada (and Tamil) newspapers or magazines (which are available mainly in Majestic and in other areas of Kannada concentration in the city), it is easy to miss out on details of regional films. The organization of urban space sets up a class and culture division across which news does not filter.

Even if regional films are reviewed in English newspapers, they are invisible to the Westernized middle classes. Many upper-middle-class moviegoers I spoke with—those with a "Convent school" education, signifying Westernized sections of the population—while extremely knowledgeable about Hollywood movies, such as the behind-the-scenes details of *Titanic*, seemed unaware of the world of regional film and of a raging controversy over a Kannada movie that had gone to the courts. Students at an elite school who were excited about a Valentine's Day dance with American rock music and a student production of a Shakespearean play were strangers to the world next door of Kannada cinema. In 2010 the sudden demise of Kannada star Vishnuvardhan, which

threw the Kannada film world into mourning, did not even register with moviegoers keen to see the special effects in the new *Sherlock Holmes*. With the
advent of electronic media, websites, and online news articles, these niches
have continued to thrive.

Because the linguistic genre of a film functions as a proxy for ethnicity and
class, theaters in certain sections of the city known for screening particular
types of film attract viewers belonging to certain ethnolinguistic and class
backgrounds.[39] Outside theaters in Cantonment that screen Hollywood movies, one sees mixed-sex groups of middle-class college students and young
professionals sporting name-brand clothing, athletic shoes, and designer
sunglasses. Students carry backpacks, and young women are in jeans, short
skirts, or designer *churidar khameez* or *salwar* and have short hair styles, once
known as "bob cuts." Not all Hollywood films attract a majority of the middle
classes, however; James Bond films and other action adventures are widely
viewed across class categories. Hollywood action films and B-ranked movies
may also be screened in run-down theaters or as morning shows in Majestic
to audiences belonging to lower socioeconomic orders.

Regional cinema draws a subset of the audience for Hollywood and Bollywood blockbusters. At theaters screening regional and Kannada films, one
sees moviegoers who belong to the (non-Westernized) middle classes and the
lower-middle and lower classes. There are a greater number of men in the
audience. Middle-class Kannadiga families selectively choose films by their
stars or directors known for making "good and decent" movies. At cinema
halls in Majestic, one sees men in simple pants and shirts; many wear *chappals*
(sandals or flip-flops). Women at screenings for Kannada films are in saris and
"half saris"; a few wore *salwar khameez*,[40] and many had strands of jasmine in
their oiled and plaited hair. Cultural diversity in the audience is aural as well as
visual. As Bollywood and Hollywood films have a wide appeal, one overhears
conversations in English and Hindi as well as in various regional languages at
these screenings. Audiences who attend regional-language cinema may not
be as ethnolinguistically diverse unless the film features a star whose appeal
transcends ethnic and linguistic divides.

In the late 1990s and into the twenty-first century, there was a widespread
perception that Kannada films increasingly appealed to the lower end of the
socioeconomic spectrum. While some filmmakers were critical of Kannada
cinema's "lowbrow" films, and thrills that catered to lower-class and rural
men, others felt the middle-classes, their prejudices, were to blame. Middle-
class audiences and those educated in English-medium schools certainly distance themselves from Kannada films and theaters that attract a lower class
of viewer. A director complained bitterly, "People don't want to see Kannada

movies because they think 'oh, all these dirty people will be at the theater.' . . . The same people will go to see *Titanic*. But people will see *Titanic* because it's Hollywood, and they will come back saying, 'we saw *Titanic*, it was so good.'"

In the late 1990s, if a Kannada film drew a broader audience, including middle classes, it was unusual enough to be commented on. When his film *America! America!* (1997) appealed to a multiethnic and middle-class audience, filmmaker Nagathihalli Chandrashekar excitedly remarked that it was "Vishesha! [unusual]. Different class of people came to see, they could identify with the film. . . . First time we have seen Sardarjis, Marwaris[41] in the theater for Kannada films."[42] Movies made by directors such as N. Chandrashekar and Nagabharana, who have a reputation for making serious films and social commentaries, and films starring Ramesh are known to draw a very mixed audience with large numbers of women and even the middle classes, while films made by Upendra in the late 1990s or that starred Jaggesh (see chap. 2) attracted men and large numbers of the lower socioeconomic classes. These films were therefore placed in theaters that would draw this audience.

A Shifting Landscape

This cinematic landscape is a changing one. Theaters are not permanently colonized by a particular film industry or linguistic genre or star, and takeovers occur. The Symphony on M. G. Road started out as an "English" theater and screened several big Hollywood films—including *The Towering Inferno* (1974), *You Only Live Twice* (1967), and the *Pink Panther* films—until the early 1980s, when its character seemed to change as a wave of B movies and action and martial arts films from East Asia altered its image. The Imperial was known for Hollywood movies in the 1970s and then closed for several years, after which it, too, screened a number of B movies and seedy adult films even as the building itself became increasingly decrepit. Residents remembered the Lido for its "English pictures" in the 1970s and 1980s, but in the late 1990s it screened mostly Bollywood films and the odd Tamil film. A Kannada filmmaker recalled the Abhinay theater in Majestic being a site for Bombay films, but after it screened *America! America!*, it became "a regular Kannada (film) theater." Similarly, the Majestic theater used to screen Telugu-language films, but after the Kannada film "*Karpoorada Gombe* [Wax Doll] released there, [and] ran for 100 days, then it became a Kannada theater. So film comes and breaks a taboo. And they always go by precedence unfortunately." The Rex, earlier known for screening Hollywood films exclusively, is now known to screen both Bollywood and Hollywood films (fig. 9).

FIGURE 9. The Rex on Brigade Road in the Cantonment. Photograph by Navroze Contractor, Bangalore, 2015.

A major source of flux and change is the disappearance of older single-run theaters. Starting in the 1980s, many of the city's older theaters, which screened the first talkies, were demolished, pointing to the "fragility" of locality and place.[43] Mr. Kashyap recollected a lost urban cinemascape: "Many theaters in Bangalore are gone now. Gita theater used to be in front of Majestic theater, Bharat theater opposite to States—all demolished! This generation wouldn't know that Bharat or Gita theater existed. The Central, opposite Nataraja theater, was demolished in the last five years. In K. G. Road there were fifty to sixty theaters." Theater owners are increasingly converting prime land to other more financially viable ventures such as shopping centers, several of which have sprung up on the sites of demolished theaters. According to Mr. Kashyap, the Alankar theater had been replaced by the Alankar Pearl Plaza, a shopping center. He felt that the Majestic theater was on its way out: "people wouldn't mind demolishing [it]" because it did not make financial sense to run these older single-run cinema halls. "Weekly shares from shopping complexes are 5 to 10 lakhs. The rent for Kapali theater is 5 lakhs per week."[44]

Since then, many more single-run theaters have been destroyed. In the Cantonment, the BluMoon and BluDiamond—"minitheaters" on M. G. Road, which in their heyday screened Hollywood films such as *Rollerball* (1975),

It's a Mad, Mad, Mad, Mad World (1963), and *The Blue Lagoon* (1980)—have been replaced by multistory commercial buildings. The Imperial was torn down, also replaced by a shopping complex. The old Lido theater is now the Fame Lido multiplex.[45] In the 1990s the city lost over a dozen theaters. As Mr. Kashyap had predicted, the Majestic theater joined the ranks of disappearing theaters. In early 2010 when I passed by the site where the theater used to be, there was a large pit and a pile of rubble. The Plaza stood dilapidated for many years until demolished in March 2010 to make room for the new metro building.

Multiplexes started appearing in 2003–2004, and there are nine in the city.[46] As multiplexes screen Hollywood, Bollywood, and regional films, they have affected the spatial distribution of cinema to some extent. Recent migrants to the city who frequent multiplexes inhabit a very different mindscape of cinema. Unaware of the older cinema halls that are still active, they do not share the experience of the city that was and is part of cinema going for older residents. A computer consultant I spoke with at the Inox multiplex had moved to Bangalore from Bombay a year earlier. She said she only saw movies at multiplexes. She confused older single-run theaters in the Cantonment, such as the Galaxy and Plaza, with theaters in Majestic,[47] an area she had never been to and had no wish to visit.

Cinematic Mindscapes

My sister and I saw few movies growing up, and the rare family movie outing is vivid in my memory. Most films we saw as children were English-language films at Cantonment theaters; I remember going to see *Tarzan* (1970) and a movie featuring Twiggy, both at the dingy, musty Imperial, and watching movies at the Plaza and the Galaxy, which meant a drive to the Cantonment from where we lived in south Bangalore. As a family we watched a movie adaptation of the Thomas Hardy novel *Far from the Madding Crowd* (1967) starring the India-born Julie Christie, as well as the historical film *Anne of the Thousand Days* (1969). Both films were screened to largely English-speaking middle-class audiences at the Lido in the 1970s. The Lido had a long curving drive and huge trees in its compound. At the canteen under the trees, moviegoers sipped tea or soft drinks as they battled the mosquitoes from nearby Ulsoor Lake. Bats would come out at dusk and swoop around near the lights on the trees. It was only in my late teens and early twenties that I saw a few serious regional art films, such as the Kannada film *Chomana Dudi* (Choma's drum [1975]) and ventured to Majestic for Hindi films.

*

For many cinemagoers, moviegoing experiences and memories of such experiences are tied to place, forming what Orvar Lofgren calls a *mindscape*: a landscape "densely populated by daydreams, images and fantasies."[48] In this mindscape, film and theater are intertwined in what becomes a "landscape of feeling."[49] M. Bhaktavatsala, a film commentator and longtime resident of Bangalore, articulates this association when he writes, "Films I liked carried my liking over to the [cinema] halls." He associates the Guru Sachidananda theater in Hospet with *Flash Gordon*; Gayathri Talkies in Mysore with *White Christmas*; BRV in Bangalore "screened *Frankenstein* and became a theater to be avoided" as the theater itself had "eerie looks." Memories of movie experiences are locked into memories of theaters and their distinct aura as well as the sensualities of the cinema that are lodged in the theater. The historic Elgin Talkies recalled this aura with its "slightly debauched look, the sepia posters, the smell, the hall which now cried out for smoke, wooden class divisions, a stamp-sized screen, open windows through which one could see the night sky."[50] The "old magic of old cinema houses" was linked to the emotional experiences of watching films in particular theaters: "crying with Dilip Kumar and Kamini Kaushal in *Shaheed* and laughing with them in that delectable comedy, *Shabnam*, in the old Majestic."[51] This romantic association of film experiences with theaters is the subject of many recent blogs and online musings following the razing of single-screen theaters. The demolishing of the seventy-four-year-old Plaza elicited this "time machine post": "I remember walking up and down to Plaza for 5 days to buy ticket for the movie *Raiders of the Lost Ark* all the way from Shivaji Nagar. Golden memories!!"[52] Thirty years after it was screened there, a lecturer at a local college recalled watching Dr. Rajkumar in a "dual role" in *Daari Tappida Maga* (1975) at the Devi theater.[53]

The erasing of theaters becomes significant for the social imagination of cinema and for moviegoers' "inner world" or "inner life." Disappearing theaters erode not only a connection to past cinema experiences but also to people's biographies. Not surprisingly, then, some see it as a sinister act. One moviegoer remarked, "I remember . . . when one venerable theater was demolished in the thick of the night."[54]

"Theater Merit": Theater as Nonstandardized Space

Given that a theater's location, its facilities, and its reputation for a certain type of film shape audience expectations and the cinema experience, distributors and producers are forced to be highly selective about theaters for a film's release. Ramesh, star of *America! America!*, and a distributor-producer friend chatted with me on the intricacies of matching films with theaters and audiences: "And if a Ramesh film now releases, they put it in theaters where the parking space is good." Ramesh pointed out that some theaters are recognized as unsuitable for films that attract the middle-classes: "Like if you have States (another theater), parking is no good, so you'll have a tough time. . . . However good the film, the car-parking audience won't come there. Your film flops!" Similar to playhouses in England in the Middle Ages,[55] a theater may almost be subcolonized by a particular star's or director's films if such films (and theaters) are thought to draw a particular class of audience. As Ramesh put it, "each actor will have his own kind of theater where the audience comes there."

The choice of theater (and its location), then, conveys information about the movie and has implications for making a film visible to the desired audience. When I asked Mr. Gupta, a distributor of Hindi and Kannada films, what his ideal theater would be for the release of a new Hindi film, he replied promptly, "I'd prefer Santosh . . . because that has got good reputation. Maintenance is good, sound is good, light is good." He conceded, however, that if he didn't get that theater he would "go to Nartaki" because "Nartaki is also good." Films and theaters draw on each other's reputation. According to Mr. Gupta, "the reputation of theater also builds up reputation of picture show. People will think 'oh, picture coming to Santosh? It must be a big movie!' See that *link* is there. That is why we want a good theater."

Theaters that have housed films that went on to become "superhits" are considered "lucky" and become prized venues. Competition is intense,[56] as stars and producers may insist on previewing their film at such theaters.[57] Consequently, even though the city had roughly seventy viable theaters in 1998,[58] the actual number considered suitable for the release of particular films came down to a mere handful. Mr. Gupta reeled off his preferred theaters, all in the Majestic area and within walking distance of one another: "Sapna is small, it's a mini-theater. I will not release it in Sapna. When the movie is very small I can release. With a big-budgeted movie, you can't go to Sapna. I can go to Nartaki. First preference Santosh, Triveni is also good. . . . Kapali is good. Sagar is good. Abhinay is there. That is how you come—you try for the best. You don't get it, you go for second best." The informal ranking of theaters and the way in which distributors and exhibitors evaluate their suitability for any particular movie points to theaters being saturated with meaning that is both local and contextual.

I was introduced to the concept of theater merit by Mr. Raman, manager of the Nartaki theater, during one of our afternoon tea sessions. He pointed out that "in Nartaki theater all Kannada picture goes very well." I asked him if this meant that Nartaki was known for screening Kannada movies. He was quick to correct me, "No! Kannada picture GOES very well. Nartaki, Santosh, Triveni, Aparna—all Kannada picture goes very well. Any damn movie no? In Triveni—four to five weeks!" Apparently any movie could be safely screened in this clutch of theaters and be sure of a respectable run because "theater merit is there." I asked Mr. Raman to explain, and he responded: "Theater merit is—certain theaters something will be there. People will say 'let's go to Nartaki.' See Sapna theater, Sapna we screen only good movies. Theater also counts. Picture may be small picture, but it will run because of theater merit."

Theaters are seen to "give off signs,"[59] and both the films screened and the audiences that attend constitute such signs, as does the theater's "merit." Certain theaters in the city become crucial indicators for the future success of a film,[60] and if a film succeeds in a particular theater, the film's market value goes up. Distributors in other parts of the state are willing to cough up huge sums of money. The producer can then sell his film to the highest bidder.[61] Theater merit can therefore have an effect on the box office for a film.

Before the arrival of multiplexes, theaters in the Cantonment that drew middle- and upper-middle-class audiences were considered "prestigious" and were able to impose "'location-centric' charges"; that is, a theater in a good location can charge a price "directly proportional to the favored environment."[62] The Plaza, Rex, and Galaxy in the Cantonment fell into this category, though multiplexes are increasingly occupying this niche now. Older single-run theaters in the City that are in a dense market area[63] and that screen Kannada and other regional films are plebeian spaces associated with the non-Westernized, non-English-speaking population, including the lower socioeconomic classes.[64]

In conversations with distributors and producers, I learned that at times films are falsely advertised in the newspapers as being screened at certain theaters when actually the film has long since been replaced by another. The hope is that out-of-town distributors will either see the advertisement in a Bangalore newspaper or learn of it and start bidding for the film. Such practices create confusion for audiences, who may show up at a theater for a particular film only to find it is no longer being screened there.

*

I visited the Nartaki theater complex (which included the Nartaki, Santosh, and Sapna theaters) multiple times and saw several movies at these theaters, frequently stopping by to say hello to Mr. Raman in his cubbyhole of an office. He would be in his uniform of open cotton shirt, which revealed a white *banian* (undershirt) and sacred thread,[65] and a white *vesti*,[66] with a towel thrown over his shoulders. Sipping tea brought by an errand boy from a nearby hotel, we would chat about various movie-related matters. On the wall behind Mr. Raman's desk was a clock with "Janumada Jodi" written on it. *Janumada Jodi* (1996) was a "superhit" Kannada film that had enjoyed an extended run at the theater. Another plaque for *Akasmika* (1993), with a photograph of the star, Dr. Rajkumar, in character, also adorned the wall. When I asked him about the clock and plaque, Mr. Raman proudly explained that both were gifts from the producers of the films, tokens to mark the films' success at the theater, now cherished mementos that signaled a golden era in the theater's history and in Mr. Raman's own career.

Theater merit therefore speaks to the biography of the theater, tying the past to the present. A theater's reputation and character includes its past glories and films screened long ago. This temporal dimension of theater merit surfaced in conversations with exhibitors: "those days Sapna was the best theater. Each movie used to run for six months! See *Kora Kagaz* (1974), *Achanak* (1973), *Amanush* (1975) [ran for] one year at Sapna!"[67] Superhits and superstars have an effect on theater merit and can alter the existing meanings of a theater as well as the mindscape of cinema. One theater manager identified "his" theater as the place where superstar Amitabh Bachchan's films had run: "When Amitabh was around, it was all Jubilee! It was Amitabh's theater." When stars and other famous people grace a theater's premises, its merit increases further.[68] Mr. Raman remembered Tamil megastar and filmmaker Kamal Hasan visiting his theater multiple times, when he was shooting a film in Mysore and again when "*Hum Kisi Se Kam Nahin*[69]—when that movie was running, he had come." He happily listed the stars who had visited "his" theater: "Almost all [big stars]— Kamal, Jeetendra, Anil Kapoor, Sunny Deol, almost all!"

Theater merit may be said to be an aura; or, as Mr. Raman put it, "Certain theaters something will be there." In its secular form, theater merit may be thought of as goodwill. It can also be understood as the theater's *punyam* (which has connotations of religious merit in Hinduism). One theater manager saw his theater's merit as clearly linked to his own career. The dusty trophies displayed in theater lobbies for successful film runs; theater awards and framed, yellowed newspaper clippings featuring the theater's glory days; faded, often garlanded photographs of stars, directors, and producers, and their families; the theater owner's grandfather—all assume greater significance as contributions to and evidence of the theater's merit, as tangibles attesting to the intangible (fig. 10).

Theater merit informs theater folklore. I first became aware of the folklore surrounding theaters when I was a student in Bangalore in the 1980s and

FIGURE 10. Trophies, plaques, and awards in Nartaki lobby. Photograph by the author, Bangalore, 2012.

was reminded of it in interviews with moviegoers when they would frequently identify theaters by their reputation, history, or past events, such as stars visiting or celebrations surrounding newly released films and rowdy fans. A theater's idiosyncrasies, physical condition, features, or oddities together contribute to its merit (or demerit) while shaping the social imaginary of cinema. When I told a college student I was thinking of going to see a particular movie, he promptly identified the theater it was running in: "Oh, hernia seats!" A middle-class woman remembered the BluMoon on M. G. Road by the many narrow winding stairs to the theater and the small workman's elevator that creaked and shuddered violently, itself an adventure. Moviegoers recalled the "frighteningly high" balcony at the Symphony and its steeply sloped seats, which "made you feel like you were pitching forward onto the screen."

Given the idiosyncratic appeal of theaters, a theater's special features may become its attraction. Abhinay theater was known for being the first (and in 1997 the only) theater with an escalator, providing what in the early days of the theater was a "fairground thrill."[70] Children treated it as a ride, and adults could be seen queuing up at the escalator to descend from the balcony on the second floor even if the short flight of stairs was relatively free of people. Some theaters had indoor gardens: one had an impressive display of cacti and succulents. Theater restrooms were also the subject of discussion; in an e-mail,[71] a college student elaborated on the facilities at a particular theater: "[my two friends] and I went to pay our respects to the toilet. . . . The best toilet that I have seen in Bangalore movie halls is in Cauvery. They have polished granite everywhere and it can be easily compared to a Five Star hotel!"

*

As Mr. Gupta explained, Santosh theater, which had "good theater merit," was of a "good" size (it seated over one thousand, like many single-run cinema halls) and had "good" light and sound. Another plus is the presence of a car park. Theaters advertise renovations such as new sound systems, new screen technology, refurbished flooring ("polished granite"), and newly upholstered seating, which improve merit. The association between a theater's material conditions and the films screened in it is seen in theaters that are run-down, that lose their merit. Dilapidated theaters become associated with second-run prints and flops.[72] As the Imperial and BRV theaters grew increasingly decrepit, for example, they became known for dodgy B movies and adult films. In the 1990s the Opera theater on Brigade Road, which also screened adult films, appeared to be crumbling day by day. Rumor had it that it was a "den of prostitution," and young women would cross the street rather than walk by that theater.[73]

Heterogeneity, Space, and Conflict

By the late 1990s, there was a crisis in infrastructure in film exhibition.[74] The number of active theaters in existence was small, the stock of working theaters was old, and new theaters were not being built. The nationwide shortage of movie theaters was reflected in Bangalore: for a city with a population of roughly five million in 1998,[75] less than a hundred (permanent) theaters were operational. In the words of a film industry insider, "whatever the theaters we have, it is all in 1950s and 1960s. . . . There is no new theaters being built." Shortages continue even with the arrival of multiplexes, which have smaller seating capacities compared with the single-run theaters that may seat over a thousand. What was viewed as a crisis in infrastructure was compounded by a lack of up-to-date information, something that continues today. I had great difficulty in finding out how many theaters were in existence and active. No such list seemed to be in existence. I pieced together a list of about seventy theaters from various sources, such as the Karnataka Film Chamber of Com merce (KFCC), newspapers, and the records of some distributors.[76] Subsequent checking revealed that some theaters that had been demolished were also on the list, and the remaining theater stock was old.

Where place and locality are significant for exhibition and for cinema going, the shortage of theater stock exacerbates competition for theaters. The life span of films are cut short, preventing them from realizing their box-office potential. Producers find their films unceremoniously bumped from theaters. Traditionally, a film's one-hundredth day of continuous screening was celebrated as an auspicious milestone. Posters of the film stamped with "100 days" could be seen plastered all over the city. Indeed, reviews commented on a film reaching such milestones.[77] However, competitive pressures mean that twenty-five or even ten days is an achievement marked with posters advertising the fact.

Theaters become sites of institutional and, given the heterogeneity of films and audiences, ethnolinguistic conflict. A distributor who deals in both Hindi and Kannada films referred to "clashes" over theaters but focused on how accommodations are negotiated: "Sometimes Kannada picture wants same theater so clash is there, but we adjust it: 'Baba, yes you come to *this* theater, I'll go to *that* theater.'" A theater manager informed us with some pride that *his* theater was so popular that directors actually fought to get it for their films. He referred to a particular director who had created a commotion in the KFCC by demanding that his film be screened in that theater and no other.

In the small Kannada film community, such fierce competition is perceived as threatening not only the survival of Kannada films but Kannada culture itself. Feeling besieged, a filmmaker observed that apart from "outside" competition from "five to six languages" (i.e., regional cinema, Bollywood, and Hollywood), "Kannada films have become enemies for Kannada films."[78] Faced with such pressures, producers may manipulate the signs of success. Some observers claim that producers make false claims of a successful run of fifty or a hundred days when the film has actually run for a fraction of that period. There are rumors and gossip that Kannada producers have paid theaters (and multiplexes) to keep films in them. One theater manager recounted an incident where he had been threatened at knifepoint by fans of a certain star if he did not stop showing a film being screened and replace it with the star's recent film. The manager complained that in the past, fans had spread rumors that the theater was owned by the star, which he said was an outright lie.

Historically exhibition sites have evolved to direct the audiences' attention to the screen and the film. The sanitized and "unobtrusive"[79] interior of the modern multiplex with its dull functionality provides a neutral environment that seeks to erase the setting from the viewer's consciousness, allowing for an uninterrupted and individualized film experience.[80] Comfortable seats, air conditioning, muted lighting, cleanliness, the control of odors (except for the ubiquitous popcorn smell) and extraneous sounds, as well as sound and light technology that claims the senses, all minimize corporeal distractions[81] and allow moviegoers to immerse themselves in the film experience.[82] This is the taken-for-granted experience of watching films and which multiplexes are designed to provide. In contrast, the physical setting is at the forefront of the cinema experience at Bangalore's cinema halls. When talking about her movie outing, a middle-class businesswoman focused on the physical discomfort she experienced: "And that theater has the most horrible seats! Soooo uncomfortable! We couldn't see a thing, ya! And the people behind us, even they couldn't see. The seats were obstructing our view. And in front there is some wooden obstruction, so even those people couldn't see!" Therefore, conflict surrounding theaters may also be fueled by the spaces themselves, their materiality, by exhibition practices, and by the heterogeneity of audiences and films.

While theaters advertise their air-conditioned interiors—"Rex, the Coolest cinema," for instance—exhibitor practices shape in-theater experience. At many city theaters, the air-conditioning would be switched off in the middle of a screening, creating a sauna effect in the auditorium. Viewers are seen fanning themselves with magazines and newspapers and wiping their faces with handkerchiefs. Reviews of the film *As Good as It Gets* in a local paper boldly attempted to promote it as a means of forgetting the surrounding discomfort: "In a nutshell it's . . . a perfect film for a hot summer day. The laughter will make you forget the heat and you will come out of the theater feeling good."[83] The absence of air conditioning is not the only issue, however. I saw movies in theaters where the floors were pitted and that had to be navigated carefully after lights out, where the seating in the balcony was precarious, and where noisy fans and cooling systems competed with the soundtrack. I suffered insect bites, as did my friends and family members who I accompanied to the cinema. Smells from the toilets were initially a distraction, though some habitués seemed to be able to ignore these things, and with time, I did, too. Poor seating appeared to be the rule rather than the exception; in several theaters seating was broken or the upholstery had been gouged out, so one had to be careful not to sit on nails or go home with splinters. Seats appeared to be of symbolic rather than functional value—indicating where the audience should sit—but in fact the seating made it difficult to do so. At some of the older theaters, moviegoers are seen wandering around the seating section, tentatively testing the seats by pressing on the seat back or gingerly sitting on it, expecting it to give way. A theater's "merit" did not always seem to guarantee cleanliness or proper maintenance. Theaters in prime locations, such as the Plaza, and that had a reputation of successfully screening hit films to middle-class audiences often had rickety seats, bugs, dirty toilets, faulty air-conditioning or cooling systems, and cracked floors. It seemed that theaters could rest on their laurels, a theater's accumulated merit countering its less desirable qualities.

Conditions that frequently draw attention away from the film and toward the material and sensual aspects of the viewing setting even provide fodder for nostalgia. A moviegoer fondly remembered movies such as *The Bridge on the River Kwai* (1957) and *The Ten Commandments* (1956) at the Plaza and wonders "how we managed to sit through the smells and the rats for hours yet enjoy the movie."[84] Recollections that focus on the sensualities of the cinema experience—the smells, the rats, the long wait in ticket queues, the food at different theaters—all show us how much the cinema experience is embedded in a given place that is part of a sensual and emotional landscape.[85]

Theater conditions are debated in local newspapers and more recently in online articles and blogs. An article in the *Times of India* begins, "If you've been to a theater this summer, you must have asked yourself, 'why isn't the air-conditioning working? why do the seats feel like a bed of nails? and why do the loos smell so foul?'"[86] Another refers to the lack of fresh air in the theaters "as films are screened continuously" and to the likelihood of contracting diseases from using the bathroom.[87] Audiences, who form a shifting population, have every chance of encountering the theaters' more permanent residents. Moviegoers reported finding bugs in their clothing and having to fumigate their homes. Certain theaters were known for their rodent population. The "film experience" at the Plaza often included encounters with rats. Following mysterious shrieks from audiences watching romance and comedy, stories circulated that some viewers had been terrorized by a rat that had "bounded across the seats" to sit on a moviegoer's lap.[88] Apparently the rats had become accustomed to the routines of screening and would wait for the film to start; when the auditorium went dark, they would emerge to look for food. Hearing of the demolition of the Plaza, a viewer became sentimental about the experience of watching movies in the theater: "As a kid I remember a rat jumping out from behind a seat while watching *Genghis Khan* at Plaza. Realized that every time there was loud clanging music, the rat would be disturbed from their (sic) normal activities. Sad to see the theater go."[89]

The Plaza also housed a community of pigeons in the ceiling, and the birds would flap around before the start of the show, making their characteristic gurgling sound. After the show began, the darkness was punctuated by dancing fireflies. Few open-air theaters can boast of such rich life-forms. Indeed moviegoers' routines may develop around the presence of theater fauna. For example, people would warn one another never to take food into theaters that were known to have rats. One movie enthusiast reported, "I would be warned at home to beware of *mootai poochi* [bed bugs] sticking on to the clothes and that always meant a quick shower after getting back from late night shows."[90]

Public criticism of theater conditions drew the exhibitors (of permanent theaters) into the debate. Placed on the defensive, theater owners and managers gave detailed accounts of measures taken to ensure proper standards of hygiene, which were duly reported in the newspapers. "Twice a month the pest control board sends someone to fumigate the place and our sweepers clean the premises during and after every show. We spend a lot of money on maintenance.... We have twelve sweepers who clean the theater in the middle of and after every show. There are no rats or termites here." Other theater managers "listed the means they use—from disinfecting the premises daily to setting traps for the rats and using termite-resistant wood for the seats to checking each seat for bugs." Some argued that theaters are in the state they are in partly *because* of audiences. A news article quotes theater managers whose theaters were described as unsanitary and uncomfortable: "What about the damage caused by patrons who tear out our seats and stick bubble gum on them? The people who complain must be having more rats and bugs in their homes."[91] In an interview, a distributor supporting this view remarked that while maintenance of theaters is "bad" and "chairs are not good," people cannot only "blame the exhibitor because audience is also very bad." He went on to describe audiences who vandalized the theater, scratched the seating with razor blades, pulled out the upholstery, and wrought other kinds of havoc.

*

In the 1990s, Bollywood films drew the middle-class audience back to the theater,[92] and the discussion about theater conditions appeared to be dominated by middle-class observers, commentators, critics, and moviegoers who were vocal about the conditions of cinema halls and the need for improvement. Prabha, a middle-class housewife in a south Bangalore suburb, voiced her displeasure with "dirty and dusty" theaters where "Bats sit on the ceiling" and with exhibitors who "don't put on the fans." She complained of "severe headaches" because theaters were "congested and stuffy" and questioned whether "any sane person" could sit there for three and a half hours. She was in favor of an increase in ticket price by "Rs 5 or more per head" to "maintain a truly high standard in the auditorium."

Public debate over theaters may be seen to express the conflict over the appropriation of theater space,[93] and in other contexts, such conflict has been interpreted as arising out of a need for the middle classes to define and dominate the space.[94] Middle-class objection to theater conditions, for instance, is also an expression of distaste for public settings that are perceived as predominantly lower class. A middle-class moviegoer disparagingly referred to a theater known to attract a boisterous and lower-class crowd as a "crummy place." Another middle-class woman called a similar theater a "sidey hall." Upper-middle-class and middle-class viewers see class differences among audiences as contributing to the poor levels of maintenance. One housewife was indignant: "Who will sit for three and a half hours, without any comforts, sweating there? My God!"[95] Yet she recognized that there were people who would do exactly that: "They [the lower classes] don't mind so what is the botheration? And we are a minority, who will listen to our complaints?" A significant section of the audience is willing to put up with even worse conditions than exist at single-run cinema halls. Autorickshaw drivers and household help—maids, cooks, chowkidars (watchmen), peons, and office boys—as well as construction workers and street vendors said that they often watched movies in tents. In rural areas, tents are literally tents or open-air cinemas where audiences either squat in the dust or on dhurries (rugs). In an urban context, tents signify informal, illegitimate spaces that exist outside regulatory frameworks applied to "permanent" theaters. Thus, the heterogeneity of the audience fuels the debate.

In 1998, the continuing popularity of tent cinema was assumed to remove pressure from managers of permanent theaters to attend to maintenance, cleanliness, and viewer comfort, as a large section of the audience is not insistent on such conditions. The problem is compounded by an absence of consensus among the middle classes about the costs of cinema going. However, distributors and filmmakers viewed tents as exacerbating competitive pressures. Located on the outskirts of cities near engulfed villages or lower-income settlements and urban slums, tents are difficult to monitor. Tent exhibitors find that it suits their purpose to side with the lower classes and the poor against permanent and legitimate theaters, the state government, and its regulatory agencies as well as the middle and upper-middle classes. In the past, movies that reached tents were second-run or older prints and did not encroach on the audience for newly released films. But according to film industry insiders and reports in the news media, even newer, hit films are being screened in tents without there being any time lag between the release of the films in regular theaters. During the 1990s, tents became more popular, leading to a loss of clientele for permanent cinemas, which were threatened with closures.[96] In 2010, tents were thought to have increased in number and to have widened their appeal.

Multiplexes have brought further diversity to the cinematic landscape. Unlike their counterparts in the West, which were introduced as a functional space that replaced the lavish movie palace, multiplexes in India are designed to offer an upmarket experience for middle- and upper-middle-class filmgoers.[97] They are being absorbed into the public culture of conflict and debate over cinema and its experience. A blog titled "The Day When Affordable Cinema Died" predicts that soon cinema will become a "luxury" rather than an everyday entertainment. The author embarks on a tirade against multiplexes:

> I get pissed off when people on television make statements like "Stop piracy. Watch movies in the theater," well, fuck you bitch—do I look like an idiot to watch that crappy 3 hour movie of yours paying Rs. 350 when I don't make Rs. 100 an hour as a software engineer? . . .

> I hate multiplexes. They have smaller screens, adopt variable pricing and excessively overcharge. . . . I don't care about the variety of crap available at the theatre. It is like saying I go to an underwear store because of the variety of sizes they have![98]

Yet it is unclear to what extent multiplexes in Bangalore have been successful in making the shift to sterile functionality and erasing space. Mall multiplexes serve a variety of food, and tantalizing fragrances waft through the auditorium. They may not have been successful in banishing other, less tantalizing evidence of humanity. After visiting one of the earlier multiplexes, a moviegoer was unimpressed and reported that "the entire corridor was stinking of urine!"

HETEROGENEITY, LOCALITY, AND THE CINEMA EXPERIENCE

Cinema is seen to be a highly local phenomenon in Bangalore as it has been in cities in India historically. One cannot speak of exhibition or of film consumption and taste without referring to place. Cinema's "taste publics" are spatialized, the city and its localities house multiple worlds of cinema, seen, for instance, in the distinctions between the cinema cultures of the Cantonment and the City. Cinema's mindscape, located in the city's space cultures, is also shaped by history, by people's relationship to locality, to each other, and by the feelings attached to such locations.[99] Kannada superstar Shivaraj-kumar remarked that while he could not walk around in Majestic for fear of being mobbed by fans, such restrictions did not apply in M. G. Road and in "Cantonment-side," as few would recognize him there.

Where a film's success at the box office depends on how effectively it taps into a particular spatial culture, a distributor's inability to secure an appropriate theater or set of theaters, can jeopardize the film's run. The competition for theaters is itself a demonstration and reinforcement of the importance of place and locality, its "relational and contextual meanings."[100] Even after the introduction of multiplexes, Kannada filmmakers continue to release films in single-run theaters that are accessible to their audiences and recognized as sites for Kannada films, though with the systematic demolishing of cinema halls, Kannada films have also made their way into the multiplexes.

Contra the expectation that there is one uniform way to experience cinema in public settings, cinema in Bangalore alerts us to the diversity and variation in its experience that is sited. Far removed from the standardized and inter-changeable spaces of the new multiplexes in the West that have evolved to provide an unremarkable setting for a placeless and individualized viewing of the film, cinema halls are sites of cultural and linguistic expression that are rich in local meaning and have distinct identities based on a combination of factors including the types of films screened, visits by stars and other VIPs, and festivities hosted at the theater.[101] All these elements together with the the-ater's "merit" influence the definition of the site and the meaning of the film, audience expectations of the movie experience, and film reception. They fuel the conflicts that center on exhibition sites. Struggles between audiences and exhibitors, between middle-class and lower-class viewers, and between exhib-itors and filmmakers become meaningful as a definition of the experience and self-definitional for audiences. They suggest that the meaning and experience of the cultural product are open to negotiation at these sites.

Given this understanding, the expectation that "Cinema should make you forget you are sitting in a theater"[102] reveals more about a particular historical and social context and culture of film viewing than about the cinema experi-ence in any general sense. Audiences at Bangalore's cinema halls and tent the-aters are constantly reminded of the materiality of the theater setting and the sensualities of these spaces. Sweating and scratching in the theater, the smells of urine and of bodies in close proximity, uncomfortable seats and noises from fans make it difficult to dismiss the collectivity and physical environment, while the inhabitants of theaters—rats, bats, bugs, fireflies, and pigeons—point to the "liveness" of the space that has to be reckoned with.

The particularities of various theaters cannot be ignored; they shape the cinemagoing experience for audiences along with the memories, nostalgia-filled accounts, stories, and debates about cinema that are place based. Indeed, the "thrills" of the cinema may have more to do with the idiosyncrasies of the exhibition setting than the film. Consequently, the film is less dominant as a determinant of the cinema experience.

CHAPTER 4

Audiences Negotiate Tickets
and Seating

I never go to Majestic because of the crowd, never sit in the lower level because of the
crowd. Don't stand in line to buy tickets. I hate that most of all.

MIDDLE-CLASS WOMAN, BANGALORE

When at first I talked with moviegoers about their film experiences, asking
them about the latest film they had seen, I was struck by their preoccupations
with what seemed to be side issues and trivia. Like Janice Radway's (1984)
readers of romance novels, who spent considerable time talking about the
act of reading and the pleasures it afforded rather than the books themselves,
in moviegoers' accounts, mundanities such as buying tickets, selecting seats,
navigating the cinema hall, and interactions in public featured prominently.[1]

These concerns are not peculiar to cinemagoers in India. In an essay in
the *New Yorker,* Edward Jay Epstein observes that "the least important commodities in American movie theaters may be the movies themselves" and that
when stadium seating was introduced at multiplexes in the United States in
the early 1990s, it attracted audiences from as far as twenty miles away, increasing attendance at these theaters by 30–52 percent.[2] The importance of such
"peripherals" is seen in the commercialization of moviegoing. Revenues from
movie theater concessions in the United States have steadily increased over
the years and bring in more than ticket sales.[3] Seats with cupholders, which
allowed moviegoers to "store their drinks while returning to the concession
stands for more food," were recognized as one of the most "groundbreaking
innovations" in movie-theater history.[4] Parking is another peripheral moviegoers in the United States and the United Kingdom consider when selecting
films and theaters,[5] and increasingly parking concerns shape the movie outings of middle-class moviegoers in Bangalore. Yet peripherals and the related
contingencies of cinemagoing have not featured prominently in either empirical or theoretical studies of cinema. Except for historical work on exhibi-

tion and market research on film consumption, studies highlight the positive meanings—the films themselves, glamor and celebrity, what may be thought of as cinema's "front stage." Active construction of the cinema experience for moviegoers involves negotiating both the physical environment and the social organization of stratified cinema halls, yet these mundane and routine aspects of the cinema experience, the "work" audiences do to accomplish an outing, are all relegated to the background as taken-for-granted aspects of the movie outing.

This chapter examines the unfolding of the cinema event by focusing on cinema's "back stage" and the "repertoire of practices"[6] that informs the social organization of the exhibition setting and audiences' navigation of such settings that are often hidden and invisible even to audiences themselves. I address audiences' negotiation of ticket purchase and seating and the attendant navigation of interactions in public settings as "creative responses to their social position" that are consequential for shaping the cinema outing.[7]

NAVIGATING THE EXHIBITION SETTING

The excitement of going to the movies at Bangalore's cinema halls is the excitement of "traditional" urban life with its "diversity and spontaneity."[8] For many moviegoers, the disorder of crowds, being jostled and pushed, having one's clothing torn, the presence of police, and dealing with scalpers represents the thrill and the "game" that moviegoing is. For others, these are risks and dangers to be avoided. To accommodate individuals belonging to different socioeconomic backgrounds, cinema halls in India pursued a strategy of separation and differentiation through their (social) organization of space. Stratified seating, inherited from British theaters,[9] allows moviegoers to watch from the stalls close to the screen for a fraction of the price of a balcony ticket. Individual ticket windows and separate queues for differently priced tickets extend the social organization of the theater into the surrounding urban space. Many theaters have separate entrances for the different ticket categories to prevent audiences from mixing as they enter the theater.[10]

Tickets, Queues, and Public Life

Especially before the advent of online ticket booking in Bangalore, queuing was part of the ritual of going to the movies. Queues outside cinema halls were a common sight in the city, sometimes indistinguishable from the general swirl of street life.[11] People stand in clumps and may resemble a gathering more than a queue. Lengthy queues and crowds outside theaters provide publicity for the film, encouraging exhibitors to delay the opening of the ticket counter.

Habitués negotiate different categories of queue. Apart from queues for balcony, stalls, and so on, the advance booking queue allows moviegoers to purchase tickets for shows later in the day or week while the current booking queue is for ticket purchase before each show. Individual theaters may vary in these arrangements. In some theaters, advance booking is available only for the evening show; tickets for matinees and morning shows must be purchased through the current booking queue. In the late 1990s, very few cinema halls had tickets available online, and Internet booking was being debated in the newspapers. Commenting on the possible inequalities resulting from making tickets available online, a theater manager proposed that tickets sold on the Internet should be priced higher in the interests of fairness, as people standing in long queues who did not have access to a computer should not have to return home empty-handed.[12] By 2009, many theaters in the city had online booking, a convenience advertised by multiplexes following which moviegoers shifted their attention to the navigation of online ticket purchase. However, one continues to see queues and crowds outside single-screen theaters. At mall multiplexes, audiences who have already purchased tickets online queue to enter the auditorium.

*

Queues and queuing featured prominently in filmgoers' accounts and memories of movie outings (fig. 11). People remember interactions in queues, the crush of crowds, and being accosted by street vendors and scalpers. Queuing is a topic for moviegoers' blogs. One blog (dated 2007) is titled *Dus ka bees, bees ka tees* (20 for 10, 30 for 20),[13] recalling a well-known scene from the Bombay film *Rangeela* where scalpers outside theaters sell "black-market" tickets, shouting out their wares like vendors of vegetables and fruit. It features comments from moviegoers (in various parts of India) pointing to the broad significance of queues and tickets for the cinema experience. A filmgoer from Jaipur (city) writes, "I have spent much of my formative years running around to get film tickets, standing in long queues, loving the FDFS [First Day First Show] frenzy. Films I can remember having a hard time getting tickets—Jurassic Park, *DDLJ, HAHK, DTPH*"[14] (November 13, 2007, 2:38 a.m.). Others share their experiences of queuing for the cinema, of buying tickets from scalpers, and fights in queues:

FIGURE 11. Moviegoers queue for the Kannada film *Raam* outside Sagar theater. Photograph by the author, Bangalore, 2010.

Hey ——, nice write-up. Brought back memories from my own Patna days, queuing up in front of Regent [cinema] . . . even buying tickets in black. (November 13, 2007, 4:54 a.m.)

I remember when I was in school. . . . Me and a couple of friends of mine used to stand in queues from the wee hours of the morning in front of Menoka cinema. (November 13, 2007, 2:50 a.m.)

Life outside cinema halls involving audience members, scalpers, footpath vendors, the destitute seeking alms, theater security staff, and, on occasion, the police, may appear random, even chaotic at first glance, but standing in ticket queues, the patterns and constants become visible. In the face of disapproval from many of my respondents and friends, I spent several mornings, afternoons, and evenings in queues of one kind or another at cinema halls in the Cantonment and Majestic. Sometimes I would go to the theater to simply stand in queues to get a sense of the interactions and activities that are peculiar to them. Frequently, the head of the queue featured the same type of people: young men of lower-class backgrounds. I heard repeatedly from various sources that the young men who scalped tickets took their place at the head of the queue to purchase tickets they would sell later that day or the next day on the "black market." Sometimes, the same men could be seen hanging around the theater and the current booking queue close to showtimes.

Queues are not merely sites of economic exchange for the purchase of tickets.[15] They are dynamic, fluid, and temporary formations that are vulnerable to the location of the theater, the movies screened, and the monitoring activities of theater staff. They may be instantly transformed into a marketplace, a pushing and shoving scrum, or a stage. Hanging around outside the Plaza on M. G. Road, I saw a footpath vendor set up shop as the queue was forming. He spread a cloth on the pavement and took packets of snacks out of a large canvas bag, then proceeded to arrange the packets in neat rows on the cloth. Within ten minutes he had made a sale. After the queue dispersed, he closed shop and moved to another location down the street. I found him there on repeat visits to the Plaza; when I asked him how often he sold items there, he said he arrived almost every day at the same time. The release of a new film meant he had to be there. That day, a man selling wristwatches from a suitcase strapped to his shoulder came and stood next to the snack vendor, creating an instant marketplace. At the Sagar theater on K. G. Road, a young man hawked Kannada film magazines to people queuing for tickets for *Raam* (2010), another youth spread out moviestar cards on the pavement, while a juice vendor selling spicy lemon sherbet made brisk sales on that warm afternoon in January.

The public and social life that embeds cinema is played out in queues. An old Bangalorean visiting from the United States watched a film at the Rex theater on Brigade Road, a favorite haunt of his student days in the city. Exiting the theater he was jolted back to the past when he encountered a pockmarked, blind man begging for alms, whom he recognized from his movie outings at the Rex fifteen years earlier. The scene could have been from an Indian film. On multiple occasions standing in line outside the Sapna Theater, I encountered its regulars: a man who appeared to be dumb begged for alms; a barefoot woman wearing a faded sari traveled the length of the queue with a young child on her hip, also asking for money; a youth desultorily hawked Kannada newspapers to people in the queue. While standing in queues, people pursue "side involvements";[16] they talk with friends, buy snacks from vendors, read newspapers, or listen to a cricket commentary on small transistor radios. People in queues are therefore often transported to other sites.[17] As a student in Bangalore, I would see school and college students with books open, cramming frantically for their examinations. Outside the Plaza and BluMoon theaters, urchins played an astonishing variety of film tunes on the bamboo flutes they were hawking. Hearing these tunes, people may remember a past movie outing or another moment in everyday life. More recently, cell phones facilitate such transcendences both through the film music that serves as ringtones and the interactions they enable.

The meaning of standing in queues differs for different types of audiences. For some, standing in line is transformed into entertainment and a means of passing the time. Young men in groups playfully push friends about, they lean on one another, slap each other on the back. For others, queuing is a tedious chore and a waste of time, to be got through as fast as possible. On a Thursday in early 1998, I waited outside the Plaza, where the James Bond film *Tomorrow Never Dies* (1997) was being screened.[18] The advance booking queue was just forming at 9:30 in the morning. The line of mostly young and middle-aged men grew rapidly. Some looked as if they might be office workers; there were also a few college students. There was a clear class division in the queue. At the head of the line were the street toughs and some urchins. For these young men, dressed in simple pants and shirts and wearing rubber *chappals*, ticket purchase is both sport and livelihood. Buying into widely held local perceptions of this group, I wondered whether they were fans or scalpers who will later sell the tickets they are buying. Some people in the queue were in uniform: chauffeurs, office clerks, and errand boys also identified by their *khaki* or other uniform-type clothing. A couple who looked like household servants had possibly been sent to buy tickets for their employers. A few who appeared to be middle-class, wearing jeans or better-quality trousers and shirts with shoes and watches, joined the queue later. There were no women.

The street toughs smoked constantly, sometimes lighting up individual cigarettes and *beedis*, sometimes sharing one, passing it from hand to hand. There was much laughter and talk interspersed with shouts and yells. Some sat on the ground, still keeping their place in the queue. They shouted, spat, pushed and jostled, hung on to one another's shoulders, leaned on one another, their antics providing a diversion for others and bringing a performative element to the mundanities of ticket purchase. In contrast to their physicality and flamboyance, middle-class queuees are staid: they stood farther apart, some talked to a friend, one man appeared to be instructing a boy (his son?) not to shout. Several checked their wristwatches, impatient for the ticket window to open. Those who smoked did so discreetly, blowing smoke down, away from the person they were talking to.

Queuees are alert to small changes and shifts in their surroundings. Those at the head of the queue are under constant scrutiny because what happens at the front of the queue provides an indication of what is to come for those farther down. From the demeanor and activities of the street toughs, others will learn whether the ticket counter is opening, how tickets are being issued, whether tickets are being rationed, and, if they are, whether there are enough to go around. On that day, there was a rumor of ticket rationing. People craned their necks to get a better view of the head of the queue, and others looked around, anticipating trouble.

Moviegoers' attitudes toward queues and activities in queues vary based on their gender and class. For the middle and upper-middle classes who seek to maintain distance and status through distance,[19] queues generate anxiety.[20] The closeness of bodies in the queue, the pushing and shoving, impinge on the boundaries of the self.[21] This is especially problematic for middle-class women, who may feel vulnerable when forced into close proximity to strangers and lower-class men. In their accounts of moviegoing, women articulated feelings of embarrassment and discomfort and of having to be "on guard" in crowded public spaces. However, not all cinemagoers seek a tame leisure experience; some enjoy a skirmish.[22] Men of a certain class may push people just for sport; the scrum creates chaos and a cover for them to brush against or "fall" on "ladies," providing a "sneaky thrill."[23]

One morning, I made plans to go to an "evening show" with Veena, a middle-class housewife. It was an outing for both our families, one of many. Veena offered to buy tickets for the Hindi film *Zor*, a new release at a theater near her home; she called me around one in the afternoon and reported, "I've got eight tickets. I stood in the queue and got them." I asked her whether she had had to stand in line for a long time. She said "no, about fifteen to twenty minutes." It was a warm day, and standing in the hot sun was tiring, but Veena did not seem to be bothered by the weather: "it was very shady in Cauvery Theater." What was more of a problem was standing in the queue close to men belonging to the lower socioeconomic orders or, as Veena put it, "ricksha fellows." She complained that the "queue was soooo long! So many people came after me. They started giving tickets only at eleven o'clock. I was the only lady there. Only men in the queue. I asked [theater staff], 'Will you have separate queue for ladies?' They said [in Kannada] 'No Ma, only one queue.' So all rickshaw fellows front and back; some decent people were also there. But it's so embarrassing, no?, if you're the only lady with all these fellows."

*

Middle-class women in Bangalore may long for the ladies' queues that further segregate them and allow them to create distance from "gents," "loafers," "rowdies," and "rickshaw fellows." Exasperated by her experience of standing in a queue and being bumped by the men standing close to her, a moviegoer informed me, "you know in Madras they have separate queues for ladies. 'Ladies queues' make it 'respectable' and 'decent' for women to stand in ticket lines." P. G. Srinivasamurthy, a journalist who has reported on cinema in Bangalore for over forty years, described ladies' queues in the city in the 1950s and 1960s.[24] Since then, theaters have dispensed with them, just as city buses no longer have "ladies seats." Bangalore has a reputation for being a progressive and liberal city with a cosmopolitan way of life, and one middle-class woman in her forties blamed the disappearance of ladies' queues in Bangalore on the feminists in the city: "It's all because of this feminist movement that we don't have separate queues. I remember ten or twelve years ago in Bangalore there were ladies' queues. Then when these feminists said 'We want to be equal, to be independent,' they said, 'No more ladies' queues!'" However, "Ladies" and "Gents" queues have reappeared at multiplexes perhaps because moviegoers are subject to security searches at malls.

ORDER AND DISORDER IN QUEUES

Moviegoers in queues are "open persons"[25] in "exposed positions"[26] and subject to the attentions of strangers, which can lead to a range of potentially unwelcome interactions.[27] People may cut into the queue, leading to confrontations. Those standing in the queue may be pushed by those behind them, prodded by security guards, and accosted by street vendors and scalpers. The tension and ambivalence that animates queuing broadly shapes cinemagoing in public settings. While most tensions are soon quelled by theater security or the police, fights over ticket shortages can escalate. There is a general understanding that fans can be especially volatile. Fans of Kannada film superstars are known to get out of control if they do not obtain tickets on the first few days of a film's release. Indeed, cinemagoing with rowdy fans and enthusiasts can be more like attending a sports match.

Queues, then, are sites for potential conflict and for confrontation between moviegoers and exhibitors and theater staff who seek to impose order. It is common to see security guards or chowkidars in khaki or gray shirts and trousers armed with a bamboo cane to discipline queuees. These guards may also turn their attention to vehicle parking and may be found directing traffic on the street in and around the theater. Ushers or theater attendants may also lend a hand at supervising the audience. At times, people who are not even directly employed by the theater may be roped in to help with crowd management and so are found monitoring queues and audiences. I watched this happen one evening in Bangalore:

> The ticket booth at Sapna theater has not opened. It is 5:30 p.m., and the show is scheduled to start in an hour. A straggling line forms in the middle of the driveway. A man wearing a red shirt and gray trousers orders people to move against the wall. Though he looks like he may be a loiterer, he has an air of authority. People in the queue shuffle obediently, responding to his instructions even though he is not in uniform. When someone asks him what time the ticket booth will open, he is brusque: "Six o'clock." He busily continues with his task of reorganizing the line and drives away some urchins who are begging. Later on I learn that he is the distributor's representative, come to oversee the collections for the show. (Field notes, Sapna theater, February 1998)

Theater staff keep a sharp eye on queues for signs of incipient trouble. When audience members enter the theater, security staff and ticket collectors position themselves on either side of the doors to regulate the flow of people. Using a style of crowd management seen at large temples and pilgrimage centers, staff may order viewers to "move along" (in Kannada, *nadi ri*), "hurry up," or "wait," and may instruct people not to push others. A fairly typical scene outside theaters screening a popular film involves crowds of moviegoers eager to enter the theater, creating a challenge for security guards.

> Outside the Majestic theater where the Kannada film *Om* (1996)[28] is being screened, the crowd thickens as it nears show time. More and more people gather in front of the theater doors, at which are stationed two men: one a security guard with an impressive military-style white moustache and another who doubles as ticket collector. Viewers inch forward till there is a wall of people, mostly young lower-class men, pressed against the doors. Some impatiently call out to the theater attendants, telling them to open the doors. One youth catches hold of the metal gates and tries to pry them apart. Finally, theater staff open the door because they can no longer keep people at bay. The crowd surges in. Staff are skilled in keeping track of and collecting tickets in this situation. (Field notes, April 1998)

Moviegoers, their bodies, are subject to social control.[29] People in queues expect to be monitored and supervised. The mass audience in particular puts up with any number of insults and even injury before entering the theater. Security guards may physically hold enthusiasts back as they push against the doors of the theater: they may shove them or grab them by their arms or shoulders, strike the ground with their bamboo canes, or shout at those who engage in pushing and starting fights.[30] If a movie is reputed to be very popular and expected to attract large crowds, a lower class of audience, or boisterous fans, theater managers do not hesitate to call in the police.[31]

Theaters also attempt to impose order with measures to discourage scalpers and black-market ticket sales, or as one manager put it, "control(ling) the black money." Taking a leaf out of rationing practices for commodities such as sugar, oil, and rice, theater staff may decide to ration tickets to discourage bulk sales, a practice that was in place in 1998 and that I observed again in 2007, 2009, and 2010. Decisions to ration tickets to two per person, for example, are often made and implemented on the spot and without warning. Sudden rumors that that only one ticket per head is being issued exasperate those waiting for hours to purchase tickets for groups of family or friends. Confrontations between staff and queuees follow; those who demand extra tickets over and above the limit set by the theater are not only refused but admonished, yelled at, or pushed away, "*Hoggu Ri! Hoggu Ri!*" (Get a move on! Shut up!). Thus ticket rationing can have the undesirable effect of exacerbating the volatility of ticket queues.

Moviegoers expect queues to be disorderly, even chaotic. Some referred to queues as "fights, wars, and wrestling matches." A blogger vividly described the process of ticket purchase in Jharkhand and the skirmishes that are a routine part of the process: "Buying a ticket from the counter is like fighting a war. First, the long queue to reach the counter and the counter had very small space in which we had to put our hands to fetch out the tickets and you have had only two second to do that otherwise your clothes will be torn."[32]

I witnessed skirmishes in queues on multiple occasions. One morning I was waiting in line with a friend and a family member at the Abhinay theater in Gandhinagar. The ticket booth was supposed to have opened at 11 a.m. for the 2 p.m. show, but it was nearing noon, and it remained closed. The serpentine queue of over a hundred people meandered down the granite stone pavement past small shops. A security guard equipped with a long bamboo stick attempted to "manage" the line, directing its structure. He instructed people not to stand in the street, moved them onto the pavement, ordered them to move to their left or right, and so on. Periodically he would relax his supervisory role and start chatting with people in the queue or with footpath vendors. People were packed together at the head of the line, which wound its way up the steps of the theater. Men clutched the shoulders of those in front of them just to keep their footing. Some held on to the metal railing next to the steps with one hand. There were several young men in this section of the queue, and many appeared to be "front benchers." I and my two female movie companions had been standing in the queue for about half an hour when suddenly there was a flare-up at the front end close to the ticket booth. We heard people yelling and shouts to "stop pushing" along with accusations of people cutting into the queue. Several such "pushing" episodes arose, during which the queue swayed and people yelled and shouted and clutched one another. A couple of people lost their footing and fell on the steps. I asked those standing nearby what had happened as we craned our necks for a better view.[33] One man had apparently hit or pushed another, and there was retaliation. People gave different interpretations of the sequence of events, a lot of it guesswork.

Suddenly there were several sharp cracking sounds as policemen's bamboo canes descended on moviegoers' backs and shoulders. Khaki-clad police brandishing their lathis (canes) shouted at people in the queue and pushed them into the line. We heard a rumor that the "fight" began when the theater started issuing only one ticket per head. After another fifteen minutes there was yet another skirmish, with the police again wielding their canes, chasing queuees who then rushed down the theater steps. Soon afterward, order seemed to have been restored, people were laughing and making jokes about the incident, and the police were seen sipping tiny cups of tea while continuing to keep a watchful eye on the queue. When the ticket booth opened, even those who had encountered the policemen's lathis bought tickets and went in to see the film in apparent high spirits (field notes, Abhinay theater, 1998; see fig. 12).

NEGOTIATING TICKET PURCHASE

Social Class and Legitimacy

Class identities and perceptions of social class are influential in the negotiations that accompany ticket purchase. Theater staff and audiences distinguish between "legitimate" moviegoers and scalpers based on such perceptions as well as the behavior of individuals at theaters. Scalpers are seen to belong to a certain (lower) class and to frequent particular theaters within their beat and so become known to both theater staff and moviegoers. I asked one theater manager how he made the distinction; he responded simply, "we know the persons, who is black [marketers], who is public.[34] We chase them [scalpers] out!" The manager's response emphasized a tacit knowledge of the terrain that is rarely articulated. He assured me, "Over the years we've got the practice [of identifying scalpers]." On another occasion when I again asked the

FIGURE 12. Crowds outside Abhinay theater. Photograph by the author, Bangalore, 2009.

manager how he distinguished scalpers from regular viewers, he responded impatiently, "We know! We know!," then elaborated, "One day we will observe. One show he will come. He will come matinee. First show [starting at 4:30] we'll observe. If he comes next day, we'll catch! We see the person, we know the family [background], just by looking." Theater managers may stand at ticket counters to see who is buying tickets and how many are being bought by one person. Theater attendants keep a lookout for individuals exhibiting certain behaviors, such as routinely purchasing multiple tickets and returning frequently to the theater.

Even though theater managers maintained that they would drive scalpers away, this appeared to be an official stance; in practice, it seemed that scalpers were tolerated as long as they were discreet and were not likely to attract the attention of the police. Habitués were cynical about what they saw as pure drama and a game. Many believed that theater staff and the police had an understanding with scalpers whereby scalpers would get their quota of tickets.[35] Scalpers become well-known figures outside theaters. In 2010 and again in 2012, when I went to the movies in Majestic, I saw scalpers very visibly hawking tickets. Everyone around seemed to be aware of who they were. Ticket rationing, however, works for the box office as it creates a buzz of scarcity that promotes the movie as a must-see.

The social class of moviegoers and perceptions of their socioeconomic and cultural background more broadly shape negotiations at theater sites with staff and strangers. Theater staff are likely to relax ticket rationing rules based on the class of the person they are dealing with. Sometimes one finds that tickets are obtainable simply by virtue of the purchaser being perceived as middle class. Middle-class moviegoers are conscious of their appearance and demeanor in signaling their status and are able to use class bias or "profiling" in ticket rationing to their advantage and to persuade theater staff of their legitimacy. Kumar, a college student, was confident that the impression he gave as a bona fide (middle-class) moviegoer meant that strict rationing would not apply to him: "If a person like me goes to the ticket counter, I can manage to get about six or seven tickets with ease because I might appeal to the manager as a person who would not sell the tickets." He explained that once when he was buying tickets for a large family group of ten, the ticket clerk was initially hesitant to give him all ten tickets at once; however, once the theater manager *saw* Kumar, he approved the sale: "There was a man standing next to the ticket counter who was controlling the number of tickets being sold to a person. . . . [He] promptly gave me four tickets for the afternoon show on my demand, but when I asked him to give ten tickets for the evening show, he had to ask the manager who was standing next to him. The manager looked at me and nodded."

Middle-class moviegoers may be approached by others in the queue who may recognize their own disadvantage in being perceived as lower class but still want tickets beyond the rationing limit. One middle-class moviegoer reported that while he was in line he was approached by three others, whom he identified as "from the lower classes," who asked him to buy tickets on their behalf. They convinced him that because he was (or looked) middle-class, "theater people would give more tickets [to him]." "So, I took Rs. 120 from one person and Rs. 40 from another person who was standing just two spaces behind me in the queue" and then proceeded to purchase tickets for them. The same thing happened when he went to see *Andamans* (1998), where "the manager was standing next to the ticket counter and administering the tickets sold. There was a repeat of the same incident when I went for the movie *Major Saabh* (1998)." Middle-class moviegoers may thus find themselves participating in dodgy deals and colluding with strangers, becoming middlemen and "false fronts"[36] in situations when they are requested to act on behalf of those lower in the class hierarchy. Again, the arrival of the multiplex, with its online booking and its ticket prices that are affordable mainly to middle-class and upper-middle-class moviegoers, has affected such negotiations and interactions.

Avoiding Ticket Queues

When I met Shanti, she was managing a neighborhood photocopying service and long-distance phone booth. In her early twenties and from a lower-middle-class background, Shanti had dropped out of college in order to work when her family faced financial problems. She had a two-wheeler that got her around the city. She spent most days at her booth, and I would visit her there to chat, usually in the afternoon, when she had a bit of down time between the morning and evening rush from office workers and students. The streets were quieter then; an autorickshaw would meander slowly down the street looking for a fare, a stray dog would amble along and curl up in the dust outside one of the bungalows. Shanti would take a lunch break and make herself a sandwich. Sitting in her cramped and airless booth, she barely had space to move but would dig out a paper packet with half a loaf of sliced white bread from under the table top, along with a cucumber, a tomato, some butter, and chili-coriander chutney from a tiny fridge. Seated cross-legged on her chair, she would set about making sandwiches. She had a flask of strong tea or coffee to go with it. Sometimes her friend would stop by, and the two would share the sandwiches. When I was there, I was always invited to a sandwich lunch. Shanti's moviegoing was defined by certain rules and preferences that had become habits. Her list of preferences revealed the parameters and constraints that middle-class moviegoers work with: "I never go to Majestic because of the crowd; never sit in the lower level because of the crowd. Don't stand in line to buy tickets. I hate that most of all!"

*

Shanti was simply expressing some of the rules of navigation of public settings that the middle classes use to distinguish themselves. Avoidance of crowds and ticket queues was fairly standard practice for women and middle-class moviegoers who often feel they simply do not have the time to wait around in queues. They also see queuing in the hot sun in dusty and congested areas as being beneath their status, or "dirty work,"[37] and devise plans for the movie outing with the purpose of avoiding queues.[38] Some may not even attempt to see a new film until a few weeks have passed to allow time for the crowds to abate. Advance booking is a boon for those who want to avoid the tedium of waiting in line and the attendant hassles of interactions in public settings.

*

I accompanied middle-class individuals, families, and groups of friends to the cinema whenever I got a chance. On these occasions I rarely stood in queues to purchase tickets. Tickets would be booked in advance or bought by others, a practice that continued in 2007, in 2010, and in 2012. Anjali, an architect in her thirties, told me that she never buys "current" tickets (from current booking queues) just before the start of a show, so she never has to stand in queues: "We buy it in the morning. We send someone in the morning to get tickets, or some friends get the tickets, it's taken in turns. So we get it in the morning for the evening show." Kaveri talked about her cinemagoing experiences as a college student with an all-girl group of classmates. I asked her how she would get tickets. She responded, "Now that's an interesting question, because now that I think about it, we never used to go [for tickets]. We used to send some guys. After all, what are they for?" The ability to avoid standing in queues or queue by proxy distinguishes the "class" moviegoer from the "mass" or "public." As the middle classes prefer to delegate queuing, advance booking queues are certain to include some people buying tickets for others. Office assistants, maids, gardeners, messengers, and chauffeurs may be sent to stand in the advance booking queue for their employers or even for the extended family and friends of their employers. In some families, organizing the movie outing began with sending the gardener or the driver to get tickets. Some middle-class moviegoers rely so much on household and office help that they may not even attempt a cinema outing if such individuals are not available. Cell phones make it easy to keep track of how the queue is progressing and for those at home to instruct those whom they have deputed to get tickets whether they should stay in line or when to give up and come home and what to do in case sudden rationing is imposed (Bangalore, 2007).

Advance booking queues can therefore be misleading, as they typically underrepresent women, family groups, the elderly, and in general a higher class of viewer,[39] and they consequently do not give a sense of the composition of the audience for the film.[40] They also do not represent the sheer volume of moviegoers, because each individual in the queue may purchase multiple tickets unless rationing is imposed. The morning I stood in line outside the Plaza for tickets to the James Bond film, I returned to the theater in the evening, half an hour before the start of the first show and found that ticket holders in the queue were middle-class, Westernized, yuppie types. Mixed groups of men and women wearing designer jeans and sunglasses chatted in English and tried to look cool as they waited for the theater to open. In 2012, middle-class moviegoers seemed only to see movies at multiplexes and cinema halls where they could book tickets online. Theater staff at the older Menaka theater in Gandhinagar complained that business was suffering because such conveniences were not available.

"Using Pull"

Getting tickets and securing seats for a popular, newly released film is difficult, because theaters may be "sold out" for days. While some moviegoers decide to stay away from crowds and the challenges of ticket purchase, others enter into the game of outwitting theater officials and circumventing rules. On a blog a moviegoer discussed "getting . . . tickets by hook or by crook."[41] Determined moviegoers are not above bribing theater staff. Another viewer recalled how he and his friends "attempted a trick" to get into the theater, which "surprisingly worked. . . . We got a chance to treat one of the theater attendants with tea [and] samosas and he agreed to allow us an entry." They were given "back door entry," or would sneak into the theater "after the genuine ticket holders" had been admitted.[42]

Moviegoers may request someone who has influence with the theater to get tickets for them, in a practice known as "using pull." Thus, organizing a single movie event may involve a number of individuals who are not part of the movie outing. Prasad, a twenty-year-old studying to be an accountant, told me that his family knew the son of a manager of a certain theater and that they were always sure of getting tickets there. He generously shared his contact with me: "No problem at all, just call him and tell him, seats are reserved." Schoolteachers whose students had parents in the movie business would be asked to get tickets for their families and friends. Even someone who knew someone who knew the police commissioner would be roped in.

It is not only the middle classes who draw on networks and people in influential positions in this way. An autorickshaw driver told me he could walk into a certain theater at any time, even after the show had started, and watch the film free because theater staff knew he was friends with a certain producer who was also an official in the Karnataka Film Chamber of Commerce. On more than one occasion I observed (lower-class) fans of Kannada film stars walk into theaters without buying tickets. They seemed to be regulars at the theaters and to know the ushers, security guards, and other staff. Theater staff appeared somewhat wary of fans who were known for their rowdy behavior and for their connections to stars and fan clubs.

After I became a familiar face at some theaters and got to know theater managers and distributors, I was offered free tickets even without my asking for them. One afternoon at the Nartaki I mentioned to Mr. Raman that I was thinking of seeing a movie at a theater not far from his. He briskly asked me what day and time I was planning to go. When I told him, he said "no problem, you come here first and collect the tickets." He said he knew the manager of that theater and would "send one boy." Then the tickets "will be ready for you." I was taken aback and not a little embarrassed that Mr. Raman thought I was angling for tickets. In the end I did not go to the movie, but when I thanked Mr. Raman he brushed it off: "We are doing this all the time. This is *mamooli* [routine] for us."

Sitting in Mr. Raman's office, I saw certain people being given preferential treatment. A man came to the manager's office forty minutes after a film had started. He appeared to be a friend, or at least an acquaintance. Apparently he had come to pick up a ticket for the movie, which the manager understood though nothing was said. The theater had put up the "House Full" sign outside, but Mr. Raman still gave him a ticket. After he left, Mr. Raman explained to me, "Police! Police!" and then said scornfully, "Who will see anything after forty-five minutes have passed? Only police! Time-pass, time-pass! Lots of policemen come. We have to oblige. Police and commercial tax [officers], KEB [Karnataka Electricity Board] employees." On another day, two uniformed policemen walked into Mr. Raman's office, joined us for a leisurely cup of tea, and then strolled into the theater well after the movie had begun. Theater managers keep discretionary seats for drop-ins and VIPs, including stars, directors, and producers who want to watch the film in theaters soon after its release. I asked whether politicians and government officials were part of this special group. One morning, when there was a long line for tickets at the advance booking booth, I had seen a white ambassador car with government license plates stop outside the theater. The chauffeur, in a white uniform with white gloves, left the motor running as he dashed into the theater. He emerged within seconds clutching pink balcony tickets. According to Mr. Raman, politicians do ask for tickets to be set aside, but "they buy tickets, no free."[43] The practice of accommodating those whose goodwill was important to the functioning of the theater continued at some theaters in 2012. At the Sagar theater, the sweeper informed me that the two men who had entered the theater before its doors officially opened to the public, circumventing the lengthy queue outside, were policemen who had come to cadge seats from the manager. Later the manager confirmed this.

*

Theater managers, staff, and distributors—and even directors, producers, and stars—are accustomed to audiences pestering them for tickets and doing favors for friends and acquaintances. Middle-class moviegoers do not hesitate to phone the theater to inquire about the availability of balcony seats. Mr. Gupta, who had produced movies and then moved into distribution, reminisced about his early days in the business and spoke nostalgically of the "excitement" that was now missing. The thrill of working in the movie business, associated with being considered influential and powerful because of insider status in a glamorous world, had become humdrum "routine work" involving "headaches" such as insistent moviegoers clamoring for tickets. "So that excitement, charm, used to be there for us. Now it's something you feel tired."

*

Theater staff become victims of the frenzy to secure tickets and expect that viewers will try to get tickets by any means. Especially in the early days of a popular film's release, an air of suspicion surrounds encounters between staff and audience members,. When I went to see *Tomorrow Never Dies*, I planned to combine my observations of audiences with an interview with the theater manager. When I asked the staff when I could meet the manager, they were very cagey about his whereabouts: "These days we can't say when he'll be coming to the theater." When I persisted, I was asked to phone and set up an appointment. I tried calling several times the next day without reaching anyone. Returning to the theater the following evening I insisted on seeing the manager. The ushers and theater attendants first dodged the issue and then quizzed me about my reasons: was it about tickets for the movie? Only after I repeatedly assured them that I was not interested in tickets and that I had already purchased tickets for the movie was I allowed into the manager's office. The manager, Mr. Mohan, a Tamil speaker who appeared to be in his late fifties, apologized immediately; he said he had instructed his staff not to tell anyone he was there because people were "pestering" him for tickets. He had taken the phone off the hook because it was ringing continuously. To demonstrate, he put the receiver back, and the phone rang immediately. He seemed to be under siege, and I began to feel sorry for him. Fourteen years later, Mr. Rao, the manager of a theater on K. G. Road, told me, "I try not to answer the phone when a new movie is released. Its always people who want tickets" (field notes, July 2012).

"Buying in Black"

Scalpers are a convenience for moviegoers who do not want to face the bother of queues or who have left ticket purchase until it is too late. Some moviegoers would boast about how they could obtain tickets from scalpers for an otherwise sold-out show. For *Tomorrow Never Dies*, the 45-rupee ticket I bought in the morning was on sale "in black" for 100 rupees before the evening show. This was a modest increase. In the 1990s, black-market tickets could be ten times the price of a regular ticket. Viewers told me that for new films starring Rajkumar, even rereleases, black-market ticket prices have been Rs. 200, 300, 400, and above. For the blockbuster *Sivaji*, The Boss, which hit theaters in summer 2007, *Businessworld* reported, "the mood . . . in Mumbai is upbeat with areas like Dharavi having seen tickets being sold in black for Rs. 1500."[44] One fan responded excitedly to the popularity of *Sivaji* as seen from the fluctuation in ticket price, which he compared to the stock market: "awesomeeeeee! . . . tickets [black] are selling in bangalore for 1500 bucks each!!! . . . i heard they touched the 7 grand mark!!!!! . . . it's kinda like the stock market man!!"[45]

Purchasing black-market tickets is not restricted to any class or group. An autorickshaw driver with whom I was discussing the fate of a film released a week earlier told me that he had been to see it that morning and had bought a black-market ticket for Rs. 40. Even if he was merely trying to convince me of the film's popularity, the ease with which he admitted purchasing a ticket in "black" suggested it was common practice. Another autorickshaw driver explained that he did not "mind buying in black," as he absolutely *had* to see any film of "Rajanna" (an affectionate name for the Kannada movie legend Dr. Rajkumar) on the first day of its release. Even though his monthly income was just Rs. 900 and Rajkumar films at the time sold tickets in black for Rs. 200, Rs. 300, "I'll buy it anyway."[46]

*

While some moviegoers refuse to buy tickets in black as a matter of principle, others are prepared not only for the increased costs but the risks involved. The hurried transactions with scalpers offer no guarantees; those who think they have purchased balcony tickets may find that the seats offer a poor view, or that they are actually in the dress circle (a lower order of seating), or somehow invalid. The purchase of black-market tickets, with all its connotations, may even increase the thrill of cinemagoing. For those unused to dealing with scalpers and the conventions and practices of "buying in black," the experience can be unnerving. My own experience was anything but routine and made me aware of the level of inside or local knowledge that moviegoers draw on in the course of a cinema outing:

My sister and I arrive at Abhinay Theater in an autorickshaw; we are planning to see the 4:30 screening of the Bombay film *Dil To Pagal Hai*. The theater is in a congested area, and there is a lot of traffic on the street. All around the theater are small shops and eateries. At 2:30 that afternoon there is a large crowd outside the theater that is spilling onto the pavement. Our autorickshaw stops abruptly. While we look for change to pay our fare, I ask the driver whether he has seen the movie. He says yes and recommends it as "a good fillum." At the same time two men reach into the auto on either side and grab the vertical metal rails. One of them thrusts an arm with a clutch of pink tickets into the auto and shouts "House full! House full!" Another waves a sheaf of blue tickets in my face and shouts "Balcony, madam? Balcony, madam?" All this is so sudden that we are taken aback and slow to react. I look toward the theater and cannot see a House Full sign anywhere. I ask whether I can see the ticket. The young man is impatient: "Hurry up! The police will catch us!" Remembering warnings of dud tickets sold by scalpers, we try to check whether the tickets are indeed for today's show. I ask how much the tickets are. The man says "70 rupees." Regular tickets are less than 35 rupees. I ask whether that is the price for two tickets, which I later realize is a ridiculous question. He looks at me in astonishment: "No, for each." He has assumed that as middle-class girls we are interested in the highest-priced balcony tickets.

The driver joins in, helpfully trying to explain, "Black, madam, black." One of the men then asks us how many tickets we want. We say two. "Here, take these two, madam, very good seats." My sister examines the tickets and says "let's take them." Meanwhile, the other man with the blue tickets keeps looking up and down the street as we are talking with his partner, who has his head inside the auto. The driver has turned around in his seat and has become involved in the transaction. He asks one of the men sternly, "Are they in the middle of the row?" The scalper, ignoring him, tells us, "Good seats, balcony seats." Then, raising his voice, "Hurry up madam, by the time you decide the police will be here!" The other man shoves him aside and, showing us the blue tickets says, "You take these, they are only 50 rupees, minibalcony." The driver, who seems to have become our advocate, says, "No! That won't be good. You take balcony, minibalcony *channage irolla* [won't be good]." We finally buy two balcony tickets. The scalpers advise us not to hang around the theater "because of the crowd. You go for coffee, relax, and come back at 4:30." The entire interaction has taken about ten minutes. The autodriver gently reminds us that we have not settled his fare. We apologize profusely and he says, "That's OK," and smiles. We decide to follow the scalpers' advice and walk around looking for a coffee place. Later, when we return to the theater, we find it is not "House Full" after all. Had we, as the scalpers suggested, got to the theater just before the movie started, we would not have known till we took our seats. We ask the ticket clerk at the box office whether the tickets had sold out and he assures us you can get tickets easily. (Field notes Abhinay theater, 1997).

Habitués are prepared to collude with scalpers and even be managed by them to make on-the-spot decisions so that the transaction remains invisible to police, security staff, and even other moviegoers. Scalpers not only have to persuade moviegoers to buy from them but also have to convince people that they are their only recourse, and they may even have to manage customers' activities before the movie to make a successful sale. By preying on our keenness to see the film and our anxiety over ticket scarcity, the scalpers that day successfully presented themselves as a last resort.

Moviegoers Sell Tickets

Habitués are not just embroiled in the intricacies of ticket purchase; they even enter into ticket sales. Given the logistics of organizing large groups, people have to find ways to dispose of "extra" tickets and recoup their costs when, for example, one or two people in a group cannot attend. Therefore, outside theaters people may be approached not only by scalpers and moviegoers seeking to purchase tickets but also by fellow moviegoers keen to resell tickets. On more than one occasion I came across moviegoers who wanted to off-load their tickets.

Kumar, who was often given the task of obtaining tickets for his extended family, frequently found himself in the role of ticket salesman. He described one occasion when three people in his group had "dropped out" and how he had managed to sell the "extra" tickets for the evening show:

I had to sell three tickets, so I went next to the [theater] door and stood there prominently showing the tickets to everyone. Then two boys approached me and said that they wanted to buy one ticket. They already had one ticket, but I said I wanted to get rid of all the tickets, and if I sell one ticket at a time, I might not be able to sell all the tickets. Then he tried to assure me, and then I gave him his ticket, and he said, "give me two tickets." He wanted the two tickets because they both wanted to sit together. Then I told him that I won't take the other ticket. Just at that time, a couple with a kid came and asked me whether I was selling tickets. So I then sold two tickets to the couple and one to the boys and was happy to have got done with it. (Field notes, Bangalore, 1998)

The account provides a sense of the complicated negotiations moviegoers enter into. They become knowledgeable about how to approach strangers, where to stand, and how to bargain. In many groups certain individuals routinely find themselves taking on the role of ticket salesmen. When we went to see *Zor*, one family member could not make it at the last minute, so Kumar was once again deputed to stand outside the theater to sell the extra ticket. This happened again when we went to see *Titanic*. Kumar, to whom the family seemed to have delegated the job of disposing of the extra tickets, returned after selling the ticket and reported that "it was no problem" and bragged, "I could have even made some money on it." Selling tickets has the thrill of doing something illegal and for young men perhaps even of trying on the role of scalper for a brief moment. However, as class identities shape perceptions of who is scalping tickets, middle-class moviegoers feel protected from real risks.[47] On another occasion one of the older women in the family group sold the extra tickets.

As seen by these examples, the negotiation of ticket purchase requires considerable inside knowledge of the terrain and of conventions and expectations as well as awareness of one's class and status, all of which play a role in such interactions and accomplishments. Moviegoers enter into complicated negotiations and transactions to get tickets, circumventing institutional rules while making up their own. Their tactics include various ways of exercising status, intimidating and bribing theater staff, cultivating film-business insiders, all to "win" entry into the theater.

THE SOCIAL ORDERING OF THEATER SPACE AND THE MEANING OF SEATING

In addition to the three main seating categories (balcony, lower level, and stalls), many theaters offer seating in the minibalcony (a section in front of the balcony or at a slightly lower level and with lower-priced tickets); the

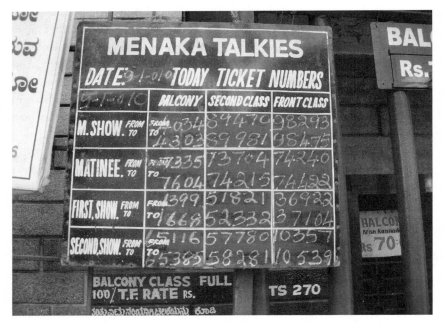

F I G U R E   1 3 . Sign showing seating classes and showtimes. Photograph by the author, Bangalore, 2012.

"deluxe" section; the dress circle (from the British theater), or second class; the mezzanine; middle class (literally the middle category or level of seating); and Gandhi class, also known as "front class" or "front stalls," all of which are differentially priced (fig. 13).

In the late 1990s people could sit in the balcony for anywhere between Rs. 40 and Rs. 100, but they could also watch the same film from the front stalls for Rs. 10–20.[48] Ticket prices also vary by theater, depending on its age, condition, reputation, and location. In 2009 I found that at older single-run theaters in Majestic, ticket pricing appeared not to have changed much over the years. However, multiplexes offered tickets at considerably higher prices for seating that is not as distinctively stratified within the theater. Multiplex ticket prices vary by their location and rank, with seating being fancier in some than in others. The PVR multiplex chain, only one of several multiplexes in Bangalore, has three categories: Classic, Europa, and Gold. In the Classic, a ticket can be purchased for Rs. 80, while Gold ticket prices can go up to Rs. 750. Ticket prices also vary by film and by day of the week, with weekend tickets priced higher.

Most audience members would agree that where they sit is linked to their enjoyment of the movie. Moviegoers put great effort into securing the seating of their choice and are willing to negotiate, bargain, and even get into confrontations over seating. Fine distinctions are made, for example, between the front section of the balcony and the back, because seats farthest from the screen are associated with a better view.[49] Sometimes viewers are able to select seats from a physical plan of the theater. Ticket clerks mark off the seats and write seat numbers on tickets. Middle-class moviegoers are overheard instructing ticket clerks, "See that you give me good seats!" or "Give us at the back in the balcony, not in front," or even, "We want aisle seating, not in the middle of the row." Those who frequent particular theaters carry a map of the theater in their heads, even down to specific seats. Moviegoers who visit theaters several times a month may know which seats in a particular theater are broken and are specific in their demands: "Give me row S, seats 12, 13, 14."

Within the stratified theater, various types of symbolic and spatial markers differentiate and distinguish the audience.[50] Divisions within the theater are maintained by sectioning off the various areas with physical barricades such as wooden railings or low cement walls between seating sections.[51] In some theaters the balcony is accessed by a flight of stairs or a ramp. Soon after entering the theater, the audience can be seen separating itself. Only those whose tickets are stamped "balcony" and that have the price displayed on the ticket are allowed to enter the balcony section. In many theaters tickets for balcony, lower stalls, and dress circle are of different colors to avoid confusion. Ushers positioned at the doors to the balcony turn away those who do not have the appropriate tickets. Balcony seating is numbered and allows ticket holders to proceed in a more leisurely fashion and be assured of their seat. Audience members with tickets for the lower-priced seating have to move toward their section with undignified speed because seating is on a first-come, first-served basis in these sections.

The seats themselves may be made of different materials, offering varying levels of comfort to the viewer. The balcony usually has upholstered seats (though I often found seats had large chunks of the upholstery torn out and the springs broken), whereas seats in stalls are usually made of hard plastic without a cushion. As a student in Bangalore in the 1970s and 1980s, I went to theaters with rows of wooden benches without backrests, or rickety wooden foldable chairs that served as seating in the stalls. In some theaters, the seats in the front stalls are placed farther apart from one another, a precaution taken by the theater to minimize rowdiness among patrons.

The difference between the balcony and the lower stalls is reinforced in other ways as well. There may be air conditioning or a greater number of fans

in the balcony, while audiences in the lower stalls have to make do with fewer
and noisier fans. Differentiation extends even to the food and drink available
at the concession counters. Many theaters have two concession stands: one
outside the balcony and another downstairs for the front stalls, or "second
class." Balcony concessions frequently have greater choice and better-quality
snacks, encouraging those seated in the stalls to migrate to the concessions
counter at the balcony level.

The differences in material comfort between the seating sections, their separation, and the varying sensibilities of moviegoers seated in these different sections saturate the meanings of seating which functions as "sign-equipment."[52]
Though they may on occasion sit in the minibalcony, dress circle, mezzanine,
or upper stalls, the middle classes associate an enjoyable movie experience with
balcony seating. Mr. Rai, a pharmacist, said he always insisted on the "quality"
of the cinema experience over "quantity" and so preferred to see fewer movies
from the balcony rather than see many from the cheaper seats (field notes, Bangalore July 2012). Talking with two college students about movies, I asked them
whether they had sat in the front seats for any movie. They shook their heads
vigorously, "No!" I asked them whether they would sit in the front stalls for
Titanic, a movie they were looking forward to. One of them laughed and said
promptly, "No! I want to enjoy it!" Indeed middle-class moviegoers may refuse
to entertain the idea that seats other than those in the balcony or its equivalent
are an option, as per the following interaction at the ticket counter:

> Outside the Rex Theater the ticket clerk at the balcony ticket window puts up
> the Sold Out sign, which immediately starts a scramble for seats. A middle-
> class woman dressed in a freshly starched and ironed cotton *salwar khameez*
> says in an argumentative and complaining tone, "Can't I get balcony seats?
> Why is that sold out?" She appears suspicious about the closing of the balcony
> section. The ticket clerk stonily repeats, "Sold out madam," by way of explana-
> tion. (Field notes, January 1998)

Last-minute decisions to see a film are often followed by a frantic search for
a theater with available balcony seats. This practice was unchanged in 2010
and in 2012, as I found middle-class moviegoers continued to consider the
availability of preferred seating as they decided which film to see at single-run
theaters.[53] Missing a good part of the movie did not matter as much as having
balcony seats. Often, by the time a theater with available balcony seats was
located, the movie would be well underway. Sudha, a middle-class housewife,
remembered similar experiences of going to the movies during or after the

intermission, halfway through the film, as it would take a good hour or so of "hunting" for a theater with balcony seats, even going from one theater to another at the last minute, before one was available. Some theaters put a "Balcony Sold Out" sign in the ticket window to forewarn middle-class moviegoers.

While moviegoers claim that balcony seating offers the best view of the screen, this is debatable and varies by theater. As an experiment, I sat in different sections of the theater and found that in many theaters the lower stalls or front stalls offered a much better view. Older cinema halls were often poorly designed, and the smallish, narrow screens were placed too far away and often at an awkward angle for the balcony audience to get a good view. Middle-class insistence on balcony seating suggests that the prestige meaning of seating frequently overrides its use value. Being seated in the balcony allows people to present themselves as respectable and of a certain status and perhaps to surround themselves with members of their own or a particular class.

Middle-class moviegoers' observations on the stratified theater revealed that they expect those seated in different parts of the theater to not only belong to different socioeconomic backgrounds but to have a viewing style that contributes to a distinct social experience of the film. Young middle-class men may indulge in "slumming" and choose to sit among "the rabble," electing to have a different movie experience from the more "genteel" balcony experience. Sudhir, a computer professional, recollected his movie adventures as a college student when he had very little money and would sit in the "cheap seats," where he had "the most interactive experience" and where "people would throw coins at the screen, and speak the hero's lines." For others, distance from boisterous viewers constitutes an enjoyable movie experience. Thus, middle-class women may forgo balcony seating for a matinee in the Cantonment but are less likely to sit at the lower level in a theater in Majestic, where they expect a lower class of viewer to predominate. Social and not just physical comfort at the theater is important to a certain class of moviegoer.

The balcony, with its social-status meanings, is the seating ideal for almost all moviegoers,[54] even those who cannot regularly afford balcony tickets. In the darkened theater, viewers may try to change seats and sometimes attempt to move into another section of the theater altogether. I would often stand at the back of the seating section or walk around inside the auditorium to get a better view of the audience. While standing at the back of the balcony section during a screening of the film *Dil To Pagal Hai*, I noticed on three separate occasions and within the space of some twenty minutes that men entered the balcony section under cover of darkness and stood at the entrance to the section looking around. They were conspicuous in the midst of middle-class groups and families. Balcony seats are numbered, but none of the men checked their ticket stubs in an attempt to locate assigned seating. Rather, they appeared to be scanning the area for empty seats. On identifying a seat, they quickly and quietly moved into it. This happened multiple times and at different theaters.

At the Sapna theater screening the Hindi film *Chachi 420* (Crazy aunt [1998]), I was seated at the lower level and saw three men leap across the wooden barricade that separated the lower stalls from the deluxe section, farther away from the screen. The theater was dark, and the usher's back was turned as he chatted with another member of the theater staff in the doorway. The men quickly located empty seats and sat down. Moving into a more pricey section of the theater grants instant if temporary upward mobility. It is a method of "honor and capture": capturing seats confers honor because it involves risk and strategy while constructing seating as a "trophy."[55] The maneuver is a demonstration of the tactics of the consumer and part of the repertoire of the consumer as "trickster."[56] Audience negotiation of theater regulations and attendant construction of meaning and experience in this case makes the movie enjoyable as a stolen experience.

The status aspect of seating may blind middle-class viewers to the choices they are making. When I asked an upper-middle-class professional about her seating preferences, she interpreted my question as being about seat numbers rather than the seating section and pointed out that one had to go with the seats assigned by the ticket clerk:[57] "Usually one doesn't have a choice here. Here, you usually buy a balcony ticket, and you're given whatever you get. So we—I've only been in balcony seats." She went on to account for the rare occasions when she or her family did not sit in the balcony. For a charity show for which her husband had purchased tickets she sat in the "lower stall." "And that's the only time. But my kids had gone the other day with friends for *Air Force One* (1997). and they didn't get tickets upstairs, because it was full and they bought tickets on the spot."

As I became aware of the stigma attached to seating at lower levels in the theater, I found that asking people about their seating habits and preferences was not always a productive way to learn about their seating practices. While some gave protracted explanations about choosing seating, others would be vague or would dodge the question. One moviegoer belonging to a lower socioeconomic class countered my question with, "Why do you want to know all these things?" Others, when asked where they usually sat, would be evasive: "We sit anywhere; wherever there are seats available," or "It depends whether we go with friends," or "Depends if there is rush." For some viewers the choice of seating may be a more flexible one, and they may be willing to sit in either the lower stalls or dress circle, hence, the open-endedness of these responses. But a reticence and hesitation in answering such questions also speaks to the taken-for-granted nature of this aspect of moviegoing, seen in the bewildered looks I frequently encountered when asking people about seating. Additionally, because where one sits is symbolic of where one is in society, questions about seating become highly sensitive, especially for non-middle-class viewers. It was embarrassing to ask lower-class viewers this question. Here, observation seemed the more reliable method.

Tensions over Seating

Being such a highly charged issue, seating often leads to confrontations among audience members and between audiences and theater staff. Tensions escalate when theaters overbook tickets, ushers guide viewers to the wrong seats, or other organizational mix-ups occur leading to the same seat number being issued to more than one viewer. Large groups who wish to sit together may find they have been issued tickets at either end of a row or across the aisle. At times people who arrive early sit wherever they please and refuse to move even when viewers who have the assigned seats show up. A combination of poor maintenance (where several seats are broken) and audience unwillingness to be flexible about seating contributes to the conflict. On one occasion I found myself with a front row seat to a conflict over balcony seating that dragged on for nearly forty minutes, providing a sideshow and a distraction from the movie.

Arriving at the Abhinay theater, we make our way to the balcony. It is a new film, and the theater is full. The usher helps us find our seats, and we sit down. The lights go off, and the movie begins. As always, there is a steady trickle of latecomers. People behind us arrive late and loudly discuss what time the film must have started, calculating how much they must have missed. A woman at the back shouts out to the usher, "This seat is not good." The usher grumpily tells her to go tell the manager. They have an argument in Kannada:

WOMAN: Fix the seat!
USHER: How am I supposed to do that? You go and complain to the manager. (He reluctantly ambles over and tries to adjust the seat.)

An elderly man sits down in another seat and falls through. The family of five talk agitatedly among themselves in Konkani[58] and then address the usher in Kannada. The usher suggests the family move to the lower stalls where seats are available. The man refuses angrily, saying he wants to sit in the balcony. After more argument, he decides to complain to the manager and leaves the auditorium to return after thirty minutes. People in the row behind are distracted by his appearance. He stumbles down the row, stepping heavily on people's feet, including mine. We overhear another heated discussion with seated family members as he informs them that he will stand, but stands as a protest where his broken seat is, blocking the view. Those seated behind him say, "Excuse me." He shouts back, "Seat is crooked!" A woman seated in a row behind begs and pleads with him (in Kannada) to stand in the aisle, "Daivittue alli ninthukoli." He turns around and tells her loudly in English, so all can hear, "He [the usher] has to give me a seat, no?" His family members, now embarrassed, make a show of examining the seat and attempting to fix it. They ask him to sit down somewhere. He relents and sits on the arm of the seat. Those seated around him crane their necks to see the screen. More people shout, "Sit down!!" He shouts back, "How can I sit down?!" Another woman shouts, "We cannot see!" He shouts back, "I cannot see also!" People grumble to one another, pointing to him. Two women start laughing. The drama and comedy in the theater, the sheer chaos of it, is more compelling than whatever is happening on-screen. The man ignores everyone and stares at the screen, standing rigidly like a soldier. (Field notes, Abhinay theater, matinee, March 1998)

Women are seen everywhere in Bangalore—driving cars or two-wheelers, riding in autorickshaws or buses, and employed in various occupations. However, they make distinctions between moving around the city for routine activities and cinemagoing and its enjoyment. Lower-middle-class women told me that they would never take an autorickshaw to the cinema hall, electing instead to go by bus or take their two-wheeler because it was less expensive and perceived as safer, but the same women seemed not to consider sitting in any section other than the balcony. Especially for women, where they sit in the theater is governed by ideas of what is respectable behavior and how they should be seen in public settings. Spending hours in the dark, in close proximity to strangers who are lower class, and to men, leaves women open to the kinds of unwelcome interactions that risk bodily boundary violations.[59]

Women navigate public settings with care, as their respectability is associated with domestic or inside spaces.[60] Sara Dickey has argued that in South India, where the home (or inside space) has meanings of purity, safety, order, and cleanliness, the anxieties attendant on the negotiation of public settings arise from associations of dirt and disorder and, therefore, pollution.[61] As the lower classes are associated with the outside and thus with such notions of dirt, danger, and disorder,[62] the middle classes, except perhaps young middle-class men, are rarely seen in the lower-priced seating sections.[63] The advice I received from a middle-class woman, to keep away from the stalls, as they would be full of "peons and autorickshaw drivers," and the characterization of lower-class individuals as "dirty people" may be explained as anxiety over "the despoilment of the body and self."[64] Middle-class moviegoers recounted incidents where boisterous audiences had ruined their viewing experience when they sat in nonbalcony seating. One woman complained about the "catcalls" at a "sidey" theater when she sat at the lower level. Other complaints had to do with people kicking seat backs and, for women, male viewers in adjoining seats "leaning" on them. But it is not only men who present a problem. Vatsala, a high school teacher, remembered an unpleasant experience when she was seated in a row of women and young children in the middle stalls rather than the balcony, her usual seating choice. The children were whining throughout the film, and the woman seated next to her had a child on her lap. During the movie the child urinated on Vatsala's sari and foot. She was irate: "[It was] Terrible! I don't think that woman even noticed!"

*

My interactions with Sujaya,[65] a lower-middle-class Kannada speaker, further illustrate the concerns cinemagoers have about seating and its significance for the presentation of self.

> I met Sujaya at a theater in Majestic one afternoon when we were both standing in line for tickets for a Kannada film. In a mixture of rudimentary Kannada and English I hesitantly struck up a conversation with her about the movie and its stars, and she in halting English enthusiastically told me about this movie and other Kannada films she felt I should see. By the time we reached the ticket counter and purchased our tickets, we had exchanged information about ourselves and our families. I learned that she had been to a local college after studying in a Kannada-medium school. The family, with retired father and mother who was a housewife, lived in Sadashivnagar and included her brother who was studying commerce. I told her I was a student and was studying cinema. She asked me many questions: where did I live? What did various members of my family do?
>
> Sujaya and I decided to meet for a movie later in the week. She said she preferred morning shows to matinees as she could get home easily in the early afternoon. Over the phone we arranged to meet for a morning show of a Kannada film at Sampige theater. The day before we were to meet, Sujaya sounded

uncertain about being able to come to the film. So my mother offered to join me to keep me company. However, Sujaya was at the theater when we arrived. She came up to us as we stood in the queue. She seemed to have bought her ticket already. So that we could all sit together, I asked her what type of ticket she had bought and she said balcony. When I got to the ticket window, I purchased two balcony tickets. As we entered the theater, Sujaya told us the clerk had given her the "wrong" ticket "by mistake," so she had to "exchange" it. She returned to the ticket counter and we went on ahead to locate seats. As the movie, a rerelease, had already been in the theater for weeks and it was a weekday morning, the theater was less than half full. Seat numbers were not indicated on the tickets, and people were left to find their own seats. The balcony section was relatively empty except for about fifteen people. However, most seats needed repairs, and it took us a long time to find three seats together that were adequate. Sujaya entered the balcony just before the lights dimmed and gave us a lengthy explanation about how she had got the "wrong ticket by mistake" and had had to exchange it. Apparently the clerk had given her a ticket for the seats at the lower level when she had asked him for a balcony seat and she had not noticed that he had given her the "wrong" ticket. She appeared flustered and repeated this information a few times as she asked me, "You didn't think I wanted to sit *down*?" (Field notes, Bangalore, February 1998)

On another occasion when I was making plans to see a movie with Sujaya, the topic of tickets and seating came up again. I told her I would go around one o'clock to get tickets and asked, "What kind of tickets shall I get?" She seemed irritated by the question: "For balcony. Remember that day I bought the wrong ticket and I had to exchange it? Don't you remember?" I asked whether she wanted "only balcony."

SUJAYA: That is best, no? Otherwise all those people will be there.
ME: What people?
SUJAYA: Lower-class people—like peons, autorickshaw drivers.
ME: Supposing when I get there, balcony is sold out?
SUJAYA: No, no! The man told me there are plenty of tickets available. [She had apparently already called and checked.]
ME: So if I don't get balcony, you don't want to go for the movie?
SUJAYA: I don't like to sit down [below].
ME: So just supposing I don't get balcony, shall I buy tickets for lower stalls?
SUJAYA: What about you? Is it OK for you? . . . Then OK—just this one time OK. Better to sit up, but this time it's OK.

However, when I got to the theater, the ticket office was closed, and when Sujaya arrived, she insisted on buying tickets for the balcony. Being keen to present herself as respectable and middle class (perhaps because she identified me as middle class) Sujaya's reaction to getting the "wrong ticket," and her subsequent irritation over choice of seating, point to a possible "performance disruption."[66]

*

It is not only viewers' decisions about seating that construct their cinema experience; people who purchase tickets for middle-class moviegoers—domestic servants, office employees, and others, often insist on balcony tickets for their employers, other types of seating not being good enough. An errand boy at an office who had been dispatched to the advance booking queue called his employer to tell her the balcony had sold out. When she asked him to get tickets for the next lowest seating category, he responded (in Kannada), "No Madam, it won't be good." Theater staff subscribe to a typology of audiences that corresponds to seating in the theater. Even scalpers share the view that appropriate seating for middle-class women is the balcony, and they press the highest-priced tickets on middle-class moviegoers. Consequently, middle-class moviegoers may find that their cinema experience is constructed by the normative world of office employees, domestic workers, theater attendants, ticket clerks, scalpers, and autorickshaw drivers.

When I saw the Kannada film *Megha Bantu Megha*, I found myself seated in a row where there were only women. The row behind me seated only men, while couples and families occupied the row in front. All these rows were in the "minibalcony." This type of gender segregation occurred on subsequent occasions when I went to the movies (to see *A* and *Kurubana Raani*) and when I bought tickets with a female friend.[67] On other occasions I noticed that men who were standing near me in the ticket lines would not always end up in the same row but were seated in a row either in front or behind me even though they had bought tickets of the same denomination and despite the fact that there is no official gender segregation at Bangalore's cinema halls. It appeared, however, that the ad hoc decisions of ticket clerks had carved out a ladies' section or a men's row—a de facto gendered seating area and resultant viewing experience based entirely on the clerks' worldview, notions of propriety, and ideas of what audiences would want.

Reading the class and social status of the viewer, theater staff routinely assumed seating preferences. When, uncharacteristically, two middle-class women asked for tickets to the lower stalls, theater staff advised them to sit in the balcony.

TABLE 1 Organization and coding of theater space

Balcony	Front stalls
Inside	Outside
Upper class/middle class	Lower class
Female/families	Male
Orderly	Disorderly
Safe	Dangerous
Pure	Impure

When I bought tickets in the advance booking line for the latest James Bond movie, the ticket clerk did not ask me what tickets I wanted. He simply assumed that I would want to sit in the balcony and charged me for two balcony tickets. On another occasion, when I arrived late at a theater screening a Tamil film with a female friend, the ticket clerks smartly informed us, "Balcony sold out madam" as soon as we approached the ticket window. When we opted for the front stalls, they looked surprised and not too happy and tried to discourage us with "channage irolla [it won't be good], madam," and offered to sell us balcony tickets for the *next* day's show. When we insisted on the tickets for front stalls, the two men at the ticket booth reluctantly gave us the tickets and exchanged smiles with one another. Then they made us wait until they had called the usher and instructed him to escort us to our seats. These experiences of going against seating conventions highlight existing shared understandings of theater space.

The actions of moviegoers and theater staff suggest that the theater is organized by the meanings attached to public and private space.[68] The balcony itself may have the meanings of a respectable "inside space" equivalent to domestic space and therefore appropriate for women and the middle classes, while the front stalls are associated with the lower classes and are coded oppositionally as "outside space," carrying meanings of the street, disorder, and danger.[69] The prestige seating of the balcony can also carry meanings of a "sacred center" that everyone desires to be close to.[70]

While the meanings of seating are frequently used to reproduce the social order and to express this as a moral order,[71] seating and the segmented spaces in movie theaters can also challenge the existing order. In his study of cinema in Benaras, Steve Derne suggests that stratified seating does not reinforce social hierarchy as completely as it may seem to and that movie theaters in India are places where class and status divisions are erased, even if temporarily.[72] This view is echoed by observations on the talkies in Tamil Nadu in the 1930s, when all audience members were accommodated under the same roof. Seating in particular was viewed as promoting equality. To quote one social commentator, "The basis of seating is not on the hierarchic position of the patron but essentially on his purchasing power,"[73] leading to the commonly held view that cinema was a "social equalizer."[74]

In addition to being an oversimplification, the view that the balcony is the exclusive domain of the middle classes may be outdated. The image of the theater as a place where social background and income levels sharply segregate the audience may need to be revised as rising incomes and increasingly segmented moviegoing are changing the practices of moviegoers. Viewers with appropriate tickets have the freedom to sit where they please. Existing stratification at cinemas does not prohibit autorickshaw drivers or owners of footpath stalls from sitting in the balcony. Especially for a newly released Kannada, Tamil, or Telugu film, the entire theater may be taken over by fans belonging to the lower social orders. This voluntary aspect of the spatial organization of audiences within the theater was emphasized by those in a position to routinely observe audiences in these settings. Theater managers and distributors remarked that generalizations could not be made that audience members from lower socioeconomic groups are necessarily confined to the front stalls or even the lower levels of the theater. As far back as 1998, a distributor informed me that "these days" the balcony audience is not limited to the middle class: "Balcony? Today what is balcony?! Today balcony audience is not same as you or I. Autorickshaw driver can go to the balcony. They are going now!" When I asked whether the expense of balcony seating was not a consideration, he responded, "What is 30 rupees? 40 rupees? Today if you go for a movie—if *you* go for a movie or if *I* go for a movie, I may not buy tickets in black [signifying an expensive ticket]. But if autorickshaw man—if he goes for a movie, or ordinary man, oh yeah! they buy ticket in black!" My own experiences of Kannada film screenings and even second-run Hindi films screened in Majestic supported these observations. In conversation, autorickshaw drivers, petty shopkeepers, and pavement stall owners said they would purchase balcony tickets, especially when seeing a movie featuring their favorite hero or director.

Seating as Tribute and Protest

The expressive function of seating is also seen in its use in both protest and appreciation. Fans and "movie incorrigibles"[75] see the same movie several times over and may be expected to sit in the cheaper seats out of economic necessity. But in talking with fans, I found that seating is used to express the fans' relationship to the star and to the movie. Fans were emphatic that they absolutely *had* to see any film with their favorite star on the first day of its release, and they are prepared to pay a significant portion of their income to sit in the theater on the first day. On the day of a new release, seating has transcendent meaning. Fans may demonstrate their devotion to a star through a no-expense-spared viewing of the film, which includes balcony seating, paying inflated prices for the balcony, or purchasing black-market tickets, all of which becomes meaningful as a tribute or offering. Fans who are unable to secure seats for a newly released film of their idol may go on the rampage, as they feel they have a right to first-day tickets.

Seating also offers a resource for moviegoers keen to express their displeasure with a film or a theater. Lower-class male moviegoers are known to rip up seating with razor blades and knives when disappointed with a film or with viewing conditions (as when electricity fails or the sound quality is poor), a lasting critique expressed in the materiality of the theater and that offers the thrills of vandalism. Anticipating audience reactions, some theaters have made the seats close to the screen out of hard plastic or wood. Indeed, I learned that in one theater all the seats in the stalls close to the screen were made of concrete.[76]

"PERIPHERALS" AND THE SOCIAL CONSTRUCTION OF CINEMA

Dealing with social difference is an inescapable part of the cinema experience at Bangalore's cinema halls. Moviegoers make the stratified theater work as a leisure space by drawing distinctions and negotiating boundaries. Attitudes about seating and the social space of the theater, tickets, and queues as well as practices that manage such contingencies distinguish moviegoers in settings where a heterogeneous audience watches the same film. They reveal the hidden and transient meanings of the mundanities that shape moviegoers' experiences and the self-definitional aspects of moviegoing that are played out in what appear to be the trivia of the movie event. Thus, cinemagoing involves stagecraft and stage management for both audiences and exhibitors, and cinema halls become spaces for the performance of self.[77]

Though their strategies may differ, moviegoers of all classes negotiate all the rules. The balcony is intended for middle-class audiences and families, yet lower-class men and "mass" viewers may occupy the balcony. Exhibitors place strict controls on ticket sales and the movement of audiences within the theater, yet audiences secure tickets in a variety of ways and negotiate theater space, circumventing rules. Though audiences are monitored and policed at exhibition settings, social control is a challenge. Moviegoers' practices and the experience of cinemagoing at Bangalore's cinema halls suggest that while "places may be scripted [but] our performances do not always follow the script."[78] Further, given that moviegoers, through their practices, are able to shape the meanings of theater space and seating with consequences for the physical environment of the theater and the social experience of cinema points not only to their inventiveness but suggests that theater space in India is also malleable or "fluid."[79]

CHAPTER 5

Families, Friendship Groups, and Cinema as Social Experience

I don't like to go to a movie alone. I don't feel very good about it. I like to watch it with people; you can discuss things, and we can chat in the middle or whatever, so I prefer the interaction with somebody.

This is almost like a social event, and I don't like to go alone.

MIDDLE-CLASS WOMAN, BANGALORE

A moviegoer described going to the cinema in his "free time" in connection with *ghumna*,[1] Hindi for "to stroll, move about, and take in the sights." For film scholars, the Parisian flaneur comes to mind. Cinemagoing is embedded in open-ended leisure, "time pass," for youth, students, those who may be in limbo before employment or marriage, and the unemployed and underemployed. Habitués even classify certain films as "time-pass movies" and go to the theater with low expectations of the film but to spend time with their friends.[2] For young men the cinema is an escape from the "surveillance of home and work," where they "[can] smoke cigarettes, eat paan . . . and enjoy horseplay and joking with their male friends."[3] Explaining his moviegoing routines, a middle-class professional recollected how as students he and his friends would "cut classes" and go to the cinema practically every weekday: "We would see every kind of movie; sometimes just go sit inside and sleep."

In April, when schools and colleges close for the summer, theaters appear to be full of students. Festivals such as Dussehra, Deepavali, and Eid, along with other holidays, are all favored times to release new films. The sociality of the family and kin group, expressed in the celebration of religious festivals, get-togethers, weddings, birthdays, anniversaries, and shopping trips also situates cinemagoing.

Distinguishing between "social" and "aesthetic" experiences, Barbara Mittman describes spectatorship at Paris theaters in the sixteenth century as "a social event, like a salon, a ball, an outing or even a cabaret," where the important thing for spectators is "to see and be seen, to make contracts, flirt, circulate."[4] Similarly, cinema in India is first and foremost a social experience. People dress up for the occasion; women wear flowers in their hair. In Bangalore, middle-class college students and young professionals in the Cantonment are seen on "dates"—public behavior that in the 1980s and 1990s was not a common sight.[5] Men bring the sociality of male friendship groups to the cinema hall; they call out to friends and "delight in . . . shouting, whistling and bawdy talk [that] the film-going experience permits."[6]

Audience research consistently identifies social relations as the single most important factor in decision making and therefore attendance at cinemas.[7] The shared opinions of coworkers, friends, family members, and others are highly influential in shaping moviegoers' decisions about what films to see, the prediction of which remains one of the hoariest problems for producers and marketers.[8] "Word-of-mouth," or WOM studies have been used to measure audience awareness of films and are used in "audience tracking" and forecasting models.[9] This film- and market-centered perspective is applied to audience behaviors such as the purchase of movie tickets at the last minute (an "impulse buy"), audiences' mood, and so on. WOM marketing even introduces "movie talk" into conversations, thereby infiltrating and colonizing moviegoers' social interactions in an attempt to "create a buzz" and ratchet up anticipation in a movie's prerelease phase.[10]

This chapter addresses the social relations of cinemagoing beyond the examination of how it affects the box office. I examine the social experience that is at the forefront of the cinema outing and that frames cinemagoing while addressing variation in the social construction of cinema events by different sections of the audience and on different occasions. Three such frameworks are explored for the movie event: the movie outing for the multigenerational family; moviegoing as "treat"; and filmgoing adventures undertaken by school and college students. To some extent the chapter privileges the middle- and lower-middle-class experience over that of other social groups. The movie event for fans is addressed in chapter 7 in connection with newly released films.

CINEMAGOING AND SOCIAL LIFE

Outside cinema halls in Bangalore, people wait in groups large and small. Friends and extended families may see films in groups of fifteen or more. Except for mass or "stunt" films, adult films (which cater to lower-class men), and particular theaters that attract such films and this audience, groups reflect the heterogeneity of the cinema audience: young men and women, people of all ages, and multigenerational and extended "families."

Studies carried out in Western societies show that a person's "immediate situation," such as the home and whether that person has children or is married, is highly influential in choice of leisure activities[11]—a finding that appears to be cross-culturally relevant. Those experiencing a change in their lives often find that their movie routines are affected.[12] Two middle-class men with families and demanding jobs looked back on carefree school and college days as the time when they saw "the most movies." Watching movies during school and college vacations, or on occasions such as festivals or weddings, when family and friends come together, is part of group life. Cinemagoing may unite people across continents: a student of Indian origin living in Boston looked forward to her annual visits to the southern India city of Hyderabad, where her parents lived, and to cinema outings with a large group of aunts, uncles, grandparents, and cousins.

Cinemagoing is so intertwined with life events and social relations that the ebb and flow of group life affects moviegoing routines. One moviegoer who said he did not watch movies all that often told me that the few he did see were either with a large group of classmates or with his cousins visiting from out of town. Just as the coming together of a group can motivate the cinema outing, an individual's ill health or absence can affect movie routines. Marriage certainly affects cinemagoing routines and habits. I chatted with a newlywed at a Kannada movie screening. She was wearing a grand silk sari with a gold border, jasmine and orange *champac* flowers in her hair, glass bangles, and gold jewelry—all of which identified her as a bride. She told me that since her marriage she had seen fewer movies, especially Hindi (Bollywood) movies, which her husband "hates . . . so now I rarely go. I haven't seen any for such a long time." Another obstacle to her frequent moviegoing was that following her marriage she had moved away from her old neighborhood; her husband had a small manufacturing business in Peenya, and so the theaters she used to visit were no longer as accessible.

While cinemagoing is universally recognized as a social event, at multiplexes in the West it is possible to see people, both men and women, enjoying a solitary film experience. In Bangalore, this is rare. There is an unspoken understanding that spending leisure time alone in public is unnatural and antisocial. For women especially, going to the cinema alone raises questions of appropriate and respectable behavior.[13] Even in a cosmopolitan city such as Bangalore, one rarely sees women alone at the cinema.

Early in my field research, when I talked with moviegoers about their cin-emagoing habits, I bluntly asked them whether they had been to the cinema on their own, which confused some and offended others. A few (middle-class) women flatly denied seeing movies on their own. Others wanted to know why I was asking them such a question. Some simply refused to answer the question. A woman accompanied by her mother and young daughter chatted with me about the Kannada film we had just seen. When I went on to inquire whether she had seen movies by herself, she gave me a strange look and walked away. A neighbor dismissed the idea with irritation—"Don't be silly, ya! What's the point (of going to the cinema alone)?"—while another woman, who had moved back to Bangalore after graduate school in the United States, also appeared puzzled by the question and emphatically denied ever going to the cinema by herself—"Never, never, never!"

In interviews, some middle- and lower-middle-class men, while admit-ting to seeing movies by themselves, qualified it with "when friends are not there," or they elaborated on other extenuating circumstances. Anthony, who worked in administration at a local school and was a fan of the Bollywood megastar Shahrukh Khan, complained that he did not have "company" to watch films starring his idol. His friends were fans of Tamil cinema and did not like Khan. Hence, he was forced to see "Shahrukh Khan starrers" on his own. Another young man responded uneasily, saying that he did not see "those kind of movies." A college student told me he had seen men singly at "lounges" where risqué and adult films are screened, responses that gave me a new per-spective on solitary cinemagoing and the implications of my naive question while bringing home the constraints I faced as a middle-class woman in the field.

Given the negative connotations associated with being at the cinema by oneself, interviews alone did not give a complete picture of cinemagoing prac-tices. Hanging around cinemas allowed me to see that while the group and so-cial experience of cinema are the typical and preferred experience, people did go to the cinema on their own.[14] On a few occasions, I encountered women by themselves at morning shows and matinees. I frequently saw men stopping off for a movie, buying a single ticket, and going into the theater. Many belonged to lower socioeconomic classes: autorickshaw drivers between fares, petty shop-keepers in the afternoon when stores are closed, household help and lower-level office workers. Middle-class male students sometimes watch films on their own, although they are more likely to be in pairs or groups. Within the theater, men who are there on their own become part of the collectivity as they join in the whistling and cheering.

THE GROUP AS CONSTRAINT AND RESOURCE

For some, movie outings are so dependent on the availability of viewing companions that when asked what movies they had seen recently, they complained, "So many movies in the theaters but I haven't seen any! No company, no?" (field notes, Bangalore, 2012). Who one sees a movie with often determines which film is seen. Habitués have to accommodate not only the tastes and interests of members of their group but also the movies that some group members have already seen. A middle-class woman explained why she had not seen the James Bond film, *Rainmaker*, and *Titanic*: "we were planning to see them together, this group of us, but we [her husband and herself] went and saw *Rainmaker* yesterday, and *Titanic* everyone seemed not so keen, at least some seemed not so keen, so I'll have to find someone to see it with."

The sociality that frames cinemagoing can explain how many people end up seeing the same movie more than once.[15] Moviegoers elect to see a film with one group and subsequently watch the same film with another set of friends or family. When I asked a middle-class housewife about her seeing a movie a second time, she explained, "I saw it again *because* I was going with a different group." Another moviegoer described how she saw a Kannada film multiple times: "I've seen it four times! Once I went with my friends from school, then second time I went with my cousin, she had come down from Belgaum, then my mom hadn't seen it so she said, 'let's go for a matinee,' and then I saw it another time—we decided to go on a weekend, all of us [a family group of about ten], so that was fun to see it in such a big group!" (field notes, Bangalore, 2007). In some families certain members vet a film for its suitability for the rest of the family. Talking with the mother in a family group of four watching the Tamil film *Billa 2* (2012) at the Lavanya theater, I learned that her two teenage sons had seen the movie the previous week and had deemed it suitable for their mother and sister.

Groups and social networks can therefore be a resource for habitués. Some rely on enthusiasts in their group for word of mouth about films. They then articulate their networks to experience the variety of cinema offerings: Bollywood, Hollywood, and regional-language cinema. Anjali, who had grown up in North India, reported that her husband, who was from South India, was not a Hindi cinema fan, so she watched Hindi movies with "a separate group," who were "always game for seeing these films and they know I am," while "English" (or Hollywood) films she mostly watched with her husband and their friends. Manjunath, who speaks Tamil at home, claimed to watch Tamil, Hindi, and English movies with his extended family of "relatives and cousins."

With his friends who did not know much Hindi, he watched Tamil movies. He often saw Bollywood movies by himself, but Hollywood movies "we all see together." (In Bangalore, English is more widely understood than Hindi.)

In a plural society where viewers are embedded in social networks characterized by linguistic and cultural diversity, groups can offer cultural resources by, for instance, facilitating access to films in different languages. Moviegoers need not rely on dubbing and subtitles, which grants authority over the experience to filmmakers; instead, their friends or family can translate.[16] Constructing the cinema event as a group outing can therefore have a direct effect on a person's experience of the film. In-theater translations for one's friends are routine in a multilingual setting. "Interpretations" or commentaries that are personal, interactive, and perhaps emotionally meaningful and contextually relevant are made available, highlighting the biographical and interpersonal nature of the cinema experience.[17] Anjali, a Hindi speaker, said she did not usually watch Tamil films but described an experience of watching a Tamil film with friends who spoke the language: "So I went with a couple of friends. . . . One is Tamil-speaking [mother tongue is Tamil], so she picked up all the nuances. The other has picked up Tamil . . . so she was able to grasp the—I should say what's on the surface, the gist of it, very well" (field notes, Bangalore, 1998). Watching the film with these friends, with translations "in stereo," allowed Anjali to negotiate the meanings of the movie and experience it through the social relations of her group. "So, one sat on one side and the other sat on the other side. So, the poetic side was given by one and the literal side by the other—so that was very nice!"

*

At the cinema viewers become sociologists and anthropologists. As well as language translations, explanations are given of cultures and customs that may pertain to certain parts of India or particular communities. Cinemagoing, its sociality, can in this way help bridge sociocultural divides. The social experiences of cinema in a culturally plural landscape therefore calls for a rethinking of the relationship between genre categorization, niche markets for cultural products, and a society's cultural resources. Cinema may even bridge, though fleetingly, the gulf in socioeconomic status. En route to a Kannada movie, a longtime resident of Bangalore told me her "driver"—who also ran errands and helped her with a variety of household tasks—was an invaluable resource as her "film consultant." Driving around the city, they would chat companionably about films. I overheard her ask him conversationally, "What movies are in theaters now?" "Did you see such- and-such film?" Or "Are tickets available for that new film?" Sometimes he asked her whether she had managed to see the latest film of her favorite star, or he offered his opinion—"Not a movie for ladies" or "The ending could be better"—and conveyed news of a film's popularity—"It's going House Full!" An animated conversation would follow (field notes, Bangalore, 2010).

SPONTANEITY, MOOD, AND GROUP TOGETHERNESS

Cinema outings are marked by spontaneity, which has led audience studies and market research to frame movie ticket purchase as an "impulse buy."[18] Moviegoers from various walks of life may decide on a movie outing at the last minute. Autorickshaw drivers on a slow afternoon slip into a theater on the spur of the moment and catch part of a film—even forty minutes of it. Household help and office workers sent on lengthy errands may also use the opportunity for a detour to the cinema. Indeed, simply spending time with others may launch a movie outing. According to one habitué, "Usually after dinner someone would start, 'let's go for a movie.'" Families and friends who routinely spend time together talk about movie outings that the group has shared and films that are currently in theaters, conversation that creates the mood to go to the cinema, which also accounts for the spontaneity of the event.

While film marketing has examined mood in connection with film content, and studies have focused on an *individual* viewer's mood in relation to a film or how a film and its content affects audiences' mood,[19] moviegoing in Bangalore points to the importance of understanding mood in the context of the sociality of group cinema outings. Mood is about shared anticipation and a shared emotional terrain. For movie enthusiasts, even talk about crowds at theaters or sold-out shows can create the mood to either see a film or simply have a movie outing.

Movie outings then often begin with "being in the mood," and for habitués, it is important to see a film while the mood is right. When in the mood they may go to any one of a number of theaters screening a range of films where they can get seats.[20] Once when I was chatting with a middle-class housewife, the talk turned to films: "[the Kannada film] *Aaptha Rakshaka* [2010] is supposed to be good. It hasn't released yet," she informed me, and then went on to say that a previous film with the star Vishnuvardhan, *Aaptha Mitra* (2004), was "very good. He has acted very well." We discussed other movies in theaters and finally went to the Kannada movie *Minnasare* (2010) at Menaka Talkies in Majestic. The film had no connection to either of the two movies discussed except that it was a Kannada film for which we could get tickets (field notes,

Bangalore, 2010). A mood may last several days, even weeks. Viewers told me that once they were in the mood, they would see movies frequently and in streaks, after which they would stay away from the cinema for several weeks.

The centrality of the social element in creating the mood to go to the cinema becomes evident from a methodological standpoint as well. When I interviewed habitués, our conversations would generate a mood to go see a movie. I heard, "Oh, I feel like seeing some movies now!" or "I wish I could see some Amitabh movies; those days were such fun!" or even "Next time you're in Bangalore, let's catch a movie!" Following a conversational interview with a journalist who was covering the launch of a Kannada film, I was invited to see the preview screening of another film for which she had passes (field notes, Bangalore, 2012).

That moviegoers emphasize the importance of mood suggests that the cinema event is about play "leaking into ordinary life," as a mood can "come and go suddenly" in play.[21] Further, the "sociability" of play, where "the pleasure of the individual is always contingent upon the joy of others" and where "by definition no one can have his satisfaction at the cost of contrary experiences on the part of others,"[22] shapes cinema experience. Talking about late-night movie outings, a woman described how, on finding a "House Full" board outside one theater, she and her friends would then "drive crazily" to another theater where a different film was being screened. "It wasn't that we were particular about the movie, it was just the fun of going out together!"

Acknowledging the interdependency that shapes an enjoyable movie experience, filmgoers recognize that being in the "wrong" mood can spoil the outing for the group, "shattering the play-world."[23] In refusing an invitation to see a film, it is enough to say, "mood seri illa" (I'm not in the mood). Anxious not to be a spoilsport or an outcast,[24] some moviegoers manipulate their mood. Film music released well before the film, as is the practice in India, is powerful in both setting the mood and in constructing shared experience. I overheard people singing and humming songs from the film they were about to see while waiting in the theater lobby. As music from the earlier show drifted out of the auditorium at the Abhinay theater in Majestic, people waiting around tapped their feet while children happily danced to the beat. Moviegoers use music to create a mood; while negotiating traffic on the way to the theater to watch a Bombay film, one moviegoer asked me to "put some music on" in the car. He had a selection of Indian film music as well as Western pop music, and I asked him what kind music to play. He promptly responded, "Let's have some Hindi [film] music; that'll put us in the mood." Other ways of creating a mood involve sharing a meal or a drink before the movie. Moviegoers who anticipate a loss of mood may resort to preventative measures. Jaya dosed herself with aspirin, explaining, "I always get a headache; it's something to do with the screen." That mood is not entirely dependent on the film or on the film's quality is seen in moviegoers' upbeat mood and jokes about how awful the movie was even after watching a flop.

The spontaneity of the cinema outing, means that habitués often wander into theaters late.[25] In all screenings I attended in Bangalore and in screenings of Indian films in the United States, late arrivals were routine. The institutional culture of exhibition in India accommodates latecomers: lights in the theater are often kept on through the opening scenes. Those who arrive halfway through the film or just before the intermission[26] are seated by ushers armed with flashlights (lately, LED lights). Elaborating on his moviegoing habits and routines, Raghu saw the absurdity and excitement in last-minute movie outings where the group routinely missed a major part of the film: "The last show was at nine thirty. . . . My grandmother would be game. We would get ready at nine thirty! [We would] go by ten thirty. Five minutes later would be the interval!" Another viewer remembered seeing (part of) *Braveheart* as an instance of one such last-minute, time-pass social event and calmly mentioned missing the "first half hour" of the film: "*That* was a nice movie! We missed the first half hour though. We went late. We didn't plan to see a movie, then we thought the matinee hour was well past. And we didn't have anything else to do, so we went to the theater, into the movie."

*

A manager of a theater in the Boston area that occasionally screened Bollywood movies to South Asian audiences observed a clear difference between American audiences for Hollywood films and South Asian audiences at screenings of Bombay films. While the former would not want to miss even five minutes of a movie they were paying for, being on time was not characteristic of South Asian moviegoers, many of whom, adopting a more informal and relaxed attitude, would come in late and wait around in the lobby or outside the theater for members of their group. He marveled at how missing part of the film did not seem to affect their enjoyment of it (field notes, Boston, 2003).

KEEPING THE GROUP TOGETHER: BOUNDARIES, INCLUSION, AND SHARED EXPERIENCE

Shared experience at the cinema may be constructed around a host of activities that have little to do with the film but that show the theater to be a multiuse social setting for audiences and where (social) boundaries are porous.[27] Before the days of "mobiles," men brought their transistor radios to listen to the cricket commentary. Scores from the match were relayed to the group, and even strangers asked about the game's progress. Before the film began and during the intermission, cheers and shouts of "Too good!" "Out!" and "Bowled!" could be heard from those huddled around transistors. I even overheard cricket commentary *during* the film. People bring in newspapers or magazines, and their viewing companions, or even strangers seated next to them, may read over their shoulder. In 2007 and 2010 I observed similar behavior with mobile phones: moviegoers looked over someone's shoulder, even a stranger's, to see what was on the screen.[28] Mobile phones appear to have heightened audience sociability, making it possible to keep in contact with friends and family not in the theater, thereby extending and complicating group boundaries and group experiences.

Viewer activities create shared experience that may be extraneous to the film. It was common to see women knitting or crocheting lace sometimes throughout the film. This was frequently a companionable activity, as women seated side by side chatted as they knitted. One woman combined film viewing, chatting with her companion, and handicrafts as she expertly wove plastic thread into a bag, pulling the thread out of a satchel next to her seat. For students, the cinema outing can be a ritual before annual examinations.[29] College students may be seen cramming from open books or copying lecture notes before the lights are switched off and during the intermission, the shared experience based on a combination of preexam anxiety and thrill. Such activities may blur the lines between play and work. Students also create shared experience by "bunking" classes and escaping to the cinema hall. Young men and women may use the cinema as a rendezvous and when meeting against parental wishes. Secrets concerning such illicit movie outings draw people together, while nonparticipants are kept out.[30] In some cases, cinemagoing has drawn group boundaries so successfully that college romances that blossomed via the cinema outing resulted in marriage.

Cinemagoing is so rooted in group life that those who miss out on an outing not only feel excluded from the event but may feel more fundamentally marginalized from group life. Unable to participate in movie outings because of his mother's curfew on his evening activities, Anthony expressed regret and frustration at being left out. "Actually, the problem is that my mother is very strict . . . she insists I have to be back by nine o'clock. . . . When all my friends go and come back at ten o'clock, eleven o'clock, I can't go. I really feel very bad."

Within the theater group, boundaries are drawn by seating arrangements. Being seated apart from one's viewing companions is seen, unsurprisingly, as an obstacle to a shared experience. Not only is one physically distant, the bodies and behavior of strangers may intrude on the group, making shared experience that much more difficult. Middle-class moviegoers frequently call the theater in advance with instructions to staff to give them seats together.[31] Talking about an upcoming cinema outing for the extended family, a young woman announced, "We booked the whole row!" Large groups and families have their seating habits and social rituals. In extended families, subgroups may be nuclear family units or family members of the same age or gender. Within groups, negotiations and adjustments over seating continue even after the movie starts and are sometimes pursued during the intermission. Individuals may decide to switch seats during the intermission to circulate within the group, rather like at a party. Even when the theater is not full, moviegoers in groups sit close together—something an American visitor to Bangalore commented on ("they sit so close") and contrasted to his own seating preferences and need for space (he liked to keep an empty seat between himself and his companions and preferred to sit where no one sat directly in front of him).

For those keen to keep the group together, disappointment with a film does not necessarily mean the end of the group event. To prolong the movie outing, its social experience, moviegoers may be willing to abandon one movie for another. Halfway through the screening of the Bollywood film *Zor* (1998), which showed signs of being a flop, I overheard people in the row behind me debating whether to go to another:

VIEWER 1: Let's ditch this movie, *yaar*.
VIEWER 2: Better than this is *My Best Friend's Wedding*. *Release ho gaya* [It has been released].
VIEWER 3: Night show? [It is 8 p.m. and the night show starts at 9:30] [*laughter, contemplating the audacity of this plan.*]

People may watch a "bad" movie through simply for the "satisfaction" of "togetherness."[32] Remedies may be sought: one viewer told me she "had to get a Pepsi in the intermission" to keep awake, as *Tomorrow Never Dies* was "Soo boring." After the intermission of a Bollywood film that displayed all the signs of being a flop, a viewer returning to her seat announced to her family group that she had taken an aspirin because "this film is so bad, it gave me a headache!"[33]

People exit the theater holding hands or hanging onto a family member's or friend's arm. Men are seen with arms thrown across a friend's shoulders;[34] the physical "keeping in touch" allows individuals both to avoid being separated in the crowd and to maintain a bridge to their group.[35] Embodied expressions of shared experience include lighting up cigarettes after the film and even before it. People go for an ice cream or for a meal after the film. The film and show timing may be chosen based on what moviegoers can do either before or after it, for example, attending a matinee so one can have *chaat* in the early evening or lunch before.

The complex interactional work moviegoers engage in, which draws group boundaries and reproduces family and group social relations at the cinema, includes criticizing or ridiculing fellow moviegoers who are not members of their group. Theater staff, ticket clerks, and ushers may be considered fair game and a foil for such boundary setting. One postmovie outing with a group of students that led to a drive-in eatery is illustrative. The group in the car was in a silly mood following a bad movie; they started to tease one another and then shifted their attention to the waiter standing outside the car taking their orders.[36] He was from another state and belonged to a different ethnic group. Some group members asked him unnecessary questions, mimicked his accent, laughed, and made jokes—interactions that drew the group together while placing the waiter outside its boundaries.[37] Boundaries are also drawn through storytelling about cinema outings, which narrativizes group social relations and experience and which I address later in the chapter.

Intermission

Three-and-a-half hour commercial films are designed with an intermission in mind, which slices the screening experience in two. The first part of the film ends with a cliffhanger: the word *Intermission* or *Interval* appearing dramatically on the screen. Intermission is so much a part of the cinema ritual that even Hollywood films less than two hours long are halted in the middle, often abruptly. During the intermission audiences confer and pass judgment on the film, share appreciation—"Good movie, no?"—or dislike—"bore!" or " slow" or "ridiculous, *yaar!*" Consensus reached during the intermission can dampen the mood for the film and generate negative word of mouth even to the extent of driving down prices of black-market tickets. The mood evoked by the film may carry over into the intermission. Exhibitors may help extend the film's mood and theme by showing stills of the star and slides from fan celebrations honoring the star during the break, adding to the variety theater format.[38] Energized fans mill about. At the intermission of *Om*, young men kissed the poster of the star in the theater lobby and clustered in groups to discuss the film and the star's performance and career. At the Plaza theater on M. G. Road, during the interval of the James Bond film *Tomorrow Never Dies* (1997), I overheard the following conversation among a group of seven young middle-class men seated in front of me. In the film, a new model BMW was unveiled, clearly a movie highlight for these men. One youth takes out *Auto* magazine from a briefcase and starts talking (in English) about the merits of BMWs—their audio systems, prices, and so on.

"It's automatic, not manual."
"231 is automatic, 280 (?) is optional automatic . . ."
[*Excitedly*] "Look at *this* and look at *that*!"
"Latest model is outdated now."
"You have diesel option."
[*The conversation becomes animated and loud. Some admonish others to lower their voices.*]
"I'll keep quiet OK? They'll put me in jail otherwise" [*Lowers voice*]
[*Resuming conversation*] "I'll request the company to get the car."
"Sandstorm—sports car lesser than 4 lakhs."
"Convertible?"
"Convertible! Two Opels coming out next year"
"Ferrari!
"Sachin (a cricket star) is for audio Audi"
"He won an audio system?!"
"Priced around 33 lakhs"
"*Yeh Dekh*! [Hindi: look at this] Suzuki!"

Two members of the group get up from their seats at the ends of the row and sit on the backs of the seats in front of them to better see the magazine and talk. They put their arms around one another's shoulders, forming a closed circle. Two bottles of Coca Cola are circulated (field notes, Bangalore, 1998).

*

Thus the interval offers an opportunity to socialize and reconnect with group members who may have been separated by engagement with the film. Clusters of moviegoers gather in the lobby, men companionably share a smoke or a "cool drink." In large mixed-sex and family groups, men may be dispatched with requests to fight their way through the scrum at the concessions counter while women and young children remain in the auditorium and in keeping with a construction of gendered "inside" and "outside." Sociality can run the gamut. One moviegoer recollected spending the entire intermission, and even after it, arguing (or as he put it, "fighting") with the concessions counter attendant over change due, causing him to miss the rest of the film (field notes, Bangalore, 2010). Other moviegoers also reported fights: "Now during the interval there was a FIGHT (a real one) near the doorway and fortunately I was just watching it from the confines of my seat."[39]

Absorbed in their social activities at the intermission, moviegoers may not make it back to their seats in time for the film. Theater staff have to find ways to lure reluctant moviegoers back to their seats. In some theaters a bell is rung to signal the end of the intermission, although viewers deep in conversation or altercations may not notice. Ushers may be dispatched to round up stragglers and shepherd them back into the theater.

Being with one's group can mean plunging into everyday life and escaping the confines of the theater during the interval. Men stroll outside with their companions and buy roasted peanuts and corn from street vendors or light up cigarettes or *beedis*. They chat with autorickshaw driver buddies parked on the street. During the interval at a Hollywood film screening, my viewing companion decided to get her watch battery replaced at a nearby store and quick-marched me up Brigade Road. At the store, she took her time and surveyed the watches in the display cases, asking my opinion in what had become a leisurely shopping trip. When we returned to the theater the lights had dimmed and the movie had begun; our places had been taken and we stumbled around in the dark to locate seats.

Storytelling

The movie experience is not a linear one beginning with awareness of films in theaters and ending with watching the film, after which people go their separate ways. Audiences look back on cinema outings and relive the experience; they attempt to connect past movie experiences to the present one in efforts to build transcendence. After her friends had located their seats, a woman reminisced about the last time the group had seen a film together. She recounted in detail the "dirty" theater and the thrill of purchasing tickets in black and the last-minute dash to the theater.[40] Watching a film at the Sagar theater, habitués tried to recollect their last movie outing together: "How long it's been!" (field notes, Bangalore, 2010). Moviegoers similarly look ahead to future outings in shared anticipation.

Stories of past movie events elaborate the social context of cinemagoing and its biographical significance. They connect the "then" and "there" with the "here" and "now."[41] People remembered going to watch all-night movies during Shivaratri[42]—an experience no longer available to Bangalore audiences because all-night screenings have been banned in the city. Fans remember watching "Rajkumar picture" and the excitement of "those days." Weaving together past and present experiences, moviegoers create tapestries of group life. Families and groups of friends who have seen several movies together may have a fund of movie lore that is carried forward in time. Favorite stories are unearthed and reviewed, like old photographs.

Uma, in her fifties, remembered her teenage years when she was living with her parents in a small town in South India. When her married sister visited in the summer, her brother-in-law would treat the entire family to a movie or two. It was a big event which involved going into town in a bullock cart. The ride was part of the fun; her brother-in-law was from the city and was unused to it. Thirty years later she associated memories of summer vacations and being with her family with these movie outings. In these recollections, the film is often long forgotten or is marginal in the retelling, while the event and the social relationships that shape it are vivid in people's memories. Storytelling in this way highlights individual idiosyncrasies, tastes, and habits and the relationship of individuals to the group. One moviegoer struggled to remember the last film she had seen at a cinema over fifteen years ago and then exclaimed, "Oh, that was the time when Raji brought that enormous box of chocolates! . . . She came late and arrived with this huge box." In an aside, "[Raji's] very generous."

Telling stories offers another means to experience the movie event retrospectively. Stories dramatize the event and extend its experience through another frame. They may highlight accomplishing the outing in the face of obstacles. Casting themselves as mythic heroes, cinemagoers apply the meanings of the contest to the outing.[43] An IT professional looked back on the thrill of schoolboy movie outings. "I remember the movie, the *Odessa File.* We pestered [my uncle, he said] . . . OK. We were in —— [locality]. We had to cross Cubbon Park. [My uncle] had a motorcycle. This one time when he was driving his cable got cut. Three of us on his motorcycle!! He took the outer cable out and tied it to his toe [then] used his toe to accelerate. . . . We got to [the theater] and came back!" The anecdote points to play "leaking in" and the thrills of danger, risk, and playing with time.[44]

From a methodological perspective, storytelling carries a bias because stories reflect selective memory even as they underscore drama and the more thrilling and entertaining aspects of the outing.[45] However, the fact that the movie outing lends itself to dramatic telling is significant for the way the cinema is collectively experienced. Stories selectively highlight good times, the group being together, the absurdities of city life, and the sensualities of the outing. They may focus on excess; for instance, a middle-class moviegoer in Bangalore described how in a single day she had "dragged" her boyfriend along to see three movies back-to-back: morning show, matinee, and first show in the evening.[46] Picking up the element of the carnivalesque that is associated with cinemagoing, many such anecdotes are about outrageous and bizarre incidents. Members of one family recalled cinema outings with their grandmother, known to all as a movie enthusiast; they pressed me to hear her stories: "You have to speak with Ajji!" or "Has Ajji told you her stories about how she used to go for movies?" A story narrated with much merriment featured Ajji's friend, whom everyone agreed was "crazy after movies." On one occasion this friend left her *chappals* (footwear) in the ticket queue as she hurried home to check on something, instructing those in line to keep her place. When she returned after about half an hour, not only did she find her "place" in the queue taken, but someone had walked off with her *chappals*! Whenever this story was recounted, it elicited peals of laughter and led to reminiscences about "the good old days." Retellings appeared to be embellished with more detail. Another favorite story was about a family friend who had found a novel and effective way of getting cinema tickets. He raised a small collection of snakes that he later established as a "minizoo" that was well known in Bangalore in the 1970s and 1980s. According to family members, when he wanted tickets for a new movie, he took his pet python with him: "The queue would just melt! People would take one look at him and tell him 'you go ahead.'" To help his friends he would obligingly "go and stand in line for them," with the snake around his neck.

Storytelling points to the ever-emerging significance of the event and its changing nature and emphasizes its sociality. At times, the social significance emerges only in retrospect.[47] Cinema experience therefore involves moving back and forth in time, creating a temporal link between experiences that are far apart, which gives each new experience greater meaning and resonance.

THREE FRAMEWORKS FOR THE CINEMA OUTING

Movie outings are constructed variously, and different frameworks organize the experience. Here I explore the movie event as adventure, the movie "treat," and the family movie outing. These frameworks are not exclusive to certain categories of cinemagoer or even to a particular outing: a high school student might construct the movie outing as adventure with his peers and then participate in a family outing, or the middle-class family movie outing may have its own transgressive thrills, such as when audience members risk purchasing tickets "in black." Thus, a movie event may involve multiple frames and meanings.

Risk, Adventure, Play

Movie events are often shaped by positive meanings of spending time with friends, going to see a favorite star, or to "see the songs" (picturized song sequences), but they may also be constructed around more ambiguous meanings. Phil Hubbard describes the attraction of the "out of town" multiplex in Leicester, United Kingdom, as offering "riskless risks"[48]—a sense of safety and comfort for an evening's entertainment in comparison to "city-center" movie theaters. Moviegoers in Bangalore address risk variously. Some choose to minimize it by electing to go to theaters near where they live or in parts of the city where they feel comfortable and by avoiding crowds at newly released films. Others embrace risk by constructing the movie outing as adventure or "dark play," described by Richard Schechner as "subvert(ing) order, dissolv(ing) frames, break(ing) its own rules."[49] Going to theaters in certain parts of the city, such as Majestic, can itself be a risk and an adventure for middle-class women (see chap. 3). High school and college students routinely complicate the meanings of going to the cinema by constructing the outing as an act of minor rebellion or protest and a means to flout parental and institutional authority,[50] which "deviant" framing aids in constructing the cinema outing as a game or contest.[51] A former teacher at a well-known private school in the city told me that she routinely came upon students, "boys in uniform," playing truant at the cinema; she would then herd them into her car and drive them back to school.

"Illicit" or "deviant" moviegoing of this kind cuts across social class. Along with students, office workers, shop assistants, and domestic servants may sneak out to a movie when they are supposedly at work, their ability to thwart being monitored by employers heightening the thrill. Middle-class housewives exchanged stories of servants telling tall tales about visiting sick relatives but going instead to the cinema. Small-town and village youth were known to run off to the city for adventure and entertainment, their travel to Bangalore facilitated by trains and long-distance buses. Watching films on such trips was seen by their parents and employers as another "bad habit" the city encouraged, on par with going to the races and visiting prostitutes.[52]

In many Bangalore households cinemagoing is a source of tension between parents and children. Apart from being seen as a waste of money, frequent cinemagoing is viewed as a "corrupting influence."[53] Consequently, pulling off a cinema outing involves enterprise, risk-taking, and even deception, trickery, and deceit.[54] The appeal of popular films in India is often attributed to their providing an "escape" for the poor and disadvantaged from lives of unremitting hardship. However, it appears that escape can be constructed variously. Young middle-class men and women reminisced about movie escapades that involved elaborate plans to "trick" parents or other authority figures.[55]

"Dark play" of this kind "may be entirely private, known to the player alone."[56] One moviegoer admitted to helping himself to ticket money from his mother's purse. Another said he would ask for money for a Balcony ticket and then use it for multiple films, buying cheap tickets, or use the leftover money for snacks. At the Bangalore racecourse, I got into conversation with a young man as he placed his bets. His love of gambling seemed to frame his cinemagoing well. While his job was to look after his uncle's shop in Majestic, he frequently went to the cinema when his uncle thought he was minding the shop. At the last minute, he would either close the shop or ask a friend to take over (field notes, Bangalore, 2007).

For middle-class adolescents, cinema outings become opportunities to craft narratives of group life. The narration of the movie event as adventure, the scramble to get to the theater, purchasing tickets "in black" from scalpers, negotiating crowded streets in Majestic, dealing with rude autorickshaw drivers and, for women, the unwelcome attentions of "roadside Romeos" or whispered hints of meeting with real or imagined male acquaintances and friends at the theater, placed otherwise quiet and outwardly well-behaved middle-class women in a new light. Saroja, now in her forties, married with two children, who went to the same women's college run by Carmelite sisters as I did, remembered, "I did things I would never have my kids do . . . like hitch [hike] to Shivajinagar. . . . There would be six or seven of us [girls]. . . . We would go for the noon show. We had to be back in college because our parents would pick us up from there, so we would attend classes from nine to eleven and bunk the afternoon and be back by four."

In keeping with the play spirit, preparations for cinema outings can involve "playing a part," masking, and other performance elements.[57] Talking about his "movie habit" as a high school and college student, Vivek, relived the "sneaky thrill" of dodging his parents and authority figures at school.[58] In what can be understood as a ritual shedding of institutional identity, both he and his friend divested themselves of their school uniform, identifiable by its crest.

VIVEK: On the school bus, change out of school uniform and into ordinary clothes . . . go to Majestic for the morning show, eat lunch there, get back to where the school bus picked up kids in the afternoon, change back into uniforms on the bus.

ME: Wouldn't your parents find out?

VIVEK: [*promptly*] We would write ourselves leave of absence, sick notes.

The strategizing and casual deception provided a "sneaky thrill," possibly enhanced by the telling of the adventure: "At ten fifteen in the morning I would leave home and *casually* walk to the corner, where a friend would be waiting on a bike. We would zip off and arrive ten minutes late. We would leave the movie theater before the film was over and come back home at noon for lunch. [Parents] would not suspect a thing because of the timing." Whether these events took place exactly as described, or whether the narration and passage of time has made them more elaborate and dramatic,[59] that people retrospectively focus on the illicit nature of the movie event and highlight the achievement of the cinema outing as a thwarting of authority offers insights into its social and biographical significance.

One movie outing I participated in began with impersonation.[60] At lunch with one of the families I accompanied to the cinema, the conversation turned to movies that were in the theaters at the time. The grandmother mentioned a new Kannada film that was to have its first screening that evening. Talk immediately shifted to the difficulty of getting tickets, which seemed to energize everyone, and there was excited discussion of whether we should all go to the movie. Grandmother quietly egged everyone on, saying she had come across a review in a Kannada newspaper and that it had been good. After more discussion, Kaveri phoned the theater for show timings. She spoke to the manager and asked him whether tickets were available: he said, "Not easily; you'll have to line up." This put a slight damper on everyone's spirits, but soon they were suggesting schemes and strategies, including calling the theater and impersonating someone. The tickets had become a prize to be won.

"Call up, say you're Rajkumar's daughter-in-law." [Rajkumar is a Kannada film icon; his son Shivarajkumar was in the movie.]

"Say you're Rajkumar's neighbor."

KAVERI: "No ya! That's stoopid! Why would they give tickets to his *neighbor*?!"

"Don't be silly!"

KAVERI: [*now confused*] "Then what shall I say?"

"Say you're from the press."

"Say you're Anant Nag's family member." [Anant Nag is a well-known independent Kannada filmmaker and actor.]

"No, No! Say you're from the US, and that you're here only for a week."

The discussion went on for some time as the meal wound down. Voices were raised in excitement, elaborate plans and ruses were proposed and dismissed, including scripting the dialogue between the theater staff and fictional members of the Rajkumar or Anant Nag families. Getting into the theater became a game, and even those who were not keen on the film joined in to try to outwit the theater manager. After many outrageous suggestions and much laughter, it was decided that Kaveri should impersonate Anant Nag's secretary and bring in the "USA connection." Kaveri was game for this performance. She called the theater and in a carefully modulated voice informed the manager that Anant Nag would like some tickets to be kept aside for his friends who were visiting from the United States. Improvising, she added that they would be leaving in a few days and were anxious to see the film before they left. As the conversation continued, she went on to say that Anant Nag would be sending his "boy" to collect the tickets. Listening to one side of the conversation, it became clear that the manager was believing it. He told her what time to send the "boy": Kaveri confirmed this. After she put down the phone, there were shrieks, yells, and more laughter: "What did he say?" "Did he ask your name?" "Who is the 'boy?'" By consensus, Raghu is chosen to collect the tickets.

The exuberance with which such movie outings are accomplished and the revisiting of such events through storytelling suggests that "fraudulently outwitting somebody else" is recognized as the "subject for a new play theme."[61] These examples illustrate audiences' (consumer) "cunning" and the tactical use of resources available to them: time and social relationships.[62] Additionally, the risk and uncertainty that shapes these cinema events constructs the outing as a gamble directed by "the question, 'will it come off?'"[63] Given that the play spirit "knows no moral function," it may explain how otherwise docile young people from so-called good families are drawn to acts involving risk and deception when they construct the cinema outing. Playing truant; deceiving parents, employers, theater staff, and other authority figures; buying tickets from scalpers that may turn out to be duds—these and other thrills satisfy a "fundamental human need" to play "for honor and glory."[64]

Hospitality and Movie Treats

For the middle classes, birthdays, anniversaries, the end of term, the successful passing of examinations, or securing a job or promotion are all worthy occasions for a movie treat, as are family get-togethers. Treating implies reciprocity and "non-economic mutuality";[65] one is obliged to treat members of one's group and return favors, thus reinforcing social relationships based on mutuality and community.[66] People feel free to demand movie treats as a celebration of some good news or simply to recall a past treat.[67] On leaving a theater, one overhears people thanking those who treated them.

Movie treats typically follow local customs of hospitality. A "group egalitarian ethos" builds shared experience; thus, food and drinking rituals are part of the sociality of movie events.[68] Cinema routines with all-male groups may involve alcohol, cigarettes, or "non-veg" food, even for those who are otherwise "vegetarian," an indication of the carnivalesque thwarting of rules the movie outing involves. One young professional described his movie outing with male friends: "In most cases, have beer, have something to eat, *then* go to the movie."[69] Theater managers told me that they had seen men in queues share alcohol on winter nights and had smelled alcohol on their breath. I often saw men at the theater sharing cigarettes or *beedis*, passing the cigarette from hand to hand companionably—or sharing a soft drink. They enjoy *paan* (brought from outside, as no *paan* was sold in the cinema);[70] I also saw a tin of Pan Parag (processed betel nut) being passed around.

People may be invited home for a meal before or after the movie, or the group's "hosts" might suggest meeting for a premovie coffee and snack in the city. According to one moviegoer, a morning show meant coffee: "usually we would have one-by-two."[71] Movie routines may involve "ghee roast [dosa]" either before or after a morning show or matinee. Matinees are preceded by lunch or followed by *tiffin* (snacks and coffee). After watching the Kannada film *Minnasare* (2010), my "hosts" decided to end the evening at a favorite ice-cream parlor, where our group of six was treated to ice creams and fruit salad. Within a fortnight we went to watch *Raam* (2010), and our host had arranged to take us all to dinner at a nearby restaurant after the film, which led to arguments over who would "treat" this time around. Framed as hospitality or treat, the film itself may become the host's responsibility. After a disappointing film, one host apologized to invitees: "Sorry, the movie was not good."

I sought opportunities to accompany people on their cinema outings and was frequently treated even when I was instrumental in initiating or encouraging the movie outing, which became a matter of some embarrassment to me.

A lower-middle-class moviegoer whom I met at a theater and accompanied on her movie outings suggested that we have coffee at a nearby hotel before the movie. She insisted on treating me, telling me firmly when I attempted to settle the check, "Next time, you can." Before going to watch *Air Force One* (1997) at the Rex on Brigade Road, Chitra, my viewing companion, dashed into the Nilgiris fruit stand next door, fought her way through the crowds of shoppers, and asked me what my favorite fruit was. She bought two bags of in-season rose apples, then offered to hide the fruit in her handbag until we got to our seats. Being familiar with such cycles of treating and hospitality, I attempted to reciprocate whenever I could with return movie outings and gifts of sweets and fruit. My role as researcher had less to do with the hospitality afforded me than my being viewed as a visitor and guest to the city, as ex-residents frequently are. Early in my fieldwork, my being a student and not having a proper job also prompted people to treat me. Other movie "guests" report similar experiences.

The Family Movie Outing

Cinemagoing with large (family) groups can be spontaneous and last minute but can also involve extensive planning and preparation.[72] Kumar gave a detailed account of one such outing that highlighted some of the logistical issues and the work involved. The family decided to celebrate his parents' wedding anniversary by treating the extended family—about fourteen people ranging in age from eight to eighty—to a movie. Kumar explained that everyone invited could not make it for the evening show, so to "include" everyone, the group was split into two: "we calculated the number of people who decided to come for the movie, and then I went to the movie [theater] and bought four tickets for the afternoon show and ten tickets for the evening."

Everyone met for lunch at Kumar's parents' home. Some had traveled from distant localities in the city in what became an all-day affair. After lunch, the first group rushed off to the theater, as they had to be there by two-thirty. During the course of the afternoon some people dropped out of the evening's plans. One group member who had to play basketball was given a ticket so that he could join the others afterward. In talking about the event, the film was mentioned only once. Much of the conversation centered on the logistics of arranging the outing, including the lunch, ticket purchase, and transportation to the movie theater.

This cinema outing cost over 1,200 rupees in tickets alone—a not insignificant sum for middle-class families in Bangalore in 1998. In 2010, multiplex prices for a single ticket ranged between 175 and 500 rupees, with some fancier multiplexes charging 750 rupees per ticket depending on the day and show-time. A family group of four can easily spend 2,000 rupees on tickets alone.[73] Even so, large groups throng the multiplexes.

*

Families may be thought of as "natural" groups with boundaries in place; however, such groups may be "family-like groups"[74] and include close friends or "family friends" who have been absorbed into the kin network. Domestic servants and other household employees may be included in the family group apart from their role as chaperone to young girls and children; in another middle-class family, the chauffeur, a film enthusiast, routinely sat with family members in the Balcony.[75]

Assembling large groups whether of peers or family is an accomplishment.[76] Individuals have to be motivated, cajoled, and in some cases even coerced. Children often play a role in motivating and persuading adults to take them to the cinema. Unlike in the United Kingdom or the United States, where children are only permitted to see G- or PG-rated films, in many families in India children are without question included in any cinema outings, just as they are at other family events. Young children, even infants, are seen at the cinema irrespective of the time of the screening or the type of film. Toddlers and infants are seen at films aimed at a "mass" audience of lower-class men. Children, often as old as ten or twelve, sit on parents' or relative's laps, a practice that has led to some theaters putting up signs mandating that tickets be purchased for children. Reflecting on her movie outings over the years, a middle-class woman said she had been going to the movies since she was five years old. Her own daughter was taken to the movies as a toddler.

Children may be taken to the theater simply because there is no one at home to take care of them. When I asked about the young children at a Kannada movie that had some violent scenes and that was a hit with the "mass" audience, I realized how out of place my question was. The theater manager looked astonished: "Where will they leave the children!? . . . No one will be at home to watch the child. So they bring the child here and put it to sleep on the ground near the seats." Standing in the doorway of the auditorium halfway through the film and against a background of children crying and shrieking, I asked whether people ever complained about viewing conditions and noise, thinking he would mention the noisy children. He said he had been asked to raise or lower the volume of the soundtrack, and there had been a few complaints about noise from the ceiling fans, or about people (usually men) kicking the seats in front of them. When I asked him pointedly about children, he shook his head emphatically, "no," he had never received complaints about children. What would he do if someone came and told him about a crying child? He sounded a bit put out—even annoyed by the question: "*That* we won't take! That is *their* lookout! Only *you* can tell your child to keep quiet!" Typically, viewers do not seem to find the sounds of children annoying or disturbing,[77] or at any rate they do not expect the theater to regulate such behavior. The ethos is one of including the family unit, making theaters community and family spaces.

In the theater, families and their interactions shape the experience for all. Children are a visible and audible presence. During the film one hears conversations between parents and children. People walk in and out during the screening with crying children or make trips to restrooms. They may rummage in bags for feeding bottles, food, even shawls to keep children comfortable. Men also attend to children in the theater, carrying them, putting them to sleep on their shoulders, offering them food, and taking them outside if they fret.

Children move around restlessly; they kick the seat back or its arms, jump on the seats, throw things on the floor, and run up and down the rows and aisles. At a Bangalore theater I watched young children and toddlers move from one adult to another during the film: from mother's lap to grandmother's lap, to grandfather and back. On one occasion when I went to the movies with a large family group, I saw a three-year old climb across a row of about eight seats to sit with her father. Family members helped by obligingly handing her over. Some who assisted were not family but were sitting in the row behind and felt free to "help out" and even fondly pinched the child's cheeks. When I mentioned what I had seen to another moviegoer, she added that she had seen this happen several times and had also seen young children "walk" down the row of seats by stepping on the armrests.

The same ethos of family togetherness shapes cinema experiences in the Boston area, in Los Angeles, and in other North American cities where South Asian families with young children turn out in numbers for Indian films.

NEGOTIATING PUBLIC SPACE

Moviegoers' preparations for the cinema are also anticipations of public space. Theaters are categorized as "outside space," with attendant meanings of disorderliness if not danger.[78] Minimizing the risks and dangers of outdoor public settings and ensuring bodily comfort and security dominate the preparations. Some make it a point to wear "something warm" when they know they are going to a particular theater, because "that theater is always cold!" One woman told me she always takes cotton wool for her ears, as "the sound is too loud." Another reported that her aunt made it a habit to wear socks and shoes (rather than the *chappals* typically worn by women), "because once there were little rats or roaches or something, because she doesn't want any creepy-crawlies on herself."

Hosting family and friends at the cinema may translate to protecting them from the dangers and discomforts of outside space. Inside the hall, people warn each other about the pitted floors and steep stairs; hosts offer to exchange seats with guests or older people, or mothers with infants when seats are broken or have exposed nails in the upholstery. The dangers of the city are emphasized: my movie hosts warned me about taking an autorickshaw home in the evening: "Even auto drivers are not safe; people have been robbed late at night. Bangalore is not safe like it used to be" (field notes, 2010). For some, ensuring the safety of their group meant dropping everyone home after the film.

Seating arrangements may be manipulated to draw boundaries of "inside" and "outside" space. Younger women and children are protected by men and older women who sit at the ends of the group, effectively enclosing them in a "family" or "inside space,"[79] insulating them from the "outside" and from interaction with strangers. Among all-female groups, such seating preferences at times lead to conflict, as some insist on sitting in the middle of the group, leaving others to occupy the more "vulnerable" outer positions. Young women may use props to separate themselves from those around them; college students told me they placed their "binders" next to their seat backs to prevent men pinching them from behind, or they used them as barricades against those in adjacent seats—again, crafting a protected "inside space." I had first seen this during my college days in Bangalore on outings with classmates to older theaters in Majestic and Shivajinagar, where even lower-class viewers occupied the balcony.

For middle- and lower-middle-class filmgoers, creating a suitable environment for family and group leisure involves extending the sociality of the domestic sphere to the "inhospitable" theater setting. Moviegoers go to great lengths to create a semipublic "inside space" in the theater. They may bring small rugs and cushions and create makeshift sleeping areas for children, placing the rugs either in the aisle or on the floor. A similar sleeping arrangement is made for children on trains. "Family space" can mean being literally surrounded by family. Kaveri had clear memories of going to Kannada movies in a small town roughly 100 kilometers south of Bangalore, where her grandparents lived: "We used to go like that, all of us . . . like when my mum's brothers and all were there; they were all staying with my grandmum. There were three uncles and two aunts and all of us kids used to go." I asked her whether the group would be around eight or ten people—the size of some family groups I had seen at cinemas. She said, "Yeah, easily! Like eight would have been a *minimum* number. . . . Like sometimes I remember a big gang of about twenty of us. Full *khandaan* [extended family]. Everybody! Whoever's around in the theater." For a child, then, going to the cinema in a large family group can offer a distinct experience of public settings. In Kaveri's memories, the theater appears to be filled with known people rather than strangers. Surrounded by family, children experience the theater as a domestic or "inside" space.

The domestic context provided by the family can aid in the navigation of public settings. For some ethnic groups, appropriate behavior for women involves shielding themselves from the public eye. Yet cinemagoers in Bangalore do not necessarily retire from public settings. Muslim women wearing the burka are seen entering the theater after lights out and with their families. One moviegoer reported seeing a group of about six children enter and sit in a row, "reserving" seats for their mothers and female relatives who came after lights out, all wearing the burka (field notes, Bangalore, 2009). In heterogeneous public spaces, family groups and even children can in this way act as chaperones and provide a buffer for women—yet another way in which the group can be a resource.

"Provisioning," an activity of caring for the family,[80] is a big part of family sociality at the cinema. Even though many theaters offer a variety of food and drink and have signs prohibiting people from bringing their own food, managers at single-run cinemas realize this is an aspect of viewer behavior they cannot monitor. Sharing food and the caring work that accompanies it allows women, especially older women who subscribe to more traditional roles, to reframe their participation in public leisure as caring for family—a domestic activity. Before the advent of the mall multiplex and food courts, when going to the cinema with habitués, I overheard elaborate discussions regarding what food to take. In some families older women in the group take charge of planning and organizing food, which may involve both taking food from home—"sandwiches and stuff"—for children to have dinner, as one moviegoer said, or purchasing snacks from favorite stores. People take feeding bottles for babies; a few times, I saw lower-class women breastfeeding infants.[81]

Families extend the hospitality of domestic settings to the cinema. Guests or invitees are taken care of just as they would be at home. When going to the movies with middle-class families and friends, I was frequently asked what I would like to eat and would be appraised of the plans for food: "Vijji is making cheese sandwiches because her sandwiches are the best. Should we pick up some chips?" Hospitality in some families meant plying everyone with food: Iyengar bakery chips, *khara* (spicy) peanuts, homemade sweets, or *pakoras* and *vadais* are distributed in the cinema hall. The "host" would solicitously inquire after guests:[82] "Please have," and press them to "take some more," helping herself only after everyone had been "served," just as she would at her home. If anyone refused food, it was offered again, and they would be asked why they were not eating. In large family groups that have been split up in the theater, I even saw moviegoers move around the darkened theater to offer food to group members seated in adjacent rows or across the aisle, split up because of seat assignments. Not all moviegoers bring food from home, and even those who do will additionally treat members of their group to soft drinks, coffee, samosas, and other snacks from the concession counter. In some families it seemed to be the duty of younger men to courteously inquire what women, elders, and children wanted in terms of food and drink from the scrum that was the concessions stand.

Organizing food and drink for the group is also about minimizing the risks and dangers of public (outside) settings. Before the availability of filtered water to buy, middle-class moviegoers brought boiled and filtered water that was "safe" to drink and sometimes hot tea or coffee in flasks. For some, the quality of food available in the theater is suspect: "I just don't know where it's made," Brinda, a middle-class housewife explained. Another said her mother (aged seventy plus) always insisted they brought food with them because "you never know what oil they use." A common complaint among middle-class audiences is that movie theater popcorn has sand in it. Anjali told me, "my maid makes very nice popcorn, so I take that along."[83]

Anxieties attendant to outside spaces have been attributed to caste society;[84] however, a comparative perspective suggests that anxieties associated with the cinema outing and public settings are more widespread and have shaped cinemagoing ever since the cinema became established as public entertainment. Phil Hubbard sees the attractions of the multiplex in the United Kingdom as directly related to the comfort and "ontological security" that moviegoers associate with such settings in the broader context of their anxieties about the city and fear of the Other[85]—his observations suggesting a need for more detailed comparative studies.

THE CINEMA AS SOCIAL EXPERIENCE

Movie outings in Bangalore are embedded in a "complex network of local social activity"[86] where satisfaction stems from being with others.[87] Sociality in the cinema hall is not "light," as it is at the Western multiplex;[88] rather, interactions with friends and family members often take precedence over the film. Stratified cinema halls in Bangalore are multiuse social spaces, like marketplaces. The range of behaviors accommodated in the cinema hall includes the public/private activities that constitute leisure for families.[89] On hot afternoons people nap in the air-conditioned auditorium,[90] and teenagers may use the cinema as a deviant thrill. Filmgoers "produce" the social context;[91] noisy children, patrons bringing in food and drink, the raucous exuberance of "front benchers," or smoking companionably in the cinema—all shape the cinema hall experience. Even the experience of the film is generated interpersonally when, for example, people watch films in a language they cannot understand with friends who can translate. Storytelling, for example, highlights the drama and biographical relevance of cinemagoing, while locating it in the mythologies of everyday life. When bloggers look back nostalgically, their "time machine" posts are focused on the social and collective experience: "I still remember the school trip from St. Patrick's (school), to watch the movie *Home Alone* in 1989, walking with friends in single line, screaming outside of teachers behind us, shouting in the Theater . . . WOW."[92]

The heightened sociality of cinemagoing in Bangalore throws into relief the film-centered experience at the Anglo-American multiplex, considered the dominant, generalizable (film) experience. Where the individual viewer's relationship with the film lies at the heart of the experience, sociality is "light," and even ritual "movie dates" become problematic. An article examining the complexities of the romantic movie outing acknowledges the "threatening level of complexity" arising from differing tastes in film leading one moviegoer to comment, "which is why I like to watch a movie alone."[93]

Cultural and social distinctions are evident even in the framing of public spaces of reception. Cinemagoing in India and the practices of hospitality, caring, and the efforts to construct inside space perhaps demonstrate a wider frame for in-theater activities relating to understandings of space in India, where "the perimeters of the inside and outside are relative, shifting and fluid,"[94] and where "the outside and inside do not entirely correspond to Euro-American notions of public and private."[95]

While the cinema hall in Bangalore is treated as "outside" space that needs to be domesticated, the Anglo-American multiplex may be understood to be a "front region"—primarily a space for adults, where the "socially incomplete,"[96] such as children, are not always welcome or even admitted.[97] In his study of movie outings in the United Kingdom, Hubbard identifies a curious contradiction: while the multiplex provides the comforts of "domestic consumption" and is promoted as a "family space," families are not actually seen at the multiplex "en masse."[98] He concludes that the out-of-town multiplex provides instead a fantasy of family leisure. Multiplexes in the United States are also highly regulated spaces that segment the audience, with consequences for the cinema experience. Some theaters have a policy of not admitting children under six, while a growing number of theaters both in the United States and the United Kingdom offer "special screenings" and "Mommy Matinees" for mothers with infants and toddlers, thus further extending segmentation and homogenization of reception settings.[99] Audience segmentation is so much taken for granted in this public culture of cinema that when special matinees were introduced in Glasgow for parents (mostly women) with young children and infants, they drew mixed reactions. Karen Boyle found that some women were appreciative of an environment that provided "solidarity" with other mothers, where "you'll be forgiven if you have a screaming baby."[100] Others expressed anxiety about what was a "strange" and new experience, with one caller to a radio show suggesting that the practice of taking babies to the cinema was a form of child abuse—all foreign notions to cinema hall audiences in India, where in-theater interactions run the gamut and point to the acceptance of family-centered moviegoing as part of a broader culture of sociability making for an intergenerationally inclusive experience at the cinema.

Cinema halls in India have been described as exclusionary spaces where considerations of both class and caste have marginalized audiences.[101] Mall multiplexes have also come in for criticism—for their inflated prices and for being elite or middle-class spaces, no doubt a valid critique. Ethnographic research in Bangalore reveals that compared with the more highly segmented "front region" of the Anglo-American multiplex, the cinema hall is a social space for a heterogeneous audience—reflected in its socioeconomic, religious, and ethnolinguistic diversity—where multigenerational families watch films and where people expect fellow viewers to have a different aesthetic of engagement with the film. Balcony audiences may see boisterous "front benchers" as part of the show. Moviegoers need not feel "out of place" because they have a crying baby with them.[102] However, the inclusivity of the cinema hall together with the heterogeneity of the audience makes it a contested and dynamic space.

CHAPTER 6

Active Audiences and the Constitution of Film Experience

The second The Hero appeared on screen for the first time: 'Wooooohoooooooooooo WOOT whistle! whistle! Shriek! whistle,' dancing in the aisles, balloons bursting everywhere, man what a thrill![1]

At the matinee screening of the Kannada-language feature *Megha Bantu Megha* (The clouds are gathering), advertisements shown before the film generate lively commentary.[2] Watching a commercial for Nirma (a detergent), a woman turns to her viewing companion: "Nirma is no good [*channage illa*]." Another commercial for Cadbury's (chocolate) depicts a cricket match and is greeted with shouts from a group of young men, one of whom yells, "Clean bowled!" In the advertisement, a woman dances sexily out onto a cricket field. The men mock the ad, "Ooh!" "Aha!" Those seated nearby laugh. Someone loudly speculates on who the actress or model might be. At the on-screen prayer and ritual invocation that typically precedes the film,[3] a woman seated next to me remarks loudly to her friend that the deity shown on-screen is "Subramani." The visual is of an altar with two lamps, with the prayer in musical verse: *vande Subramaniam*.[4]

For a large section of the moviegoing public, there is a sense that watching visuals on-screen is incomplete entertainment. Expectations of "film experience" extend beyond the film to the reception context. Much like sixteenth- and seventeenth-century Paris theater and opera in the Old Regime, both described as "more social event than aesthetic encounter,"[5] where "the greatest pastime . . . was conversation,"[6] audiences are talkative, even noisy. An Indian moviegoer who had watched films in India as well as in the United States distinguished in-theater customs and aesthetics as follows: "With Indian audiences you feel you can talk more; [with] Americans it's hard to talk; you feel it's rude. With Indians it's OK to have normal conversations; people behind you will be talking." Historian James Johnson observes that in seventeenth-century

Europe, operagoers' "horizon of expectations" led them to hear music very differently from the way contemporary audiences hear music. Similarly, in cinema halls habitués watch "within the boundaries of expectation,"[7] which shapes their experience of the film. Reception practices in Bangalore constitute a "cinema of interactions and distractions."[8] After watching the Tamil blockbuster *Sivaji* (2007), a moviegoer commented on the noisy audience: "People were shouting so much we couldn't hear the dialogue only!"[9] Moviegoers may look forward to spectacle provided by a lively and participatory gathering, even seek out such experiences.

This chapter explores the ways in which the social aesthetic described in chapter 5, audiences' expectations of film entertainment and their embodied and participatory practices of engaging with film, shape in-theater experience and the "contingent character" of film.[10] Rather than framing reception as interpretation and meaning making (of texts), I explore how film and in-theater experience of viewing is constituted by the play spirit, its sociality, and by performance.

PARTICIPATORY, INTERACTIVE, AND CONVERSATIONAL VIEWING

Elizabeth Hahn describes the cinema experience in Tonga as one where the film is subordinated to the social experience in the setting. People watch sitting in their church groups, leading to a curious "intimate quality" in exhibition settings.[11] While cinema halls in Bangalore seat between eight hundred and a thousand-plus viewers, a similar social atmosphere prevails as moviegoers watch in viewing clusters.[12] Participation and interaction run the gamut; moviegoers not only talk with each other, they talk to characters on-screen—warning the hero of danger, exulting in his triumphs, and voicing involuntary expressions of fear, pity, hurt, embarrassment, and jubilation on his behalf. The hero's pursuit of the heroine and exchanges with the villain are marked by enthusiastic whistles and catcalls. While scenes of high drama may momentarily silence viewers, they applaud the resolution of dramatic tension, the improbable happy endings, or when good triumphs over evil. Audiences watching Bollywood's *Hum Aapke Hain Kaun* (1994) are reported to have given a standing ovation to a dramatic scene toward the end of the film in which Tuffy, the family dog, carries a letter intended for one character to another, which leads to the reuniting of the hero and heroine. Moviegoers are equally unrestrained in expressing disappointment. They hiss, boo, or shout advice, providing instant feedback.[13]

The same social and interactive aesthetic shapes reception of English-language Hollywood films. At the screening of *Air Force One* in the Cantonment, moviegoers talked throughout the film. A scene where a woman and a young girl get out of a car prompts the speculation—"Must be the family." Meanwhile, two men loudly discuss the absence of a member of their group. Following a line of dialogue in the film, "What if the president is not on the plane?" a viewer exclaims, "He's going to do something now!" When the American president is tied up on the floor at the feet of the terrorists and spots a piece of glass nearby, a viewer exclaims, "He's seen the glass piece!" His group speculates on what the president will do with the piece of glass. At another tense moment in the film, viewers worry that the fax sent from the hijacked plane is lying unnoticed in Washington. Audiences "explain" scenes and plots to companions without being asked—the objective is the interaction.[14] Audience talk is often more audible during Hollywood movies, which are not equipped with soundtracks that drown out the audience.

While audience comments may be "interpretive" with a view to achieving shared understanding of the film (discussed later in this chapter), commentary is not always geared to a faithful interpretation; rather, moviegoers add local flavor and humor and embroider the film, an aesthetic that is evident even in theaters screening Indian films outside India to NRI audiences. In a melodramatic scene in the Hindi film *Bombay* by award-winning director Mani Ratnam—known for making quality films on serious social issues—the hero's son, born of a marriage between a Hindu and a Muslim, is lost in the city torn by ethnic (religious) conflict. The boy comes across an urchin. Recognizing hunger and exhaustion on the boy's face, the urchin offers him a grimy piece of bread shaped like a bun. The soundtrack swells to express the high drama of reverse compassion between rich and poor. The boy hesitates for a moment before accepting the bun. In this space, a young middle-class man in the audience yells, "Gimme hamburger!" His friend shouts, "Fries and a large coke!" They laugh and argue about whether the coke should be large or small. Others join in their laughter while some attempt to silence them: "Sssshhh!" An inconsequential act such as a character lighting a cigarette can set off irrepressible moviegoers who seize opportunities for play. At a screening of a Bollywood film, which viewers dismissed half an hour into it as a "B grade movie," a character enters the scene to loud music, smoking a cigarette. A viewer yells, "Hey! Smoking is bad for your health, idiot!" Another, having decided the film is a flop, yells, "Don't kill yourself; the movie will be over soon!"[15] Here again, like Tongan narrators who "recast" film into a "lively exchange for the assembled gathering," humorists in the audience become performer-narrators, making the film relevant to the immediacy of the social context (of reception).[16] These examples suggest that the playfulness that characterizes in-theater experience with habituated audiences provides a shifting mood, a "force" in the theater that "erupts and one falls into it" and which "may come and go suddenly seizing the players, then quickly subsiding—a wisecrack, a flash of frenzy, risk."[17] Audiences therefore do not necessarily experience the film in the frame provided by the filmmaker or the story. Habitués engagement with a film and its scenes may be marked by irony and distance. Even a "bad" film can provide opportunities for play. This "performative element" shapes cinema experience in other cultures as well. We learn from Elizabeth Hahn, for example, that for Tonganese moviegoers in the 1980s, enjoyment of the film rested on having a good "narrator," who, like a "master of ceremonies or storyteller," entertains the gathering with witty remarks. Narrators "embellish and personalize the story . . . crack jokes and provide a local context." They make random comments that "depend on [the narrator's] whim or mood of the film."[18] The exchange "epitomizes . . . the Tongan sense of humor and delight in repartee."[19]

Where the social aesthetic is dominant, attention is not closely focused on the film or performance. Theatergoers in eighteenth-century Europe "wanted to see the stage, wanted to see the actors; but above all they wanted to see each other, and . . . take in every detail."[20] Similarly, in cinema halls in Bangalore people take in the atmosphere, scan their surroundings, and comment on fellow audience members, a sensibility of being in public that is perhaps associated with streets and markets—heterogeneous spaces in which people are immersed socially and sensually and constantly aware of their surroundings.[21] Habitués then experience the movie "in terms of the overall gathering in the theater."[22] When exchanging notes about their movie experience, people talk not only of the story but of the audience, too. People may say of a mediocre film, "It was entertaining; people were passing comments in the theater," or, of a member of their group admired for his wit, "This guy has to pass comments always!" A Kannada movie enthusiast wrote in a blog, "After writing the review, if I don't write the crowd response then it wont give you a picture."[23] Talk of "a good crowd" and "atmosphere" points to the enjoyment of cinema as spectacle, which incorporates the audience and an aesthetic of performance and participation. Focusing on the "crowd reaction" when talking about his experience of watching *Mungaru Male*, a moviegoer described it as "something amazing. They were cheering for each and every dialogue of Ganesh . . . As usual, when JOG SHOTS appeared on the scenes, everybody were cheering and clapping in disbelief (*sic*). They didn't forget to whistle when Devdas arrived on the scene."[24]

Exhibition spaces are nonstandardized (see chap. 3), and some theaters are known for their boisterous and rowdy audiences, who provide the "attraction."[25] The "film experience" then includes the "show" by the audience. In the stratified cinema hall, "front benchers" sitting close to the screen are expected to be overtly participatory, even rambunctious. A student of Indian origin living in the United States describes going to the cinema in Bombay: "In India, those seated closest to the screen—lots of whistling, shouting, rowdy audience. They'll shout *ladki aa gayee*! [the girl is here] when the heroine appears on-screen, holler when she's wearing a short skirt." Stratified cinema halls then offer a kind of class and gender voyeurism; middle-class moviegoers and the "balcony audience" may view the antics of "front benchers," or the Gandhi class, with distaste, but they nevertheless anticipate diversion and entertainment from them. Talking about people in the lower stalls throwing coins at the screen,[26] a middle-class woman remarked, "What CTs [cheap thrills] people get!" Vivek, a software engineer, elaborated on the distinctive practices of the audience he called "the rickshawala crowd": "[They] Love fight scenes! They whistle when the hero or villain gets beaten up, when the girl [heroine] comes on-screen, when a character makes a decision; when there's a turning point, they'll clap. After a period of misunderstanding when he [the hero] makes a speech, one of those dialogues, very cliché? 'Profound?' They'll clap."

Moviegoers pursuing a local experience seek out theaters and showtimes that provide the atmosphere they seek. To counter the problem of a quiet audience, a moviegoer recommends a change of venue to a fellow enthusiast for the "atmosphere" and suggests Bangalore's Urvashi theater, where "the crowd was pretty good in terms of whistling and clapping."[27] He comments on a friend who "watched it 2–3 times in a theater in KR puram and I can go on and on about the atmosphere he experienced."[28] Even write-ups on the films frequently include audience reaction and the "performance context." The audience or "crowd" and the sensualities of the setting shape the total experience of film reception. For another moviegoer an online post jogged a "pleasant" memory of the cinema that had more to do with a "smelly" crowd and an equally smelly theater rather than the film.

The post evoked some *vairy romba* [extremely] pleasant memory: may [*sic*] years ago, my second cousin and I went to to [*sic*] LoKal Piccher . . . it was some arbit [arbitrary] Tamil movie but man what an experience! The theater was a large shed, with a canvas siding . . . The place reeked of batsh*t, the crowd was sooper-sooper enthu [enthusiastic] and super dooper smelly—it was a hot summer afternoon in Cuddalore . Even today, the whiff of batsh*t takes me back in a nanosecond to that experience![29]

Expectations of a lively atmosphere in the theater and local experience extend to screenings of Indian films outside India, where nostalgia for cinema experiences "at home" can shape moviegoing. Screenings of Indian films in the United States to largely Indian audiences offer the opportunity to recapture to some degree the liveliness of the cinema hall experience. At these screenings there is almost a sense that watching the film attentively and being absorbed by it is a "social faux pas"[30] committed by those "who don't know how to watch."

"WHAT STORY?" SELECTIVE VIEWING AND FILM AS AMUSEMENT

After watching a fight scene in the Bollywood film *Jeet*, a viewer said half-jokingly to his partner, "Now I've got my money's worth. We can go [home] now." Vivian Sobchack observes that film, though objectively presented to viewers, "may be subjectively taken up in a variety of ways, not only in its entirety, but also in its parts."[31] Her observation is illustrated by the aesthetics of viewing with habitués. For some moviegoers, going to the cinema can be equivalent to going to the fights; others are drawn by the promise of dance spectacle and the glamor of the stars. At a screening of the lavishly produced *Devdas* (2002), a woman said she had "heard the costumes were very nice, so [I] came to see the saris and jewelry." Another moviegoer who had heard the film's music at home remarked that his sole purpose in watching the film (in the theater) was to see "how the song was choreographed" and "where it fits in the story."

Habitués thus do not necessarily engage with the film through its narrative or seek to become immersed in the story. Indeed, the traditional song-and-dance film does not present audiences with a seamless narrative. Similar to variety theater and early cinema, where a series of acts followed one another and were appreciated as discrete performances by a participatory audience, the films offer a collection of favorite scenes and performances loosely strung together, something like a Spanish zarzuela. People go to the cinema to see a favorite performer; the attraction of the film's story is secondary, if that. Stars provide spectacle, and the "star effect" is very powerful.[32] Robert Hardgrave, who has studied the culture of Tamil cinema, observes that most fans "see the film as a sequence of scenes—fights, romance, songs, cabaret. Continuity is provided only by the star." For many, "the story fades into the background, even if fully comprehended."[33] After watching *Sivaji*, which starred the Tamil superstar Rajinikanth, a fan at a New York theater is quoted as saying, "we are here for our hero, who cares about the plot?"—a sentiment echoed by an autorickshaw driver in South India, who, when asked about the film's story is reported to have said, "What story? Rajni [the star] is the story."[34]

Selective viewing or attention complements film as an assemblage. When, after a Kannada film, I asked a fan, "How was the movie?" he responded by enthusiastically endorsing the star: "Puneet [Kannada star Puneet Rajkumar] is too good!" Moviegoers then apply different levels of attention to different parts of the film: they switch "on" and "off" without losing enjoyment.[35] Frequently conversation on-screen—unless it is the hero or villain delivering "punch lines"—serves as a signal for audiences to "take a break" from the film and have conversations of their own. Lately, conversations on-screen appear to function as a signal for moviegoers to talk on their cellphones. Selective appreciation and engagement shapes film experience for the collectivity; applause following the hero's dialogue often drowns out the heroine's (or other character's) response. Realizing that audiences watch a film piecemeal and that "selective viewing" is located in a broader aesthetic of watching film as spectacle and amusement,[36] filmmakers invest a great deal in providing the expected ingredients. Their belief that a hit song in a film can save it from flopping speaks to the aesthetic of selective and fragmented viewing.

Aesthetic appreciation of a film and its scenes also demonstrates selective attention and engagement. People hum along with a tune or tap their fingers to the music even when it is background for a tense or tragic scene. Each star or director has his or her trademark style, which audiences look for. After watching *Sivaji*, a moviegoer reports, "The movie had its share of Rajni one-liners . . . the usual sunglasses trick, the coin trick, a new addition is the shifting of the gun from right hand to left."[37] It is not only heroes who receive applause; audiences may perversely cheer a favorite villain. While watching *Agni Sakshi* (Fire as witness [1982]), audience members laughed uproariously and applauded the villain's dialogue even though he was terrorizing the heroine; both characters were played by popular stars. Responding aesthetically to witty dialogue and voicing support for a favorite artist or performance rather than responding morally to evil[38] is evidence of the play spirit that "has no moral function"; and where "the valuations of vice and virtue do not apply."[39] Many stars have acquired a following for their portrayal of charismatic villains, Amjad Khan's portrayal of the *dacoit* (bandit) Gabbar Singh being one example.

In addition to the structure of the film, the organization of screenings makes piecemeal viewing possible. The intermission lends itself to selective

engagement. In what appears to be a strategy that can garner a broader audience, the pre- and postintermission "halves" of the popular film are often
designed like two separate films. Following the break there is a shift in the
story, which is frequently accompanied by a change of location, and that satisfies the expectation that the film provide travelogue. New characters and
"new" stars are introduced. For example, the "first half" of the blockbuster
Kabhi Khushi Kabhie Gham (2001) locates the story ostensibly in "India"
(represented by sets), while postintermission, the story moves to London,
and the film introduces a new star (Kareena Kapoor). In older films, the
"second half" would often project the story twenty years or more into the
future.

Selective viewing is so much a part of the reception aesthetic that film reviews underscore the elements that appeal to an audience engaged in it. For,
example they highlight audience reaction to specific scenes. In a review of the
Kannada film *Raam* (2009), the synopsis of the plot reads like an afterthought
and is only a couple of lines long. The bulk of the review (here abridged)
focuses on whether or not the film delivers elements that audiences want and
that cater to selective viewing. The review points out, for instance, that there
were only a couple of "good songs." It refers to a "first half" and "second half,"
and pre- and postintermission sections of the film, indicating the way in which
audiences "see" the film. Multiple references are made to the star playing the
hero and his performance.

PUNEET STARRER "RAAM" MONEY'S WORTH

Raam is a laugh riot and has *lots of commercial ingredients* to entertain the
audience. . . .

Puneet is a big star in Kannada, Madesh has centered the film on him and
roped in National Award winning actress Priyamani to play his love interest. . . .

The real strength of the film is its *second half* that engages the audience with
its *comedy elements*. In many films this year, the *first half* had been very good,
but the *second half* was very weak. But "Raam" is different as the film's *second
half* appeals largely to the audiences. . . .

The film not only moves at a faster pace, it has lots of *sequences that make
audiences laugh continuously*. Another plus point is that *each actor has excelled
in his performance and comic timing*.

The film's sore point is its music. Hari Krishna has delivered *just two good
songs*. The older songs are ordinary. Even the camera work doesn't match up
to the standards of top Kannada films released this year. . . .

Puneet has effortlessly carried his role and his fans will certainly enjoy his performance in the film. He proves that he will *excel in comedy* roles in future also. He is at ease in the *dance and fight sequences.*

Priyamani has gelled well with Puneet and *showcases her talents in dancing.*

Both Puneet and Priyamani *impress with their dances in songs* "Hosa gaana bajaana" and "Neenedhare nanagishta."

Talented Rangayana Raghu *makes audiences laugh with every dialogue.* Sadhu Kokila, Doddanna and Shobharaj are impressive too.

In short "Raam" is a "paisa vasool" [worth your money] film.[40]

A review of the Tamil film *Endhiran* (2010) focuses similarly on the star, on spectacle, and on popular elements such as thrills, stunts, and jokes.

Anyone who has seen a Rajnikanth film understands that often it is not the story that makes the film a success, but Rajni's antics. There are plenty of them in the film. . . .

There are gravity defying stunts, shooting with a finger, running horizontally at high speed on the side of a train, flying cars and bikes, corny but hilarious dialogues—e.g. After grabbing and pointing scores of guns at the police, he says 'Happy Diwali' before firing a salvo of bullets; or when the robot is asked his address he gives his IP address. It's not just god, the universe and its logic itself is recreated in the film.

Director Shankar who has a penchant for double image, multiple images and split images of his heroes returns this time with hundreds of images of Rajinikanth.[41]

"Seeing the Sights": Documentary Viewing

In what may be understood to be a form of selective involvement, audiences look beyond the film's fictional world to the underlying reality.[42] At a screening of a Bollywood film two women commented on a star: "My god! He's grown so fat after his wife died!" Scenes in natural landscapes, gardens and parks generate curiosity about the actual locations. Adopting an aesthetic of sightseeing viewers are overheard speculating on locations: "See, it's Melkote (where the scene was filmed), so beautiful!," and "we can go there on a picnic all of us," or "This was shot at Jog Falls. Have you been?"[43] Locations in the film are not always recognizable or marked, however, and viewers wonder aloud as they look *through* the fictionalized story to the reality beyond: "Where was this shot? In India?"

Habitués do not suspend disbelief; during the interval of the Tamil film *Indian*, I overheard people comment upon Kamal Hasan made up to look like an elderly man: "What fantastic makeup! They got someone from Hollywood to do the makeup," and "Terrific acting! You can't tell it's the same guy!" (The star had a double role in the film.) In a mode of viewing that may be described as "looking-as-in-everyday-life," moviegoers dismantle a scene, relating fragments to their lives. While watching *Kurubana Raani* at the Sagar theater, during a tragic scene in which the heroine had just swallowed a bottleful of sleeping tablets to escape the attentions of the villain, a middle-class woman, disgusted by the heroine's physical condition, asked her friend, "Do you see her flab?" Her companion, who had recently renovated her home and was looking for furnishings for her dining room, commented on the decor: "That table is nice, we should get one like that." Women examine costumes with a keen eye for fashion. In another scene, where the heroine is recovering from her suicide attempt in the hospital and the hero is nearly out of his mind with grief, a viewer remarked loudly, "I really like that brocade blouse," worn by the heroine, and then proceeded to discuss the suitability of the blouse for a wedding she was invited to. Men, too, appreciate style and attitude; fans were admiring of the portrayal of "rowdies" (criminals) in the film *Om* (1996), and some turned up for the screening mimicking the dress of the rowdies in the film. Fans watching "Rajinikanth starrers" are there mainly to soak up the star's attitude and style.

Documentary viewing of fictional film is not specific to habitués of Indian cinema, as evidenced by the fashions generated by popular film and television programs worldwide and by film-related tourism, also a global phenomenon. What is perhaps distinctive to the Indian setting is that documentary viewing is part of an aesthetic of in-theater engagement that involves different kinds of attention, and that become visible because of an overtly interactive and social aesthetic.

An aesthetic of watching live entertainment shapes moviegoers' attitudes and experiences. Wedding scenes and dance sequences may be enjoyed as celebrations. The film *Lagaan* (The tax [2001]) set in Victorian India, which featured a cricket match between oppressed villagers and British colonialists, drew wild cheers and applause from cricket enthusiasts in the audience. This aesthetic is evident in audience reaction to screening preliminaries. When the lights are switched off, viewers applaud, cheer, and whistle enthusiastically, similar to theater crowds applauding when the curtain falls. For a "good" film, people applaud when the lights come on at the end, again similar to theater audiences applauding the curtain. Audiences talk of stars "coming on" or "coming out," as if onto a stage.[44] The dramatic "arrival" of favorite star-characters on-screen is greeted with thunderous applause and whistling, which can go on for several minutes. When the star looks at the audience or walks toward the camera,[45] pandemonium breaks out. The din in the theater has to be heard to be believed. Uninhibited audiences whistle, cheer, shout out to star-performers: deafening screams and yells of "Talaivaaarrr!" ("head" or "chief" in Tamil) and "Superstaaarrrrr!" greet Rajinikanth's arrival on-screen.[46] At theaters in the Boston area, audiences burst into applause, cheers, and whistles when the Bollywood stars Kajol, Rani Mukherjee, and Amitabh Bachchan made a "surprise guest appearance" in a wedding song-and-dance sequence in *Kal Ho Na Ho* (2003)—the response similar to that of audiences at performances of Bollywood stars on live concert tours in the United States and the United Kingdom. By delaying the entry of the star, films keep viewers in suspense, encouraging such participation.

Audiences may "talk to" and interact with performers on-screen even to express their disappointment and take them to task. The film *Khamoshi* (Silence [1996]), surprisingly, featured the actor Nana Patekar—generally admired for his "dialogue delivery"—as a deaf mute; casting that initially stunned the audience into silence as well. Nasrin Kabir reports that when moviegoers recovered from seeing their beloved Nana using sign language, they responded by imploring him to talk, and then by booing and shouting. According to the film's director, Sanjay Leela Bhansali, who was watching the film at the Liberty theater in Bombay along with the audience, "The audience in the lower stalls starts shouting "'Nana! Talk! Please speak!' . . . They continued shouting, 'We want to hear you speak, *yaar*, come on, speak!' as if Nana could hear them, and Nana was going to start speaking."[47]

"Walking through the Film"

The generalized experience and expectation of film viewing in public settings at any Anglo-American multiplex is that audiences are silent and immobile. Film viewing that is equated with absorption and with "reading" or "interiorizing the story" is a private and individual experience of identification with characters.[48] The physical organization of the theater, with seating in rows, is designed to keep audiences in their seats and to direct their attention away from one another and toward the screen, the sole source of light and sound. This understanding of film and in-theater experience and the spatial relations that accompany it, the dominant understanding of film reception, is thrown into question at cinemas in India where, rather than being "pinned to their seats,"[49] moviegoers walk in and out of the theater in an ambulatory viewing style. Audiences' mobility is not involuntary, as might have been the case with early audiences and the famous "train effect" (where spectators are reported to have run away, "panicking," from the oncoming train on the Lumières' screen),[50] but considered and deliberate. People stroll, walk, and browse together, bringing the aesthetic of the street and marketplace to film viewing.[51] Their mobility brings them closer to the spectators of the Ram Lila, performed in the open air in North India, who are described by Richard Schechner as walking all over town, following its mobile enactment.

Using their bodies to carve out routes through the film, ambulatory audiences reinvent the film; their mobility and its "rhythms and gestures"[52] shape film experience while making visible the ongoing process of constructing a bricolage.[53] These "shortcuts and detours"[54] have an effect similar to hitting the fast-forward button on the remote, allowing audiences to avoid scenes they consider "optional," thus reshaping the film. People may exit the theater before a song-and-dance sequence and return after ten minutes anticipating a shift in scene. Often at the start of a song sequence, seats are heard snapping back, and a series of thuds and creaking springs announce people exiting the theater singly or in groups. Here again, there is variation among heterogeneous audiences as to which scenes they choose to avoid. Some wander out when there is conversation on-screen and return to watch a dance.

The film *Indian* (1996), for example, was being debated by members of the intelligentsia as an ideological piece with a controversial social and political message. An academic at a local university reported excitedly, "[the film] critiques democracy in India!" Yet a section of the cinema-hall audience demonstrated an interest in exotica and eagerly anticipated "Telephone Manipol"—a song sequence set in Australia that had "become the buzz." At the Lido theater I followed a group of young men into the theater lobby after the song ended and overheard them exclaiming about the kangaroos in the scene and the Sydney Opera House. At a screening of *Jeet* near Los Angeles, I saw groups of viewers exit the theater, thereby avoiding a "serious" conversation between the hero and the heroine, and return cheering and whistling when the scene shifted to a fight. At Kannada films in Bangalore, fans gathered in the theater lobby and, keeping an ear open for the soundtrack, rushed back into the auditorium when a favorite scene with the hero began. From groups sitting out song sequences, or "slow" scenes, one person is dispatched to check and "see whether the song is over" or whether the scene has shifted. This piecemeal viewing was evident at almost every screening I attended both in India and in the United States where Indian films are screened to South Asian audiences.

Mobility frees viewers not only from any preexisting narrative order or structure the film may have but also from the constraints of the "disciplinary" or organizational space of the theater,[55] with consequences for collective experience. Barbara Mittman has observed that the mobility of the theater audience in seventeenth-century France challenged the separation of audience and players, making for a participatory and interactive gathering.[56] In the cinema hall, people watching the film "in parts" do not feel compelled to be in their seats when it begins; they wander in, locate their seats, and even call out to friends well after the film has begun.[57] Indeed, the traditional masala film with an introductory song-and-dance sequence appears to anticipate and accommodate late arrivals. If missed, it will not be critical for those wishing to follow the loosely constructed narrative. The two "halves" of the film also lend themselves to such piecemeal viewing and liberation from rules of having to be in one's seat. Moviegoers talked about walking in late, even arriving during the intermission and missing the "first half" entirely, which did not seem to be a deterrent to an enjoyable experience.[58] Schoolboys in Bangalore who plan to "catch" the movie once classes end also anticipate missing the "first half." Not only do viewers enter the theater once the film is underway, they may exit before the last scene has played out. Many films I watched in the late 1990s and into 2000 did not air credits after the film. Instead, a freeze frame of the star appeared on-screen accompanied by a popular film song in anticipation of audiences rushing out of the theater.

REPEAT VIEWING

At a screening of *Air Force One* in Bangalore's Cantonment, people waiting for theater doors to open called out excitedly to friends and family. I heard "Harrison Ford" mentioned several times, along with the name of the director, "Peterson." Phrases such as "Too good!" and "Whatta plane!" filled the air, suggesting many had seen the film before. Moviegoers differentiate between "good" films—"It was good" or "It was fun"—and mediocre films—"It's OK, it can be seen *once*." When I went with a group of four to see the Kannada superhit *Mungaru Male* (2007),[59] I found one of them had seen it twice; another had seen it three times.

Movie talk often involves sharing details about the number of times one has seen a film or plans to see it and is a topic for online musings on films. In one online forum a moviegoer congratulated a film commentator on his well-written review, then wondered, " How many times have you watched this movie?" Another enthusiast announced, "Phhhhhhhew finally watched it . . .

its just the best movie . . . i think i may see it another 2 . . . hmm no 3 . . . no maybe 5–6 times."[60] A third revealed that he had paid a total of Rs. 305 to see the film four times but planned to see it ten times in total and provided details of date, ticket price, and theater:

7th Jan Rs 50 @ Nalanda
8th Jan luckily Rs 30 @ Nalanda
14th Jan Rs 80 @ Pramod
15th Rs 35 @ Uma.
4 times and it continues till 10 I think.

While it may be argued that these online posts could be authored by fans or by the star's friends or family or others seeking to promote the film rather than by audiences, they nevertheless point to the practice of repeat viewing.

*

Repeaters can prolong the life of a film at the box office, which explains how some films remain in theaters for months on end. Movies such as *Bangarada Manusha* (1972), *Sholay* (1975), and *Hum Aapke Hain Kaun* (1994) enjoyed a run of a year or more and owe their superhit status to repeaters. The Hindi film *Dil Wale Dulhaniyan Le Jayenge*, which premiered in 1995, set a record as the longest-running film in the history of Indian cinema due to the enthusiastic patronage of the repeat audience. According to some reports it was still playing at the Maratha Mandir theater in Bombay in 2011.[61] The presence of repeaters is seen as evidence of a film's success, and both distributors and exhibitors highlight the adoption of a film by the repeat audience. An e-mail advertisement from the distributors also plays up the presence of the repeat audience (see fig. 14).

A theater manager attributed the success of the Kannada film *A* (1998) to its having drawn more than the usual number of "repeaters." Apparently, the men who made up the majority audience for the film were returning to watch it ten, even twenty-five times. Ticket clerks and ushers believed that the violence in the film was drawing lower-class men and that this "mass" audience of uneducated men had difficulty following the film and so were coming back to watch it repeatedly—the film makes liberal use of flashbacks, "flash-forwards," "cutaway shots," and other such camera angles and representational styles. However, these attractions were not articulated in the informal conversational interviews I had with men at the theater. Roughly three weeks after the film's

FIGURE 14. "Super Star Rajini's ENDHIRAN / ROBO. Prices reduced to $11 and $7 due to enormous requests from REPEAT audience!" (Imoviecafe e-mail, dated Friday, October 15, 2010, 12:02 a.m.)

release, few moviegoers were first-time viewers. One youth exiting a matinee screening told me he had seen the movie three times already because it was "different," echoing the description of the film on the marquee behind him: "Different . . . different . . . different."

While fans are known to watch films of their stars multiple times, viewers of all classes and ages as well as both men and women are seen to engage in repeat viewing. An elderly Anglo-Indian lady in Bombay claimed she had seen *The Sound of Music* more than eighty times.[62] It is also unclear whether motivations for repeat viewing vary by the viewer's social class or whether narrative is equally important across class and educational background—a determination that is beyond the scope of this study. A middle-class professional in Bangalore posted on her social media page that she was buying ten tickets for *Inception* (2010) because she had been unable to figure it out the first time and so planned to watch it over and over again till she did.[63] Some admitted to seeing all films starring their favorite actor several times over. For fans, each encounter with the film allows enjoyment of a particular performance or "act." Hardgrave's observation of Tamil film fans supports this understanding of repeat viewing:

A fan of Tamil film legend M. G. R. said that he had seen an early M. G. R. film 31 times—an impressive record, but hardly rival to that of middle-aged Brahmin homeopath cum travel agent, who saw one devotional film 116 times. One young man, waiting to see *Nam Nadu*, for the third time, said he fully expected to see it 15 times. 'The first time I go for the star, the second time for the songs, the third time for the acting and then again and again for the fights."[64]

When a film remains in theaters for an extended period, or when it achieves the status of a superhit, repeaters outnumber "first timers," and their participation shapes collective experience. Seeing a film the second, third, or twenty-fifth time affords a vastly different involvement and emotional engagement.[65] Being familiar with the terrain of the film, repeat viewers are free to play. Not only do they talk back to the screen and sing along with the songs,[66] they loudly "predict" what will happen next and respond to each line of dialogue with dialogue they have memorized or that they make up on the spot. Repeaters and first-day audiences are consequently identified with a particular aesthetic and mood. A distributor anticipated the audience for a Friday evening screening of a popular Tamil film: "Tonight's 9:50 p.m. show will have the repeat crowd and the crowd who wants to celebrate." Viewers, too, are alert to repeaters in the audience and comment on the phenomenon when talking about their film experience, seeing it as evidence of the film's success.[67]

Repeat viewing is evidence of the centrality of social relations in making film experience meaningful. As discussed in chapter 5, people sometimes watch a film multiple times, as they attend with different groups of friends or family. Repeaters demonstrate, for example, that viewing clusters are not merely "interpretive communities";[68] they share emotional experiences and may even perform collectively in the theater, contributing to the celebratory mood. When narrating a movie outing with his group of twenty-five college friends, a student excitedly relived the experience of seeing a film he had seen at least once before: "we knew all the songs; in the theater about ten of us were singing the songs—*starting* to sing before the song came on. There would be excitement because we know the song is coming, we had seen the movie before. Even the catch line: we know he's gonna say it, some poetry right now, you basically are waiting to say it!"

*

Rather like soap-opera audiences, repeaters develop a relationship with characters. A newspaper article reviewing the hit film *Satya* (1998), about Bombay gangs, comments on the changed orientation of repeaters to the film.

In the first week of July, when the film was released and coincidentally underworld killings were at its peak, movie-goers emerged from theaters dazed, stunned, still trying to assimilate the cinematic experience. By the fourth week, the same people—what trade pundits call repeat audience—had established a camaraderie with the film's characters. In loud stage whispers, they informed one and all what was going to happen next, giggling delightedly each time another expletive was uttered.[69]

Familiarity with the film and its characters allows repeaters to experience the film as a social world in which they are one of the inhabitants. Their interactions and participation elaborate the film's mood and theme. A woman who had seen *Hum Aapke Hain Kaun (HAHK)*, a story about a Hindu joint-family wedding, six times, explained that she liked it "because it was like going to a family wedding."[70] In more general terms the cinema offers an experience much like a wedding celebration,[71] which has a known structure in which sociality is at the forefront. After *HAHK* had been in theaters for over a year, watching the film became an entirely social event. One viewer observed, "everyone who went to see it had seen it before. . . . People were passing coffee, talking, [they] knew when the songs in the film would come on and they would join in. There was continuous talking, like there was a marriage in the theater. People would say, (referring to the heroine's costume), 'that backless blouse is nice, I got one stitched like that.'"[72] Repeat viewing in this way allows audiences to elaborate the meaning and experience of the cinema event and to bring it into their lives. This may involve participating in the film's aesthetic. According to a news report, "Women in the city of Jaipur are known to have gone back to see *HAHK* in the clothes and jewelry they wore when they got married."[73] These examples suggest that moviegoing is as much about experiencing community and locating oneself in a social reality as it is about *escaping* a social reality, the latter frequently given as an explanation for why popular cinema with its song and dance, fantasy, and spectacle has such widespread appeal in India.

Repeat viewing is not a phenomenon one hears much about in the West. Richard Caves observes of (Western) audiences, "People—adults, anyhow—seldom read a book or view a movie twice."[74] Yet when I presented field data on repeaters to academic audiences in the United States, I was questioned about the movie *Titanic*, which is known to have drawn repeat viewers worldwide, many of whom were teenage girls, fans of Leonardo DiCaprio. However, films such as *Titanic* and *Star Wars* (1977), it may be argued, fall into a particular niche or subculture within the mainstream movie culture in the West.[75] *Star Wars*, for example, achieved cult status with legions of fans. Films that are either based on known events or on stories people are familiar with—popular novels, comic books, or long-running television shows—already have an engaged audience that watches with foreknowledge.[76] In this respect, they resemble the majority of commercial, formula-driven Indian films that draw on Indian mythology and folktales, even on past films, to present audiences with familiar stories and performances. In India, repeat viewing is a phenomenon that is fairly routine and cuts across social class, gender, even age. Engaging with a story that is familiar—such as the Hindu epics, the Ramayana or Mahabharata, or the many folktales and poems that are widely known in India—is something that Indians have been doing for generations. Practices of participatory and repeat spectating are very likely rooted in a tradition of spectatorship that has its origins in folk theater and traditional cultural performance.[77] These modes of viewing call for further research into cultural forms of spectatorship.

ANTICIPATORY VIEWING AND "LOOKING AHEAD"

In a general sense, anticipation and the need for foreknowledge shape film experience. Trailers tap into and fuel this anticipation. However, how much should be known about a film before one actually watches it varies between audiences and different cinema cultures. Anticipation for popular Indian films that present audiences with known storylines, with favorite stars in familiar roles, may not have the same taboos against plot "spoilers." The formula films provide the pleasures of engaging with a familiar world. Habitués watch by anticipating outcomes, a way of following along by "looking ahead"—an aesthetic they apply to Bollywood as well as to Hollywood films. Halfway through Bollywood's *Hameshaa* (1997), a young man who had been predicting the outcome of various scenes remarked to a member of his group, "I knew what would happen as soon as the film started; there have been no surprises." When in *Zor* a character is sent to prison, a viewer loudly predicts, "They've put him away for good." During *Air Force One*, I overheard a viewer say to another, "You thought he would jump off the plane? I knew he was still there!" Even children are socialized into this viewing aesthetic, where they anticipate the playing out of the formula. Foreseeing a failed romance between the character played by her favorite hero, Hritik Roshan, and his love interest, an eight-year old stood on her seat and jumped up and down, "I know he won't marry her; he'll marry the other girl" (field notes, Bangalore, 2007). Anticipatory responses arising from familiarity with the formula film may intentionally ironize it. When watching *Hameshaa*, Priya, my viewing companion, rolled her eyes and sighed, "now there'll be a song." The scene was in a "hunting lodge" at night, where the hero and heroine were taking refuge from being chased by the villain. Priya went on to explain that all the ingredients were there: "ladka, ladki, aur fire [boy, girl, and fire]."As per her prediction, the scene morphed into a romantic song-and-dance sequence.

For repeaters, the removal of all unknowns facilitates anticipatory viewing in an extreme sense. Repeaters mouth dialogue before it is spoken by characters. They "predict" what characters will say, willing them to say or "repeat" what the viewer has articulated. Predicting involves movement, and "looking ahead" allows viewers to move ahead, to set the pace in anticipation of the film's unfolding. Repeaters applaud and cheer moments before an event on-screen. They provide sound effects that preview the scene for others and that make sense to first timers only after a scene has shifted, for example, making a sound ("Zoop!") of a gun (with a silencer) being fired before it actually is. Anticipatory viewing is therefore yet another expression of the play spirit, where a viewer demonstrates that he or she has seen through the strategy of the filmmaker and therefore has won the game.[78] Anticipations and predictions therefore can also be a performance for the group; repeaters demonstrate that they are ahead of the "game" (of viewing) and other viewers, and that they have anticipated filmmakers' intentions, rendering them transparent. Yet there is no consensus that they are spoiling the film experience for others.

Habitués at times "look ahead" to the point where they move outside the frame of the film. Looking ahead to the intermission, viewers are sometimes impervious to preintermission scenes of crisis and melodrama, even violence. During a violent scene in *Indian* (1996), an audience member, anticipating the interval as he would the halftime break at a sports event, announced companionably to his group, "It's getting on for halftime. I'm feeling hungry. I'll have a samosa; what'll you have?"

REMAKING THE FILM AND ITS EXPERIENCE

Audiences' overt engagement makes visible the collaborative "finishing" or reworking of the film in the theater. Moviegoers are seen to craft entertainment out of the "raw material" of the film.[79] Embodied practices such as singing or humming along with the songs and providing "sound effects" to accompany visuals allow audiences to move closer to the film and to amplify its "effects." Audiences, for example, make the sound of a train to accompany images of a train on-screen; fight scenes prompt sounds of punches, groans, and gunshots from the auditorium.[80] Such vocal participation allows habitués to inhabit a scene: in *Kurubana Raani*, when a character bumps into another, a viewer "entering the scene" responds with "Idiot! Look where you're going!" Habitués repeat the hero's or the villain's lines after watching the film more than once, each occasion becoming an opportunity to "learn one's lines" as they take on the roles of various characters. While watching *Air Force One*, during a banquet scene, a young man who was clearly a "repeater" applauded along with the banquet guests; anticipating the dialogue he loudly declaimed,

"Ladies and gentlemen!" which was then "echoed" by the character in the film giving a speech. When the speech ended with, "we will no longer tolerate it! We will no longer be afraid!" he shouted "Bravo!" then clapped, following the applause on-screen. In this case participation allowed the viewer to become part of the scene and a member of the audience *in* the film.

Audiences improvise and "write" new dialogue for characters and shout out their version. The film *Bombay* presents a familiar Hindi movie plot of a romance that transcends differences in sociocultural background. The hero, a Hindu, after overcoming multiple obstacles, finally manages to come face-to-face with the heroine, a young Muslim girl. As the two gaze at one another, the scene builds to an emotional pitch. Two young men chose to comment on the melodramatic quality, overstatement of tension, and lack of subtlety in the scene by chanting coquettishly "yes," "no," "yes," "no," in turns till the tension was broken by a shift in scene. Other viewers laughed at this byplay. Later in the film the hero's father, an orthodox Hindu, now estranged from his son, visits him and his family in Bombay. He knocks on the door, his uncertainty and anxiety evident, as he has not seen his son in years. The door opens and he announces, "I have come." At this instant a middle-class viewer in his twenties or thirties, the same age as the son, shouts, "Why have you?" followed by "Go home!"[81] The remark is followed by (supportive) laughter from audience members and scattered applause. In such cases, apart from introducing spontaneity and unpredictability, commentary by viewers shapes collective experience by providing an alternate thread of (audience-generated) meaning, a rescripting of the film, and a way to experience it that was not intended by the filmmakers. "Passing comments" and "dropping remarks" may transform lowbrow melodrama into comedy and satire. The Bollywood film *Hameshaa* had a scene where the hero threatens to jump off a precipice when he learns the heroine will not return his affections; this prompted viewers— who did not like the star playing the hero and had criticized him for being a "lousy dancer"—to shout scornfully, "Kood ja! Kood Ja!" (Jump! Jump!), again drawing laughter from fellow viewers.[82] Viewers may assume the role of the director and "instruct" actors. During a fight scene in *Kurubana Raani* when the villain shows signs of trouncing the hero, there are shouts of encouragement and instructions: "now thrash him," "hit him nicely!" In another scene where the heroine is playing the role of a movie star shooting a scene in the rain, she catches cold and sneezes—an audience member immediately shouts "Pack up! Pack up!" "becoming" the character of the director in the film within a film. Here, the audience member not only becomes part of the scene but seems to command it.

Audiences even edit the film in the theater, their practices recalling an era of prenarrative cinema when film entertainment was crafted in the theater by exhibitors who at the time were closer to producers.[83] Besides embodied practices such as walking in and out of the theater, the film is also edited when adults "censor" scenes for children by instructing them, "Now close your eyes!" or when they place their own hands over the children's eyes or ears. Taking over the role of editor and exhibitor, audiences may demand favorite parts of the film be shown repeatedly. During a screening of *Hum* (1991), audience members created a commotion and demanded that the popular song "Jhooma Chumma de de" be shown repeatedly. Theater officials were made to rewind and replay the song multiple times until moviegoers were satisfied. Audience control over exhibition in this way happens more often than might be imagined. Fans pressure theater staff to "repeat" certain parts of the film and which reshape the flow of the film.[84] A moviegoer reports that audiences watching a Tamil film starring Rajinikanth appreciate the "classic Rajni entry songs that are common to all his films . . . they even ensure that it is repeated."[85] Another moviegoer writes in an online forum that while watching *Mungaru Male*, the "crowd went berserk for 'Anisuthide Yaako Indu' songs. Many were cheering 'once more,' 'once more' for this soul stirring song."[86] Bored with a film, people may "instruct" the exhibitor (or director) by shouting out, "comedy hakruppa!" (bring on some comedy).[87] Using laser pointers, viewers reach out and "touch" images, projecting their gaze while literally highlighting the visuals on-screen.[88] Fans watching *Kurubana Raani* directed laser lights on the hero's and heroine's faces and on the heroine's bare midriff, which allowed them to effectively highlight and eroticize the images, revealing where their gaze lay and directing the gaze of others.

There appear to be few aspects of "producing" film entertainment that moviegoers do not engage in. They even manage props and sound effects. At a theater in Majestic I watched a man in the front stalls helpfully throw what looked like a knife "to the hero" (at the screen) when the latter was disarmed by the villain in a fight. When the hero against all odds wins the heroine's affections or gets married, audiences, in addition to throwing flowers and coins at the screen, blow conches and ring bells as if at a real wedding. At one screening a group of women college students had brought plastic whistles with them to greet the hero's arrival on-screen. Audiences ring bells and blow horns to participate in scenes of ritual worship on-screen. They are known to perform *arathi*[89] in front of the screen and light incense in a ritual worship of the star. "Confetti" is manufactured in the theater by tearing up rupee notes and lottery tickets, which audience members throw at the screen or in the air. An electrical outage at the Sangam theater near the bus stand provided an opportunity for audiences to take charge of the screen and the entertainment. The film being screened was *Titanic*, and there had been problems with the sound from the start, which drew shouts of "Sound! Sound!" from the restive audience. Suddenly the theater was plunged into darkness, not an unusual occurrence in Bangalore. Amid irate shouts of "refund!" and "lights!," hooting and more whistles, a few enterprising young men entertained themselves and the collectivity by "chasing" each other across the darkened screen with the laser lights they had brought along, generating laughs as they brought the "show" into the theater. The film resumed, censored scenes drawing loud protest, following which the men trained the red pinpoints of light on the heroine's face and breasts, adding lewd commentary to an otherwise tame film, and seeking to perhaps compensate for the removal of risqué scenes.

These are just some of the ways audiences appropriate the film, transform emotional and collective experience in the theater, and introduce "improvisational participatory performance."[90] In the process they destabilize and rework the film.[91] During tension-filled moments in *Air Force One*, such as when Harrison Ford's character is hiding in the aircraft a few feet away from a terrorist guard, viewers whistled piercingly and made popping sounds. In a scene where gunmen appear to have cornered the president of the United States, a viewer shouts "Meeooww!" Those seated nearby laugh. At another tense moment in the film, a young man lets out an exaggerated yawn "Hooooaaahh!"—again drawing laughter. Such interactions reveal a fight over the film and the audience in the theater, a contest over who controls the experience.

Filmgoers register their dissatisfaction with the film instantly and vocally. They may attempt to take charge of viewing conditions in the theater with shouts of "Volume! Volume!" "Focus!" or "Lights!" A certain section of the audience does not hesitate to exact revenge for a film that falls short of expectations or for theater conditions that fail to satisfy; male viewers who anticipate risqué scenes based on rumor or advertising and instead find scenes have been censored, may slash the upholstery with razor blades and knives or even trash the entire theater in protest.[92] The thrill of vandalism taps into the carnivalesque, adding to other transgressive pleasures of the movie event.

AUDIENCES' PROBLEM OF SHARED UNDERSTANDING AND EXPERIENCE

Given the differential appeal of multigenre films and the varied responses of heterogeneous audiences, shared experience of a film can be elusive. This may sound contradictory given that Bombay cinema has produced a shared culture that is not only national but increasingly global and that incorporates active engagement. However, in stratified theaters in which audiences engage with the film and its "attractions" based on differing worldviews and lifeworlds, commercial films that seek a broad audience, rather than homogenizing viewers have the effect of articulating difference. A scene that one viewer experiences as profoundly moving may appear exaggerated or ludicrous to another.[93] The volubility of the audience can itself be a distraction and an obstacle to achieving shared experience. A remark that draws a family member or friend closer may also reveal differences between strangers who find their views are not shared. Watching *Khamoshi*, viewers who were critical of what they saw as the film's clumsy portrayal of a family where both parents were hearing impaired overheard others commenting on how "touching" the film was. Differing perspectives can arise within families and can be especially jarring. After watching *Titanic*, members of a family group standing in the cinema car park waiting for the crowd to disperse discussed the film. One asked another what the "moral" of the "story" was. A young woman said in a satisfied tone, "First love is the best." Her brother quipped, "Always travel First Class!" His joke was greeted with laughter and "Oh you're so cynical!"

Audiences reveal some of the complexities of intersubjective experience of the film where in the darkened cinema people are "open" to interactions with strangers. Moviegoers "drop remarks" initiating oblique interaction,[94] using the film as a resource or a foil. Men repeat provocative lines of dialogue, which allows them not only to remark on the scene but to make suggestive comments to women seated nearby. Those who are moved by a film may experience anger and irritation with others who remain skeptically aloof. A university student reported being amused by the clichéd and melodramatic portrayal of womanly devotion in a Telugu-language film where the heroine, a nurse in love with the hero, a surgeon, assists him when he has to carry out surgery by candlelight. The heroine shields the flame with her bare hands, which become blistered as the operation proceeds, but she staunchly carries on. Those who laughed at the scene faced the disapproval of others; one woman turned around in her seat and admonished them: "Have you no pity?"

Aesthetic conflict, a reflection of divergent sensibilities and tastes, then, is part of in-theater experience. "Taste wars" erupt as groups seek to appropriate or hijack the film for that instant and win over fellow viewers to their interpretation and sensibilities. People may actively use engagement with the film to underscore the differences between themselves and others. Conflicts also emerge from moviegoers' desires to drive home to others that they are not "taken" or "done" by what to them is overwrought emotionality or an unconvincing scene.[95] They may use scenes to taunt fellow moviegoers: watching *Khamoshi* in Bangalore, two men in the audience pretended to weep in imitation of a woman who sobbed audibly during an "emotional" scene, leading those witnessing the interaction to laugh.

The film can therefore stand in the way of shared experience and can even erode social relationships.[96] Anthony described an embarrassing experience when he took his coworkers to a movie starring his idol, Shahrukh Khan. As Anthony tells the story, his colleagues did not like the film and proceeded to "tease" him about it, making him vow "never" to go with them to a movie again.

> They somehow didn't like it; they kept telling me "what a stupid movie you've brought us for." I felt so embarrassed. I told them, "next time never again ask me to take you for a movie!" Laughing with embarrassment, he recollected the incident: "Really, I took them for such a nice movie because I really like Shah Rukh Khan a lot. And I couldn't find anything upsetting in that. I was really feeling very bad when they told me what a stupid movie it was." . . . Even now they keep telling me. And I told them next time they ask me to take you for a movie, I'll never take them! (Field notes, 1998)

Why should multiple and divergent perspectives and ways of engaging with a film become provocative? After all, audiences are engaging with a fictional world. One explanation is that as viewers use their experiences of everyday life and their biographies to both make sense of the film and make it personally relevant, divergent understandings and responses reveal the difficulty of achieving intersubjective understanding in everyday life, which can lead one to appreciate why romantic couples involved with one another may ignore the film.[97] The play element, in which "sustaining a mood" is important, suggests another explanation. The "play mood" is "labile," and the shifting, multiple, and interrealities of play create volatility.[98] Play knows no boundaries; it can destroy itself;[99] multiple and divergent perspectives may lead to "a collapse of the play spirit, a sobering, a disenchantment."[100] This might explain why viewers sometimes find others' comments and reactions at odds with their own to be not only provocative but disturbing, as within the play world, "the spoilsport shatters civilization itself. . . . Therefore he must be cast out for he threatens the existence of the play community."[101]

Attempts to homogenize differences in viewing aesthetics may lead to confrontation; for instance, when a section of the audience attempts to police or educate fellow viewers on proper viewing etiquette. In theaters in India and in Canada (Toronto), audience members are reported to have stood to attention when the Indian national anthem played during the last scene of the film *1942, A Love Story* (1994), while those who remained seated were chastised and made to stand. Requests are heard to "please stop talking," or simply "Ssssh!" Restless viewers are instructed to "just sit down!" (*sumne koothkoli*). These attempts to shape the gathering into an audience can have the unintended consequence of fueling further confrontation, as irrepressible fellow viewers may refuse to be quelled, and yell "SSHhhhh!" in response, laugh loudly, or drop snide remarks, thus seizing the opportunity for repartee and play. In this way aesthetic conflict adds to the spectacle and entertainment, grounding reception in the local context.[102]

Moviegoers also differ in terms of whether they participate or elicit participation and in the type of participation they consider desirable and appropriate. Those who enjoy a boisterous and exuberant atmosphere whistle loudly and applaud, partly to encourage fellow viewers to join in the din. In an online forum, a moviegoer writes that his experience "sucked" because "most people in the theater were family types and me and my friend Prashanth were the only ones whistling and clapping for every one of Rajini's killer dialogs."[103] At the same time, middle-class attendees recounted incidents where the raucous audience had ruined their experience. A woman complained about "rowdies" and "catcalls" at a theater when she sat in the lower level.[104] Another was disgusted by the "kissing sounds" made by men in response to on-screen romance, which she found "so obnoxious and cheap!"[105] What is play for one section of the audience can prove a revolting and sadistic display to another;[106] in theaters screening *Bandit Queen* (1994), some men are reported to have cheered scenes of a gang rape, "with the whistles and foot stamping with which they applaud sexy dance sequences," leading middle-class women to hastily exit the theater.[107] In these settings, achieving a shared or "common perspective" or experience is an accomplishment.[108] Through repeated attendance at multiple screenings, I identified audience practices that sought to build a common perspective within their viewing clusters, starting with the construction of the movie outing as a social event (as discussed in chap. 5). Here, people do not rely on the film to provide shared experience; they do interactional "work" to accomplish it.

Viewers feel free to voice their confusion with a scene or ask for clarification. People translate the film's dialogue for companions with a different linguistic background. When watching the Hindi film *Chachi 420* (1998) from the lower stalls in Majestic, I sat next to two young boys, barefoot urchins in baggy shorts, who were there by themselves. They talked and laughed loudly, moving around excitedly in their seats throughout the film. During the interval the older boy explained various scenes to his younger companion, who appeared to be confused by the scene shifts and the relationship between the characters. The challenge for moviegoers, then, is to determine whether they "see the same thing."[109] People direct the attention of members of their group (or even strangers seated near enough to overhear) by making comments that could be described as "pointing talk," which coordinates "joint looking."[110]

Common perspectives on the film arise from emotional (and embodied) shared response to the film. Comedic scenes evoke explosive laughter. People rock back and forth in their seats. They look at one another rather than at the screen.[111] Helpless with laughter, they lean toward one another or *on* one another. Enjoying the joke, men slap each other on the shoulder, back, or leg, using their bodies to bridge any gap between them. Even strangers become a resource for constructing shared experience of the film. Anthropologist Freddy Bailey remembered a stranger seated next to him, slapping his (Freddy's) thigh as he convulsed with laughter when the hero made a witty remark.[112] Another moviegoer said that during a tense fight scene, he found his arm gripped by the man in the next seat.

By letting others know where they are, emotionally and experientially, audience members ensure that a gap in experience does not develop between themselves and their viewing companions. Crying in the theater may be a more private or hidden experience than laughing is. However, some moviegoers sob audibly while others talk about tearing up. While watching the Kannada film *Megha Bantu Megha*, during a scene when it becomes clear that the hero and heroine's love is doomed, a woman seated next to me sighed heavily and remarked, "So sad! So disappointing!" Her friend nodded and sighed, expressing her dismay, "Tch Tch Tch!" A pivotal scene in the film has the hero locked in a room with a young girl who is betrothed to another man, but the incident throws doubt on her character, and he is compelled to marry her to save their reputations. At intermission my viewing companion for the film, Sujaya, distressed at the turn of events, expressed herself in local idiom: "I'm feeling so sad, why should they mistake [misunderstand]. Always they mistake! When they know each other so well, why should they mistake? Because they saw them in one room! You know there is a saying in Kannada, 'If you drink buttermilk under *echala mara* [a toddy palm] people won't believe it's buttermilk' [they will assume you are a drunkard]."

Audiences expand the frame for shared experience beyond the film's story. Applying a documentary aesthetic, people provide "background knowledge" to their viewing companions. They are overheard situating a scene for friends: "This is Russia" or "This is the Malnad region."[113] Supplying background knowledge is not about interpreting film content and narrative alone; rather, moviegoers attempt to ensure that their viewing companions are familiar with the "local social world" [114] of the film, which situates the viewing experience. Even if people understand the story, their viewing companions may feel they need to give additional context and resources toward a common perspective. Repeaters are well positioned to guide first timers through the film, provide them with a 'map' of the film's highlights, and 'show them the sights.' They exchange information about the film, its making, the number of days the film has been in theaters, or the star's rumored remuneration.

Gossip about the stars and the film industry provides shared experience for habitués. A dramatic scene in *Kurubana Raani*, where the heroine has taken an overdose of sleeping tablets, prompted a woman to give her viewing companion information about the actress: "Nagma is a Muslim; Hindi film heroine who didn't make it in Hindi film." My movie companions felt they needed to ensure that I, a novice, had the necessary background to appreciate what I was seeing. A young woman who had already seen *Mungaru Male* twice proceeded to tell me about the star, Ganesh: "you know his father is from Nepal? He was a *gurkha*." Another moviegoer informed me that it was the first Kannada film to "run continuously for 180 days!" During the interval of the Kannada film *America! America!*, my viewing companion leaned over and provided me with "relevant" background: "Ramesh is old [established] star, Hema [heroine] is new, so is Akshaye [second hero]. But now, I think they will come [act in more movies]. This movie was made one year ago. It was very costly." Given the broader sociality that frames film viewing, interactions that "explain" scenes or that sort out characters are as much a means to connect with one's viewing companions as they are attempts to follow the film.

An extension of "seeing what I am seeing" is "scanning," or looking around to see what others are seeing (or hearing). Glancing at one another and seeing that a viewing companion is enjoying a scene or realizing that one's perspective is shared by the group increases enjoyment. Conscious of the reactions of fellow audience members that reinforced his own experience, a college student said he liked *Titanic* because "It was so real! When they show the water in the movie, all the kids [seated nearby] jumped out of their seats! . . . They went, "unnnnhhhh!" and went back in their seats [he makes a movement as if he is falling backward]. The water looks as if it is going to fall on you. It was so real!" Our conversation was overheard by another member of the group who said she had heard people questioning the special effects in the row behind her: "People behind me were saying, 'Oh, they're just swimming in a swimming pool.' All sorts of things they were saying. You didn't hear?" "Scanning" the audience can aid in building a shared perspective even if what is shared is a contagious enjoyment and not necessarily a shared understanding or appreciation of a scene. In an online forum for the Kannada film *Bellary Naaga* (2009), starring Vishnuvardhan, a moviegoer remarks, "There were 3 ppl [people] siting in front of me . . . who were all *pukka vishnu abhimani's* [diehard fans of Vishnuvardhan] for the first 10 minutes [of the film] they started enjoying the getup and style."[115]

The beginning and ending of a film may be thought of as transitional or liminal times when audiences move in and out of engagement with it. The instability of beginnings and endings also rests on audience activities that remake both. In keeping with the "in process" nature of works of art, where "things might not stop at the ending,"[116] film experience continues to be constructed after moviegoers leave the theater. On the way home after watching a film, audiences interactively and retrospectively (though not self-consciously) reconstruct shared experience. After watching *Titanic*, members of a family group asked one another whether anyone had cried during the movie. A woman in her twenties said emphatically, "*Of course* I cried! Towards the end. Even now, I'm just holding it! I'll go home and cry on my pillow!" Another viewer commented on a humorous scene: "How we laughed when he said that! We couldn't control ourselves!" Habitués look back on the film, repeat jokes and dialogue, sing and hum the songs, and share their thoughts and reactions to particular scenes. After watching *Kurubana Raani*, urbanites shared a laugh at the lack of sophistication of dialogues based on a rural dialect, "'Bandli'! Aay-yoh!" In the film the hero's mother calls him "koosey" ("child" or "infant"), which is intended to be comic: he is a hulking man in his twenties, though with a childlike air.[117] This group of viewers decided it was too "silly" to be taken seriously even as they proceeded to appropriate the term into their lived experience. One remarked, "Oh, I got so fed up with her saying 'Koosey, koosey,' that too for that Lump!" Another, gesturing toward her teenage son, sitting in the front seat of the car responded, "This is MY koosey! Even if he is a lump!" Her remark was greeted with loud laughter. Moviegoers can in these ways reconnect with the group, resolve differences in perspectives, and perhaps achieve reinforcement of their experience.

"MAGICIANS OF TEARS AND LAUGHTER"

Audience practices and reception aesthetics reveal there is more to film viewing than engaging with a story with a beginning and end that is constructed by filmmakers, an assumption that has shaped the study of narrative cinema and its reception. In cinema halls the film on celluloid provides only part of the entertainment; audiences and their doings actively shape mood and collective experience in the theater, making them the "magicians of tears and laughter."[118]

The notion of artworks forever evolving or play that is ongoing or "unfinishable" and transformative[119] is useful in thinking about what happens when a film is screened. Rather than "receiving" a "finished product," audiences participate in "film in process," making cinemas "cottage industries"[120] where film is remade and transformed through interaction.[121] As collaborators, or "partners"[122] in the entertainment, moviegoers overcome the status of being a distant and passive viewer while illuminating the artificiality of the distinctions between widely held notions of "production" and "consumption."[123]

Play and performance provide overarching frames for reception. For example, when women dress up in their wedding saris and jewelry to watch *Hum Aapke Hain Kaun* in the theater, it may be seen to be an expression of festive play.[124] In keeping with the play spirit, audiences experience film through multiple and shifting frames.[125] Play involves movement and fluidity; it is unbounded and unconstrained and introduces surprises.[126] A Bollywood film that addressed terrorism and was praised by critics for its serious themes nevertheless provided the thrills of a circus sideshow. In the theater, playful viewers amused themselves by looking for glimpses of the star's misshapen thumb whenever a scene showed his hands: "There! Can you see it?"

Movement can be argued to be central to the play spirit and to performance and its multiple realities. It remakes the film, subverts its meaning and its intended effects, and even upturns the social organization of the cinema hall and therefore the intended delivery of film experience. As "travelers"[127] or wanderers, habitués move freely in and out of the theater and among the roles of spectator, filmmaker, character, playback singer, and critic as well as different "frames"—of story, spectacle, performance, and social event. Film experience continues to be recast after the screening when audiences discuss it with fellow moviegoers; repeat viewing may be seen as yet another opportunity to recast the film experience, all of which forms of engagement lead to the question, when does a film end?[128]

As with performance, the immediate and local context cannot be ignored. Theater experience routinely dominates "film experience," which in Anglo-American contexts is typically associated with the bygone eras of the nickelodeon and the picture palace.[129] Humorists in Bangalore's cinema halls become performers or narrators who make the film relevant to the viewing context. Indeed, audiences opt for local entertainment as they seek out particular theaters for the audiences that are known to frequent these sites and the "atmosphere." Practices such as scanning, ambulatory viewing or browsing, "dropping remarks," and so on that elaborate film in context may also be rooted in a public culture of performance and spectacle that links cinema experience to precinematic entertainment and its social experience with overtones of the market or fairground.[130] Exhibitors localize film entertainment by contributing to the "show" either intentionally, as when special effects are located in the theater or by regulating the time for intermission, or unintentionally by introducing variability and unpredictability through electricity shutdowns and disruptions involving technical problems with projection. The use of local cultural metaphors for film experience—likening it to going to a wedding or comparing it to eating a *thali* meal[131]—call for a new vocabulary for understanding film and its reception, one that moves beyond the rapt viewing, "reading," or "interiorizing" of the story that has grown around the Western experience and has limited applicability and relevance here. The identification of audience practices in this chapter seeks to contribute to this effort.

The reception aesthetics of Indian audiences may be rooted in an expressive culture of performance of religious epics, dance drama, and folk theater, where the performance context and its sensualities shape enjoyment. Various types of folk theater, such as *Tamasha*, *Bhavai*, and *Nautanki*, "cater to large audiences . . . are secular and full of fun and noise. Staged in the village square, they are frequently interrupted by whistles and catcalls from spectators."[132] Open-air enactments of the *Ram Lila*, for example, incorporate song, dance, and skits and last several days in some locations. Annual dance-drama performances of *Ram Lila* and *Rasa Lila* theater, which present audiences with stories they have known from childhood, are improvisational and locally situated and are constructed for participatory spectating. The lines between performance and spectators are often blurred. Audiences join in and "clap in time with the music"; they also respond at given points when their participation is solicited. In the *Rasa Lila*, the leader of the performing troupe shouts a slogan, "Radhaiaiai!" and the audience answers, "Shyam!"[133]

The noted commonalities in reception experiences and aesthetics with audiences in other times and places and the shared aesthetics of spectatorship that bridge film, live theater, and performance call for further study of spectatorship that explores the interconnections between theater forms, cultural performance, and contemporary cinema.

CHAPTER 7

"First Day, First Show":
A Paroxysm of Cinema

Even today if Rajanna's[1] film comes to a theater, say Santosh, I'll go there and I HAVE
to see the first show! The Morning Show I have to see! I HAVE to see it! I don't mind
buying in black.

AUTORICKSHAW DRIVER AND KANNADA FILM FAN,
BANGALORE (TRANSLATED FROM KANNADA)

The "First Day, First Show" (also referred to as FDFS in the era of text messaging
and blogs) is a special event. For the new film of a well-known star or director, a
big-budget film long-awaited by fans and ushered into theaters with a great deal
of fanfare or controversy, theaters are packed. Crowds and long lines outside
theaters announce a new release. Seats are frequently oversold; inside, people
may be camped out in the aisles or watch the film standing in the doorways.
Theaters hosting new releases, many of which are either next door or around
the corner from one another in the localities of K. G. Road and Gandhinagar,
are decorated with garlands of marigold and roses, fragrant tuberose and jasmine, tinsel, pennants, and lights. Neighboring buildings, even nearby trees,
may sport posters and streamers. Similar to the Ram Lila festival, where effigies
of gods and demons look down on devotees and their world, colorful cardboard
and plywood "cutouts" of the stars in costume loom fifty to seventy feet above
the theater. Together with the brightly colored posters, billboards, or "hoardings" that announce the film, they bring the dreamworld of cinema onto the
street. A Kannada producer, referring to the phenomenon as a "craze," told me
that in the past, cutouts of Dr. Rajkumar up to 150 feet tall had been erected.

*

Film in its festival avatar is elaborated with processions, bands, and fireworks.
Similar celebrations attend certain milestones in a film's career, such as the fif-

tieth or hundredth day of continuous screening. As with festivals, a heightened emotion and sensory experience is associated with the new release.[2] A fan described going to a newly released Rajinikanth movie as being "part of a festival. The mood in the theaters is electric and the fans are at their emotive best."[3]

Of cinema in Egypt, Walter Armbrust notes, "the theater district always had a touch of the carnivalesque."[4] He describes a "liminoid territory out of the grasp of institutions," where social norms are relaxed to some degree and where people engage in "experimental behavior," a "temporary liberation from . . . the established order."[5] The thrills of the new release have much to do with the carnival aesthetic. First-day screenings in Bangalore, especially of regional and Kannada cinema, attract boisterous fans, the "mass" audience (mostly men), school and college students, and *cinema paithyam* (lunatics), known for their obsessive interest in films. These enthusiasts delight in the crowds and commotion. An autorickshaw driver described going to see a film soon after it was released as *tamasha* (fun); another autorickshaw driver and Kannada film fan became nostalgic about the atmosphere that surrounded the release of new films in the 1970s and 1980s, a period of heightened fan activity by all accounts: "Avattu full galata!" (those days were crazy), "channage ittu!" (it was fantastic). Colloquially, *tamasha* refers to "fun" and "play," while *galata* carries meanings of commotion, danger, and fluidity.[6] Both speak to the aesthetic of excess, frenzied excitement, disorder, and even mayhem that attend the release of popular films.

This chapter selectively maps the new release as a distinct form of the "cinemascape,"[7] where cinema, its reception, is shaped by an indigenous culture and local aesthetic. At this stage in its "career," film is "in transition," moving from one set of social relations and spaces (of production) to another—a complex and hybrid form with elements of festival, performance, and the experimentation and volatility of carnival. The new-release events examined here are typically associated with regional-language films of popular stars that have fan followings—this is nonelite cinema characterized by spectacle. The chapter concludes with descriptions of the in-theater experience at two newly released Kannada films.

THE MOOD OF THE NEW RELEASE

Habitués judge a new release by its "House Full" status and the crowds it attracts rather than by the film alone. Crowds, "House Full," and "Sold Out" theaters are seen as indicators of the popularity of the star and of a successful "launch." A filmgoer and enthusiast disagreed with a glowing review for

FIGURE 15. Excited fans mob the star on arrival at the theater. Photograph by Navroze Contractor, Bangalore, 2015.

the Kannada film *Pancharangi* (2010) based on the evidence of a half-empty theater: "I think this idiot has not seen the movie . . . the theater was filled by only 40% of audience."[8] The *visibility* of crowds and the sensory experience of the "massing of people" shapes the highly charged atmosphere associated with a film's successful debut. Like other events where masses of people take over public space, the new release is "vortexed, whirling, full of shifting ups and downs, multi-focused events generating tensions."[9] Crowds further the sense of the "unexpected" associated with the new release, imparting a sense of "giddiness."[10] One news report, for example, described the Kannada film *Super* (2010) as "a huge crowd-puller" and noted the "craze" for the movie on the first day of its release with "followers of the star going bonkers."[11] Crowds facilitate carnivalesque thrills and transgressions. Pickpockets and "eve teasers" avail themselves of the opportunities provided by the crowds, as do footpath vendors.

Fan activities and enthusiasm shape the mood and the aesthetic of newly released regional films. Fans are seen to contest order and authority, to be "crazy," "rowdy," and generally unmanageable (fig. 15).[12] Robert Hardgrave notes of fans of Tamil star and icon M. G. Ramachandran that their " enthusiasm . . . in itself often approaches pandemonium. . . . Stampedes occur when gates are opened and people die."[13] Passions fueled by ticket shortages have damaged theater property and nearby stores as fans stone storefronts, even passing buses.[14] A producer told me about fan hysteria in the 1970s and 1980s, when fans, desperate to see a first-day screening of a film starring Dr. Rajku-mar, used the hundred-foot tall cutouts of the star to voice their protest: "the police would be there, and if people didn't get tickets, they would go up and *jump*!" Fans, producers, theater managers, and Kannada stars all recollected similar incidents.

Word of mouth, public discussion and anticipation contribute to building up the fervor for a new film. By highlighting the "upbeat" mood at theaters,[15] newspaper reports heighten the scale of the event and its volatility even as they participate in the word-of-mouth culture. Thus, reports of a new release often highlight "crowds," "mobs," "rush," "rowdies," "mania," "hysteria," and "frenzy," which all form part of the vocabulary of the new release. For the release of *Endhiran*, a headline read, "Endhiran mania . . . has gripped the whole of India."[16] An aesthetic of excess even shapes the reporting of atten-dance, ticket prices, and sales. News that "tens of thousands . . . mobbed movie theatres for tickets,"[17] "About 60,000 people are expected to watch the movie in Chennai city alone everyday," tickets are sold out for fifteen days straight, or across the state of Tamil Nadu ticket bookings for the film *Sivaji* began at 6 a.m. and queues were "longer than visa queues before the US consulate"[18] transforms even the mundanities of ticket purchase into spectacle. Film reels arriving at the theater in procession and on elephants or in horse-drawn car-riages[19] and fans breaking coconuts or bursting firecrackers at exhibition sites are fodder for news stories and gossip.

References to volatility and disorder may be seen as evidence of film's fluid-ity and the contagion that is part of the new-release phenomenon. *Galata* may spread outward from the focal point of the theater to the streets and even to other parts of the city or to screenings in different parts of the country. A pro-ducer in Bangalore described how, during one of these instances of fan frenzy at a "Rajkumar film," the star's sons—themselves major stars in the Kannada film world—were picked up and carried off into the crowd on fans' shoulders. The perception that new releases are potential trouble spots is consequently widespread. One moviegoer, when asked about the "first show," remembered a newspaper report on scaffolding falling from the cutouts outside theaters, which injured viewers and passersby. At the first-day screening of a Kannada film, a distributor prevented a female friend and me from going to the lower stalls, where we could hear fans shouting slogans and whistling. As he directed us to the balcony, which he said would be "calm" (in English), he warned us (in Kannada), "Be careful! These people you can't say what they will do. They may snatch the video camera or do something. They see you are young girls."

New releases are frequently associated with clashes between the police and fans. Newspapers report lathi (cane) charges outside theaters. Called in to deal with crowds, police at times even patrol inside cinema halls.[20] The mood is labile. On his recent experience of watching *Mungaru Male*, a blogger writes, "the most shocking thing was awaiting us when we came out of the theatre. A mini riot took place inside the theatre campus . . . the crowd was increasingly growing impatient with the nonavailability of the black (market) tickets. Police had to arrive on the scene to bring the crowd under control."[21] A news report described a brawl and shooting at the first-day screening of the Bollywood film *Jeet* that started as a row over tickets. The theater was reported to be under siege for over four hours until the police stepped in.[22] While such extreme outcomes are infrequent, the stories, reports, and rumors become part of the public narrative of the new release, which frames its experience.

*

First-day screenings, then, are memorable events. One afternoon over tiffin at the home of one of the families I accompanied to the cinema several times, the talk turned to movies currently in theaters. While my interest certainly acted as a catalyst for these conversations, habitués needed little encouragement, and talk would often drift toward films. That afternoon I asked whether anyone was interested in going to see *Titanic*, which was being screened at the Galaxy and Sangam theaters, which prompted an animated recollection of a first-day outing at the Sangam twenty-five years ago to see a film starring the Hindi-film star Vyjayanthimala.

The new release carries different meanings for different sections of the audience. One eighteen-year-old said attending a "first show" gave him the sense of being a pioneer: "There's something about seeing a movie the first day. It's style! You know you're the first to see *Titanic* in Bangalore." Highly anticipated films, those starring Indian cinema's superstars, draw audiences keen for the experience. Fans see attendance at the new release as a tribute to the star and may revel in the adrenalin rush of crowds and clashes with theater staff and the police. For the "class" audience, women and families, the same crowds are a deterrent. Hence, new releases offer audiences opportunities to distinguish themselves based on their attendance rather than the film alone. Middle- and upper-class moviegoers who prefer a more "leisurely" movie outing may avoid the first-day crowds, an exercise that signals their respectability. Describing first-day audiences as "the people that are crazy after movies . . . [who] have to see it as soon as it comes," Shanti said she liked to wait for the rush to die down, "rush" being code for crowds and disorder. After remarking that "First two days are really bad," Kaveri expressed her preference: "I've *rarely* gone for those rushed movies. You know, movies where there's a big crowd. Or in the first week, the first show, very rarely have I managed to go. Or *bothered* really to go for it. [I] take my own sweet time and go for it after the crowd is gone." Some middle-class men also expressed their distaste for crowds. A lower-middle-class youth said that though he always tried to see a "Shahrukh Khan starrer" on the first day, "because I'm so crazy about it," he didn't like to go "if the theater is crowded." Yet I found people who articulated such preferences on occasion became caught up in the excitement of the new release and even took pleasure in the challenges of dealing with crowds and ticket scarcity.

THE FAN-STAR RELATIONSHIP AND THE PRODUCTION OF THE NEW RELEASE

Fans are forever hanging around cinema halls. In Majestic and K. G. Road, the small eateries, coffee shops, and street corners near cinema halls become a rendezvous for fans and "a center for their social life."[23] Fan devotion is oriented toward the top male stars,[24] and when they get together, fans talk about the star's films, praise him, his performance, anticipate future "releases," denigrate rival stars and their fans, and gossip about the film industry.[25] Affiliation with the star and with fellow fans shapes a community; at theaters fans chant slogans in praise or support of the star, raising their voices together in a display of loyalty and fellow feeling.

Hollywood films, while very popular in India, do not attract the same kind of celebratory fan culture. In the case of regional cinema, ethnicity in terms of regional culture and language plays an important role in mobilizing fans.[26] The home state of the star or the region that has "adopted" him or her becomes a site of intense fan activity,[27] evidence of cinema experience that is local. Many Kannada fans identify themselves as *abhimani* (admirers) and turn out in numbers for films of their favorite stars. They are especially visible City-side and in Majestic or Gandhinagar. Tamil and Telugu fans are also active in Bangalore, though their activities tend to be centered at theaters such as the Lavanya and Naga theaters in the Cantonment and other theaters where Tamil films are screened in what used to be a predominantly Tamil-speaking area. Films of Tamil superstars Rajinikanth,[28] Kamal Hasan, and to a lesser degree Vijay and Ajith as well as the Telugu megastar Chiranjeevi and others, are received with great excitement in the city, although the frenzy generated by their films reaches a peak in the neighboring states of Tamil Nadu and Andhra Pradesh, respectively.

Fan presence itself speaks to the liminoid status of the new release, as fans occupy ambiguous spaces in society. In Bangalore, large numbers of self-identified fans of Kannada, Tamil, or Telugu films belong to the lower socioeconomic orders and include the unemployed and underemployed, the illiterate and semiliterate, though the class of fan varies by the star. Among those identifying themselves as fans, I encountered autorickshaw, bus, and taxi drivers; petty shopkeepers and shop assistants; waiters; government and bank clerks, chauffeurs and household workers for middle-class households; as well as lower-middle-class school and college students. Shekar, a fan of Shivarajkumar, was in his late twenties and lived with his elderly parents and unmarried sister. He said he had studied until eighth class and spoke some English. When I met him, he was trying to get a job as a door-to-door salesman for vacuum cleaners. Another fan, Suresh, managed a footpath stall in Majestic with his brother. The stall was close to many cinemas and thus facilitated last-minute movie outings.

Fan Involvement and "Face"

The fan-star relationship plays out in an intense fashion on the occasion of the new release. Fans territorialize the theater and in large numbers even take over the streets. While many fans are marginalized in society, their visibility and influence is one of the "inversions" of the new release.

Fan involvement in film releases and related promotion of the star has been attributed on the one hand to devotion and on the other to self-interest.[29] As they are caught in webs of affect and obligation, fan attendance at "first shows" is a ritual demonstration of their affiliation and their closeness to the star. A Rajinikanth fan explained, "Watching a Rajni film on the first day of its release has become a part of my life; I have been doing it for 25 years."[30] Mundane activities surrounding the new release carry transcendent meanings for fans. The effort involved in getting tickets, standing in long lines, sometimes for a major part of the day, braving crowds and clashes with the police becomes a duty and a ritual.[31] Where inflated ticket prices and sold-out theaters are testimony to the popularity and charisma of the star, a no-expense-spared viewing of the film, which includes prestige (balcony) seating or purchasing astronomically priced black-market tickets also carries meanings of devotion, trust (*vishwasa*) and affection (*preeti*) that both fans and stars like to feel marks their relationship. "I go first day morning show for Shivarajkumar picture," explained an autorickshaw driver and Kannada film fan: "*Kurubana Raani* I saw morning show. *Andamans* is releasing on the tenth. I'll see it even if I have to buy in black!" (translated from Kannada).

Fans sometimes "skip a meal for a ticket,"[32] borrow, or otherwise obtain the money. They may imbue the purchase of a ticket at an exorbitant black-market price with meanings of giving the star a gift. Another autorickshaw driver made it a point to say that money is no object: for a film starring Dr. Rajkumar; he would purchase a ticket "in black" at over a tenfold increase in ticket price.[33] "Rajkumar films sell tickets in black for Rs. 200, Rs. 300, but I'll buy it anyway. See—I make a pittance driving this auto. I pay so much to the owner, for the license, etc. Then I get a few hundreds. But what I want is to see Rajanna's picture. For that I'll buy in black because of the affection and trust he has for people like me. That's what it means for me." (translated from Kannada).

The new release presents the fan-enthusiast as producer, participant, and devotee. Select groups of fans may host the new release, collaboratively "produce" the event, and organize many of the inaugural activities and festivities that usher in the new film. The need to be seen as involved and visible certainly motivates the young men who have a collective identity as *abhimanigalu* (fans). They participate in the festivities, take on guardianship of the star's image, even assume responsibility for the successful launch of the film, all measures of their affiliation and investment in the star's "face."

The notion of "face" explains the significance of "mundanities" such as ticket prices and sales. "House Full" theaters, long lines, and crowds outside theaters are as much about the star's (and fans') "face" as they are about publicity for the film. A crowded theater becomes a tribute to the star or filmmaker—even to fans themselves, as many are involved in producing crowds and therefore atmosphere at theaters. These meanings are shared by film-business insiders: Bollywood superstar Shahrukh Khan expressed concern about his films opening to less than full theaters, saying that he "would die" if his movies were quietly screened in the half-full tiny multiplexes that Hollywood movies are screened in in the West and where audiences can easily obtain tickets on the first weekend.[34] Inflated ticket prices are seen as evidence of the star's worth and appeal. Fan engagement in "face-work"[35] may lead them, sometimes in collusion with distributors and producers, to manipulate the box office by purchasing tickets in bulk, striving for a "sold out" buzz for the film. Some theaters give fan clubs the responsibility for ticket sales for the first week.[36] Fan clubs block-book theaters and buy out the seats to sell them on the black market, thus enhancing respect for the star.[37] For the theatrical release of the Tamil film *Sivaji* (The boss) at the AVM Rajeshwari theater in Chennai, the Rajinikanth Fan Association booked shows for three days in advance.[38] Such reports allow fans to take credit for a film's successful launch.

Their affiliation with the star and involvement in the proceedings may lead fans to consider the film and the theater "theirs" and assume a proprietorial stance. I found on multiple occasions that fans did not purchase tickets but sauntered into the theater as if they owned the place. Fans who are known to stars, theater staff, and producers may acquire a special status at new releases and theaters hosting the films of their idols. In Kannada cinema circles in the 1990s, Shekar was among the small group of fans who was seen to be a friend of the superstar Shivarajkumar, and he easily gained entry to theaters and film sets. The rest of his group followed. This was a matter of annoyance to some theater managers. As they "own the show," fans feel they can extend the hospitality of a free screening to "guests." Meeting me before the film, fans would attempt to escort me into the theater. On a couple of occasions, in 1998 and again in 2012, finding I had already purchased tickets, they chastised me, "Why did you buy tickets?" and then, grandly, "When you are with us, you don't have to buy." These meanings attached to the new release allow reports on fans' activities to be seen in context. For example, a recent news item on the Kannada film *Super* reports that "in many theatres" fans "forced their way in without tickets."[39]

Fans constantly perform loyalty and closeness to the star. Their expressions of affiliation can play out in conflicts. Involvement in the star's face leads fans to do battle for the star,[40] to preserve his honor, and to make sure that he is given respect. Publicity for the film, including the festivities surrounding its release, is seen as "due" to the star and a tribute to his charisma as well as evidence of public affection. Fans may demand that distributors and exhibitors organize a grand welcome for the film; in a sense, maintaining the star's "face" or "giving face" to the star requires it, and its absence poses a threat to the star's face while creating a state of "ritual disequilibrium or disgrace."[41] Fans may take key decisions as to when and where the film should be released. When I was in Bangalore in 2010, commotion and controversy surrounded the release of *Aaptha Rakshaka*, starring Vishnuvardhan. The star had passed away suddenly, shortly before the film was due to be released, sending his fans and many in the Kannada film business into mourning. Grieving fans were said to be "visibly angry" at the "lack of prerelease publicity." According to a news report, "hundreds of agitated fans . . . forced the producer to postpone its [the film's] release by a week" by sitting in *dharna* (sit-down strike) outside the distributor's offices. Some even went to the Karnataka Film Chamber of Commerce and demanded that the president "stall the release." [42]

In the spirit of contest, rival fan associations may fight over theater space or over the promotion of a newly released film at a particular theater.[43] When a film stars two major actors, fights erupt inside the theater between rival fans.[44] More recently, such conflicts have surfaced in online interactions where fans freely criticize and hurl insults at fans of other stars and their idols. Maintaining face includes the thrills of defacing the posters and billboards of rivals.[45] Fearing disorder and violence, stars frequently implore fans to restrain themselves and, taking on the role of father or elder brother,[46] encourage them to act responsibly. Anticipating "public nuisance" by fans eagerly awaiting the release of his film *Sivaji*, Rajinikanth issued a series of "directives" entreating them not to "disturb the public by engaging in extravagant celebrations, not to burst crackers on the road disrupting vehicular traffic, not to put up welcome arches . . . not to write messages hurting anyone . . . and not to disturb the audience while watching the film in theatres."[47] That stars make such calls for peace and assume responsibility for fans' actions is also evidence of the "face" shared by fans and stars alike, where the bad behavior of fans can have a bearing on the star.[48]

FILM AS FESTIVAL

Ritual Welcome and Audience as Devotee and Guest

Scholars have observed that in South India, where a "personality cult" shapes cinema (and politics), stars are propitiated like gods.[49] For many fans, attending the first show is a ritual activity akin to a religious experience—a kind of pilgrimage similar to going to the temple when there is a religious festival and for *darshan* of the deity.[50] Referring to the release of a film starring Rajinikanth, an exhibitor remarked, "a Rajini release is like God descending on earth and so is worth all the efforts for the festivities."[51] Newspapers highlight the devotee-deity relationship and refer to fans as "worshippers."[52] Describing audiences as "devotees," the *Times of India* went on to report, "In Mumbai people had started queuing from two-thirty the previous night to 'buy their darshan of Rajni Saar [sir].'"[53] Assuming the role of devotee, fans may seek divine help for a film's box-office success. According to the *Hindustan Times*,[54] in an act of penance, about a hundred fans of "Superstar Rajnikanth" climbed the 1,305 steps of the Sholingur Temple on their knees to perform a special *puja* for the success of the film. This was not an isolated incident. In Mumbai, fans prayed for the film at a local temple and offered the film reel in worship before its screening.[55] For the Kannada film *Godfather* (2012), I was informed on the eve of the film's release that its reels were being taken to the producer's home, where a priest would perform *puja* for an auspicious launch.

Other practices attendant to worship are transferred to the theater. Exhibitors, distributors, and moviegoers talked about fans breaking coconuts in front of the theater and the film's posters and cutouts to propitiate the gods and the star to signify an auspicious occasion.[56] Fans break coconuts on their own heads and perform *uralseve*—rolling on the ground outside the theater or even inside it. They light incense in front of billboards, perform *abhishekham*[57] by pouring milk or water on billboards carrying the star's image. Rajinikanth fans are known to bathe cutouts of the star with beer and cola as well as milk. Even film trailers may merit such a welcome.[58]

The model for new-release celebrations being religious ritual, festivals, and weddings, moviegoers at new releases may be welcomed as devotee-guests. Gift giving, sharing food, and other such activities help reinvent film as festival. Just as at temples, where devotees are given *prasadam*—auspicious gifts of food or flowers that have first been offered to the deity—many of my interviewees referred to recent history, between five and eight years ago, when audiences for the first, seventh, fiftieth, hundredth, and two hundredth days of continuous screening of a film were given sweets at the behest of the star and the producers. "Sweets distribution" marked the height of the Rajkumar era: "*Laddu* they used to give—at the main gate, one packet each, every twenty-five days," a theater manager recalled. Becoming nostalgic for "those days," a sweeper/janitor at the Sagar theater remembered people being given "*jalebis*, *bahadurshah* and *Nandini peda*."[59]

The festival being an "occasion for the circulation of wealth,"[60] stars, producers, even fans hosting the new release organize the distribution of food and gifts. Gifts for the audience may include clothing. Ramesh was known for making quality cinema that attracted women and middle-class audiences. I learned that women going to see a "Ramesh picture" about a wedding were given gifts of glass bangles, a "blouse piece,"[61] and strands of jasmine for their hair, simulating the experience of going to a Hindu wedding. In 2012 the tradition of gifting seemed to be going strong. At the release of the Kannada film *Godfather*, which starred Upendra in a triple role, fans positioned at the theater entrance handed out a *laddu* (sweet) in a plastic wrapper and a free CD with songs from the film, the producer's gift to each attendee. Also like festivals, new releases are occasions for charity and "poor feeding." Audiences were given free meals on the hundredth day of a Rajkumar film organized by the star. "Full *kotidare!*" (he has given in full), the sweeper at the Sagar theater, also a fan, told me approvingly, emphasizing the star's generosity. Fans gift theater staff with clothing; they even donate blood and pledge their eyes on the occasion of a film release.[62]

Gift exchange binds together exhibitors, producers, stars, fans. and audiences. Fan clubs may present commemorative gifts to exhibitors, producers, and stars. According to Hardgrave, at the first-day celebration of the Tamil star MGR's films, fan clubs presented "a gold-plated shield to the producer as congratulations."[63] The shields, plaques, inscribed clocks, and other mementos proudly displayed in cinema halls are demonstrations of respect, affection, and affiliation. Gifts, ritual practices, relationships, and dates all contribute to the transcendence of the experience. The Kannada film *Mylari* (2010), starring Shivarajkumar, was launched on April 24, his father Rajkumar's birthday. At a special ceremony held at a temple, fans presented Shivarajkumar with a silver statue of Dr. Rajkumar, which was reported to weigh "6.350 kilograms." Shivarajkumar is said to have become "a little emotional as he held the statue."[64]

The transcendent meaning of the new release is seen even in its timing and the significance attached to it when it arrives in theaters. Films are often released to coincide with festivals; Kannada films sometimes have their inaugural screening on the *Ugadi* (Kannada new year) festival, which resonates with the regionalist, pro-Kannada sentiment of fans. The release of *Godfather* in summer 2012 coincided with the *Varamahalakshmi* festival.[65] The date on which a film is released is often chosen for its significance for both the star and his fans. Shivarajkumar's films, for example, were released on the birthday of his father Dr. Rajkumar or on his wife's birthday, which was considered lucky for him. Films are also released on the "lucky number day" of the star. The new release then draws on other auspicious events and times to build meaning and resonance as an auspicious event itself. Transcendence shapes all aspects of the new release. Even the death of fans seeking entry to the theater assumes transcendent meaning in the context of the new release.

Decorated Theaters

Audience experience of the new release is also shaped by elaborate ornamentation of the theater. To host *Mughal E Azam*, a theater was transformed to look like a Mughal palace. According to a "publicity coordinator," "The picture [*Mughal E Azam*] ran for almost a year because all Muslims in Tamil Nadu came to see the film like a pilgrimage."[66] In Bangalore, decorated theaters bring spectacle onto the street. Banners and posters on theater facades scream "Hat-

FIGURE 16. Nartaki theater complex decorated for new release with statue of Dr. Rajkumar looming above the awning. Photograph by the author, Bangalore, 2010.

trick Hero Shivarajkumar," "Golden Star Ganesh." The familiar "titles" recognized by fans refer to the star's performance record or his traits, locating him in a popular mythology.[67] Shivarajkumar, for example, made a name for himself via his three consecutive "superhit" films—hence the cricketing term *hat trick*—while the late Dr. Vishnuvardhan is referred to as "Sahasa Simha" (Fearless Lion), perhaps because of the fearlessness with which he is known to have tackled daring stunts in his films. Ganesh earned the title "Golden Star" after the unprecedented success of *Mungaru Male* (2007), which established him as the star with the Midas touch. The film remained at multiplexes for an entire year, rewriting box-office records for Kannada films.

In 2010 the Nartaki-Santosh theater complex exemplified the festival/ fairground aesthetic (fig. 16). A concrete statue of Dr. Rajkumar towered above the parking lot. Within a few feet of it, a fifty-foot cutout of Ganesh, whose film was being screened at the Santosh theater, vied for attention. Streamers, banners, and small flags transformed the theater exterior. Billboards on the side were garlanded; posters proudly announced: "100 days." Down the street at the Sagar theater, where another "film festival" was in progress for the Kannada film *Raam* (2010), massive garlands of roses and tinsel adorned a towering cutout of "Power Star" (because of the energy and "power" with which he jumps and dances, a fan explained) Puneet Rajkumar.[68] Such decorations provide a changing landscape of spectacle[69] as old decorations fade and are refreshed when new films arrive at the theater or when a film reaches the fifty- or hundred-days milestones.

Decorations and celebrations also serve to make the threshold space of the theater hosting the new release auspicious. Invariably, when I spent time in Majestic, I came across a newly decorated theater, banana plants on either side of its awnings, garlands of electric orange marigold looped around the entrance gates, rows of mango leaves strung above the entrance arch, and *kolam* on the ground[70]—all auspicious symbols seen outside marriage halls for Hindu weddings, in Hindu homes on festival days, or at temples and shrines.[71] Again, following the ornamentation of awnings outside weddings halls, which spell out the name of the bride and groom in flowers, decorations on theater awnings display the name of the film, the star, and often the producer and director along with a greeting, "Suswagatha" (Very warm welcome). A theater owner in Mumbai actually compared his grandly decorated theater to a "marriage venue."[72] Decorations for Kannada films often have a red and yellow theme—the colors of the (unofficial) flag of Karnataka, sported by Kannada activists.

Where large numbers of moviegoers are illiterate or semiliterate, such visual spectacle may be effective in terms of publicity. I came across autorickshaw drivers and footpath-stall owners who could not read the lettering on posters yet knew which film was being advertised, along with minute details of its cast, production, and so on. This way of evaluating a film through spectacle and firsthand accounts of crowds, ticket prices, long lines, and celebrations has taken shape in an environment where films lack extensive marketing budgets or campaigns of the Hollywood variety,[73] where publicity derives from word of mouth, and where the aesthetics of festival shape film experience, underlining its local and situated character.[74]

The city's cultural geography locates the activities attendant to a new release. The festival/fairground aesthetic seen in Majestic is absent at theaters screening Hollywood films in Cantonment and at mall multiplexes. Of the two theaters screening *Titanic* in Bangalore in early 1998, it was the Sangam near the interstate bus terminus in Kalasipaliyam that was decorated, though minimally. Tiny colored lights hung down from the roof and were wound around a clump of giant aloe cacti next to the driveway. The cacti also had eggshells covering their leaf tips, which gleamed in the light. Many believe eggshells to be a remedy for removing the evil eye (the theater had recently undergone renovations). On the other side of town, the Galaxy, where the same film was being screened for the Cantonment audience, lacked this festive air. Moviegoers were greeted with the bumpers of rows of cars and two-wheelers in the parking lot out front. Hidden inside malls, multiplexes today present a standardized and sterile neon and glass facade, a stark contrast to the vibrant festivities in Majestic.

"Om" and the Festival/Fairground Aesthetic

Popular films that are "rereleased" are at times welcomed with the fanfare attached to new releases. The Kannada film *Om* achieved superhit status when it was first released in 1995. In 1998 a distributor managed to obtain an old and scratched print for its rerelease. I learned from fans and theater staff that the distributor had spent his own money—"100,000 rupees!"—to have a grand opening of this "superhit" film. The distributor, who was supervising last-minute arrangements at the Majestic theater, confirmed this backstory, and with quiet triumph described the negotiations that had led to his acquiring the print. His hope was the film would draw fans back to the theater. Many fans planned to see the film, although some had already seen it twenty times and more when it was first released. They urged me to go see it.

Acting on fans' recommendations I went to Majestic Talkies on a warm Sunday afternoon in March. The theater, which some dated to the 1950s, was all done up with colored streamers, pennants and banners, paint, lights, and flowers. A large balloon with the distributor's name and the name of the film in Kannada trailed into the sky like a miniature blimp. Streamers from the theater to the buildings across the street extended the festival atmosphere to the surroundings. A string of lights trailed across the top of the theater, and a multicolored awning made of flowers arched over the metal gate spelling out *Suswagatha* (Most warm welcome). Even film credits were brought outside the theater and etched into the urban landscape: the decorated arches spelled out the names of the distributor (Radhakrishna) and producer.

The film was a family venture, and the theater facade presented a tribute to the Rajkumar film family. Toward the bottom of the building was a large poster of Parvathamma, producer of the film, mother of Shivarajkumar, the star of the film, and wife of Dr. Rajkumar, the star's father. Directly above this poster, rising above the building and silhouetted against the sky, a bust cutout of a benevolent and smiling Dr. Rajkumar graced the venture. To the right of the cutout, a forty-foot tall cutout of the star of the film, Shivarajkumar, in the role of "rowdy" menaced onlookers with a machete in his raised hand. The collection of posters and tributes to the star and his parents created a larger kin atmosphere to which Upendra, the director of the film, with a fan following of his own, was admitted as evidenced by *his* poster on the facade. Talking to fans that day, it appeared that they felt part of this family and were invested in the film's successful rerelease. They informed me that *Annavaru* (elder brother, i.e., Rajkumar) had *himself* sung some of the "superhit" songs for the film.

The theater had a small "car park" in front of the building; however, there were no vehicles in the area. Here knots of young men gathered, keeping a watchful eye on the closed entrance doors. Immediately in front of the theater doors, a small fountain spewed purple water. It was surrounded by pots of ornamental palms and crotons arranged in concentric circles. The crush of young men around the fountain made it difficult to see it. There was a lot of talk and laughter, pushing and shoving. One youth had removed his *chappals* and was dipping his feet in the purple water. Others shouted at him and attempted to pull him out.[75] Some men stood around and gazed open mouthed at the vivid posters that were plastered on all available wall space. They craned their necks to view the looming cutouts.

Edging past the crowd at the gate, I went closer to photograph the posters. I had to find my way through the matinee crowd of young men who were pressed against the theater doors waiting for them to open. The security guard, who doubled as ticket collector, glanced at the camera around my neck and asked whether I was "press." I said that I was at college and was writing a book about Kannada cinema. After questioning me about what I was writing, whether I knew the star, which seemed the critical piece of information, he moved aside and held out his arm, "go ahead." Inside the theater, streamers in metallic green, magenta, yellow, and blue formed a grid across the ceiling in the lobby. The double doors at the entrance to the lower stalls were framed on either side with banners that seemed to be of a silklike material and that carried the same image of a fierce-looking Shivarajkumar with a machete.

Later that evening when I went to see the film, the theater had the look and feel of a fairground at night. All the lights were on; white globe-shaped lights that had *Om* written on them blinked alternately in sequence: Om-Om-Om-Om. . . . Another set of tiny multicolored lights were strung all over the front of the theater and across the posters and plywood cutouts of the stars. (Field notes, Bangalore, March 1998)

Film in Procession

Described as "ritual[s] of intensification,"[76] processions are part of public culture in India, marking celebration as well as protest and demonstration. Religious festivals are celebrated with processions in which devotees participate.[77] In North India, the wedding party takes to the streets in celebration; the groom is brought to the wedding venue in procession, riding on a horse.

Along with decorated theaters, crowds, and fan activities, processions bring film reception outside the theater. As an expression of ritual welcome, of "happiness," and "an idealized public performance,"[78] they frame the star as god or king, constituting a kingly welcome. Processions allow audiences to be at once participants and observers[79]; they bring people together around spectacle, provide a performative space for fans, and are "expressions of community and devotion enacted on city streets."[80] Even the rerelease of a favorite film may be inaugurated with a procession. As one producer put it, "Some twenty-year-old film was [re]released in the theater. And they had a procession from here with stars, four months back."

Film processions are multidimensional and, as both an event and a practice, difficult to make sense of.[81] They may be seen as an expression of films' liminality and fluidity and may serve to both question and establish the film's boundaries.[82] Similar to processions at Ram Lila festivities described by Richard Schechner, processions inaugurating the new release trace a "ceremonial path" expanding the terrain of the film (as festival) to encompass the theater surroundings, the street, even the city. Speaking excitedly and at top speed, a moviegoer somewhat incoherently described the activities of fan associations at new releases, focusing on their processions with drums and "huuuge garlands"[83] and decorating the theater facade with banners and papier-mâché stars. The enthusiasm in his account captures the mood and effervescent atmosphere.

Kamal Hasan starrer on a Sunday; they will take a whole big banner and all that, stars and all that—every area has an association for these actors, OK? So, they carry these stars with the photographs of the actor stuck on that to the theater, and they put *huuuge* garlands on these banners. Mr. Kamal Hasan and Rajnikant movies, definitely! It will be on a Sunday only. They take their drums and go, and they carry it right from their area to the theater. . . . Huge banner will be full of garlands; lots of hero worship for Kamal Hasan movies. (Field notes, Bangalore 1998)

Processions frequently involve a band of sorts, and sometimes even horses and elephants. According to news reports in a small town in South India, "the box containing the trailer reel was taken in a procession on a caparisoned elephant through the town, accompanied by a band playing music"; "chariots" and "horse-drawn carriages" transport film reels or even the film's trailer. [84] Fans, in the role of devotee chant slogans in favor of the star, set off fireworks, even dance in the street.[85] The procession ends at the theater, where billboards and cutouts are garlanded.

Fans see processions and attendant *galata* as an achievement and evidence of the power of the star and of their own influence in shaping city events. A fan proudly predicted that if a film of Dr. Rajkumar is released, "there will be Bangalore *bundh* [strike, city closure] for three days!" The *bundh* becomes a symbol of Rajkumar's power among this group of admirers and of their own enthusiasm, devotion, and influence.[86] Processions may create disruptions in the city when they block streets and affect public transport. Sections of the city may even be brought to a standstill. A producer discussing the theatrical release of a Kannada film starring Dr. Rajkumar recalled such incidents: "He came back with a film called *Jeevana Chaitra*. There was a major blockage throughout Bangalore. BTS buses were not passing by, and they had to be stopped because of processions on the road carrying the stars and garlands. You know they have these forty-foot garlands and big medals?"

Regional-language nonelite cinema is often invisible to sections of the population that flock to Hollywood and Bollywood films; large numbers of this audience are non-Kannada speakers—in-migrants from North India and Westernized middle classes. Consequently, first-day festivities, crowds, excitable fans, police intervention, roadblocks, and traffic diversions are significant as an inversion that makes film visible even outside the smallish community of fans and habitués. For fans, these events are a culmination of their efforts at hosting, planning, and strategizing to welcome the star and the film–expressions of their affection and loyalty. They are moved by the occasion, even ecstatic. The night before a film's release, the core group of fans in charge of decorations sleeps rough, sometimes on the ground within the theater compound after working into the early hours of the morning; some drink, but all revel in the camaraderie.

FIRST DAY FESTIVITIES AT KURUBANA RAANI, SAGAR THEATER

The crowds and volatility surrounding the new release presented challenges for fieldwork. I routinely received warnings to stay away from new releases—

especially those films and theaters that would attract fans and rowdy audiences. After telling me the time and place where fans were expected to gather, the manager of a theater in Majestic said that he regretted having given me the information and attempted to dissuade me at the last minute: "They're all loafers! Drunkards! *Simply* they will create *galata* [commotion]. You should not go! Don't take camera!"

Even more of a problem was the lack of information about the event. Most people I spoke with seemed to know of the existence of new-release celebrations and processions, yet few were able to locate them in advance with any certainty. Many middle-class residents, especially those new to the city and who did not watch regional-language films, seemed oblivious. By talking to exhibitors and audiences for Kannada films, I learned that processions "usually" take place on Sunday or Friday and "usually in the afternoon." However, pinning down the time and place ahead of the event proved difficult. The common understanding seemed to be that these events were random, and their timing and location were up to the fans who organized them. Contacting theater staff about new-release events was itself difficult. Theater managers often would not answer the phone, so I could talk with them only by going to the theater. A couple of times I expressed my wish to see a procession only to have theater managers tell me I had just missed one by a day or a few hours. Even fans I spoke with who were involved in such celebrations seemed vague about times and places. I later realized this was in keeping with the spontaneity and transient nature of such events and the foreknowledge that was shared by a small "inside" group.

In a desperate attempt to witness new-release festivities, I asked practically everyone I encountered for information: middle-class moviegoers, domestic servants, autorickshaw drivers, shopkeepers, footpath-stall owners, ushers, and ticket clerks. From longtime observers and participants of the cinema scene I learned that processions would start at points in the city where the fan associations had their offices or where fans lived, then wind their way to the theater in the late afternoon while gathering numbers along the way. I was urged to meet Mr. S. R. Govindu, an ex-president of the Rajkumar fan association,[87] who was also influential in the Kannada film world. I had a plan to ask him, among other things, where the offices of fan associations were located and how I might witness a procession. From our phone conversation, it appeared that Mr. Govindu had *his* office either near or in a hotel in Gandhinagar.[88] Meeting him was in itself quite a feat, requiring repeated phone calls and waiting around for weeks for an appointment: he traveled a lot in the state and was involved not only with the Kannada film business but with local and regional politics. He quizzed me at length before granting me audience. On the appointed day around 10:30 a.m., I found my way to the address given for the hotel in Gandhinagar—a modest establishment, like many in the area. Small boys played cricket in an open space opposite, framed by ancient rain trees. A group of five men sat on the railings near the street, scuffing the dust with their *chappals*. They stared at me. When I asked them whether they knew where I could find S. R. Govindu, their demeanor changed, and they helpfully directed me to the hotel. The desk clerk rang the room and told me Mr. Govindu was at *nashta* (brunch) and would be down shortly. Mr. Govindu appeared in the lobby after half an hour: a short man with a moustache and an air of having many things to do. Our meeting was brief. Mr. Govindu was courteous and businesslike. He briskly confirmed that processions and related celebrations usually took place over the weekend for Kannada films. He did not know of any such scheduled processions but asked me to keep an eye out for them at theaters in Majestic. He referred me to the Karnataka Film Chamber of Commerce and to a couple of distributors, whom I had already contacted. When I asked whether I could call him again if I needed information, he readily agreed but then told me he would be out of town organizing some event for the next couple of weeks. I never saw him again, and though I was able to contact him by phone a couple of times, conversations were always brief, given Mr. Govindu's hectic schedule.

After many such dead ends, I decided to hang around a couple of theaters in Majestic on weekends on the off chance that I would stumble across such celebrations. The breakthrough, however, came one afternoon at the home of one of my respondent families. Family members would routinely ask me whether I had seen any movies or had met the stars. That afternoon they asked me whether I was planning to see the new Kannada movie *Kurubana Raani*, which had received favorable reviews in Kannada newspapers. When I mentioned that I wanted to see processions and celebrations, Kaveri called the theater to inquire. The theater manager confirmed the likelihood of a procession that very day, as the film would draw fans of the star. He encouraged us (middle-class women) to come *after* the excitement had died down in a few days. When we insisted we wanted to see the film that very evening and witness the processions, he suggested we get to the theater early in the afternoon, as processions would start around three o'clock. Family members decided that the best plan was for me, accompanied by a couple of people, to go to the theater around two thirty, as there was a consensus that I should not go alone. Then the rest of the family would meet us at the theater that evening in time for the first show.

Accompanied by three family members and taking along a camera I had borrowed for the occasion, I waited outside Sagar theater that afternoon, hoping to see festivities in progress. The theater being in the dense commercial area in Gandhinagar, we were in the middle of a thriving market. Although a long line of moviegoers waited in the sharp afternoon sun for the ticket booths to open, there was no sign of any fan activity at three o'clock. We hung around outside the theater for the next hour or so, taking in the scene, asking various people whether they had seen a procession. They shook their heads, "no." Yet many were hopeful that a procession would still happen. It was very warm, in the high 80s at least. In late January and February, Bangalore suddenly becomes hot and temperatures can reach into the 90s. My companions suggested going home, resting, and returning closer to showtime but I was reluctant to leave and miss out on anything—were anything to happen, that is.

Outside the theater the crowd was getting thicker. Standing across the street it became difficult to see up to the theater doors over a sea of heads. There was a palpable and growing excitement. People shouted out to one another; young men in groups leaned on one another; some crossed and recrossed the street. People started lining up on the sidewalk, and by four o'clock it was difficult for the traffic to proceed because the crowd was spilling onto the street. A uniformed traffic policeman materialized and was soon shoving people back onto the pavement. At four thirty we heard the sounds of drums and shouts that drew closer. Then all of a sudden the crowd surged, and it became difficult to see the street at all. Men craned their necks eagerly. Some climbed the lampposts to get a better view. Suddenly, there were sharp cracking sounds followed by the smell of something burning. A man on a two-wheeler who had stopped for the traffic light wobbled and nearly fell with the suddenness of it. Firecrackers had been set off within a few feet of him and the traffic policeman. The beat of drums grew louder as a group of about fourteen men came into view: a smaller group than I had anticipated. Some carried large six-cornered papier-mâché stars that displayed the film's title in Kannada and on which were stuck photos of the star. A few in the procession beat drums and chanted slogans in favor of the star Shivarajkumar and his father, Dr. Rajkumar. Rounding the corner, a few of the men broke into dance. What we could not see at the time were the giant garlands of fragrant tuberose, rose, marigold, and jasmine, each of which was about forty feet in length, which were also brought ceremonially in procession and were being set out underneath the sixty-foot tall cutout on the theater facade that loomed above all this activity. A heavily built man with a moustache who had accompanied the procession dashed about sticking flyers on the poster stand outside the theater. He had a bulky black satchel slung over his shoulder and was doubled up under its weight. From the satchel he produced flyers and posters, which he proceeded to stick on all available surfaces. Many in the crowd surged around him asking for posters, which they received along with a brightly colored sheet with the star's photograph on it.

*

My position across the street was not the best vantage point, given the density of the crowd, but moving closer did not seem to guarantee any better visibility. I was also warned by family members and by other gawkers not to go closer. A member of our group ventured across the street, came back, and reported: "Lot of them are drunk!" and "very excitable." At intervals, the crowd would break into shouts and slogans: "Shivarajkumar ki Jai!" (Long Live Shivarajkumar!). The mood was electric.

By taking photographs we had drawn attention to ourselves and had become part of the spectacle. A small group of interested onlookers gathered around and passed the time by quizzing us—"Why were we taking photographs? Were we Press? Part of the distributors or producers? Did we know the star?" When I moved across the street, this group followed me in order not to miss out on any action. We were suddenly engulfed by the crowd.

Closer to the theater there was frenetic activity. The policeman appeared fully occupied with regulating traffic when he was not watching the spectacle. The crush of onlookers grew and pressed closer. Two of the men started climbing the scaffolding that supported the cutouts, and instructions were shouted out to them from below. The man with the flyers, whom I later came to know as Suresh and who identified himself as a fan of both Shivarajkumar and Rajkumar, continued to paste flyers outside the theater and distribute them. Meanwhile, the men had climbed to the top of the scaffolding, and the papier-mâché stars were winched up to them, then tied to the cutout of the hero. When each star was hauled up and secured, cheers erupted from the crowd. Garlands were then lifted, a laborious process as each was several feet long, unwieldy, and judging by the many hands needed to lift it, very heavy. However, the men all seemed practiced at what was clearly routine activity. When the first garland was fixed around the neck of the poster of the hero, a massive roar went up from the crowd.

I asked several people who was in charge and was directed to others. People again asked me whether I was "press." While I was thinking about how best to make myself understood, Raghu started explaining that I had come from

America to study Kannada films. This announcement seemed to make an impression, and I suddenly found myself face-to-face with a heavy young man who appeared to be a leader of sorts. His height and pale coloring made him stand out in the crowd. The man with the moustache encouraged me to talk with him. Shouting above the noise, I hesitantly introduced myself and my interest in cinema in Bangalore. He asked me briskly, what did I want to know? I replied I was keen to know more about the procession and who had organized the events. I asked him whether I could contact him at another time. He responded by asking me where I lived, what I did, and so on. When I explained I was studying Kannada cinema and was in college, he asked where I was based. Upon hearing I was in Bangalore from America, he shouted excitedly, "But I'm not American, I'm Indian!" explaining that people mistook his pale skin for his being American (he was an albino). He repeated this to me a few times in case I had not heard or understood. His face flushed, he introduced himself and the knot of men around him, "We are all *abhimanigalu!*" (fans) of Shivarajkumar.[89]

A sizeable crowd, there for the spectacle, had gathered around to listen in on our conversation. They moved closer and leaned in on us. Several people seemed to want to both ask and answer questions, and some answered the questions others asked of me on my behalf. One individual who was part of the group organizing the celebrations warned us we would draw the attention of the police (I later realized that fans in large numbers and amid crowds were always wary of the police); he pushed us into an alcove outside the theater. About a hundred fans and onlookers squeezed themselves into the tiny space, making it difficult to breathe. The rest waited outside. Clearly I had an interested audience and was expected to perform my role of interested observer and interviewer. However, the crowd and noise made it impractical, to say the least. The heat and smell of sweat was overpowering. There was also a strong smell of urine. However, people were determined not to miss out on the event. I asked a few questions about the fan club, where it was located, whether such events were organized for most Kannada films, and whether they hoped to see the star today. I had taken along a tape recorder, and the fans and other onlookers were fighting to talk into it. Periodically, people would get carried away by the fervor of the declarations of others. They set up a chant, and several voices joined in. Many declarations of loyalty were shouted directly into the recorder:

"We are fans of Shivarajkumar, we will give our whole lives for him!"

"We will do *anything* for him and for the Rajkumar family!"

"We don't want anything in life, we just want to see him!"

"I have come all the way from —— [on the outskirts of the city] just to see this picture of Shivarajkumar, because I am such a great fan of his and of his father!"

Following these declarations, someone asked, "Is it being recorded? Are you certain?" I was asked to play back the recording as proof, which received applause and more cheers. After this performance, fans looked at me expectantly. I had become the audience. Not knowing quite what to do, I applauded them and their loyalty. There was a good feeling all around. Some wanted to know, "What will you do with the information?"

A lot of this exchange was in Kannada, and a few young men who looked like students, hearing my hesitant Kannada, decided to helpfully provide English translations: "He's saying, madam, he will die for Shivarajkumar." More people seemed to have joined us, and given the state of enthusiasm bordering on hysteria among those gathered, I thought it better to leave but did not know how to, and everyone seemed to want to talk. I tried to get the name of the fan who had declared he was not American. He readily gave me his name, Shekar, and a phone number where he could be reached as well as the names of some of the other organizers who during the course of my fieldwork became known to me individually.

As we edged out from the alcove, there was a sudden commotion and lots of shouting. The crowd scattered, and people ran toward the theater. I thought for a moment the police had arrived but was told, "He's here! He's here!" and then "Come this way!" The crowd rushed to the doors of the theater and surged up the steps. The guard at the door attempted to close the iron security gate against the crowd. Sandwiched in the middle of the group of fans, we were propelled up the steps. I remember asking Raghu, who suddenly appeared, what was happening, and he—caught up in the excitement—shouted, "He's here! Shivarajkumar is here!" As we were yanked into the theater, the guard put his hand on the face of the man behind us and pushed him down the steps. The man did not fall because of the wall of people behind him.

A young man whom I later discovered was a member of the theater staff ran up the winding stairway and indicated that we should follow. We dashed up the steps and arrived breathless in the theater lobby, which was flanked on one side by the concessions counters. The man ran into the auditorium, from which sounds of the movie reached us accompanied by whistling and cheering. Raghu, longtime Kannada film enthusiast, followed him into the auditorium; I heard respect and admiration in his voice: "I'm a great fan of your father's. I've seen all his films, sir." The man coming down the steps looked vaguely familiar. I suddenly realized who this was from his likeness on the poster. He kept ruffling his hair, which stood like a cockscomb on top of his head. He was dressed in jeans, very casually. Thoroughly disoriented and not knowing what to say, I clumsily asked him, "Are you Mr. Shivarajkumar?" If he was offended by my blunder, he did not show it. He simply smiled and nodded "yes," following which there were introductions all around. The theater manager turned to me encouragingly, "You can ask him [questions] now."

*

Throughout this time there was clearly no question of me as the fieldworker being in charge of the situation. People around me were taking decisions and creating situations that I had to respond to. Finding myself face-to-face with the star of the film who had been told I wanted to ask him questions, I had to improvise. After expressing my gratitude, I asked him about his role in the film and whether he often attended first-day screenings. He answered readily. Watching the film with the first-day audience seemed a routine; he said he always liked to get a sense of how the audience was responding. In the background we could hear the shouts and whistles from the auditorium. I asked, "What did he think of today's audience?" He smiled and said they were enjoying the comedy. After chatting for about fifteen minutes, during which time he graciously posed for photographs with us, he said he would get back to his viewing of the film from the projection box. When I asked whether I could speak with him at a later date, he agreed and promptly gave his phone number. He invited all of us to the projection box: "there are good seats and coffee and tea there." The theater staff were very courteous to us after that and offered us coffee on the house.

Unfortunately, I was not able to observe a procession from its inception. However, this experience at the Sagar theater gave me a visceral sense of the new release, the passionate involvement of fans and the extent to which spectacle and spontaneous performance dominate the event. Performance and spectacle provide the metaframe, co-opting everything, even reframing fieldwork.

FIRST DAY AT THE RERELEASE OF *OM*, MAJESTIC THEATER

On the first day of a regional film's release, the theater is transformed into a community space for fans. Fans attend expecting to bump into their friends and other followers of the star. Occupying theater space physically and turning out in numbers is important as a display of loyalty to the star and solidarity with other fans.[90] New releases therefore offer opportunities for fans to express their sense of belonging. Fans may therefore feel obligated to present themselves at new releases and at rereleases. Feeling the mood and energy of the place is itself a draw. Even if they do not intend to see the entire film, fans participate in the revelry. To celebrate the occasion they sometimes have a few drinks before coming to the theater.[91]

*

On the last Sunday in March, around five o'clock in the evening, I took an autorickshaw to the Majestic theater for the rerelease screening of the film *Om*. As I neared the theater, I saw Shekar and his buddies crossing the street; they seemed to be heading in the same direction. I had chanced upon many of these fans at multiple venues since our first encounter: on film sets, at inaugural film shoots (*muhurtam*), and in theaters in the Majestic area. At the Sagar theater, it was evident that Shekar and his friends had had a few drinks to celebrate, their clothes smelling of alcohol. This was not the case today. When I get down from the auto, I find Suresh there. He greets me with, "Namma boys yelli?" (Have you seen our boys?). I see another familiar face, which I later recognize as Harsha, who smiles, " You here?" He seems pleased to see me in attendance. I reply that I have come to see the movie. He asks approvingly, "So you are still here? Still writing?" I routinely encountered appreciation of what was seen as my commitment.

As I direct the video camera at the posters, Shekar strolls toward me. He waves and shouts hello, "Yen ri Madam!" His face is horribly magnified through the lens as he moves toward me, smiling. Shekar's buddies gather around and we greet one another. They are in high spirits. They ask me whether I have seen the movie, and I say I am going to the six o'clock show. They are pleased at this appropriate response.

Fans admire the decorations on the theater. They praise the cutouts of Dr. Rajkumar and Shivarajkumar. Some tell me with pride that they participated in garlanding the cutout and affixing *kumkum* powder on the poster on Dr. Rajkumar's forehead. Behind us, activity on the theater facade continues as Rajkumar's cutout is garlanded with roses. Shankar, another fan—slimly built with an anxious air about him—announces he is climbing up on the scaffolding behind the cutout and tells me he wants me to "tape" him. He rushes off and disappears into the crowd. A couple of the men ask how I like the decorations, and I tell them they are excellent (*baala chaanagey idey*)! It is a matter of collective honor that the film be properly hosted at the theater. Later, and in private, a few fans confessed their displeasure with the decorations.[92]

Fans see the film's rerelease as an event in its larger career in which they are participants and therefore are very invested in the film's successful launch. They educate me about its history; I learn that the film, a "superhit" when it was first released, has "real rowdies" starring in it. They praise Shivaraj-kumar's acting: "First class! . . . He has acted as a rowdy." There is general agreement about his talent. While describing the violence in the film, there is disagreement. Some feel others are misrepresenting the scenes, presenting the star in a poor light.

Where physical presence is important as a show of loyalty, fans' attendance is also to satisfy the expectations of fellow fans. Within this close community, fans keep tabs on one another. Shivarajkumar fans kept track of who attended which event. Hanging around film sets and producers' offices, I learned that the star and his family, as well as others associated with the star, received reports on whether fans had attended and patronized his movies. For a while I became part of this circle and found it both intrusive and claustrophobic.

Not seeing the film or being absent from a first show requires a valid excuse. That afternoon Shekar and his group had decided they would swing by the theater, stay for a bit, and then, having done their duty, leave, much like going to a party. This meant they had to account for their early departure. I, along with other fans, received elaborate explanations and excuses for why they were not staying for the whole movie: they have seen it multiple times when it was first released in 1995, they were planning to stay for the beginning and for the first song because it was "First Class!" They recommended it to me: "You must see it; it is very good!" However, as they were planning to visit the star *at his home* and take him sweets—it being the auspicious Ugadi (Kannada New Year) festival, they could not stay for long. Making it known that they would be visiting the star's home not only legitimized their absence from the theater but also allowed them to present themselves as moving closer to the sacred center.[93]

Within the theater, people were in a highly excited state. The packed auditorium was largely occupied by repeaters who had seen the film several times before. Many appeared to be emulating the star, his character of a "rowdy" in the film. They sported an unshaven look and wore checked shirts with short sleeves. A kerchief twisted around the neck completed the "rowdy" attire. People seemed to know one another; young men shouted out to friends, stood chatting in the aisles, and vaulted over the seatbacks to "visit" with their buddies. Given the large number of repeaters in the auditorium, the film becomes a backdrop, allowing audiences to relive the excitement of past viewing experiences through which they engage with one another.

As the titles play, audience members continue to talk and mill around. Those who enter the darkened hall shout out to friends who respond with "Come here, *putta!*" (an affectionate term for friend or child). Then, seeing us easily identifiable interlopers to the community, "Be careful; *ladies* are here!" (in Kannada). Six men shout across the aisle to their friends. More climb over seat backs to sit with their group, falling on their friends amid much laughter. The theater resonates with cheers and slogans expressing fans' support and eternal allegiance to the star, "We will never forget you!" The intimacy and feeling in the cinema hall, shouts, whistles, laughter, smoke from cigarettes and *beedis*, the closeness of bodies, the smell of sweat and of urine wafting from the toilets made the setting very far removed from the clinical placelessness and anonymity of the multiplex.

Looking down on the lower stalls from the balcony section, I can see viewers close to the screen put their feet up and light cigarettes, cheerfully ignoring the "no smoking" rule in the theater. Throughout the film people chat, speak the hero's dialogue, and sing the songs. It is very difficult to keep one's attention on the screen. A man in his thirties seated next to me, who identified himself as an *abhimani* (fan) of the star Shivarajkumar, struck up a conversation in Kannada after he was told by other fans that I was "writing about films." Upon hearing that I had not seen the film multiple times, as everyone else in the theater appeared to have done, he appointed himself my guide and proceeded to educate me, pouring out statistics about the film's "collections," its controversy, other prominent films of the star, the director, and the star's famous family. He informed me that "real rowdies" (criminals and gangsters) had been cast in the film—"See, he's Satish. He's a real rowdy. He has killed so many people"—drew my attention to well-known scenes, "hit" song sequences, and fight scenes, and told me about the "hat-trick hero's" past films and his "action-hero" background.[94] During a fight scene he repeatedly pointed to the star on-screen and then jabbed at his forearm and shouted above the soundtrack, "Rad idey! Rad idey!" It took several attempts on his part and the help of his friends seated nearby for me to understand that the star had broken his arm while exercising and had a metal rod inserted in it, but even so he was able to do fight scenes without a stunt double.

During the intermission people greet one another and talk animatedly. Men move around, again leaping over seat backs to sit with their friends, slap each other on the back, and laugh loudly. Some more fans recognize me and come over to say hello. They want to exchange addresses, send me photographs of the star. They say they are doing it out of friendship and that seeing their star is like seeing a god (*devatha*) and that he is "that kind of man." Once again there are many demonstrations of loyalty: "We are prepared to do anything for Rajkumar family!" In this context offering to send photographs may be understood to be an expression of faith and communitas while at the same time a performance of loyalty and affiliation that they hope will reach the star.

Fans wish to extend this community feeling and its shared emotional high. Before one film event ends, they look ahead to the next. That day, fans tell me I must attend the birthday celebrations of Dr. Rajkumar on April 24.[95] On this auspicious and significant date, the film *Swastik*, starring Dr. Rajkumar's middle son, Raghavendra Rajkumar, is scheduled for release. Eagerly anticipating this event, fans inform me it is "Upendra direction." I tell them regretfully that I have to go back to college, which means leaving Bangalore. They ask whether I cannot delay my departure for this important event: "Can't you explain to them that it is important? That it is *Rajkumar's birthday*?" I repeat my regrets and some look annoyed. They persist, "It would be really nice if you could attend the celebrations on the twenty-fourth and also the release of *Andamans*, Shivarajkumar's next film." Toward the end of the film, when everyone was standing and watching the last scene, a fan remarked to the theater at large—an anonymity that was no longer anonymous—"Next we'll meet at *Andamans*!" The star's next film was timed for release on April 10. The remark met with cheers, laughter, and applause.

AUDIENCES PUT ON A SHOW

Inversions, experimentation, and improvisation all shape the in-theater experience of the new release.[96] The film's "effects" are elaborated, contributing to the carnival aesthetic, recasting the film as show or performance. Fans take over the theater, rewrite the rules of spectatorship, and produce entertainment spectacle while routinely overturning the order that separates film space from theater or audience space.[97] Celebrations outside the theater continue inside. I heard rumors of fireworks being set off *inside* the theater as part of the festivities. Historian Randor Guy describes the experience of going to see a film starring M. G. Ramachandran in Bangalore: "They were lighting camphor and bursting [fire]crackers in the theater. The smoke was so thick I couldn't even see the screen and the theater had to be evacuated."[98] Exhibitors collaborate in producing such "effects." When the popular song "Kabootar Ja Ja" (Fly away dove) from the film *Maine Pyar Kiya* (I fell in love [1989]) played in some theaters, the special effects involved releasing pigeons in the auditorium.[99]

The devotional aesthetic seen in processions and prerelease ritual shapes viewing and is seen in a range of practices that may be described as "pentecostal"[100] (viewing or) engagement with the film, a crossing over from social respect (of the star) to worship. Similar to the Ram Lila festivities described by Schechner, where the *swarups* are worshipped, audiences respond to stars playing the role of gods as if seeing gods on the screen; the experience borrows from *darshan* at the temple.[101] A Bangalore resident remembered that in the 1970s, "for Rajkumar films . . . a shrine would be erected in the [theater] lobby and moviegoers would be given *thirtham* [holy water] and *prasadam*" (field notes, 2011). Incense and oil lamps may be lit in front of the image of the star on-screen (even for nonmythological films), just as they are at temples and in Hindu homes in front of images of deities. More recently, fans performed *arathi* in front of the screen for the "trailer release" of *Endhiran*. When exhibitors projected slides of superstar Rajinikanth onto the screen, fans "performed a full-fledged *pooja* [along with a priest seated in the front stalls] before the projector rolled."[102] Again, in practices transferred from Hindu worship, where the deity is propitiated with flowers, coins, and incense, people throw flowers, coins, and torn-up rupee notes or lottery tickets at the screen when, for example, the star makes a grand entry in the film, vanquishes the villain, or makes a passionate speech about morality or "social uplift."[103]

Reception is performance using the film as backdrop. Audience activities highlight the theatricality of the experience while contributing to its volatility. They actively transform the film experience or "perform its interrealities."[104] A popular song from the Bombay film *Hum* (1991) had audiences in various parts of India on their feet and singing and dancing in the theaters. One viewer remembered her experience of watching the film soon after it was released: "People were going crazy . . . it was so chaotic! People were shouting, jumping from the Balcony, making them [theater staff] rewind the song and show it again and again!"[105]

I came across multiple reports of audiences spontaneously singing and dancing in theaters and on the occasion of a newly released film. The manager of the Plaza theater talked of people dancing in the aisles and while standing on their seats when *Grease* was shown in Bangalore's Cantonment to middle-class viewers and college students. Consider this report of audiences at the new release of *Sivaji*, The Boss: "It was mind-boggling. When his [Rajnikant's] entry, a close-up of his shoes, was beamed, the pandemonium in the theatre was deafening. People actually got up and began to dance in front of the screen."[106] These expressions of joy and collective effervescence at the cinema have remained in place over the years. The Bollywood icon and superstar Amitabh Bachchan comments on the reception for his film, *Major Saab* (1998): "During the song sequence, a friend called me on his mobile from the theater and said, 'Here, listen! People are dancing in the aisles and throwing money at the screen.' I could hear the cheering on his mobile."[107] Given the strong devotional fervor of fans, whistling in the theater, throwing coins, or singing and (ecstatic) dancing may be viewed as performance that is also act of devotion.[108]

The possible presence of stars and film-business insiders at the theater and the knowledge that fans were likely to report on "how the first day went" to the star encourages fans to "put on a show" in yet another inversion that shapes in-theater experience. Fans crave visibility and may be in costume, while stars may attend incognito. In an interview, the actress Priyamani reflected on her experience of watching *Raam* (in which she starred as heroine) in the theater. This excerpt, when reported, functioned as both review and advertisement for the film: "What a great experience it was! I saw people clapping, whistling and even dancing in front of the screen during the *Hosa Gaana Bajaana* song. The audience enjoyed the comedy, song picturisations and fights. Watching the film with the audience was thrilling."[109]

*

The first shows of *Kurubana Raani* and *Om* in 1998 displayed many of the characteristics of new-release events. At the Sagar theater on K. G. Road, the evening show of *Kurubana Raani* began at 7:30 and went on till 11:00 p.m. The theater proudly displayed the "House Full" sign outside. Inside, every seat was occupied, tickets were oversold, and some youngsters sat in the aisles. Ushers and other theater staff clustered in the doorway, eager to watch the spectacle of reception. Every now and then anticipatory whistles cut through the chatter. When the lights dimmed there was a deafening roar, applause, and whistling, which continued for several minutes. This was repeated when Shivarajkumar, the star, appeared on-screen: "Wheet! Wheet! Wheet! Whooooo!" People sprang to their feet to applaud. On the screen there was a freeze shot of the hero leaping in the air; viewers shouted out "to" the star, and again whistling continued for over a minute. In the midst of this pandemonium, latecomers were being seated by the usher, whose torch flashed intermittently as he directed people to their seats. There was a muddle over seating; people complained that someone was in their seats.

Throughout, the audience was viscerally aware of fellow viewers' reactions. The energy, noise and activity in the theater made it impossible to remain detached or focus on the film exclusively. Audiences adopted selective viewing; humorous scenes were greeted with raucous laughter; people fell about in their seats enjoying the scene, they repeated dialogue to one another and shouted out to the characters. The hero's grand gestures received standing ovations. Fans whistled and shouted for the sheer pleasure of it. Much of the film's dialogue was lost in the noise. My viewing companion, a middle-class Kannadiga woman who earlier claimed that she preferred to avoid first-day shows, commented on the hubbub, "this is like Bangalore bus stand!"

Certain scenes received a more intense response. Viewers whistled for ten minutes nonstop during a scene where the hero waits in hospital for the heroine, who is recovering after an overdose of sleeping pills that she took to escape the villain. Someone appeared to be beating a metal object, and a loud clanging sound was heard above the applause. Luckily, there was no conversation on-screen, as no one would have been able to hear it. Whistling continued as the hero, Kencha, visits the shrine of Lord Ganesha, the elephant god, and breaks coconuts on his head in a form of worship.

Suddenly, during a scene when Kencha beats the villain, light from the screen picked up objects in the air followed by a clattering sound. The attention of audience members is diverted. Some people in the Balcony stand up and attempt to look over the balustrade. My companion nudges me: "See—they're throwing coins!" Soon after, I see small pieces of paper fluttering down in front of the screen. She again draws my attention to it: "See—they're throwing money!" Her cousin seated next to her adds, "Must be lottery tickets!" Pandemonium when the hero beats up the underworld kingpin. During this fight scene, viewers again throw confetti into the air, making it a celebration of the hero's victory. Later, as we exit the theater, I ask the sweeper, "What do people throw?" He says, "They throw anything: paper, lottery tickets, rupee notes, coins, even flowers."

This was the first time I had witnessed this level and intensity of embodied participation by the audience. When I saw the film two weeks later, the theater was less full, relatively quieter, and there was no such activity. Three weeks after this, there were hardly thirty people in the theater for a matinee, although the evening show was still half full. A couple of men dozed under the ceiling fans, and a few stray whistles merely drew attention to the lackluster experience.

The film *Om* achieved something of a cult status with legions of Kannada fans when it was first released in 1995. In the film the hero, the son of a priest, falls in love with the heroine, a "middle-class college girl." The story follows the hero as he becomes a gangster ("rowdy") and is then reformed. The movie was controversial because it cast numerous well-known real-life rowdy-sheeters (criminals and gang members)"[110] It also gained a certain notoriety for its portrayal of many of the "real-life incidents of Bangalore's gang world" and for its violence.

The first-day screening of its rerelease (in 1998) involved an even more rambunctious audience than at the first show of *Kurubana Raani*. In a blurring of "film" and "performance" that lasted throughout the screening, audiences transformed film experience into participatory spectacle. Repeaters shouted out lines of dialogue that they knew by heart, and sang along with the songs. They invaded 'film space' multiple times, breaking up the distance between the film on-screen and audience space and taking over the entertainment with improvised performances of their own. It started quietly. When the star's image came on-screen at the start of the film, audiences responded almost as if the star had manifested in the theater. People jumped to their feet, whistled and applauded, shouting out to the star. In a scene where the camera moves slowly up the body of the hero, it first focuses on his feet, drawing whistles and shouts. Suddenly there is a shadow on the screen. The print is so scratchy that at first glance it looks like a defect in lighting. Then it becomes visible as a raised human arm. A viewer has climbed onto the ledge protruding from the screen[111] and is raising his arm to touch the hero's feet, an expression of respect and devotion. Another man joins the first on the ledge and, as the camera moves up the character's body, he leaps up to touch the star's face.

As the film progresses, more viewers leave their seats to move closer to the screen. At one point, about seven men jump on the ledge. Five of them dance in a group "with" the star on-screen; two others dance facing one another. With the film as backdrop, its gigantic images and lighting, the entire scene is surreal—an effect that may otherwise be carefully choreographed at a club or discotheque. This improvised performance was repeated for most of the song sequences, following which viewers returned to their seats, some lighting up cigarettes or *beedis*. They again moved to the front of the auditorium or climbed onto the ledge to dance near the screen when the next song began. A couple of men in the stalls danced standing *on* their seats, encouraged by applause from those seated nearby.

When the heroine, portrayed as a Westernized, middle-class girl, "kisses" the hero, there is uproar in the theater. The scene does not actually show them kissing, as it would not be permitted by censors; rather, the backs of their heads are shown close together, facing one another. Following the "kiss," a momentous occurrence for the hero, he falls down, overcome by emotion. Fans "fall" in front of screen in imitation, which prompts shouts and whistles from those seated.

Audience participation reached a peak when at the start of the song "Mehbooba" (Beloved), about twelve men left their seats to dance in front of the screen—the largest number so far. The fan seated next to me, who had appointed himself my guide, leaned over and shouted excitedly over the noise, "This is a superhit song!" Fans clambered onto the ledge to get closer to the screen. They mimicked the visuals, embodying the emotions and rhythm of the song. When the hero "Satya" rolls on the stone floor of the temple, having taken a vow (*uralseve*), viewers lie down on the ledge and roll in front of the screen. They stretch out their hands to the screen to touch the hero's image. Although their actions are entirely spontaneous, "unscripted," and spur of the moment, having seen the film multiple times before, it seems almost as if they "perform" by agreement. A heavily built khaki-clad security guard suddenly emerged and, waving a bamboo stick used to keep order in ticket queues, struggled onto the ledge, attempting to push fans off it. The men on the ledge appeared unfazed and used the intervention to improvise their "performance." A "chase" scene unfolded *in front* of the screen, and those seated whistled and fell about laughing as they shouted encouragement to the performers. A young fan nimbly danced out of reach and leapt about as the guard chased him down the length of the screen. Meanwhile, on-screen, a scene at a local movie theater on K. G. Road, is greeted with howls of delighted recognition and cheers. The security guard chases a couple of fans to the edge of the raised platform, and they flamboyantly leap off the ledge to enthusiastic whistles from "front benchers." A lone fan evades the guard, saunters down the length of the screen, and tries to touch the image of the star. On-screen, the hero, while singing, takes off his shirt with a flourish: a fan standing in front of screen also takes off his shirt and whirls it over his head while dancing, a move that once again is greeted with shouts, howls, and whistles. A couple of men seated close to the screen remove their neckerchiefs and wave them above their heads in response. Another fan, also seated, removes his shirt and twirls it. At end of the song, the lone fan on the ledge returns to his seat. All the while, those who remain seated clap in time to the music. Lights in the auditorium are switched on before the film actually breaks for the intermission—a signal for restless viewers to exit before the intermission sign actually comes on-screen.

First-day reception offers some insights into "film experience" as performance and an illustration of what is otherwise tacit—the corporeal experience of the film. Mimicking the hero's actions, for example, is a way of following and experiencing his emotional journey in the film and a means for fans to get close to, and affiliate with, the star/hero and the film.

A MULTIDIMENSIONAL EXPERIENCE

If festival is the "paroxysm of society," the new release is the paroxysm of cinema. The meanings of festival and performance saturate first-day screenings. Like all festivals it is "a summation, manifesting the glory of collectivity"[112] seen in the exuberant crowds, fans, and processions. There is a heightened emotion and sensory experience and an intense community-building and ecstatic mood.[113] "Riotous happiness and collective unity, . . . ecstatic dancing,"[114] dark play, "masking,"[115] and "inversions" are associated with the experience. New-release festivities are even more elaborate and extreme in the South Indian states of Tamil Nadu and Andhra Pradesh.

As with festivals, the sensualities of the new release—the visual spectacle, sounds, and smells—make it an immersive "total experience."[116] Also like festival (and cultural performance), the new release transcends indoor and outdoor distinctions, taking over the street, which may become its stage.[117] Decorated theater facades and fan celebrations elaborate film to incorporate elements of *mela* (fair) while bringing spectacle outside the theater. Other features of cultural performance associated with festivals are evident: "gift giving," the sharing and consumption of food, and a "festive atmosphere" with "snacks and tea and familiar faces."[118] Paraphrasing Schechner on the Ram Lila, on the occasion of a new release, and especially for fans and enthusiasts, "the mind and body are full [of cinema]. . . . There is no respite from it."[119]

At the reception threshold film is in a fluid and expansive phase, refusing to be contained by the screen or by the theater. It is film in transition, both "start" and "finish," and therefore a "dangerous [place] for groups involved."[120] The activities that usher in the new release and that seek to construct it as an auspicious event are efforts to contain and define and at the same time elaborate this unstable and volatile form. Ritualized celebrations address cinema's liminality at the site of exhibition.[121] Dramatic events, volatility, and chaos shape its multiple realities.

Processions can be seen as efforts to both elaborate cinema and establish boundaries, while decorations make the threshold spaces of the cinema hall auspicious for this volatile avatar of film. The instability and fluidity of the new release is seen in variations in in-theater experience over the career of the film. As the days and weeks go by, the theater is no longer full, fans relinquish theater space, and exuberance wanes. The progressive damping down of participation and collective response is accompanied by a shift from collective to more individual experience, from "show" involving the audience to "film." Thus, the new release questions existing distinctions between film and cinema and cinema and performance that are based on dislodging film experience from the reception context.

The in-between quality of the new release brings together audience and performer, "consumer" and "producer," spectator and participant. Opportunities to "turn the tables" and change the equation between those identified as producers and consumers present themselves. Audiences are hypervisible, part of the entertainment spectacle, while stars become spectators. The raucous reception of the film is itself a performance or "show" that is privileged over the film and is a source of pleasure for the gathering.[122] The "totality of effect" and entertainment includes the audience as attraction.[123] Through such performances audiences attempt to "finish" the entertainment, once again using the film as raw material.[124] Participatory audiences remind us that the "formalized separation" of actors on the stage and performers in the West is a recent phenomenon and the result of historical processes.[125] The porosity between spectators and performers is again similar to that of Ram Lila and Rasa Lila performances.[126]

The new release featuring middle- and lower-middle-class fans and their activities is becoming a global phenomenon as many Indian films are now released simultaneously in many countries. For the global blockbuster *Endhiran* (2010), tickets across the United States were sold out for weeks. Fans in the United States, Australia, Singapore, and other countries welcomed the film with inaugural rituals that included lighting incense and lamps at the theater, ceremonial cake cutting, anointing a pumpkin with *kumkum* powder and breaking it outside the theater, chanting slogans in praise of the star, and singing songs from the film. Thus the "local" aesthetic of the new release is now exported with the films.

CHAPTER 8

Conclusion

I think to experience the real feel of Indian cinema, one must watch movies in single screens. The whistles, catcalls and claps are an integral part of the whole cinematic experience here.

ANONYMOUS MOVIEGOER[1]

At a screening of *Thelma and Louise* (1991) in the Boston area, an Indian viewer connected with a scene in which the characters drive through Oklahoma, where he had gone to university. His excited shouts of "Oklahoma! Hey guys, it's Oklahoma!" met with disapproval. People seated in front of him turned around and shushed him. When the theater emptied after the film, a woman tapped him on the shoulder and said both she and her companion were "very upset" by his behavior. She then advised him on proper etiquette: "If I were you, I would show some courtesy to others who are watching the movie." American students who were assigned to watch Bollywood films in theaters in the United States found the talkative and multigenerational gathering (including children and infants) "annoying." Some said they "couldn't stand it" and had to leave the theater. Indian and South Asian audiences who have grown up accustomed to the cinema hall culture may find the same audiences to be tame; an Indian moviegoer watching a Bombay film in a Massachusetts suburb with an exclusively South Asian audience found that the "quiet" audience did not meet his expectations. He remarked loudly for all to hear, "This gang doesn't know how to watch!" and followed his comment with a piercing whistle as the heroine appeared on-screen in a miniskirt. At moments like these, when cultures collide, the broader culture and aesthetics, the conventions of film reception in public settings are thrown into relief. On his television news show *Hardball*, Chris Matthews spoke glowingly about the film *Argo* (2012), then showing in theaters, and wondered at the spontaneous applause at the end of the screening, given that it was a film. The question would not arise in India, where cinema is embedded in performance culture.

The anthropologist Karin Barber has argued that we cannot predict "the nature of audiences and publics from the nature of the medium"; instead, "ways of being an audience are made possible only by existing ways of being in society."[2] By examining a non-European cinema tradition, exploring cinema's articulation with indigenous customs and traditions and investigating local "appropriations,"[3] including a lived culture of filmgoing, this book has sought to address some of the limitations in existing approaches to cinema film that are rooted in models of communication, social organization, and aesthetics that are identified as Western.[4] The objective of the study of cinema and its reception in Bangalore and with habituated audiences is a societal perspective that makes visible variation in the contemporary social experience of cinema and its "making," and in doing so highlights the importance of place and culture.[5] It seeks to inform abstract understandings of film that assume its universality and that are based on the normalization and idealization of a particular Western (Anglo-American or Western European) setting and minority experience yet have been generalized and extended cross-culturally.

THE CONSTRUCTION OF UNIFORM "FILM EXPERIENCE"

In the West, cinemagoing has become progressively segmented and homogenized following Hollywood's aggressive niche marketing to age, gender, ethnicity, and other demographic categories. Silent and rapt viewing by an audience of individuals, the dominant and preferred aesthetic at the contemporary multiplex, may be seen to be the product of concerted efforts by the film industry to elevate the film, standardize its experience, and make it the center of the audience's experience. This style of viewing is also rooted in broad societal shifts in entertainment culture and public life.

In the early 1900s, cinema was an "attraction." Films were screened as part of variety entertainment that included nonfilmic acts: live skits, amateur wrestling, and song-and-dance performances. Film consumption was situated in a broader amusement culture in which "people from all walks of life came together."[6] Reception settings for early cinema were "places of chaotic mingling" for a boisterous crowd, not yet a "movie audience."[7] Film viewing in the silent era was interactive, more a "theater experience" where audiences flocked to the show in the theater rather than a "film experience" and therefore subject to variation and instability.[8] Heterogeneity characterized early cinema entertainment; even the sites where films were consumed were nonstandardized: "amusement arcades, music halls and fairs," even churches and barns, served as venues for exhibition, and the "meanings of the locations affected the meanings of activities within them."[9]

As the film industry matured, efforts to legitimize film entertainment and grant film authority involved shifting attention to the film. Exhibitors were directed to remove live performances from the entertainment lest they detract. Attention to lighting, innovations in sound, improved seating, and comforts such as air conditioning were also geared toward "minimizing (audience) awareness of theater space" and removing distractions.[10] The lavish picture palaces themselves came to be seen as a distracting spectacle and were replaced with the more functional multiplex.

Creating a homogenized film experience also meant subduing the spontaneity and "liveness" that could undermine the uniformity of film experience. Voluble and restless audiences drew attention to the theater and to themselves and away from the film, potentially destabilizing the film; therefore, silencing and disciplining the audience was crucial for legitimizing film entertainment. Silencing and homogenizing the audience in the theater was also key to standardizing and creating uniformity in film experience that was needed to widen the market for film across divisions of class, ethnicity, and culture.[11] Film that addressed an "anonymous and undifferentiated public" and whose experience was uniform and transcended place could potentially reach an infinite audience,[12] thus satisfying the logic of mass appeal.

Some have argued that efforts to standardize film entertainment were also fueled by the need to create sameness in public life and in entertainment culture[13] involving "subdu(ing) social and ethnic diversity" and "destroy(ing) ethnic theatrical engagement."[14] In America, early silent films, the mixed program on which they appeared, which included live acts and attracted working-class and immigrant audiences who knew little English,[15] was seen as lowering the tone of film entertainment. The campaign to, as Adolph Zukor put it, "kill the slum tradition in the movies" stemmed from social and moral concerns associated with cinema as low-class entertainment and a corresponding desire to gentrify cinema.[16]

Cinema thus evolved in ways that systematically dislodged it from place and from the local. The films themselves were reworked to this end; early "actuality films," which often presented audiences with local events and happenings, were replaced by fictional and narrative film, which offered a self-contained story. The arrival of narrative film marked the "celebration of film as a new universal language" and required a shift in audience attitude.[17] The objective was a "totality of effect," a type of fascination that would subdue social and cultural distinctions among viewers and turn them into a homogeneous group of spectators, "a tense, well-knit, immobile mass of human faces, with eyes fixed alertly on the screen."[18]

These changes highlight the significance of the spatial and social organization of film viewing. Earlier, the presence of lively spectators watching variety acts blurred the boundaries between "film space" and "theater space," but now the aim of narrative cinema was to absorb the viewer into "film space" and detach audiences from "theater space," in effect "blotting out" a person's physical and social space.[19] Disciplining audience members to remain in their seats throughout the screening even meant getting rid of the practice of having a film play all day so that the audience could enter and leave at any time, distracting others but retaining control over their experience.[20]

In all these ways the heterogeneous publics of early cinema were gradually homogenized, socialized, and manipulated into the silent, immobile, and atomized viewers that are seen at contemporary multiplex cinemas in the West. Yet change in audience engagement with film was uneven, and even in the 1920s audiences continued to be attracted by the theater rather than the film. Localized studies have demonstrated that greater variation in reception did exist that was based on place.[21] Commenting on cinema in the United Kingdom in the 1940s, before television siphoned off a large section of the audience, Christine Geraghty describes an audience that is "wide and heterogeneous" and boisterously social. Yet she observes that by the 1960s there was a shift from the cinema as a multiuse social space that was public and for the mass audience to a semiprivate space for a more homogeneous and narrow segment of the moviegoing public.[22] The development of genres, ratings, and niche films further homogenized audiences and served to make experience in the theater more uniform.

Once Hollywood became increasingly "nationalized and centralized, . . . the production of popular culture receded from both local control and local view."[23] The growth of theater chains and the vertical integration of the movie business further concentrated ownership and made theaters "much less localized and individualized," limiting patrons' influence on them.[24] The multiplex or megaplex, its sound and screen technologies, its "nondescript" and "self-effacing"[25] interiors designed for a standardized delivery of an individualized experience of rapt viewing to an undifferentiated audience[26] was yet another step on the road to the homogenization and universalization of film experience.[27] Hollywood's increasingly product-centered focus—where the meaning of cinema is constructed around the film, its own authority, that of the director and the narrative, and star power—implicitly constructs audiences as objects of the films, a faceless mass of revenue generators. Events like the

Oscars, which so celebrate the films and their makers and highlight glamor and celebrity, contribute to this construction.

BEYOND UNIVERSALISM

Karin Barber has drawn attention to the assumptions that have shaped understandings of audiences historically and offers insights into taken-for-granted ideas about film and its experience today. Film as mass medium may be seen to be rooted in the notion of the imagined "equivalence and interchangeability" of individuals that Barber observes was attendant to ideas of the public as an "indefinitely extensible horizon of anonymous and interchangeable individuals."[28] The uniformity of film experience then rests on assumptions of the "sameness" or duplication of individuals, ideas that Barber traces to social formations in Western Europe, to "new disciplines of the body in space" that accompanied social change following the industrial revolution.[29] Therefore examining how these "disciplines of equivalence" have been adopted by different populations and in different places becomes critical. Barber cautions that while ideas of "'the public' or 'the mass' . . . as a new form of coming together" are "powerful," they need "to be carefully qualified."[30] In Africa and Egypt, for example, where "imported disciplines of equivalence," of "time and space," encountered a "heterogeneous mass" that was differentiated by religion, language, family, tribal affiliation, place of origin, and occupation and by "popular philosophies of irreducible human difference," they were "creatively modified" by local populations, "adopted and parodied" in the popular culture, used "selectively and creatively," and made "locally relevant." "The public though addressed as anonymous and undifferentiated did not really function like that."[31] Therefore, detailed empirical studies that examine "specific forms of address, use of space, modes of staging and expectations and interactions of performers and spectators" are needed.[32]

In India, where cinema encounters a population of startling heterogeneity and articulates a variety of regional and ethnolinguistic cultures, the assumed standardization and universalization of film experience is thrown into question. To understand cinema in this context one has to understand how it is "taken up" by this diversity and by filmmaking practices that are deeply rooted in cultures of performance and in traditions of theater and storytelling that are centuries old as well as by social change and institutional development before and since independence.

Film experience here is not a mass experience, and "the audience does not respond as a mass."[33] Reception is characterized by spontaneity and unpredictability that speaks to the difficulty of standardizing and containing "film experience."[34] Interactive audiences destabilize the film, challenging received understandings of film experience as universal and something that transcends reception contexts. Different sections of the audience experience film variously and "on their own terms";[35] for some, film experience is about "moments of pleasure"[36]—a "get thrills quick" experience[37] that is supported by a loosely organized narrative or plot, a collection of favorite scenes, and spectacle. Many may not even watch a film in its entirety. These practices collectively point to the limitations of textual or narrative analysis as the sole method for understanding the nature and significance of film and its reception. Explanations that viewers use interaction and participation solely to "resist" or subvert the (dominant messages in) film appear narrow and simplistic and attribute an intentionality that is questionable.

Unlike the experience Phil Hubbard describes of going to a multiplex in Leicester where social diversity is minimized, moviegoers in Bangalore expect to encounter social and cultural difference, evident in their expectation of the cinema hall experience and in their strategies to deal with such difference. Theater staff distinguish the audience by social class, status, gender, or ethnic identity, as seen in their differential treatment of moviegoers in issuing tickets, crowd control, and so on (see chap. 4, 5, and 7).

*

Rather than the address of the film, its narrative structure and positioning of shots and so on that shape understandings of spectatorship in film studies, what is most useful for a grounded perspective and holistic understanding of cinema film is "the concept of the audience's work of appropriation and self-positioning to receive it."[38] When we examine cinema as a collective act, as I have done here, we see that audiences become a collectivity by electing to participate.[39] As in the case of performance, this collectivity is "variably constructed, emergent and continually undergoing redefinition and expansion . . . [yet] a powerful active organizing principle in people's experience,"[40] thus calling for an understanding of reception not as films "addressing" audiences who are "out there awaiting address" but as "performance" that convenes "those congregations" and that "constitutes those audiences as a particular form of collectivity."[41] Cinema may be seen as multiple performances coming together.

Hyperlocal distinctions have been significant for cinema, its exhibition, and its reception. Cinema halls are not standardized, interchangeable, and impersonal spaces. In chapter 3, I described how the area of the city where the theater is located, its history and reputation, and the audience that frequents it saturate the meanings of the site while shaping a local aesthetic and the collective experience of watching a film in that theater. Indeed, audiences opt for "local entertainment" as they seek out particular theaters for the audiences that are known to frequent these sites and the atmosphere.[42] The new release examined in chapter 7 is an extreme instance of the local experience of cinema that is received into a community. New-release celebrations steeped in an indigenous culture of performance and festival and intertwined with the spaces of the city question distinctions between film and cinema that are based on dislodging film from place and context. It is unclear whether ethnolinguistic cinema with ties to the local, which I have studied here, can be equated with alienating mass culture imposed from above and that is understood to fragment groups and communities.[43]

The film scholar Madhava Prasad has described film production in India as "a heterogeneous form of manufacture," a process similar to watchmaking in that it involves an "assemblage of pre-fabricated parts."[44] This study has demonstrated that film, rather than being delivered to audiences as a standardized and finished product with a stable set of meanings, is "reassembled" in encounters with audiences and at the reception-exhibition threshold, where it is elaborated and reinvented as theater, performance, and festival. This ongoing transformation and "making," which takes place through a series of negotiations and microproductions, lasts throughout a film's career.[45]

Indeed, cinema may be better understood as play, which in India is understood to be a cycle of creation and destruction, fundamentally "unfinishable."[46] According to Richard Schechner, play generates "multiple play-worlds that are the slippery ground of contingent being and experience."[47] "'Playing' as a process is off-balancing, loosening, bending, twisting, reconfiguring and transforming the permeating, eruptive/disruptive energy and mood below, behind and to the sides of focused attention."[48] Understanding cinema as play and playing therefore captures the fluidity of film. Reception is "microplay" that destabilizes the film and its experience while recreating localized entertainment. Play is also contest: different social groups fight over the film and over collective experience in the theater as they seek to appropriate the film and its experience. Play and the festival aesthetic explain the "inversions" that occur when a film is released and "appropriated" and on the occasion of the new release, for example, described in chapters 6 and 7. Cinema may therefore be understood as "the performance of inter-realities co-existing on different scales simultaneously."[49]

Mobile spectators encountered at the cinema are also characteristic of open-air or "environmental theater," a traditional theater form in India,[50] as well as religious festivals where devotees move through space in processions and pilgrimages. The "feeling of movement . . . the sense of adventure, exile and danger followed by a triumphant return home"[51] shapes the cinemagoing experiences of habitués as it does festival attendees. Audiences wander in and out of the auditorium; fans celebrate new releases with processions. Within the larger frame of performance and festival, getting to and from the theater itself is part of the adventure and performance, as I described in chapters 4, 5, and 7. Bangaloreans described the pleasures of cinemagoing in years past when the city was more easily navigable and when they would walk several miles home after a late show, enjoying the night air. Film itself moves from one set of social relations and spaces to another as it enters the reception threshold. Like traveling performance, it circulates from one theater to another over the course of its "career" and to eke out its social existence. Posters, cutouts, new-release celebrations, processions and crowds, and film music extend cinema to "the streets, back lanes and courtyards" that "become theaters."[52]

Thus, cinema, like festival, offers a "rich mix of experiences" that are "multidimensional" and "multi-sensory."[53] Scripts for films that focus on developing a unique story are less important. Like festivals, cinema events, especially new releases, may be seen as "a happy 'time out' from ordinary life"; for fans, such events are "part [religious] obligation and part vacation."[54]

THE CHANGING LANDSCAPE OF CINEMA IN INDIA

Current reports on cinema in India echo the drumbeat of change. By all accounts the film industry is in a high-growth phase.[55] Filmmaking is being taken over by large production houses, and the ongoing corporatization of the industry is transforming the business. Collaboration with international studios is growing, and an increasing number of Hollywood stars and international celebrities have been featured in Bollywood films, as have Indian stars and actors in Hollywood and other international productions. Further, technological developments such as digital filmmaking, the increasing use of special effects, and so on are altering the way films are made and marketed. To add to this, rapidly differentiating audiences and segmented markets continue to offer challenges to an industry that for decades sought the "all-India hit." The expanding middle classes in India, the spread of satellite television and the greater accessibility of Hollywood films are all influencing audience tastes and are believed to be creating a market for independent films or "new age cinema" that does not follow the song-and-dance formula.

Exhibition has seen a sea change with the phasing out of single-screen cinema halls—the dominant exhibition form in all major cities in India in the late 1990s and into the twenty-first century. Even in the late 1990s older cinema halls in Bangalore were being razed to make room for more profitable "shopping centers." Starting in the early 2000s, news articles forecasted the end of cinema halls,[56] and between 2000 and 2014, many of the cinema halls where I watched films for this study were demolished as mall multiplexes proliferated. In 2012, exhibitors of the remaining cinema halls whom I spoke with were unsure whether their theaters would survive week to week; collections were down, and some gloomily reported that even hit films were not filling their theaters as they used to. The skyrocketing real estate values in the city are a major factor in the closing of cinema halls. According to a recent news report, the Kapali theater, the city's first and only Cinerama theater and one of the largest single-screen theaters in Asia with a seating capacity of 1,465, will be torn down and replaced by a multiplex. The land on which it stands is simply too valuable for a cinema hall.[57] Film-business insiders list a number of other reasons for the demise of cinema halls, including a lack of good movies, increased competition from other entertainment options, new technology such as LCDs (and DVDs), the availability of movies on television, home theaters, and the many taxes that exhibitors are required to pay, all of which make the cinema hall unprofitable.[58]

With up-to-date screening technologies and conveniences such as online ticketing, food courts, and other attractions, the mall multiplex is siphoning off a section of the cinema hall audience. Multiplexes are seen as civil spaces for the "class" audience and the upwardly mobile who seek out these "clean" and "decent" spaces.[59] Watching a film at the multiplex, a "high-end" experience removed from the hubbub of the street, is a status symbol for many. For filmmakers, having their film screen successfully at the multiplex is an accomplishment. A current preoccupation with filmmakers is producing the ideal "multiplex film." Especially for Kannada films, with their smaller markets and significant percentage of audiences from the lower socioeconomic orders, having a film run at a multiplex is a sign of the industry's upward mobility. Thus, reports proudly announce that a given film "ran for four weeks at the multiplex!"

In the United States, multiplexes "introduced retail marketing to the movie business and encouraged audience fragmentation."[60] The contemporary multiplex in the West has been described as a "frighteningly homogeneous,"[61] "exclusionary," "public non-civil"[62] space where the "cult of the individual" finds expression. Sociality at the suburban multiplex is seen to be "shallow" or "light": moviegoers have only minimal interaction with strangers, and even those are highly scripted.[63] In these settings, atomized and homogenized audiences approximate the "equivalent" and "interchangeable" individuals Karin Barber describes. Thus, multiplex cinemagoing in the West together with the niche marketing of films "does away with the need to deal with difference."[64] Moviegoing in America, for example, is recognized as a middlebrow activity where one has a greater chance of being seated next to a college graduate than to a high school dropout.[65]

In the West, multiplex auditoriums are rarely full; there are simply too many screens and films. Phil Hubbard observes that in the United Kingdom, most films are shown at multiplexes where occupancy rates are under 30 percent; thus audiences can choose to sit apart from others for a more private and predictable viewing experience focused on the film.[66] Even if the multiplex is crowded, "there is nothing collective" in these spaces of "individualized consumption."[67] If cinemagoing in India follows this model, the movie experience will change qualitatively. Currently, multiplexes cater to a largely upper-income and middle-class audience who seem to prefer these more homogeneous spaces where they need not encounter boisterous "front benchers" and where they might have a more individualized "film experience." Social control at the mall/multiplex in India affects filmgoing experiences; audiences are closely monitored, at the entrance to the auditorium moviegoers are subject to "security searches," and food and camera batteries are confiscated, thus changing the meanings of being together in public settings. Multiplex auditoriums with a seating capacity of 150 to 300 seats simply cannot provide the experience of cinema halls that can seat 850 to 1,000 people or more. Therefore, multiplexes offer a social experience that is different from the cinema hall. The latter's disappearance may signal a shift from audience as public to audience as a collection of homogenized and atomized individuals. Those who revel in the "House Full" experience may soon find it no longer exists.[68]

Yet contradictions and surprises suggest the need for a more detailed examination that addresses complexities on the ground. The Bollywood megastar Salman Khan, known for his mass appeal, recently predicted the end of the "mass entertainer" film,[69] yet his own film *Kick* (2014) drew "House Full" audiences and broke box-office records nationwide; single-screen cinema halls were reported to be "overflowing."[70] While there are plans to introduce the next generation of multiplexes or megaplexes in India, tent theaters that cater to low-income moviegoers and the urban poor are also reported to be on the rise in many cities, including Bangalore, their status as unregulated and "illegitimate" theaters making it difficult to monitor such trends. Single-screen cinemas were also reported to be embarking on ambitious remodeling plans to offer the comfort and conveniences of multiplex cinemas, or "the multiplex feel," but at more affordable prices.[71] Multiplexes may be facing their own problems. According to a recent report, some malls have closed and with them multiplexes because of poor location planning and zoning.[72] M. Bhaktavatsala has commented that multiplexes have "no staying power," and in that respect, "they are like pubs, the crowd will go to the newest."[73]

Multiplexes pricing systems are the subject of controversy[74] and are seen to further polarize the audience.[75] Multiplexes signal a departure from an era when movies were affordable by everyone.[76] The elevated prices at the multiplex make moviegoing out of reach for even a large section of the salaried middle classes[77] and are seen to create an "imbalance between the rich and the poor."[78] In response to moviegoers' demands, some multiplex exhibitors have lowered ticket prices to make them more accessible. In Chennai (Madras), for example, multiplexes have adopted the stratified pricing of cinema halls with the first three rows being priced at Rs. 10, in effect creating "front bench" seating. Reverting to the cinema-hall model, they have fixed the price of seats, unlike the variable price seating adopted in Bangalore, which can drive up ticket prices for a blockbuster released during a festival or for weekend screenings. Following Chennai's pricing reforms, Bangalore moviegoers submitted a petition to lower multiplex prices in their city.[79]

Except for the nostalgia blogs and forums that bemoan the disappearance of old cinema halls and news reports following the raising of yet another cinema hall, public discussion has largely been framed by market economics, issues of affordability, and so on. Yet a section of the movie audience prefers the cinema hall and not just for its affordability. In 2007 and again in 2010 and 2012 I came across Bangaloreans who saw the multiplex as a sterile space that could not deliver the excitement of watching a film at a cinema hall. Moviegoers in search of "authenticity" in their movie experience and fans seek out the "electric atmosphere" of the cinema hall and the first-day screening experience, which they recognize "cannot be matched by any multiplex."[80] Therefore, very real social and policy concerns regarding the nature of Indian cinema and its heterogeneity are being overlooked. As cinema shifts to the multiplex, we can expect to see a more homogeneous audience, with a section of the audience excluded. An immediate question is what will happen to the "front bench" audience? In 2012 many existing cinema halls had removed the inexpensive seats closest to the screen, there being no takers for this seating. Will the audience that occupied the lower stalls and the Gandhi class be relegated to watching films in tents and therefore be displaced to the city's outskirts and low-income areas? Even lower-middle-class moviegoers may become invisible in settings such as the multiplex, where the upper-income and professional classes seek leisure. A news report in the *Hindu* quotes a man who runs a medical shop saying that where the "common man has to shell out at least Rs. 1000 to watch a film with his family," he would prefer to "wait for that particular Kannada film to be shown on television."[81]

Historically, changes in public settings for leisure have gone hand in hand with changes in public life. In the late 1800s in the United States, the disappearance of existing spaces and settings for public amusement led to lasting changes in public culture. Audiences for vaudeville, melodrama theater and amusement parks were "huge and heterogeneous crowds" that were "drawn from all walks of life."[82] This era was followed by a progressive segregation and fragmentation of the population in a change that led to the loss of a particular "sense of civic sociability."[83]

What then do current shifts in Indian cinema mean for the public culture of cinema in India? for the distinctive aesthetics and practices of filmgoing and engaging with cinema that were observable in India for decades? Change in this context is unpredictable and nonlinear yet constant. Many questions remain. If cinema's "spatial organization is central to its social life,"[84] what does it mean to locate cinema in the consumer spaces of malls? How does the move indoors affect cinema's social existence, its sensualities and meaning? Given that cinema is intertwined with urban life and the urban landscape, as this study has shown, how will such changes affect the city? At risk is much of the pageantry associated with cinema seen in the vivid posters that line the street and in the decorated theater facades and garlanded "cutouts" that bring cinema outdoors. New-release celebrations, the participation of fans, the elaboration of cinema through processions, and the spectacle of crowds, all of which transform cinema into participatory festival and carnival, will likely disappear, as will localized filmgoing and the meanings of cinema that center on the idiosyncrasies of particular theaters and their location in urban space.

Many questions have to do with the future of the Indian film business and with the experience of cinema. For example, will the film business develop along the lines of the Hollywood model and standardize, homogenize, and delocalize both product and film experience? Will this mean a less "live" cinema experience, less associated with the active audience and the social aesthetic that characterizes in-theater experience at the cinema hall? From cinema that may be scriptless and improvisational, will filmmaking in India shift to having scripts vetted by computers with a view to maximizing the box office, an emerging practice in the United States?[85] Can the Hollywood model of niche filmmaking, segmented multiplex viewing with homogeneous audiences, and individual "film experience" accommodate Indian cinema's heterogeneity, the heterogeneity of its audiences? What will happen to the social world of cinema that exists outside the multiplex and that includes regional cinema and its audiences? Clearly more detailed field studies are needed of cinema's lived culture both in India and elsewhere.

NOTES

1. On the occasion of the continuous screening of his film *Dil Wale Dulhaniyan Le Jayenge* (DDLJ; The braveheart will win the bride) for five hundred weeks. From disc 2, special features (Mumbai: YashRajFilms, Home Entertainment, 2006), DVD.

2. Mishra 1995, 69.

3. Hardgrave 1975.

4. Larkin 2008, 149 on cinema in Nigeria.

5. M. N. Srinivas identified a bias toward the "book view" in Indian academia of the 1930s and a "deep hiatus" between the "book view" favored by Indologists and the "field view" of the anthropologist. Srinivas's fieldwork in rural India led him to question the "relation, or its lack between the book-view and the field-view" while he noted that "one of the most difficult problems in the study of civilizations is to relate these two different views in a meaningful way with the aid of historical and regional studies" (Srinivas [1966] 2002, 573).

6. See the work of Stuart Hall (1973), David Morley (1980, 1986) and other scholars associated with the Birmingham School (Willis 1978; Hebdige 1979; Fiske 1986; Brundson and Morley 1978).

7. Curran 1990. For McQuail (1997), it is a flawed concept. Miller and Philo (2001) describe it as a "wrong turn" in audience research and as "naïve relativism."

8. Fuller 1990, 75.

9. Armbrust 1998, 413.

10. See Stoller 1989, 4–7 and 9, on a sensory ethnography.

11. Reimer 1977.

12. Srinivas (1966) 2002; Narayan 1993.

13. Others identify Madras as the city with the largest number of theaters (Dickey 1993; Hardgrave 1975).

14. Some place the number between 25 and 30. Palahalli Vishwanath, "The Heydays of Bangalore's Movie Halls," *Citizen Matters*, September 19, 2009; K. N. Venkatasubba Rao, "City's Cinemas Have Many Firsts," *Hindu*, February 23, 2010.

15. After the aromatic sandalwood tree, genus *Santalum*, native to the region.

16. Jancovich, Faire, and Stubbings 2003, 24.

17. "Four Billion Tickets Sold and 1000 Movies Each Year? Not Hollywood, Silly. . . ." *Blog-critics*, http://blogcritics.org/four-billion-tickets-sold-and-1000/. In 2009 India is reported to have produced 1,101 films; Indian films sold 3.6 billion tickets. The comparative figures for Hollywood are 739 and 2.6 billion (Shabnam Mahmood and Manjushri Mitra, "Bollywood Sets Sights on Wider Market," *BBC News*, June 25, 2011, business sec., http://www.bbc.co.uk/news/business-13894702). In 2011, 1,255 films were produced in India (or certified) and 3.3 billion tickets were sold (Lecuyer 2013). It has been suggested that around five billion annual visits are made to movie theaters in India, four times as many as in the United States (Dudrah 2006, 35).

18. Nandy 1981.

19. The next of kin.

20. Pandian 1992, 17.

21. Nair 2005, 234, 396.

22. Appadurai and Breckenridge 1988, 6; see also Ortner 2013, 8.

23. Ortner 2013, 8.

24. Hughes 2003.

25. Hannerz 2010, 544.

26. Hahn 1994, 103.

27. Press 1996.

28. Sobchack 1992; Hanich 2010.

29. Shashi Tharoor, "India's Odd Enduring Patchwork," *New York Times*, August 8, 1997. Yet beyond the twenty-two official languages, there are several regional languages. The number of dialects was recently reported as 1,652 (Lecuyer 2013).

30. In 2001, the country's literacy was 64.8 percent with 304 million illiterate. *IndiaSpend*, July 30, 2013, http://www.indiaspend.com/sectors/at-270-million-indias-poverty-equals-illiteracy-75570. In 2011, 74% of the population was literate with approximately 273 million illiterate.

31. Vishwanath, *Heydays of Bangalore's Movie Halls*.

32. See Becker et al. (2006, 16) on the need for variation for expanding the conceptual strength of explanatory frameworks in the social sciences.

33. Hahn 1994; Barber 1997.

34. Becker et al. 2006, 6.

35. Barber 1997, 349.

36. Adorno and Horkheimer 1972; Rosenberg and White 1957.

37. Barber 1997, 348.

38. Ibid., 348, 353.

39. Ibid., 350.

40. See Boyle 2009, 262.

41. Hahn 1994, 103.

42. See Dickey 1993, 5.

43. Rajadhyaksha 1986; Rajadhyaksha and Willemen 1999; Vasudevan 1999; Ramachandran 1985; Kabir 2001; Mishra 2002; Dwyer 2002; Vasudev 1995; Das Gupta 1991; Thoraval 2001.

44. Hughes 2003, 2; See Srinivas 1998, 2002.

45. Sivathamby 1981; Dissanayake and Sahai 1992; Nandy 1981; Vasudevan 1991, 2000; Booth 1995; Thomas 1985; Gokulsing and Dissanayake 1998; Gopalan 2002; Raghavendra 2008.

46. Madhava Prasad 1998; Nandy 1981; Bharucha 1994; Niranjana 1994; Chakravarty 1989, 1993; Vasudev 1995; Thomas 1995; Inden 1999; Rajadhyaksha 1993, 2003; Rai 2009.

47. Pandian 1992, 1996; Jacob 2009; Srinivas 2000a, 2000b; Dwyer and Patel 2002; Vasudevan 2003; Sharma 2003; Bhowmick 2009; Mazzarella 2013.

48. Grimaud 2004; Booth 2008; Ganti 2012.

49. Chakravarty 1993; Nandy 1998; Dissanayake 1997; Dissanayake and Sahai 1992; Uberoi 2001; Rajadhyaksha 1998; Kasmi 1999; Rajadhyaksha and Willemen 1995; Derne 2000; Mishra 2002. Vasudevan 1995 and Rajadhyaksha 1994 (see Hughes 2003 for a critique).

50. Hardgrave 1975; Uberoi 2001; Pfleiderer and Lutz 1985; Pandian 1992; Srinivas 2009; Punathambekar 2008 on online fan communities. For exceptions, see Dickey 1993; Athique 2009; Hughes 1996.

51. Hughes 2003, 1.

52. In terms of "audience reach," the market is growing at an impressive 15 to 17 percent annually. In comparison, Hollywood audiences are growing at 5 to 6 percent a year. Mahmood and Mitra, "Bollywood Sets Sights on Wider Market." In 2012 the Indian film industry was reported to have grown at 21 percent.

53. Lecuyer 2013.

54. The early work of theorists such as Christian Metz established the study of film as a "cinema semiotics" and "in terms of codes and textual systems" (Metz 1974; in Stacey 1994, 256). Screen theory further emphasizes text-based analysis of film with less attention paid to the study of context for film production and reception (Dudrah 2006; Hughes 2011). In the 1970s, apparatus theory examined how the physical conditions of cinematic space and its machinery gave spectators the illusion of authoring meaning. See the work of Metz, Heath, Baudry, Mulvey, Silverman, and Doane (Williams 1995, 1).

55. Sobchack 1992, 269; in Williams 1995, 1.

56. See Stacey 1994, 23, on feminist film theory and distaste for the messiness of "empiricist research"; Allen 1990.

57. Mulvey 1973; Doane 1982. See Stacey's critique of film studies (1994, 23, 35–36) and Press 1991.

58. Kuhn 2002, 3. See Guru and Sarukkai (2012) for an important discussion of the ethics of theorizing and representation.

59. Even in media audience research, the study of film audiences has lagged behind the study of audiences for other media such as television or radio (Reisman and Reisman 1952, 202).

60. Dickey 1997, 416.

61. Austin 1989; Hill 1997.

62. Hanich 2010; Larkin 2008.

63. Epstein 1998, 112.

64. In India Hindi-language Bombay films attract a national audience, many of whom may not follow Hindi all that well, if at all. See also Larkin (1997) on Nigerian audiences watching Bollywood imports.

65. Hahn 1994, 108.

66. Ibid., 103–4.

67. Ibid., 108, italics in original.

68. Ibid., 108.

69. See, e.g., Hanich 2010, 67; Sobchack 1992.

70. Friedson 1953, quoted in McQuail 1997, 22.

71. McQuail 1997, 22.

72. Kakar 1980, 12.

73. Caves 2000, 175, 3.

74. Barber 1997, 355.

75. "The pleasure people get from a night on the town depends on the presence of other people at the event itself and the shared residue of memories of the experience" (Caves 2000, 175). See Simmel on sociability (1949, 257).

76. Hanich 2010, 51.

77. "Sociability is the play-form of association" (Simmel 1949, 254).

78. Jancovich, Faire, and Stubbings 2003, 27. In feminist film theory, for example, audience "pleasures" have been dismissed as "false consciousness," either "voyeuristic" or "fetishistic" (Stacey 1994, 21).

79. Dudrah 2006, 23.

80. See Blumer's ([1933] 1970) Payne Fund Studies; Friedson 1952, 1954; see also Spitulnik 1993, 299.

81. The work of Stuart Hall, David Morley, Paul Willis (1978), Brunsdon and Morley (1978), Hebdige (1979), and others.

82. Liebes and Katz 1990; Seiter et al. 1989.

83. Spitulnik 1993.

84. Grossberg 1987, 34; in Spitulnik 2002, 349: "the force of the mass media changes with the context and the accompanying activities."

85. See Jancovich, Faire, and Stubbings 2003; Allen 1990; Gomery 1992; Fuller 1996; Hansen 1991; Waller 1995; Ogihara 1990.

86. Jancovich, Faire, and Stubbings 2003, 1; Allen 1990, 351.

87. Gomery 1992, 43; quoted in Jancovich, Faire, and Stubbings, 2003, 1; Fuller 1996 on early cinema.

88. Jancovich, Faire, and Stubbings 2003; Waller 1992, 1995; Rosenzweig 1983.

89. Larkin 1998, 46, quotes Diawara 1992 and Okome and Haynes 1995 (italics in original).

90. Watts 1996. Much of the work on media and cultural imperialism is based on this assumption.

91. See Hahn 1994; Powdermaker 1962.

92. See Hubbard 2003b, 259; Boyle 2009; Corbett 1998; Jancovich, Faire, and Stubbings 2003; Srinivas 1998, 2002; Athique 2009; Hoek 2013.

93. Hubbard 2003b: 258–59. See also Boyle 2009.

94. Hubbard 2003a, 2003b; Boyle 2009; Jancovich, Faire, and Stubbings 2003.

95. Press 1996, 114. For exceptions, see Hahn 1994; Dickey 1993; Pandian 1992.

96. Jancovich, Faire, and Stubbings 2003. Even works described as cross-cultural have addressed the reception of Hollywood films in Britain, for example (Stacey 1994; Klinger 1997, 127).

97. Jancovich, Faire, and Stubbings 2003, 1; Allen 1990, 351. Early sociological studies attempted to address the "social situation" of film reception (Blumer [1933] 1970; Friedson 1954). Following cultural studies, context has been variously introduced into reception analysis as the social background and identities of audiences, domestic settings, and everyday contexts for television viewing or discourse (Morley 1980, 1986, 1992; Brundson and Morley 1978; Silverstone 1994; Lull 1990; Lindlof 1987). David Morley's studies of television for example were driven by concerns regarding the differential interpretation of content by audiences belonging to different social backgrounds or positions. On a more macro level, historical and political contexts have located the study of media and film reception (Staiger 1992; Klinger 1997; Larkin 2008, Abu-Lughod 2005).

98. Klinger 1994; in Jancovich, Faire, and Stubbings 2003, 7.

99. McEachern 1998. Alternatively, culture has been examined as differences in values and belief systems, history, national or ethnic cultures, and ideologies that are reflected in audiences' interpretations of texts and styles of engagement. Liebes and Katz 1990; Ang 1991; Stacey 1994; Shively 1992; Klinger 1997; Mankekar 2002.

100. McEachern 1998, 259.

101. Barber 1997, 353.

102. Ibid., 356.

103. Becker 1982, 7

104. Becker, Faulkner, and Kirshenblatt-Gimblett 2006, 6.

105. The concept of a career is "imported . . . from the study of occupational careers" and refers to "typical sequences of movement and change in the story of any artwork. . . . These sequences provide, analytically, a series of points at which . . . the work might have gone differently . . ." (Becker, Faulkner, and Kirshenblatt-Gimblett 2006, 5–6).

106. See Klinger 1997, 108–9; Arnold 1990; Spitulnik 1993.

107. Schechner 1993.

108. Singer 1959, 972.

109. See Spitulnik (1993, 301) on " the constellation of processes that include direct responses to media content, decodings of media messages, phenomenological comportment toward media technologies and appliances, social relations among groups of media users; and the material, economic and cultural conditions of media ownership and use."

110. Ang 1996, 67, 165; Radway 1984, 1988; Hughes 2011, 292.

111. Allen 1990, 352.

112. Stacey (1994, 48) on the "striking absence" of discussions of method in film studies.

113. Stacey 1994, 12. The "sheer productivity of textual analysis often rendered any reference to actual audiences redundant as the audience-text relationship became unproblematically inferred from a particular 'reading' of the by now extremely problematised text" (Brunt 1992, 70).

114. McEachern 1998, 258. For example, the "family television" studies of the Birmingham Cultural Studies Group. Morley 1986; Lull 1988, 1990; Lindlof 1987; Morley and Silverstone 1990; Silverstone 1994; Hughes 2011, 303.

115. See Boyle 2009, 26; Jancovich, Faire, and Stubbings 2003 for a critique.

116. Jancovich, Faire, and Stubbings 2003, 27.

117. McEachern 1998.

118. Spitulnik 1993, 302.

119. McQuail 1997, 22. See also Becker, Faulkner, and Kirshenblatt-Gimblett 2006.

120. Katz 1988 on background and foreground factors; McEachern 1998.

121. Csikzentmihalyi and Kubey, quoted in Liebes and Katz 1990, 19.

122. Jowett and Linton 1980.

123. Brunt 1992, 69.

124. Bird 1992, 251.

125. Brunt 1992; McEachern 1998. See Staiger, 1992, 2000. Historical ethnographies of film audiences and reception, for example, necessarily rely on retrospective accounts of events that took place decades ago and on self-reports in viewer diaries, letters, even survey responses. Stacey 1994; Kuhn, 2002.

126. McEachern 1998; Ang 1990; Spitulnik 1993; Abu-Lughod 2005.

127. For example, Liebes and Katz 1990. Seiter's work on television audiences is based on twenty-six interviews of sixty-four participants divided into groups. Interviews were short, and the research took three weeks. See McEachern 1998, 257.

128. McEachern 1998, 259.

129. See Michel de Certeau (1984) on "hidden operations," the "secondary" or clandestine production by consumers (xiii), which is "dispersed," "hidden," "insinuates itself everywhere silently and almost invisibly" (xii).

130. Hughes 2003, 1: "a unique interaction of people and projected media at a specific place and occasion." Dickey 1993: 12; See Srinivas 1998, 2002.

131. Abu-Lughod 2005, 19.

132. Ibid., 26.

133. Pfleiderer and Lutz 1985.

134. Dickey 1993.

135. Derne 2000.

136. Hardgrave 1975, Pandian 1992, and more recently Srinivas 2009.

137. English-language studies are mostly of cinema in the United States and England. See Hansen 1991; Jancovich, Faire, and Stubbings 2003; Waller 1995; Fuller 1996; Geraghty 2000; Gomery 1992; Hubbard 2003a, 2003b; Boyle 2009; exceptions are Dickey 1993; Hughes, 1996, 2000; also Hahn 1994; Larkin 2008; Himpele 1996.

138. Keil's 1966 landmark study of blues musicians and performances, for example; Levine 1988; Johnson 1995; Nasaw 1999; Papp and Kirkland 1988; Mittman 1984.

139. Klinger 1997, 123.

140. See George Marcus on "follow(ing) the thing" for a multisited ethnography in Abu-Lughod 2005, 35; Larkin 1998 on media circulations.

141. Film scholars themselves have called for greater attention to cinema at the "interface" of exhibition. See Hughes 2003. Comolli has argued that "the cinema is born immediately as a social machine," acknowledging the social function of exhibition (Comolli 1980, 122; in Arnold 1990 46). See also Srinivas 2002.

142. Hubbard 2003b: 258.

143. Becker 1982, 38.

144. As per map of Bangalore theaters drafted by Dr. B. G. Kulkarni for my research.

145. See Hannerz 1969, 16, on the selectivity that shapes the "field situation" and ethnographic research.

146. See Hannerz 2004, 13, on "polymorphous engagements" in fieldwork.

147. The study is therefore a departure from reception research that examines a particular subculture or audience demographic. For example, men's filmgoing (Derne 2000), women (Stacey 1994), children, or a particular ethnic group (Shively 1992).

148. Stoller (1989, 7) calls for "sensual immersion in the field" and for "tasteful fieldwork."

149. Ibid.

150. See Bestor 2004, 41.

151. Jancovich, Faire, and Stubbings 2003; Spitulnik 1993; Allen 1990.

152. Natural history, a "fundamental concept of the Chicago School," refers to a "temporal process" or "pattern" that "could be understood as a whole, beyond the contingent details"; it carries a sense of "unfolding" according to an "internal logic" (Abbott 1997, 1154).

153. Becker (1982, 34) describes an "art world" as "a network of cooperative links among participants."

154. See Stoller 1989 on an ethnography of the senses.

155. What Paul Willis has characterized as ethnography's "profoundly important methodological possibility—that of being surprised, of reaching knowledge not prefigured in one's starting paradigms" (Willis 1980, in Brunt 1992, 71). See also Willis and Trondman 2000.

156. See Becker, Faulkner, and Kirshenblatt-Gimblett (2006, 6–11) on endings and the "finishedness" of an artwork.

157. See Madhava Prasad 1998.

158. Marcus 1998, in Abu-Lughod 2005, 20.

159. Abu-Lughod 2005, 24.

160. See Hannerz 2004, 7, on "on and off-site conversations."

161. The social class of fans varies by the star (Hardgrave 1975). I have referred to the class background of people in Bangalore using local identifications and ways of thinking about class and of assigning and displaying class status that encompasses levels of education or literacy, fluency in English, language(s) spoken, occupation, place of residence and home ownership when known, and attire and demeanor, all of which factor into identification of respondents as middle- or upper-middle class, lower-middle or lower class, or recent members of the new business classes, the newly wealthy in urban centers. See Dickey (1993) for a discussion of why precise class labels and classical Marxist terminology are difficult to apply in India.

162. See Derne 2000.

163. M. N. Srinivas, conversation with author, 1998. Wacquant describes his "total 'surrender' to the exigencies of the field" and quotes Kurt Wolff (1964) on the concept of "surrender" in ethnography as "total involvement [in which] a person's received notions are suspended" (Wolff 1964; in Wacquant 2004, 11). See also Stoller on anthropologists' tendency "to allow [our] senses to penetrate the other's world rather than letting our senses be penetrated by the world of the other" (1989, 39).

164. See Grimaud 2004.

CHAPTER 2

1. This chapter is derived in part from an article published in *South Asian Popular Culture* in 2005.

2. Booth 1995; Kabir 2001.

3. Mishra 2002.

4. "Film-Making Accorded Industry Status," *Times of India*, May 11, 1998.

5. Dickey 1993; Dwyer and Patel 2002; Hardgrave 1975; Bose 2006; Grimaud 2004; Ganti 2004; Uberoi 2001; Thomas 1995.

6. See Becker 1982 on the "collective act."

7. See Madhava Prasad 1998.

8. Grimaud 2004, 32 (translated by Jack Katz; personal communication with author, 2011).

9. Ortner 2010, 222; See also Gans 1999; Gitlin 2000.

10. Gabler 1989

11. Dickey 2006, 126.

12. Dickey 2006.

13. Achal Prabhala, "Making A while the Sun Shines," *Time Out Bengaluru*.

14. Dwyer 2002; See also Kabir 2001.

15. "A Film Maker's Satya," *Times of India*, July 9, 1999.

16. M. Bhaktavatsala, personal communication, 2007.

17. Theatre personalities who influenced Kannada cinema include B. R. Panthalu, H. L. N. Simha, Subbiah Naidu (father of the actor Lokesh), and R. Nagendra Rao.

18. "Showbiz Is 80 Per Cent Greed," *Sunday Review,* August 4, 1996. See also "Flop Show," *Sunday Herald* (Bangalor), July 19, 1998.

19. Grimaud 2004, 63.

20. Ibid.

21. "Showbiz," 1996.

22. Thomas 1995.

23. I did visit the set of one director who worked with a prepared script.

24. Interview on Koffee with Karan. http://www.youtube.com/watch?v=FcQCIt5Bt08 (accessed June 30, 2010; no longer posted). See also Ganti 2012 on filmmaking in Bombay.

25. Interview on Face the Review. http://www.youtube.com/watch?v=z16xwxjk3Xs&feature =channel (accessed June 30, 2010; no longer posted).

26. Starting in 2005, some of the larger corporate film producers, such as UTV and Yash Raj Films, "insist on a written and bound script before they discuss any project" (Kohli-Khandekar 2006, 125).

27. "Showbiz."

28. Howard Becker (1982, 7–9) on the "fine division" of labor in in the making of large-budget films.

29. Hardgrave 1975, 111–12.

30. Grimaud 2004, 65.

31. Pandian 1992, 46.

32. Hein 1959, 89.

33. Gargi 1966; Hein 1959, 74.

34. Lutgendorf 1991, 84.

35. Hein 1959, 74, 89.

36. See Faulkner and Anderson (1987, 884) on the "gambling instincts" of Hollywood film-makers and the "perpetual worry" that is part of filmmaking.

37. Hardgrave 1975, 94.

38. Madhava Prasad 1998.

39. Grimaud 2004. See also Kohli-Khandekar 2006, 120.

40. Liu 2006.

41. Risk and failure as characteristics of the film business and the business of popular media transcend time and place. An article in the *Economist* ("How to Manage a Dream Factory," January 16, 2003) describes the Hollywood entertainment business as an "odd industry. . . . Firstly, it is hugely hit driven. Most of the films flop, most records fail, most TV series fail. A single hit . . . can transform profits. The fizzling out of a hit . . . can drag down an entire division." See also Ohmann 1996.

42. Top bidding refers to those films for which distributors bid the most. Distributors offer a price for releasing films in particular "territories" where they own a share of profits.

43. Typically the ratio of success to failure (or hit to flop) was 20:80, and every year saw fifteen to twenty films enter the top bidding range, but in the first quarter of 1998, out of forty-two films released by Bollywood, thirty-eight were reported to be "total washouts" ("Panic Sets In among Bollywood Filmmakers as Several Big-Budget Movies Crash," *India Today*, June 29, 1998 [http://www.indiatoday.intoday.in/articlePrint.jsp?aid=262990]; "Bollywood's Flop Parade," *Outlook*, May 4, 1998). According to Taran Adarsh, editor of *Trade Guide*, over 95 percent of releases in 1998 were "disasters" at the box office ("*Titanic* Sinks Bollywood Films," *Indian Express*, May 29,1998).

44. "Flop Show."

45. Madhava Prasad 1998.

46. Hardgrave (1975, 106) reports a rate of 60 percent in the Tamil film business.

47. A reference to the "black" or underground market.

48. Grimaud 2004, 57.

49. Bose 2006, 20.

50. Ibid.

51. Shekar Hooli, July 29, 2010, http//www.filmibeat.com/kannada/news/2010/khc-stay-auction-rajendra-home-280710-html.

52. While organizations such as the Film Finance Corporation may fund nonmainstream cinema, they do not appear to be involved with commercial films.

53. See Ganti 2012 for an in-depth discussion of film financing and liberalization reforms.

54. The government's series of economic reforms aimed to "open up" the Indian economy—thus far crippled by regulations, controls, and bureaucracy—to the global economy. Import controls and rules for foreign investment were relaxed, and the industrial licensing system was abolished. The "liberalization package" (Varma 1998) included a host of radical policies that sought to make it simpler to start businesses, to import and export goods, and to shift the emphasis from state-owned to private enterprise.

55. The reach of television jumped from 9 percent in 1991 to 74 percent in 1995 (Varma 1998, 178).

56. Varma 1998.

57. Uberoi 2001; Kohli-Khandekar 2006.

58. In 2006–2007, over 60 percent of moviegoers were under age thirty. Kaveree Bamzai, "Freaky Fridays," *India Today International*, April 30, 2007.

59. Kohli-Khandekar (2006) reports that revenues from overseas markets played a large role in changing the way the film industry functions. Even though NRIs spend a fraction of their total entertainment expenditure on Indian movies, as a market segment they are becoming increasingly influential. In 2001–2002, the overseas market was estimated to account for 11 percent of total film revenues. The export of Indian films earned Rs. 9 billion in 2001–2002, *Times of India*, October 9, 2002.

60. Anupama Chopra, "Sliced Success," *India Today*, August 17, 1998.

61. V. Shankar Aiyar and Anupama Chopra, "Boy Meets Girl," *India Today*, January 31, 2000.

62. Gitlin 2000; Ohmann 1996.

63. Daniel Fierman, "Off-Track Betting," *Entertainment Weekly*, November 17, 2000. See Eliashberg et al. 2000 on the "pre-release forecasting model."

64. Even as early as the mid 1980s, *Dirty Dancing* (1987) was produced for less than $6 million and marketed for $10 million (Jowett and Linton 1980, 58).

65. Austin 1989, 23. *Jaws* was one of the first films for which marketing campaigns began over a year before production (Jowett and Linton 1980, 60). In 2005, *King Kong*'s initial budget of $150 million rose to $207 million, and its marketing and promotion costs were $60 million. Bernard Gordon, the Hollywood director who was blacklisted during the McCarthy era, describes the Hollywood of today as a place run by lawyers, accountants, and business people: "moneymen" rather than "the film-makers who founded the industry"; interview on MSNBC, May 20, 2004.

66. Epstein 1998, 34–37.

67. Austin 1989, 9–23. See also Jowett and Linton 1980; Handel 1950.

68. Eliashberg et al. 2000; Eliashberg and Sawhney 1994. Electronic and social media play an increasing role in tracking and publicity and are used to elicit feedback from audiences before a film is released.

69. Derek Bose (2006, 50) mentions preview screenings for Bollywood films in the late 1990s where a sample audience would be invited to preview a film and rank their approval on a scale of 1 to 10. However, such previews were invariably flawed as predictors of box-office success.

70. Uberoi 2001, 301.

71. See Kohli-Khandekar 2006, 120.

72. Bharati Mandapati, personal communication, 1999. The counterpart in the United States during the early years of the nickelodeon was the ballyhoo wagon. In addition, loud music played outside nickelodeon theaters and barkers shouted out to passersby (Fuller 1996, 59).

73. Contrast this approach with the release of Hollywood movies such as *Radio* (2003) and *I Am Sam* (2001), where, through a variety of advertising and publicity efforts, the audience knows exactly the type of role to expect for Cuba Gooding Jr. and Sean Penn as well as the departure these roles represent from the actors' previous work.

74. Eliashberg et al. 2000 on similar reluctance to use formal and scientific marketing and "forecasting models" in Hollywood.

75. Austin 1989. *The Player* is a satire of Hollywood that shows how the process of movie-making is prioritized toward marketing and the business end of things at every stage.

76. Malcolm Gladwell, "The Formula," *New Yorker*, October, 16, 2006.

77. Gabler 1989.

78. Hardgrave 1975, 94. In interviews and after award ceremonies, Hollywood stars consistently express their gratitude for their good fortune and luck, partly to indicate their humility but perhaps also as a belief.

79. Recent Bollywood films dispense with the auspicious scenes and instead display the names of their business partners and promoters in the initial credits. In *Om Shanti Om* (2007), the villain—an Americanized NRI producer, Mike—ridicules these customs and practices of filmmaking as nonsensical and old fashioned.

80. Sivaji, *Truth and Fears*, Friday April 20, 2007; http://entertainment.oneindia.mobi/tamil/top-stories.

81. "Shivaraj Kumar Getting Rs. 91 lakhs for Mylari?" http://www.filmibeat.com/kannada/news/2010/shivaraj-rs91-lakhs-myalari-140410.html.

82. Ibid.

83. "Raam Releasing on 25th @ Sagar," *Deccan Chronicle,* December 28, 2010. http://maja.up-with.com/sandalwood-suddhi-f24/raam releasing-on-25th-sagar-t1476225.htm (accessed January 5, 2011; no longer posted).

84. This is a well-known fact about Karan Johar; see http://en.wikipedia.org/wiki/Karan_Johar.

85. http:www.entertainmentandshowbiz.com/we-are-family-what-do-astrologers-predict-about-kareena-kapoor-kajol-film-2010090169852 (accessed August 30, 2010).

86. Derek Bose (2006, 49) writes of a Bombay filmmaker inviting the "families of his cook and chauffeur" for "an accurate barometer of public response."

87. Gabler 1989, 28.

88. Austin 1989, 4.

89. Thomas 1995, 164.

90. Kabir 2001, 203, 214–15, on Bombay film directors and stars visiting theaters.

91. http://maja.up-with.com/sandalwood-siddhi-f24/raam-releasing-on-25th-sagar-t1476225.html (accessed August 5, 2010; no longer posted).

92. http://movies.ndtv.com/movie_story.aspx?from=bottomrelated&ID=ENTEN20100130894&Keyword=bollywood (accessed June 30, 2010).

93. http://www.bollywood.com/abhishek-bachchan-does-marathon-promo-raavan (accessed June 30, 2010).

94. Jowett and Linton 1980.

95. Ibid.

96. Liu 2006, 75.

97. Gladwell, "The Formula."

98. For a more detailed discussion of both background factors and the phenomenological foreground, see Srinivas 2005. On audience classifications, see also Grimaud 2005; Athique 2009.

99. See Kakar 1980. Himpele (1996) makes a similar observation about cinema in La Paz in the 1990s.

100. Bose 2006, 24–25.

101. While the examples here are from the Kannada film industry, similar distinctions in language and address distinguish films and audiences in other film industries in India.

102. "Love Bites," *Express Magazine*, May 25, 1997.

103. See Athique 2009; Srinivas 2002.

104. See Hansen 1991; Gomery 1992, 29.

105. Anupama Chopra, "Bye Bye Bharat," *India Today*, December 1, 1997.

106. Young Fans Won't Get to See Mrityudaata," *Times of India*, April 25, 1997; Bamzai, "Freaky Fridays."

107. Chopra, "Sliced Success."

108. Revenue sites are inexpensive plots of land that fall outside the urban metropolitan jurisdiction and (temporarily) lack services such as piped water and paved roads. In this context the phrase refers to the lower socioeconomic classes (Rukmini Srinivas, personal communication, 2009).

109. Kakar 1980.

110. 1 crore = 10 million; given the exchange rate in 2010, Rs. 1 crore was roughly equivalent to $225,000.

111. See Becker 1982, 28, on artistic conventions and emotions.

112. Thomas 1995, 164.

113. Hardgrave 1975, 101.

114. M. N. Srinivas, personal communication, Bangalore 1998. Before currency went metric in India, one anna was equivalent to twelve paise and was a sixteenth of a rupee.

115. This proposed relationship between filmmaker and audience needs further examination in the context of ongoing changes in filmmaking. On the patron-client relationship, see Srinivas (1966) 2002, 65.

116. A term that seems to be routinely used in anticipation of a film's success; "Young Fans."

117. Hardgrave 1975, 104.

118. Becker 1982, 32.

119. Aiyar and Chopra, "Boy Meets Girl."

120. Pandian 1992, 46.

121. Kakar (1980) sees the Indian audience as the author of the film text. See also Thomas 1995.

122. From the term *hat trick*, which in cricket refers to a bowler dismissing three batsmen in a row but is used more broadly for three wins or successes in a row.

123. Booth 1995; 2008, 175; Richmond 1990.

124. See Booth 1995, 2008; Lynch 1990 on the social construction of emotion in India.

125. Hardgrave 1975, 97.

126. Gomery 1992: 33.

127. See Grimaud 2004; notes on filmmaking in Hollywood by Jack Katz (personal communication with the author, 2011).

128. Dissanayake 1997.

129. Hardgrave (1975, 2) refers to a "vast system of popular beliefs and behavior" or a "folk culture of cinema." Cinema in the West also had its roots in vaudeville and variety theater, as well as in the thrills of the fairground (Gunning 1989).

130. This includes regional theatrical forms such as the Yatra of Bengal; Ram Lila and Krishna Lila, best known in Uttar Pradesh; the Tamasha of Maharashtra; Nautanki in Rajasthan; Bhavai of Gujerat; Terakootu or folk street theater; and the company drama of Tamil Nadu, along with Vithinatakam of Andhra Pradesh and Yakshagana of Karnataka as well as nineteenth-century Parsi theater (an eclectic mix in itself) and Victorian theater (Dissanayake 1997, 718).

131. Booth 1995.

132. Gargi 1966.

133. Kohli-Khandekar (2006) calls it a new business. See also Ganti 2012.

134. See http:www.hindustantimes.com/india/it-took-us-over-a-year-to-decide-on-we-are-family/story-MTWVZBHTCu9jCRrXPI6Vel.html.

135. Becker 1982, 7.

136. "Crowd Funding: An Emerging Trend in Bollywood," *Times of India*, March 11, 2012.

CHAPTER 3

1. See Gomery 1992 and May 1980 on makeshift theaters for early cinema in the United States and the importance of space and setting for the gentrification of cinema and Epstein 1998 on the contemporary multiplex.

2. Verena Dobnik, "Marcus Loew: The Movie Man Who Changed Pop Culture," *Associated Press*, May 6, 2004.

3. Certeau 1984, 115.

4. See Appadurai on locality and the local as a "phenomenological property of social life, a structure of feeling" (Appadurai 1996, 178, 182, and Larkin 1998.

5. The "opposition between the 'native town' and the cosmopolitan colonial sectors of the city" that is relevant to the spatial organization of cinema has been observed by Vasudevan (2003, 4, 6) and Hughes (2003) in the Indian context and by Larkin (2008) in Nigeria.

6. Demolished in 1999.

7. Nair 2005.

8. Ibid.

9. Open parkland named after Sir Mark Cubbon, an officer of the British East India Company who became the Commissioner of Mysore State and moved the capital from Mysore to Bangalore. Nair 2005.

10. Srinivas 2001.

11. Ibid. See also Nair 2005.

12. Palahalli Vishwanath, "The Heydays of Bangalore's Movie Halls," *Citizen Matters*, September 19, 2009.

13. Ibid.

14. Palahalli Vishwanath, "Early Days in Beantown," *Citizen Matters*, November 5, 2008.

15. Srinivas notes, "In a culture and society such as India's, 'the other' can be encountered literally next door" (1966) 2002, 571–87.

16. Srinivas 2001.

17. Roadside eateries serving Bangalore's fast food.

18. A term used locally by residents and English-language newspapers for men who make advances to and harass women in public spaces.

19. The young men who are described as either unemployed or underemployed and in low-paying jobs who "lived on the streets"; frequently referred to as "lumpen elements" in English-language newspapers and described as "engaging in semi-criminal activities" (Inden 1999, 53). See also Derne 2000. See Dhareshwar and Srivatsan 1996 for an ideological analysis.

20. Vishwanath, "Early Days."

21. M. Bhaktavatsala, personal communication, 2009.

22. K. N. Venkatasubba Rao, "City's Cinema's Have Many Firsts," *Hindu*, February 23, 2010.

23. Ibid.

24. With cinema halls such as Himalaya, Kempegowda, Kapali, Menaka, Kalpana, Alankar, Majestic, Sangam, Sagar, Nartaki, and Santosh (Ibid.).

25. Others place the number in the Majestic area at between fourteen and forty (Ibid.). While there were fourteen theaters in Majestic in the 1970s, by 2009, only two of the original theaters remained. Palahalli Vishwanath, "The Heydays of Bangalore's Movie Halls," *Citizen Matters*, September 19, 2009.

26. The Alankar, Kalpana, Menaka, Abhinay, Kapali, and Tribhuvan were added in the 1950s and 1960s.

27. Although second-run theaters in the city such as Vijayalakshmi and Bharat Talkies screened English films (Vishwanath, "Heydays of Bangalore's Movie Halls").

28. Rao, "City's Cinemas."

29. There are any number of permutations and combinations: some theaters may screen Malayalam and Telugu movies in the morning and Kannada or Hindi movies for the matinee and evening shows.

30. "Bangalore Cinemas," *Ninaivugal . . . Thoughts* (blog), June 3, 2010, http://whowrites .blogspot.com/2010/06/bangalore-cinemas.html accessed.

31. Grimaud (2004) found a similar arrangement with local distributors in Bombay.

32. Theaters that were known for screening such films are Vijayalakshmi in Chickpet and Bharat Talkies on J. C. Road (Vishwanath, "Heydays of Bangalore's Movie Halls").

33. Convenience, ease of access, and comfort are powerful shapers of movie events (Hubbard 2003a, 2003b).

34. Vishwanath, "Heydays of Bangalore's Movie Halls". See Vasudevan (2003, 5) on the connection between neighborhoods and cinema halls in Delhi in the 1950s and 1960s.

35. Vishwanath, "Heydays of Bangalore's Movie Halls."

36. Phone communication, 2004.

37. Field notes, 2010.

38. Hughes (1997, 90), writing of Madras in 1928, finds that film exhibitors at the time "identified locality as the main determinant of audience composition at any given cinema theater," which led to the various cinemas each charting out a policy and program of films to suit the tastes of their particular audiences (see Vasudevan 2003).

39. On neighborhood theaters and class in Worcester, Massachusetts, in the 1900s, Rosenzweig (1983, 212) notes that even after movies became an interclass and mass entertainment, "Many working class people continued to view movies within their own neighborhood theatres."

40. This had changed in 2007, by which time more women appeared to be wearing *salwars* or *churidars*.

41. Ethnic groups identified here as non-Kannada.

42. Since then, Kannada films may have expanded their appeal. However, detailed studies are needed to track the audience for regional films over time.

43. Appadurai 1996.

44. One lakh is 100,000 rupees.

45. "The Select theatre was renamed Gita and demolished in the early 1990s. . . . Well-known cinemas on J. C. Road—Bharat, Shivaji and Minerva, made way for commercial establishments in the early 1980s. The drive-in was replaced with the IT park." Rao, "City's Cinemas."

46. Namely, PVR Cinemas, Vision Cinemas, Inox Leisure Ltd., Fame Lido Cinemas, Fun Cinemas, Innovative Multiplex, Urvashi Cinema, Manoranjan, and Ajantha.

47. Garuda Mall, conversational interview, Bangalore 2010.

48. Lofgren 2002, 2.

49. See Appadurai 1996, 199.

50. Bhaktavatsala 1997.

51. Ibid. See Larkin (1998, 47) on the emotional experience of cinemas in Nigeria.

52. "Ground Zero for Plaza Theater on M. G. Road," *Deccan Herald*, Bangalore, March 28, 2010. http://www.deccanherald.com/content/60785/ground-zero-plaza-theatre-m.html. These viewer memories were posted on March 29, 2010.

53. "'Devi' Demolition," Chitraloka.com (megaportal for Kannada cinema), March 16, 2006, http://www.chitraloka.com/sections/action_cut/devi_geetanjali_06.shtml (accessed July 12, 2010; no longer posted).

54. Vishwanath, "Heydays of Bangalore's Movie Halls."

55. Papp and Kirkland 1988.

56. In 2008 and again in 2010, the Santosh and Sapna theaters, part of the Nartaki complex, were at the center of controversies over the location and the films shown there.

57. "Re: Raam Releasing on 25th @ Sagar," *Deccan Chronicle*, December 28, 2010. http://maja.up-with.com/sandalwood-suddhi-f24/raam releasing-on-25th-sagar-t1476225.htm (accessed January 5, 2011; no longer posted).

58. As per the count I made in 1998. Others placed the number between seventy and 100, but there appeared to be no official count that was agreed on and verified.

59. Goffman 1959.

60. A counterpart to the symbolic value of the theater is the value of the first-weekend audience. Film marketing in the United States creates the audience for the first weekend through saturation advertising, wide-screen release, and other strategies. A heavy first-weekend or first-week turnout has high symbolic value and is read as an indicator of the viability of the film (apart from the actual revenues from ticket sales). There are signs that in India, too, the shift is to the first-weekend "collections" from the earlier "100 days" indicator for a film's success.

61. Srinivas, 2010b, 201.

62. "Bangalore Cinemas."

63. Similar to the organization of theaters in other cities in India. Theaters in Delhi that screened English films to a "socially complex audience" of English-speaking middle classes and the elite were considered "upmarket," while theater(s) close to "fish and chicken markets" were seen to cater to "the poorer sections of the old city" (Vasudevan 2003, 5).

64. Though the class of the audience will depend on the theater, its location, and the film itself.

65. Worn by upper-caste men to signify twice-born status.

66. A sarong-style unstitched garment worn by men in South India.

67. Comment by Mr. Raman referring to legendary hits of the 1970s.

68. In 1941, "the famous Prabhat cinema was inaugurated by the then Diwan Mirza Ismail. . . . Watching a film at Prabhat was said to be a prestigious event in those days," *Hindu*, February 23, 2010.

69. *Hum Kisi Se Kam Nahin* was released in 1977.

70. See Gunning 1986, 1989 on early cinema.

71. Received 2005.

72. A moviegoer observes that run-down movie theaters lead to flops. http://www.ourkarnataka .com/Kannada/movie/blore_theaters.html (accessed August 9, 2010; no longer posted).

73. Larkin (1998, 51) identifies "stories" about theaters as part of the moral economy of cinema in Kano.

74. An article in the *Times of India* (Nikhat Kazmi, "More than Awards, Films Need Viewers," January 28, 1998) noted that while "the country may be the largest film producer in the world, it has only 13,500 theaters." In 2000 there were 12,900 theaters for an annual theater attendance of five billion, of which only 10,000 were permanent theaters, the others being touring cinemas. The ratio of screens to population is one of the lowest. While in the United States there are 117 screens per million and in the United Kingdom there are thirty screens per million, in India there are only thirteen screens per million (Anderson 2000; see Ganti 2004, 25; 2012, 71–72).

75. As per Government of India. However, other estimates place it over six million.

76. A. Raman (1994) noted ninety theaters in Bangalore in the mid-1990s. According to the Karnataka Film Chamber of Commerce, eighty cinemas in the category of permanent and semipermanent (including multiplexes) are currently active (Rao, "City's Cinemas").

77. For example, "Yaare Neenu . . . Makes It to 100 Days," *Asian Age*, August 28, 1998; "Apatha Rakshaka Completes 25 Weeks," August 9, 2010. *Sampurn Wire*, "Porki Runs for 100 Days, *Sampurn Wire*, May 8, 2010, http:www.thaindian.com/newsportal/entertainment/porki -runs-for-100-day 100360522.html.

78. At the time, Kannada cinema was exempt from entertainment taxes, and movie tickets for Kannada films sold at 20 rupees for the balcony and 10 rupees for lower sections. Compared with Hindi and English films, tickets were 40–50 rupees and 30 rupees, respectively, but even such measures have proved ineffective given the other constraints. Since then, further protectionist measures have been put in place.

79. See Hanich 2010 on the phenomenology of in-theater experience.

80. Hanich 2010. See also Epstein 1998 on multiplex design.

81. Hanich, 2010.

82. For example, stadium seating, an innovation in the late 1990s, was designed to provide a clear view of the screen irrespective of where one was seated in the theater: "every row of seats is elevated about fourteen inches above the row preceding it, allowing all customers to have an unimpeded view of the screen" (Epstein 1998).

83. "A Laugh Riot," *Sunday Times of India*, April 26, 1998.

84. Vishwanath, "Heydays of Bangalore's Movie Halls."

85. See Appadurai 1996; Lofgren, 2002.

86. "Give Tax Holiday If You Want Better Theatres," *Times of India*, April 10, 1998.

87. "No More Worry about Bad Theatres Thanks to New Bill," *Times of India*, April 16, 1998.

88. "Rats or Sharks: Take Your Pick at Any City Theatre," *Times of India*, May 1, 1998.

89. In response to the news of the demolishing of Plaza theater; http://churumuri.wordpress .com/2010/03/29/saturdays-girlfriends-popcorn-just-memories/.

90. "Bangalore Cinemas."

91. "Rats or Sharks."

92. Uberoi 2001; Kohli-Khandekar 2006.

93. Apart from noting one instance of conflict over theater space for a Kannada film, I have not examined in any detail the contestation of theater space by the Kannada film business, its filmmakers, and audiences.

94. Similar debates over theater conditions surfaced in Worcester, Massachusetts, in the mid-1800s to early 1900s. According to Rosenzweig, "movie theater conditions accorded with the realities of working class life." Middle-class observers reacted to the run-down and ram-shackle theaters, as well as to "large numbers of working-class people who acted, looked and smelled differently from themselves" (Rosenzweig 1983, 203).

95. However, talking to various middle-class viewers, I found little agreement over what they were willing to pay for improved theaters. Many were critical of increasing costs in newer and fancier theaters.

96. "Tents Eat into Permanent Cinema Profits," *Bangalore Times Supplement*, June 5, 1998.

97. Sharma 2003.

98. N. R. Akshay, "The Day When Affordable Cinema Died," http://arbitblogs.wordpress .com/2010/07/24/the-day-when-affordable-cinema-died.html.

99. See Appadurai for an examination of locality as a "phenomenological property of social life, a structure of feeling" (1996, 178, 182) and on embodying locality and the localization of space and time (179–180); see also Larkin 1998.

100. Appadurai 1996, 178, 182.

101. Discussed in chap. 7.

102. Attributed to Roman Polanski.

CHAPTER 4

1. This chapter is derived, in part, from an article published in *South Asian Popular Culture* in 2005.

2. Epstein 1998, 34–37.

3. By 1997, revenue from sales of concessions had overtaken revenue from ticket sales. According to Epstein (1998, 35), the theater chain Hollywood Theaters made $22.4 million on sales, and $26.7 million on concessions.

4. Epstein 1998, 35.

5. See Hubbard 2003a, 2003b.

6. See Hubbard 2003b, 259.

7. Slater 1997, 184.

8. Nasaw 1999, 2.

9. See Jancovich, Faire, and Stubbings 2003.

10. An arrangement shared by theaters in other times and places. In 1895 and 1897, The Grand and the Theatre Royal in England attracted a wide variety of audiences; the way the theaters were designed ensured that the classes did not meet. The "pit" had its own entrance and the different classes of patron were not only spatially segregated within the theater but did not mingle while they were queuing to enter. In 1911 in Nottingham, England, such divisions were seen in "the plans for the Harwich Electric Palace. . . . The seating near the screen had its own entrance and box office down at the side of the cinema so that audiences would not be queuing at the front of the house or frequenting the lobby area" (Jancovich, Faire, and Stubbings 2003, 74).

11. Queues are characterized by their blurred boundaries. Brady 2002, 162.

12. *Indian Express*, Bangalore, February 21, 1998.

13. http://passionforcinema.com/dus-ka-beesbees-katees (accessed July 2010; no longer posted).

14. *Dil Wale Dulhaniyan Le Jayenge, Hum Aapke Hain Kaun,* and *Dil To Pagal Hai*—three superhit Bollywood films.

15. Mann 1969; Brady 2002.

16. Goffman 1963, 165.

17. On transcendence, see Katz 1999.

18. The dates of films do not coincide with the dates they are in theaters, as in the late 1990s, Hollywood films did not arrive in theaters in India as soon as they were released in the United States and other international centers.

19. Simmel (1950, 321) refers to a "sphere of honor" for those of high status.

20. Queues everywhere are sites of anxiety (Hubbard 2003a, 2003b), but in a caste society perhaps more so. See also Pandian 1996, 950.

21. The appeal of the modern multiplex is attributed to its providing safeguards against "boundary violations" and anxieties about "defilement of the body and self" (Hubbard 2003b, 261).

22. Similarly, hardcore football fans in England enjoy a "fight situation." Dunning, Murphy, and Williams 1986, 222.

23. See Katz 1988, 53.

24. P. G. Srinivasamurthy, personal communication, Bangalore, 2010.

25. West and Zimmerman 1987.

26. Goffman 1963, 127–29.

27. For contrast, consider Hubbard's (2001a, 2003b, 2003) description of the multiplex.

28. *Om*, made in 1996, was rereleased in 1998.

29. Hubbard 2003b, 257.

30. On physical "abuse" of audiences by theater staff and security, S. V. Srinivas (2000b) notes "cane-charges to control crowds" and the "manhandling" of audiences by ushers and other staff in coastal Andhra Pradesh.

31. Policing cinema audiences was observed as early as 1939 (Srinivas 2000b).

32. Dipankar Giri, *Dus ka bees . . . bees ka tees* (blog), November 13, 2007, http://passionfor cinema.com/dus-ka-beesbees-ka-tees (accessed July 2010; no longer posted). Such skirmishes in queues were observed over 60 years ago. In a historical essay, S. V. Srinivas (2000b) observes that "people, in their anxiety to purchase tickets, fall on one another, tear the shirts of others and pick the pockets of others."

33. Those in the queue have a local perception of the queue, where "often the front of the line is wholly invisible to those in the rear," which contributes to the "vulnerability" of queues. Brady 2002, 162.

34. *Public* is the term used to describe the mass audience (see chap. 2).

35. Needless to say, it is difficult to get verifiable evidence of such matters.

36. Goffman 1959, 59, 79.

37. Ibid., 44; Hughes 1971 on "dirty work."

38. Strategies of avoidance create boundaries between self and other (Hubbard 2003b, 267).

39. "In both class-conscious and relatively class-free societies the privileged classes circumvent the line altogether and get their tickets through agents or other contacts. . . . Queuing is confined largely to the less-privileged groups in society" (Mann 1969, 353).

40. Exactly how misleading the queues can be was brought home to me when video clips of advance booking queues led students in the United States to comment on what they saw as a gender asymmetry—"they're all men"—and to ask whether women went to the movies in public settings in India.

41. http://passionforcinema.com/dus-ka-beesbees-katees (accessed July 2010; no longer posted).

42. Ibid.

43. In Andhra Pradesh, theater managers gave "'free passes' to the family of the neighbor of a doctor. . . . Government officials too were given free passes. A 'regime of complimentary passes'" had institutionalized bribery (Srinivas 2000b).

44. S. Kalyana Ramanathan and Vatsala Kamat, "Sivaji's Global March," *Business World*, http://www.businessworld.in/content/view/1971/2034 (accessed April 5, 2009; no longer posted).

45. "Shivaji—The Boss . . . The Big Boss . . . The Mega Boss!," *Oxygen Flow* (blog), http://www.oxygenflow.net/shivaji-the-bossthe-big-bossthe-mega-boss/ (accessed August 2010).

46. In 1998, regular balcony tickets for Kannada movies cost around Rs. 75–100.

47. See Hubbard 2003a, 2003b, on "riskless risks" in cinema going.

48. In rural areas and in "tent" cinemas the "seats" close to the screen are in the mud where children squat, sometimes on a dhurrie (carpet). If a visiting VIP is present, some sofas or chairs are placed for them.

49. Similar seating arrangements existed in Nottingham cinemas, where "the balcony tended to have the better seats than the gods because the view was better from there. The seats got more expensive . . . the further they were from the screen" (Jancovich, Faire, and Stubbings 2003, 74).

50. In sixteenth-century London, theaters offered prestige seating (with cushions) for an extra penny in the gallery section, while the "groundlings" gathered in the yard (Papp and Kirkland 1988, 142). This pattern of stratified seating continued into music halls and movie theaters, where "seats at the back of the auditorium [were] . . . accessed through the main doors, and they had their own toilets. There were also little differences between the seats, in which some sections sat on benches and others on upholstered chairs." Possibly reflecting "Victorian attitudes toward class and/or a reflection of the reduced working class expenditure in that period," differentiated seating remained into the Edwardian period, where benches appeared as part of gallery seating (Jancovich, Faire, and Stubbings 2003, 74). Graded seating was also characteristic of vaudeville in America in the 1800s (Nasaw 1999).

51. Spatial divisions within the theater shaped the movie experience in Nottingham in the 1900s, where "the front seats were divided from the back seats by a wall" (Jancovich, Faire, and Stubbings 2003, 74). See Srinivas 2000b.

52. Goffman 1959, 36.

53. At multiplexes where seating sections are undifferentiated, middle-class moviegoers prefer to sit at the back of the theater furthest from the screen, a space they associate with the balcony.

54. "In most stratified societies there is an idealization of the higher strata and some aspiration on the part of those in low places to move to higher areas" (Goffman 1959, 36).

55. The trophy was the first consumer good: "What is stolen by conquest is desired not as an end in itself but as an indication of a man's honor, a sign that his role in life is to assert his prowess rather than carry out functional labor and that he is successful in this" (Slater 1997, 155).

56. See Certeau on "tactics" and on planning raids and deception (1984, 37).

57. This is actually not the case, as many moviegoers do make demands for and are able to secure seats according to their preference.

58. Konkani is spoken on the western coast of India, including North and South Karnataka.

59. Hubbard 2003a, 2003b. See Rosenzweig 1983 for a description of moviegoing under conditions of "class mixing."

60. Seizer 2000. See also Dickey 2000, 471.

61. Such anxieties relate to caste society (Seizer 2000; Dickey 2000; Douglas 1966; Kaviraj 1997), but a comparative perspective suggests they are more widespread. The popularity of the multiplex theater in the United Kingdom has been traced to its providing moviegoers with "ontological security," which ensures the safety of bodily boundaries (Hubbard 2003b).

62. The "concepts of inside and outside are particularly class marked. . . . People who are viewed as lower class both come from and stand for the outside" (Dickey 2000, 482).

63. Derne (2000) observes the same broad, gendered segregation of theater space in the 1990s in Benaras: "Young, unmarried men who attend with their friends tend to sit in the inexpensive crowded seats in the front of the theater" (33), and while women regularly attended movie screenings at Benaras cinemas, "they rarely watched from the cheaper floor seats" (37).

64. See Hubbard, 2003a, 2003b.

65. Along with Sujaya's name, some personal details including her residential locality have been changed to maintain confidentiality

66. Goffman (1959, 208–9, 212) identifies such "performance disruptions" as "incidents" when a person is "likely to react by becoming flustered, ill at ease, embarrassed and nervous." As performances are "delicate and fragile," they can be "shattered by minor mishaps" (56).

67. Unlike cinema halls in Tamil Nadu, which had designated "ladies seats" (Sara Dickey, personal communication, 2010).

68. The seventeenth century Paris theater was also a space ordered by class and gender. In 1727, a guidebook to Paris, one "intended for well-off visitors," advised that "at the theatre, a man of quality views the play from the stage, from a lower box or from the parterre, rarely from the second boxes, intended for the bourgeoisie, never from the amphitheatre where all the rabble assembles" (Mittman 1984, 27). "Viewing the play from the stage had evolved into a male prerogative. Women did not normally venture onto the stage although they did sit in the loges de balcon or stage boxes after these were installed in the 1670s. The stage seats proper were occupied by men alone" (Mittman 1984, 25). See Waller (1992) on racial segregation and the cinema experience in America.

69. Dickey 2000; Seizer 2000; Kaviraj 1997.

70. Goffman 1959, 36.

71. Slater 1997, 148.

72. "For the young men who are seated in the cheap floor seats the darkened hall provides equal opportunities to shout, laugh, clap and whistle. The loudest, not the eldest or richest, is heard" (Derne 2000, 63).

73. Sivathamby 1981, 18–19.

74. However, there is little in the way of published research on the inclusion and/or exclusion of audiences in movie theaters. The extent to which all audiences were accommodated under the same roof appears to have varied over time and across rural and urban settings and is the subject of debate. See Pandian 1996; Srinivas 2000b, 2003; Hughes 1996.

75. Such terms describe those who virtually live in cinema halls. Kesavan 1995.

76. CNC Unni, personal communication, Bangalore, 1998.

77. Mittman 1984, 27–32, on Paris theaters in the seventeenth century. Goffman 1959.

78. Hubbard 2003b, 259.

79. Dickey 2000, 471; Daniel 1984, 108.

CHAPTER 5

1. Derne 2000, 35.

2. Ibid., 33; See also Dickey 1993, 36.

3. Derne 2000, 33. *Paan* is betel nut and leaf.

4. Mittman 1984, 27–28.

5. In Egypt in the 1990s there is no social custom of single males and females socializing in an unchaperoned setting (Armbrust 1998, 419). In metropolitan centers in India, mixed-gender groups do go out in public settings; however, for a large section of the population, there is no custom of cross-gender socializing over leisure that is outside the kin group.

6. Derne 2000, 34, 63. See Nisbett 2009, 940, on male group sociality.

7. Austin,1989: 72–73. See also Katz and Lazarsfeld (1955) on 'personal influence.'

8. See Austin 1989; Handel 1950.

9. Eliashberg and Sawhney 1994. Forecasting models such as MOVIEMOD have had some success (see also Eliashberg et al. 2000).

10. Liu 2006, 74, on WOM marketing and buzz and the success of films such as *The Blair Witch Project, My Big Fat Greek Wedding, Star Wars: Episode I—The Phantom Menace.*

11. See Kelly 1978.

12. There has been little attention to lifecycle as contextualizing leisure activities such as movie outings (see Kelly 1975, 188). According to Derne, "Once married, men may see films exclusively with their families" (2000, 35).

13. Sebastian Pradeep, "The Magic of Movies," *Deccan Herald, Sunday Magazine,* March 25, 2012. Dickey (2000) argues that for Tamil women, their behavior in public reflects on their respectability and "family honor."

14. See Derne 2000, 36.

15. Ibid., 33.

16. See Liebes and Katz, 1990, 83, on "mutual aid." Subtitled commercial films are not released in theaters, and few dubbed films are released in Bangalore, perhaps because of the linguistic and cultural plurality of its population, as audiences and film-business insiders explained.

17. See Hahn 1994 on traditions of commentary and repartee in Tonga.

18. "A *Los Angeles Times* study found that 45% of its sample usually made their decisions to go to a movie on the same day they actually went" (Austin 1989, 6). See also Liu (2006) on the "impulse buy."

19. Marketing studies on "hedonic consumption experiences" focus on individual consumer moods in relation to particular films or genres. Eliashberg and Sawhney, for example, describe their "forecasting model" as a "framework to predict individual differences in the enjoyment of a movie" (1994, 1170).

20. On cinemagoing in Madurai, Dickey writes, "People are willing to see any movie that is worth seeing [and to most people this means almost any film], and do not think of it as a chance to see a particular chosen film" (1993, 36).

21. Schechner 1993, 41; "playing continually squeezes in through even the smallest holes of the worknet. . . . No matter how hard people try, play finds its way through" (ibid., 42).

22. Simmel 1949, 257.

23. Huizinga 1955, 11.

24. Ibid.

25. Timeliness is not a characteristic of exhibitors either, as films frequently start late.

26. Commercial Indian films are three to four hours long; it is common practice for theaters to institute a fifteen to twenty minute "interval" halfway through the film.

27. Larkin 2008, 134.

28. Contrast this with Katz's (1999, 96) description of families at the amusement park in Paris.

29. Corroborated by Arthur Pais, personal communication, 2012.

30. Nisbett (2009, 945) observes that in Bangalore, "shared participation in slightly illicit behaviour (drinking alcohol), discouraged, if not forbidden by their parents, was also further fortifying of the fellow feeling of [their] middle-class masculine friendships."

31. This has changed with some of the newer multiplexes, where a ticket entitles one to any vacant seat. See chap. 4 on how moviegoers negotiate seating.

32. Simmel 1949, 255.

33. DeVault 2000.

34. See Derne 2000, 34.

35. On the interactional construction of intersubjective experience, see Katz 1996.

36. Teasing in male friendship groups has been described as a negotiation of hierarchy (Nisbett 2009).

37. "The reaction of the nonplayers is a big part of what gives dark play its kick" (Schechner 1993, 38).

38. Hansen 1991 on early cinema.

39. "Cogito Ergo Sum: Sivaji—The Boss, Whose Boss I ask!," *The MBA Who's Also a Blogger!*, http://www.abhijith.in/20070601archive.html (archived entry, Friday, June 15, 2007). See Simmel (1949) on argument and sociability.

40. "The individual . . . participates in an interpersonal grid of spectators who discuss the meaning of past experience with mass communication and the anticipated significance of future experience" (Friedson 1953, 310). Liu (2006) observes a correlation between the "level of WOM" and movie memories, where greater WOM makes the memory last longer, thus increasing the likelihood that a moviegoer will talk about the movie after seeing it.

41. Katz 1988 152, 112–13.

42. *Shivarathri* is a Hindu festival celebrated in the month of *Maagha*, involving offerings to Lord Shiva, fasting, and all-night vigils.

43. Huizinga 1955.

44. Schechner 1993, 36–38, 42. Some details have been omitted for confidentiality reasons.

45. Grazian 2008.

46. Facebook entry 2010. Tulasi Srinivas, personal communication.

47. Jackie Stacey's (1994) and Annette Kuhn's (2002) ethnohistories of cinema going and audience experience in Britain, for example, draw substantially on such retrospective accounts in interviews and audience letters.

48. Hubbard 2002.

49. Schechner 1993, 36–38.

50. There is a tradition of framing popular culture consumption as rebellion and protest—as an expression by the marginalized against the establishment. Such framing is seen in studies of the widely influential Birmingham School.

51. Huizinga 1955, 52.

52. On the ambiguous moral position of cinema in Nigeria, Larkin writes, "As illicit moral spaces commercial cinemas repelled respectable people, attracting only the marginal, the young or the rebellious" (2008, 138, 143–44).

53. Dissanayake and Sahai (1992, 98).

54. Schechner 1993, 36; Huizinga 1955, 52 on heroic contests and winning by trickery.

55. Armbrust (1998, 432)observes of cinemagoing in Egypt that "the group most attracted to this realm of potential experimentation are those who are in flux," "young people," and "students escape into a realm in which social order is reversed or rearranged." Their behavior "verges on the carnivalesque" (Bakhtin 1984, 10, in Armbrust 1998, 420).

56. Schechner 1993 36.

57. "Masking is very important [to dark play]—sneaking off, not being recognized, playing out selves that cannot be displayed at work or with family" (Schechner 1993, 38).

58. See Katz 1988, 52–79.

59. In his study of nightlife in Philadelphia, Grazian (2008, 200) argues that the experience of risk is invented by participants and that in "re-tellings" of nightlife adventures "thrill-seekers often attribute an exaggerated amount of risk to social situations that are relatively safe"; this "illusory sense of danger" is incorporated into "accounts of their nightlife experience in highly scripted ways." See also Goffman 1974, 83.

60. See Goffman on "fabrications" (1974).

61. Huizinga 1955, 52.

62. Certeau 1984.

63. Huizinga 1955, 47.

64. Ibid., 6, 62.

65. Rosenzweig 1983, 60.

66. Conrad Arensberg describes drink rituals in Ireland being "firmly embedded in a reciprocal life style that governed at least some social relationships in the Irish countryside . . . Treating thus provided the nineteenth-century Irishman with a crucial means of declaring his solidarity and equality with his kin and neighbours" (Rosenzweig 1983, 59).

67. M. N. Srinivas ([1966] 2002, 68) notes that *dakshinya* (obligation) was important in village society and governed social relationships. *Dakshinya* gives people a claim on others whom they have hosted or given gifts to: "Because of 'obligation' one is frequently called upon to do things one does not want to."

68. Nisbett 2009, 941.

69. See Nisbett (2009) on the "cycle of treating and sharing" (947) in male friendship groups in Bangalore, frequently involving "an afternoon or an evening's drinking in a local bar, restaurant or *dhabha*," *dhaba* being a Punjabi roadside eatery (941, 945). See also note 30.

70. Betel leaf and nut. In India and in other parts of South Asia, betel leaves (*Piper betle*) are chewed with processed areca nut (*Areca catechu*) and lime.

71. "One by two" refers to the well-known custom of splitting a cup of coffee between two people.

72. See chap. 4.

73. At the time the exchange rate was around Rs. 45 to US$1; however, moviegoers are prepared to spend a considerable part of their income on the cinema. An autorickshaw driver making Rs. 2,500 month told me he would pay for a black-market ticket to see a Rajkumar film, upward of Rs. 500 in the 1980s.

74. DeVault 2000, 490.

75. It could be argued that domestic servants are associated with the family and with inside space and therefore do not carry the potential danger of lower-class strangers.

76. See DeVault (2000, 487) on the family movie outing to the zoo.

77. The soundtrack is also set very loud to drown out the audience.

78. See also Seizer 2000; Kaviraj 1997. "The concepts of inside and outside are aligned with a number of parallel constructs, including family/not family, like/different, close/distant, affection/distance, safe/unsafe, protected/unprotected, clean/dirty and private/public" (2000, 470, 471).

79. Dickey 2000; Seizer 2000.

80. DeVault 1991.

81. See Boyle (2009) on special "baby screenings" in Glasgow.

82. *Vicharaskolodu*, or "courteous enquiry"—also seen at weddings and other "functions."

83. Eating at restaurants or buying food cooked outside the home is a relatively recent phenomenon in India. Middle-class and upper-caste women and families did not eat out at restaurants until the 1950s. M. N. Srinivas, personal communication, 1998; Tulasi Srinivas, personal communication 2009.

84. Seizer 2000; Dickey 2000; Douglas 1966; Kaviraj 1997.

85. Hubbard 2003b, 266–67.

86. Friedson 1953, 310.

87. See Simmel (1949, 255) on sociability, "a satisfaction in . . . the fact that one is associated with others and that the solitariness of the individual is resolved into togetherness, a union with others." See also Caves 2000.

88. Hubbard 2003b, 262.

89. Families often create "a sphere that has a 'private' character" even in a "densely crowded public setting" (DeVault 2000, 498).

90. "A marketplace can be 'a sleeping place'" (Masselos 1991, 40; in Dickey 2000, 471). See also Jancovich, Faire, and Stubbings 2003.

91. DeVault 2000.

92. See chap. 3, n. 52.

93. Sonya Sorich, "Why a Simple Movie Date Can Be Complicated," *Ledger Enquirer*, March 12, 2009.

94. Dickey 2000, 471. See also Daniel 1984.

95. Dickey 2000, 471.

96. On "front" and "back" regions in Western societies, Goffman (1959, 123) observes that "social adults" routinely occupy the front region, while "the socially incomplete—domestics, delivery men, and children—enter through the rear."

97. "Public places in Britain are not necessarily experienced as baby-friendly" (Boyle 2009, 269). Debates in the United States over the absence of appropriate fare for family viewing are evidence of the segmented nature of the popular culture experience and of the success of narrowcasting in dividing up the audience.

98. Hubbard 2003a, 70–71; 2003b, 268.

99. News report on the Century 20 at Jordan Creek Town Center, Iowa. "Movie Theater Offers Mommy Matinees, Special Snacks, Films Cater to Children, Mothers," WeatherNet5.com February 15, 2005. Viewers are reassured, "don't worry about arriving at exactly 1 pm . . . they give parents some slack by starting a little late," and "You're welcome even if baby fusses," or "If

anybody cries nobody has to leave." "Taking Baby to the Movies," *The Mom Beat*, OregonLive .com, June 17 2008.

100. Boyle 2009, 267.

101. See Srinivas 2003 on cinema in rural Andhra Pradesh. Others have lauded the democratic inclusivity of the cinema hall (Sivathamby 1981).

102. Part of the appeal of special baby screenings is that "anxieties of 'being out of place' can be set aside" (Boyle 2009, 268–69).

CHAPTER 6

1. http://kalyan.livejournal.com/230006.html (no longer posted).

2. This chapter is derived in part from an article published in *Visual Anthropology* in 1998.

3. Where a Hindu deity, usually Ganesha or Lakshmi, is propitiated (Booth 1995). Lately, ritual beginnings involve displays by corporate sponsors, financiers, and producers.

4. For the deity Subramaniam.

5. Johnson 1995, 10.

6. Mittman 1984, 28.

7. Johnson 1995, 3, 12.

8. See Boyle 2009.

9. Seventeenth-century Paris theater spectators were so loud that they frequently drowned out the actors (Mittman 1984, 29).

10. See Becker, Faulkner, and Kirshenblatt-Gimblett, 2006: 5.

11. Hahn 1994, 105.

12. Chuckles, comments, and laughter from "scattered pockets of people" are heard in the Tongan cinema theater (Hahn 1994, 106).

13. Hahn (1994, 110). Throughout history, the liveness and volubility of theater audiences has shaped performances. See Mittman 1984; Johnson 1995, 27; Papp and Kirkland 1988, 144; and Hansen 1991, 65, on the immediate feedback from working-class audiences during the nickelodeon era who "take charge of the screen."

14. Liebes and Katz (1990, 92) on the "phatic function" of "mutual aid."

15. Mittman (1984, 27) observes that uninhibited theatergoers in seventeenth-century Paris held "running dialogue" during the play: "Much of the time the play was overshadowed by the by-play which surrounded it," creating confusion between the actors and the audience.

16. Hahn 1994, 108–9. See also Hansen 1991.

17. See Schechner (1993, 36, 41) on playing as a "mood" and an "attitude."

18. Hahn (1994, 107). Narrators were also known to entertain audiences during the nickelodeon era (see Hansen 1991). In Japan, professional performers (*benshi*) provided live narration, often in theatrical style, for silent film. See Ogihara 1990.

19. Hahn 1994, 109.

20. Baumann 1956, 61, quoted in Schivelbusch 1988, 208.

21. "West Indians are acutely aware of their human surroundings." Public settings in Barbados are characterized by "constant scanning and attention to others" (Reisman 1974, 114, in Fisher 1976, 229). See Hansen (1991, 65) on the nickelodeon experience.

22. Hahn 1994, 103.

23. http://www.viggy.com/forum/topic.asp?TOPIC_ID=3597 (posted January 22, 2007, 8:26:29 p.m; no longer posted).

24. Capitals in original. This refers to scenes of the picturesque waterfalls known as Jog Falls, a favorite filming location in Karnataka state. http://www.viggy.com/forum/topic/asp? TOPIC_ID=3597 India 1721 (posted January 21, 2007, 11:17:12 p.m.; no longer posted).

25. See Hansen 1991 on prenarrative cinema, voyeurism, and a heterosocial audience for early cinema.

26. A practice traceable to Hindu worship where the deity is propitiated with flowers, coins, incense, and camphor.

27. http://kalyan.livejournal.com/230006.html (posted May 9, 2008, 8:48 a.m.; no longer posted).

28. http://kalyan.livejournal.com/230006.html (posted August 21, 2007, 9:32:00 a.m.; no longer posted). K. R. Puram is considered a lower-middle-class (or even a low-income) area by Bangaloreans.

29. http://kalyan.livejournal.com/230006.html (posted May 9, 2008, 8:48 a.m., accessed November 2010).

30. See Johnson 1995, 31, on the etiquette at the opera in the mid-1700s in France.

31. Sobchack 1999, 252.

32. See Shively 1992, 728, on "Native American" audiences and the "star effect."

33. Hardgrave 1975, 114.

34. S. Kalyana Ramanthan and Vatsala Kamat, "Sivaji's Global March," *Business World*, http://www.businessworld.in/content/view/1971/2034 (no longer posted).

35. Of the Tongan cinema audience, Hahn notes, "people sat in distinct groups and paid attention to the movie in varying degrees of intensity" (1994, 107).

36. See Johnson 1995, 23, on the attitude of operagoers in seventeenth-century France.

37. "Cogito Ergo Sum: *Sivaji, the Boss*, Whose Boss, I Ask!," http://www.abhijith.in/2007/06/Sivaji-boss-whose-boss-i-ask.html (archived entry, Friday, June 15, 2007). Audience expectations of Tom Cruise in the *Mission Impossible* films—in terms of the action, thrills, and stunts—or of Sean Connery in the James Bond films point to a similar viewing aesthetic.

38. Similar reactions were in evidence at screenings of *Delhi Belly* (2011) and *Kaminey* (2009).

39. Huizinga 1955, 6.

40. http://www.india-forums.com/bollywood/hot-n-happening/12155-puneet-starrer-raam -money-worth-kannada-film-review.htm, italics added.

41. Satyen K. Bordoloi, "Movie Review: 'Robot'—Rajnikanth Scores Again!," *Bollywood .com*, http://www.bollywood.com/movie-review-robot-rajnikanth-scores-again, italics added.

42. Sobchack (1999, 251) argues that the "documentary is not a thing but a subjective relationship to a cinematic object. It is the viewer's consciousness that finally determines what kind of cinematic object it is.". See also Srinivas 1998, 2002.

43. See Gunning (1986, 64) on "attractions" and the "Lumiere tradition" of "putting the world within reach."

44. S. V. Srinivas (2003) writes that professional translators whose job was to translate from one language to another introduced the star upon his arrival on-screen.

45. Babb (1981, 393) on darshan and the exchange of glances between deities and devotees.

46. Keil (1966, 162) on patterns of applause for Blues performers: "B. B. King walks into the spotlight, picks his guitar once, and bedlam reigns."

47. Kabir 2001, 203–4.

48. Hahn 1994, 108.

49. Elsaesser 1981, 271, quoted in Hanich, 2010, 70.

50. This is debated: Gunning 1989; Bottomore 1999.

51. See Schwartz (1995) on mobile viewing and the flaneur.

52. Edensor (2000, 82); see also Certeau (1984, 98) on "carv[ing] out spaces of enunciation."

53. Just as the countryside is produced and reproduced by walking through it, "walking articulates a relationship between pedestrian and place, a relationship which is a complex imbrication of the material organization and shape of the landscape, its symbolic meaning, and the ongoing sensual perception and experience of moving through space. Thus . . . walking can also (re)produce and (re)interpret space and place" (Edensor 2000, 82).

54. Certeau 1984, 84.

55. Certeau 1984, 97. Walking in the British countryside was associated with notions of "freeing the body," of releasing it from "restrictions experienced by bodies in the city" (Edensor 2000, 84–85).

56. Mittman 1984, 3, 27.

57. In eighteenth-century Europe, etiquette demanded that operagoers were fashionably late, and some "maintained it was bad form to stay for the entire opera" (Johnson 1995, 31, 9).

58. See chap. 5.

59. The exact meaning of *Mungaru Male* is debated, with some translating it as the "mango showers," premonsoon rains, and others contesting this interpretation.

60. "The Rediscovery of India: Movie Review: *Mungaru Male*," April 5, 2007, http://www .sandeepweb.com/2007/04/05/movie-review-mungaru-male/ (no longer posted).

61. http://en.wikipedia.org/wiki/Dilwale_Dulhania_Le_Jayenge.

62. Paul Hockings, personal communication, 2014.

63. Tulasi Srinivas, personal communication.

64. Hardgrave 1975, 114.

65. See Kakar 1980.

66. In the mid-1700s, French operagoers sang along with the chorus and hummed to the music (Johnson 1995, 27).

67. http://www.viggy.com/forum/topic/asp? TOPIC_ID=3597 India 1721 Posts (posted January 21, 2007, 11:17:12 p.m.; no longer posted).

68. A term coined by Fish to "account for modes of literary criticism within the academy" (Radway 1984, 8). Radway argues that the concept is "insufficiently theorized to deal with the complexities of social groups or to explore how, when and why they are constituted precisely as interpretive communities" (ibid.).

69. *Satya* review, *Sunday Indian Express*, August 9, 1998.

70. Srinivas 2002, 168.

71. See Grimaud 2004.

72. Srinivas 1998, 336; 2002.

73. *Times of India*, May 21, 1995. See Srinivas 1998, 336.

74. Caves 2000, 84.

75. Although an increasing number of films—*Lord of the Rings* (2001), the Harry Potter films, and even the Twilight series, as well as a rash of films based on comic books—seem to be tapping into the market advantage of presenting audiences with stories and characters they are familiar with.

76. MSNBC anchor Chris Matthews announced he had watched *Game Change* (2012) twice and might watch it again twenty times, it being so good (*Hardball*, March 10, 2012).

77. "Some genres predicate performance on audience familiarity with the material being presented" (Beeman 1993, 383).

78. Huizinga notes, "closely connected with play is the idea of winning" and of competition and contest (1955, 50, 14).

79. Becker, Faulkner, and Kirshenblatt-Gimblett 2006.

80. Action movies featuring fights and gunshots were popularly referred to as "*dishum dishum* movies," possibly based on audience-generated sound effects.

81. Srinivas 1998, 340, 344.

82. In seventeenth-century opera, Johnson writes, whistles and shouts from the parterre, drowned out the singing. "The parterre's antics shattered any sort of dramatic engagement the performers might hope to encourage. When Caron demanded a coin from a shade crossing over to Hades in a performance of Lully's *Alceste*, a spectator called out, 'Throw him a banknote'" (Johnson 1995, 27).

83. Jancovich, Faire, and Stubbings 2003; Hansen 1991; Gomery, 1992.

84. Srinivas 2009, 38.

85. "'Rajinikanth' Once a Superstar, Always a Superstar," August 25, 2010 (blog post no longer available).

86. http://www.viggy.com/forum/topic/asp? TOPIC_ID=3597 India 1721 Posts (posted January 21, 2007, 11:17:12 p.m.; no longer posted). Miriam Hansen (1991, 67–68) describes working-class nickelodeon audiences "taking charge of the screen."

87. http://www.gandhadagudi.com/forum/viewtopic.php?f=1&t=3382&start=360&st=0&sk=t&sd=a.

88. Fans are reported to throw "balloons before the projector's beam to cast giant shadows on the screen" (Srinivas 2009, 37).

89. Hindu religious ritual in which the deity is propitiated with lamps (light), flowers, and with water in which turmeric and kumkum may be dissolved. Songs are sung.

90. Schechner 1993, 10.

91. "Playing is a creative destabilizing action that frequently does not declare its existence, even less its intentions" (Schechner 1993, 40).

92. Arthur Pais, in conversation, 2012. See Papp and Kirkland (1988, 144) on spectators of Shakespearean plays wreaking "revenge" on "hangings, stools, walls and whatsoever came in their way very outrageously."

93. "The audience does not respond as a mass, for some the comments hit home and not for others" (Hahn 1994, 106).

94. See Fisher (1976, 229) on oblique communication.

95. See Katz (1999, 121–23) on the shift from "doing" emotion such as laughter to being "taken" or "done by" it.

96. The sociological problem of intersubjectivity is one of "how to establish a 'common world' which transcends private experiential worlds" (Heritage 1984, 55).

97. "Why a Simple Movie Date Can Be Complicated," *Ledger-Enquirer*, March 12, 2009, http://www.ledger-enquirer.com/392/story/6466071.html (no longer posted).

98. Schechner 1993, 26.

99. Schechner 1993.

100. Huizinga 1955, 21.

101. Ibid., 11.

102. Aesthetic conflict is described in other entertainment and performance settings that accommodate vocal spectators from a variety of social backgrounds. Of concert audiences in the mid-nineteenth century France, Johnson notes, "fighting in the theater [in 1913] was one of several possible responses expressing extreme divergence in taste" (Johnson 1995, 4). During the recital of the violinist Lafout, "One half of the hall acted as police, so to speak and demanded silence" (ibid., 232–33). Barbara Mittman (1984, 32) describes "aesthetic conflict" in a pattern of "disruptive opposition between the stage and the pit" in Paris theaters of the mid-seventeenth century.

103. http://kalyan.livejournal.com/230006.html (posted August 21, 2007, 9:32:00 a.m.; no longer posted).

104. Hahn reports a similar dynamic in Tonga, where "deafening shouts . . . annoy the Europeans who sit upstairs drinking cokes" (1994, 110).

105. E-mail communication, 2010.

106. See Schechner on "dark play" (1993, 27).

107. Uberoi 2001, 268.

108. Katz 1996; Heritage 1984.

109. Katz (1999, 97, 41) on "intersubjective seeing."

110. DeVault (2000, 492) on "Talk that organizes a collective experience"; "A way of looking in everyday life which creates a shared perspective" (491–92). See also Heritage 1984, 56, 53.

111. See Katz (1999, 96): "The relationship necessary for eliciting laughter . . . is not simply for one to gaze at another gazing at the mirror, the two must appear to each other to see the same thing"; "the sensual awareness of our seeing" is necessary for laughing together.

112. Freddy Bailey, personal communication, 1999.

113. Anyone familiar with MTV's "pop-up videos," which provide background information on the making of a music video and biographical information on the artistes and bands, will recognize that this is a spontaneous and interactive audience practice that has been imported to the video.

114. Schutz 1964, in Heritage 1984, 62.

115. See Schivelbusch (1988) and Mittman (1984) on audience as spectacle in the baroque theater. http://www.gandhadagudi.com/forum/viewtopic.php?f=1&t=3382&start=360&st=0 &sk=t&sd=a (posted January 4, 2008, 3:42 p.m., accessed June 7, 2009).

116. Becker, Faulkner, and Kirshenblatt-Gimblett (2006, 5).

117. "The country rube was a stock character in vaudeville, comic strips and other popular media" (Hansen 1991, 25), and made his way to early cinema.

118. Huizinga 1955, 181.

119. Schechner on play (1993, 39). Becker, Faulkner, and Kirshenblatt-Gimblett (2006, 5) distinguish between artworks that are "done" and those that are "finished": "'Finishedness' is an empirical problem whose investigation shows us the processes at work in the invention, making, communicating and preservation of art" (7).

120. Filmmaking in America during the nickelodeon boom has been described as a cottage industry (see Hansen 1991, 93; Musser 1983).

121. "Viewing (an artwork) . . . is constitutive of it. The work wouldn't be what it is, if no one viewed it" (Becker, Faulkner, and Kirshenblatt-Gimblett 2006, 5).

122. Hahn 1994, 108.

123. See also Michel de Certeau (1984, 166), and Hirsch 1972, quoted in Jacob 1998, 312.

124. Huizinga 1955, 13.

125. An alternative explanation to "rupture" in "fictional consciousness" (Sobchack 1999, 246)—an analytic construct that privileges the fictional narrative.

126. Schechner 1993.

127. For Michel de Certeau (1984, xx), "readers are travellers."

128. See Becker, Faulkner, and Kirshenblatt-Gimblett (2006, 5) on artworks.

129. See Hansen 1991.

130. Gunning 1986; Schechner 1993; Schivelbusch 1988; Mittman 1984.

131. Grimaud 2004, 107–9 (translated by Jack Katz; personal communication with author, 2011; see also Srinivas 1998, 2002). A *thali* meal offers a variety of prepared items, a full complement of foods to diners who combine various items on the plate to create their own taste combinations.

132. Gargi 1966, 20.

133. Ibid., 22. "Call" and "response" performance is also seen in blues performances. See Keil 1966.

CHAPTER 7

1. Affectionate name for Kannada film icon Dr. Rajkumar meaning "elder brother." Rajkumar is also referred to as "Annavaru," another term for "elder brother." See also Hardgrave 1975, 100.

2. See Beeman 1993; Schechner 1993.

3. Poornima Swaminathan, "Horse Carriage for Robot Reel at Aurora," *Mid-day*, October 1, 2010, http://www.mid-day.com/articles/horse-carriage-for-robot-reel-at-aurora/96774.

4. Armbrust 1998, 417.

5. Bakhtin (1984, 10) in Armbrust 1998.

6. Tamasha is a traditional art form from Maharashtra that incorporates song, dance, and variety entertainment. There is even a Galata movie portal: http://kannada.galata.com/entertainment/kannada/livewire/id/Shivarajkumar_7401.html.

7. Appadurai 1996 on mediascapes.

8. "Pancharangi: Kannada Movie Review," September 4, 2010, http:www.cinefundas.com/2010/09/04/pancharangi-kannada-movie-review (no longer posted).

9. Schechner 1993, 46–47.

10. "To allow people to assemble in the streets is always to flirt with the possibility of improvisation—that the unexpected might happen" (Schechner 1993, 47; see also 26).

11. H. M. Chaithanya Swamy, "Upendra's *Super* Draws Huge Crowds to Theatres on Day 1," *dna* (India), December 4, 2010, http://www.dnaindia.com.

12. Srinivas 2009, 12; post-1990s, "Some view . . . [fans] as criminals"; police refer to them as "rowdy-sheeters" (56). Dhareshwar and Srivatsan 1996.

13. Hardgrave 1975, 112; Schechner (1993) on "dark play" (36) and risk (27).

14. Srinivas on rioting fans (2009, 36).

15. S. Kalyana Ramanathan and Vatsala Kamat, "Sivaji's Global March, 2007," http://www.businessworld.in/content/view/1971/2034 (no longer posted).

16. "Endhiran Festivity Starts in Mumbai," September 22, 2010, *IndiaGlitz*, http://www.indiaglitz.com/endhiran-festivity-starts-in-mumbai-tamil-news-60266.html.

17. "Shivaji Mania: Theatres Out of Tickets," *Economic Times*, June 15, 2007, http://articles.economictimes.indiatimes.com/2007-06-15/news/28463123_1_sivaji-ticket-prices-book-tickets.

18. "Chennai Theatres Run Out of Tickets for Rajni's Sivaji." *Hindustan Times*, June 11, 2007.

19. The owner of the Aurora cinema in Mumbai, G. Natarajan, quoted in Swaminathan, "Horse Carriage."

20. Hardgrave 1975, 112; Srinivas 2009, 36.

21. http:www.viggy.com/forum/topic.asp? (posted January 21, 2007; no longer posted).

22. "Theatre Manager Triggers Orgy of Violence Leaving One Dead, *Times of India*, August 24, 1996.

23. Hardgrave 1975, 114.

24. Ibid., 95.

25. Dickey 1993, 150; Hardgrave 1975, 95, 122.

26. Localism and regionalism motivate many fans of Kannada films. For many, loyalty to stars and to Kannada cinema translates into seeing themselves as guardians of Kannada culture and language. Rajkumar fans participate in pro-Kannada agitations in Karnataka (see Nair 2005).

27. MGR, Rajinikanth, even Rajkumar are examples of such "adopted" stars.

28. While Rajinikanth is associated with Tamil films, his stardom is at a national and international level.

29. See Srinivas (2009, 24) on "conditional loyalty." Dickey (1993, 157) describes fan devotion as "a mix of passionate devotion and respect." Hardgrave 1975, 16.

30. Rajinikanth fan quoted in Indo-Asian News Service, June 11, 2007.

31. According to Beeman (1993, 380), "attendance at a ritual may be considered a cultural duty."

32. Hardgrave 1975, 113.

33. In 1998, a Kannada film could be seen for less than Rs. 10 for a stalls seat in regular theaters; tents had even lower ticket prices. Regular Balcony tickets for Kannada movies in 1998 were around Rs. 20.

34. Interview on Shah Rukh Khan's *Inner World*, DVD.

35. Goffman 1967.

36. Hardgrave 1975, 119.

37. Srinivas 2000, 309.

38. *Hindustan Times*, "Chennai Theatres Run Out of Tickets."

39. However, fan associations in cooperation with the police also helped remove these troublesome fans from the theaters. Swamy, "Upendra's *Super* Draws Huge Crowds."

40. Goffman (1967, 14) on defensive versus protective orientation.

41. Ibid., 9, 19.

42. IANS, "Vishnuvardhan Fans Force Postponement of His 200th Film," *Thaindian News*, February 11, 2010, http:www.thaindian.com/newsportal/entertainment/vishnuvardhan -fans-force-postponement-of-his-200th-film. The "feelings about face sustained for the other participants . . . constitute an involvement in the face of others that is as immediate and spontaneous as the involvement (in one's own) face" (Goffman 1967, 6).

43. See Srinivas (2000, 309) on the battle between rival Chiranjeevi and Balakrishna fans to claim certain theaters for their fan activities.

44. Hardgrave 1975, 98, 112; Dickey 1993.

45. "A person's attachment to face gives others something to aim at" (Goffman 1967, 39).

46. Dickey 1993, 169 on "personal closeness" of fans to stars. Hardgrave (1975, 100) has noted that Tamil superstar Shivaji Ganesan "entertains (fans) at his house."

47. Agencies, "Rajnikanth Cries Halt to Fans' Frenzy over 'Sivaji,'" May 26, 2007, http:// www.apunkachoice.com/scoop/downsouth/tamil/20070526-0.html. See Srinivas (2009, 55) on stars' "disciplinary intervention."

48. See Goffman (1967, 42) on trusting one's self-image to others and embarrassment.

49. Hardgrave 1975, 113; Jacob 1998, 2009; Dickey 1993, 187; Srinivas 2000a. Hardgrave (1975, 95, 122) distinguishes between the poor, who make up the majority of the audience for Tamil films and for whom the stars are like gods, and the middle classes, who gossip about the stars and their scandalous lifestyles.

50. Alexander Zaitchik, "India: Where a Movie Star Is More Than a Movie Star," April 20, 2006, http://www.spiked-online.com/newsite/article/214#.Vh0kZ27P_zg. Of Tamil film fans, Hardgrave (1975, 119) notes, "The devotion of fans is stirred by [stars] personal appearance." The devotional dimension of the fan-star relationship finds expression in temples built to stars.

51. "Endhiran Festivity Starts in Mumbai," *IndiaGlitz*, September 22, 2010, http://www .indiaglitz.com/endhiran-festivity-starts-in-mumbai-tamil-news-60266.html.

52. Swaminathan, "Horse Carriage."

53. Meena Iyer, "The Rajnikant Effect: Non-Tamils Too Catch the Fever of Sivaji," *Times of India*, June 27, 2007. "For Hindus, gazing at images of the deity, the 'sight' or 'vision' (*darshana*) of the deities, is one of the most important things they do" (Fuller 1992, 59–60). When the devotee looks at the deity, the belief is that the deity looks back and "sees" the devotee (see Babb 1981). The "seeing" of the deity confers on the devotee "good fortune, well-being, grace and ritual merit" (Fuller 1992, 59–60). See also Babb (1981, 390–93). By "joining gazes" with the deity, "the devotee can gain access to a benevolent power": as "gazes 'unite' and 'mix,' the devotees' spirit is 'drawn up'" (Babb 1981, 391). See also Jacob 2009.

54. "Rajni's Fans Seeking Divine Help for *Endhiran*," *Hindustan Times*, September 22, 2010.

55. "India's Most Expensive Film Sets Box-Office Record," AFP, October 6, 2010. Worshipping film reels or film "cans" is not a new phenomenon. In rural Tamil Nadu, fan clubs

have been observed taking the film cans around the town in a cart and doing *puja* before them (Hardgrave 1975, 119).

56. Coconuts are broken at Hindu temples as part of worship and by devotees who wish to propitiate the deity routinely as well as on festival days and for wish-fulfillment.

57. *Uralseve* is an act of worship where devotees roll on the ground. *Abhishekham*, also known as *Angapradakshinam*, is part of *puja* (ritual worship) where priests pour water with camphor, milk, honey, turmeric water, etc., on the deity's image, in effect "bathing" it. All these practices are seen at Hindu temples.

58. Ibid.

59. Sweets made with milk, flour, and sugar syrup often served on special occasions.

60. Schechner 1993, 48.

61. A gift of a cloth for a sari blouse is considered auspicious at it marks the married state.

62. Srinivas 2009, 35. See also Hardgrave 1975, 121.

63. Hardgrave 1975, 121.

64. "Fans Make 6.350 kg Silver Statue of Dr. Raj," *Filmibeat*, April 5, 2010, http://www .filmibeat.com/kannada/news/2010/rajkumar-silver-statue-050410.html.

65. Hardgrave 1975, 113, on the *Pongal* festival release for MGR films.

66. Jacob 1998, 310.

67. Tamil film superstar Rajinikanth is contracted to have "Superstar" in his title. Grady Hendrix, "Superstar Rajinikanth," *Slate.com*, September 27, 2010.

68. "Power Star" was also the "handle" for Telugu film star Pawan Kalyan in the late 1990s (Srinivas 2009, 10).

69. Jacob (1998, 2009) on the visual spectacle of cinema.

70. *Kolam* refers to intricate floor designs made of rice flour traditionally found at the entrances of homes and in doorways to make such spaces auspicious.

71. See Goody 1993, 340–41, on the culture of flowers in India and their importance as a signifier of auspicious events. See also Srinivas 1976, 324–28, in Goody 1993, 341).

72. Swaminathan, "Horse Carriage."

73. While some film financiers believe that lavish spectacle is effective as publicity, in the 1990s there was also a sense that the local nature of such spectacle itself was a drawback because it was largely confined to the theater surroundings (Jacob 1998, 310–11). The ongoing corporatization of the Indian film business has meant a gradual change in the way big-budget films are marketed.

74. An aesthetic similar to *Ram Lila* enactments described by Schechner 1993.

75. The "carnival state" is associated with "jocularity, masking and public performance" (Consentino 2004, quoted in Addo 2009, 220).

76. Booth 2008, 65.

77. In India, processions shape Hindu, Muslim, and Sikh religious festivals (Booth 2008). At Hindu temples, deities are taken in procession, accompanied by ritual chanting and *nadaswaram* music. Even St. Marys' feast in Bangalore is celebrated with a procession.

78. Booth 2008, 74.

79. Beeman 1993, 384.

80. Booth 2008, 65.

81. Kratz 1994; in Booth 2008, 64.

82. Processions themselves being a liminal space where "the behaviours of participants are sometimes at the edges of social acceptability" (Booth 2008, 69). Men in the *baraat* (wedding procession) are often intoxicated (ibid.).

83. Jack Goody describes India as "the land of garlands" (2003, 345, 339).

84. Pushpa Iyengar, "Chennai Corner," *Outlook*, October 1, 2010, http://www.outlookindia .com/article/chennai-corner/267318.

85. Booth (2008, 68) describes a "performative space" within the North Indian wedding procession or *baraat* in which participants engage in "ecstatic dancing."

86. When Dr. Rajkumar passed away in 2006, Bangalore and other cities across the state saw days of riots and "bloody clashes" between fans and the police. The city ground to a halt as fans "demanded immediate cessation of all traffic and business activity"; Zaitchik, "India."

87. Named the Akhila Karnataka Dr Rajkumar Abhimanigala Sangha and described as a "quasi-political" organization; Anupama Katakam "The Eternal Kannada Icon," *Frontline* 17, no. 24 (November 25–December 8, 2000), http://www.frontline.in/static/html/fl1724/ 17240160.htm.

88. According to S. V. Srinivas (2009, 13), most Telugu film fan associations do not have regular offices. Public places or homes usually become de facto "offices."

89. I learned later that there was no formal association, and the group of people who called themselves fans did not want to start any formal organization for various reasons.

90. Madhava Prasad has also commented on fan activities being "community-forging" (quoted in Srinivas 2009, 30).

91. See Beeman 1993, 372, on preparations for performance; Schechner 1993.

92. Fans are loath to publicly criticize anything having to do with their favorite star (Srinivas, 2009: 31–32).

93. Visiting the star's home is not unusual for fans. On Tamil megastar Shivaji Ganesan's birthday "in 1969 3000–4000 fans representing fan clubs were received at Shivaji's home. (The count was kept by the distribution of Coca Cola)" (Hardgrave 1975, 119).

94. See Hahn 1994 on professional narrators in Tonga.

95. See Hardgrave (1975, 119), "Shivaji's birthday Oct. 1, is the yearly occasion for homage by the fans. In 1969, Shivaji received at least one thousand garlands."

96. Schechner 1993, 72.

97. Schechner (1993, 15) quotes Awasthi (1989, 48) on "theater of roots," rejection of the proscenium stage, and closer contact between spectators and performers." See Hansen (1991, 28) on "the segregation of film and theater space."

98. Jacob 1998, 309.

99. "Carnival . . . [is] characterized by a ludic undermining of all norms" (Stam 1989, 86; quoted in Armbrust 1998, 415).

100. I thank M. N. Srinivas, who alerted me to this way of viewing fans' performative activities.

101. See also Babb 1981, 390–93. In films featuring the story of Lord Rama, or Lord Krishna, when the stars appear in character as gods on the screen, "men and women in the audience

prostrated themselves before the screen" (Barnouw and Krishnaswamy [1963] 1980, 15; quoted in Jacob 1998, 309). Audiences going to watch the goddess film *Jai Santoshi Maa* were reported to leave their footwear outside the theater, as devotees do at Hindu temples (Lutgendorf, 2003: 19).

102. "'Rajinikanth' Once a Superstar, Always a Superstar," August 25, 2010 (blog post no longer available).

103. Hardgrave 1975, 104.

104. As, for example, with the Ram Lila. See Schechner 1993, 32, on avant-garde theater and "celebratory performance."

105. Srinivas 1998, 336.

106. "Neetu Chandra, Bollywood Heroine," *Times of India*, June 27, 2007. See Babb (1981, 395) on the symbolism of the deity's feet.

107. Kabir 2001, 215.

108. A journalist hinted it was all increasingly a show encouraged by producers and stars (field notes, January 2010).

109. R. G. Vijayasarathy, "People Were Whistling while Watching Raam," *Rediff*, http://movies .rediff.com/slide-show/2009/dec/28/slide-show-1-south-interview-with-priyamani.htm.

110. https://en.wikipedia.org/wiki/Upendra_(film). Some of the real gangsters who acted in the film are Jedarahalli Krishnappa, Bekkina Kannu (Cat Eye) Raajendra, Korangu, and Tanveer. According to reports, some "convicts had to be bailed out just to act in this movie."

111. Approximately 5–6 feet high.

112. Callois 1959, 125–26; in Schechner 1993, 48.

113. Gotham 2005 (quoted in Addo 2009, 229): this mood attends "festive and public events like carnivals."

114. Booth 2008, 74.

115. Schechner 1993, 36, 78.

116. Schechner 1993 on the Ram Lila.

117. See Jacob 1998; Schechner 1993.

118. Schechner 1993, 161.

119. Ibid.

120. Ashley 2001, 17; in Booth 2008, 66.

121. See Armbrust 1998, 416; Turner 1982, 41. "Film events" in Egypt are described as "provid[ing] a point of entry into the "carnivalesque" or "liminoid" (Armbrust 1998, 415–16).

122. "Spectators derive pleasure from spectacles of themselves looking at or consuming others" (Kirshenblatt-Gimblett 1998; in Addo 2009, 228).

123. See Hansen 1991, 38; Boyle 2009 on the audience as "attraction."

124. See Srinivas 2002; Becker, Faulkner, and Kirshenblatt-Gimblett 2006.

125. Theater audiences in the sixteenth and seventeenth centuries in France provide one such example where "historically there was not a formalized separation between performers and the public" (Mittman 1984, 2).

126. A characteristic of "cultural" performance in India is that performers were and are drawn from spectators who have watched the performance time and again (see Gargi 1966; Schechner 1993). Addo 2009, 228; Beeman 1993, 372.

CHAPTER 8

1. Quoted in Suhas Yellapantula, "Affordable Cinema Experience," *New Indian Express*, July 29, 3014, http://www.newindianexpress.com/cities/hyderabad/Affordable-cinematic -experience/2014/07/29/article2354188.ece.

2. Barber 1997, 348.

3. Barber 1997.

4. Hahn 1994; Barber 1997; Spitulnik 1993.

5. Mark Jancovich, Faire, and Stubbings 2003, 20, observe that variation is underplayed even in historical studies that overlook localized differences in reception. See Waller 1995. See also Hubbard 2003b, 258, on "non-representational theory."

6. Nasaw 1999, 2.

7. Jancovich, Faire, and Stubbings 2003, 43. See Hansen 1991, 36.

8. Hansen 1991, 99; Jancovich, Faire, and Stubbings 2003.

9. Jancovich, Faire, and Stubbings 2003, 38; Fuller 1996.

10. Hansen 1991, 84; see 96–98 on distractions.

11. Ibid., 84.

12. Barber 1997, 350.

13. Up until the 1950s, films made outside the Anglo-American film circuit were screened to ethnic groups. See Ogihara 1990 on the screening of Japanese and English-language films to Japanese immigrants in Los Angeles; see also Hansen 1991; Rosenzweig 1983.

14. Hansen 1991, 103. When French Pathé films became popular, they received opposition from both social reformers and American manufacturers . Once sound arrived, all movies made in Hollywood were in English (Thissen 1999). Gabler (1989) begins his fascinating study of the origins of Hollywood by identifying a paradox: Hollywood was founded by Eastern European immigrants who saw in the industry a way to transcend their immigrant backgrounds. They constructed a popular American culture in order to inhabit it.

15. Hansen 1991; May 1980; Gomery 1992.

16. Harry Geduld 1971, 57; in Hansen 1991, 64.

17. Hansen 1991, 61, 79.

18. "Lux Graphicus," *Motion Picture World* 5 (September 4, 1909): 10; in Hansen 1991, 66.

19. Hansen 1991, 83–85, 93.

20. Geraghty 2000.

21. Film historians are far from unanimous on the composition of the nickelodeon audience and the successful standardization and homogenization of film experience; see Jancovich, Faire, and Stubbings 2003. Gregory Waller has challenged the thesis that there was a "standardization of recreation" in which "provincialism" was eroded by a homogenized American culture; Waller 1995, in Jancovich, Faire, and Stubbings 2003, 12. Other scholars have argued that nickelodeon audiences were more middle and lower-middle class: Singer 1995; Waller 1995; Allen 1990.

22. Geraghty 2000, 1–2; see also Jancovich, Faire, and Stubbings 2003.

23. Rosenzweig 1983, 219.

24. Ibid.

25. Eleftheriosis 2001, 181–82, in Boyle 2009, 262.

26. See Hubbard 2003a, 2003b on the homogeneity of the multiplex audience.

27. In 1997, "six major movie companies supplied one theater chain not only with films but with the essential marketing campaigns that accompany them"; Epstein 1998, 111. Commercials that play in theaters and advertise the chain are produced by the chain and distributed throughout the country.

28. Barber 1997, 348.

29. Barber traces the origins of the idea of identical and equivalent audiences, the basis for any mass media, to the social transformations of the industrial revolution where "collectivities were no longer united by kinship, co-residence and cooperation," where workers "severed from ownership of the means of production" could be "boiled down to their labor power in the open market," which made them exchangeable by "the sheer fact of human interchangeability." In English schools "in the 1820s the 'simultaneous method' of teaching" made pupils seated in rows and sorted by age into an audience that was a uniform group of seemingly interchangeable and equivalent units (Barber 1997, 348). Similarly, "in the second half of the 18th century when European armies wore uniforms and in the 19th century when church congregations began to give up differentiated seating" and so on, "new disciplines of the body in space" were brought into being that involved "the imagining of human beings as in principle equivalent to each other" (Barber 1997, 348).

30. Barber 1997, 353.

31. For example, "disciplines of space and time associated with the church and school were introduced with a regulatory intent" but were "taken up differently by local populations" (Barber 1997, 350).

32. Barber 1997, 350, 353.

33. Hahn 1994, 106, on the Tongan audience.

34. The case even with appointed narrators (Hahn 1994) and film "lecturers." See also Hansen 1991, 97–98.

35. Peter Van der Veer (1992, 555) describes Hindus participating in the celebrations of a Sufi saint's day as doing so "on their own terms."

36. Johnson (1995, 19) on the popularity of the "opera-ballet" performances in eighteenth-century France.

37. Nickelodeon theaters are described as "get-thrills-quick-theaters" (Hansen 1991, 65).

38. Barber 1997, 356.

39. Ibid., 355.

40. Ibid.

41. Ibid., 353–54.

42. Jancovich, Faire, and Stubbings 2003, 30, on Nottingham cinemas; Waller 1995.

43. Adorno 1991; Adorno and Horkheimer 1972.

44. Madhav Prasad 1998, 43. Marx provides the example of watchmaking as a heterogeneous form of manufacture.

45. Barber 1997, 358–59; Becker, Faulkner, and Kirshenblatt-Gimblett 2006.

46. Schechner 1993, 34, 39; See Becker, Faulkner, and Kirshenblatt-Gimblett 2006, on the "finishedness" of artworks.

47. Schechner 1993, 34.

48. Ibid., 43.

49. Ibid., 33.

50. Ibid., 176.

51. Ibid., 160.

52. Ibid., 72.

53. Ibid., 133.

54. Ibid., 162.

55. In terms of "audience reach," the market is growing at an impressive 15 to 17 percent annually, making it attractive for foreign companies. In 2012, the Indian film industry was reported to have grown by 21 percent (*INA Global*, November 26, 2013). In comparison, Hollywood audiences are growing at 5 to 6 percent a year. *BBC News*, business sec., June 24, 2011.

56. *Times of India*, March 16, 2004.

57. "For India's only Cinerama Theatre . . . The End," *Bangalore Mirror*, October 1, 2013, http://www.bangaloremirror.com/bangalore/others/For-India's-only-Cinerama-theatre-The-End/articleshow/23314311.cms.

58. "No Housefull, It's the End," *Times of India*, March 16, 2004.

59. See Athique and Hill 2011.

60. Gomery 1992; Paul 1994.

61. Nasaw 1999, 1.

62. Bauman 1956; quoted in Hubbard 2003a, 71.

63. Hubbard 2003b, 262.

64. Ibid., 267.

65. Gomery 1992, 114–12; Katz-Gerro 1999.

66. Hubbard 2003b, 263–64.

67. Cf. Bauman 2000; in Hubbard 2003b, 264.

68. "No Housefull, It's the End," *Times of India*, March 16, 2004.

69. "Salman Khan: Mass Entertainer Films Will Die Totally," *Indian Express*, October 2, 2013.

70. "*Kick* Takes Bumper Opening: Housefull Already," *Box Office India*, July 25, 2014, http://www.boxofficeindia.co.in/kick-takes-bumper-opening-housefull-already/.

71. "Single Theatre Owners in a Dilemma in City," *Times of India*, February 22, 2012.

72. "Mall Closures, Theater Taxes Stunt Growth of Indian Multiplexes," *Variety*, May 14, 2014, http://variety.com/2014/film/news/mall-closures-theater-taxes-stunt-growth-of-indian-multiplexes-1201180902.

73. *Times of India*, "No Housefull."

74. "The Worst Experience," http://bangalore.burrp.com/establishment_inox-multiplex/review-theaters (accessed August 5, 2010; no longer posted). "The Day When Affordable Cinema Died," http://arbitblogs.wordpress.com/2010/07/24/the-day-when-affordable-cinema-died/ (accessed July 24, 2010). "Movies, Me and the Markets," *Preran*, February 18, 2008, http://bangalore.metblogs.com/2008/02/18/movies-me-and-the-markets/ (accessed August 5, 2010). "Saturdays, Girlfriends, Popcorn and Other Memories, http://churumuri.wordpress.com/2010/03/29/saturdays-girlfriends-popcorn-justmemories/ (accessed August 5, 2010).

75. Ticket prices at multiplexes range between Rs. 175 and Rs. 500, making them unaffordable for a large section of the moviegoing public. In some Bangalore multiplexes, a ticket on a weekend or on occasion of a "festival release" can cost between Rs. 400 and Rs. 750.

76. "The Day When Affordable Cinema Died," http://arbitblogs.wordpress.com/2010/07/24/the-day-when-affordable-cinema-died/.

77. Multiplex tickets can be $3–$10 compared with prices of a few cents at single-run cinema halls. Multiplexes have also hiked the cost of popcorn and other concessions.

78. "Normal Theaters Giving Way to Multiplexes: Is This a Good Sign?," *Praja*, September 29, 2007, http://praja.in/hi/discuss/2007/09/normal-theatres-giving-way-multiplexes-good-sign.

79. "If Chennaites Can Watch Films in Multiplexes for Rs. 10, Why Can't We? *Bangalore Mirror* November 21, 2013, http://www.bangaloremirror.com/bangalore/others/If-Chennaites-can-watch-films-in-multiplex-for-Rs-10-why-cant-we/articleshow/26108263.cms.

80. *Ninaivugal . . . Thoughts.* 2010; "The Day When Affordable Cinema Died."

81. "Is the Show Over for Single-Screens?," *Hindu*, August 2, 2013.

82. Nasaw 1999, 2.

83. Ibid.

84. Jancovich, Faire, and Stubbings 2003, 16.

85. Gladwell 2006; Josh Eliashberg, "Can Computers Pick Better Movie Scripts?," *Forbes*, December 4, 2006, http://www.forbes.com/2006/12/03/hollywood-dvd-writers-guild-ent-sales-cx_kw_1201wharton.html.

REFERENCES

Abbott, Andrew. 1997. "Of Time and Space: The Contemporary Relevance of the Chicago School." *Social Forces* 75 (4): 1149–82.

Abu-Lughod, Lila. 2005. *Dramas of Nationhood: The Politics of Television in Egypt.* Chicago: University of Chicago Press.

Acland, Charles R. 2000. "Cinemagoing and the Rise of the Megaplex." *Television and New Media* 1 (3): 355–82.

Addo, Ping-Ann. 2009. "Anthropology, Festival and Spectacle." *Reviews in Anthropology* 38 (3): 217–36.

Adorno, Theodor W. 1991. *The Culture Industry.* London: Routledge.

Adorno, Theodor W., and Max Horkheimer. 1972. *Dialectic of Enlightenment.* New York: Herder and Herder.

Allen, Robert C. 1990. "From Exhibition to Reception: Reflections on the Audience in Film History." *Screen* 31 (4): 347–56.

Anderson, Arthur. 2000. *The Indian Entertainment Industry: Strategy and Vision.* New Delhi: Federation of Indian Chambers of Commerce and Industry.

Ang, Ien. 1990. "Culture and Communication: Towards an Ethnographic Critique of Media Consumption in the Transnational Media System." *European Journal of Communication* 5: 239–60.

———. 1991. *Desperately Seeking the Audience.* London: Routledge.

———. 1996. *Living Room Wars.* London: Routledge.

Appadurai, Arjun. 1996. *Modernity at Large.* Minneapolis: University of Minnesota Press.

Appadurai, Arjun, and Carol Breckenridge. 1988. "Why Public Culture?" *Public Culture* 1 (1): 1–24.

Armbrust, Walter. 1998. "When the Lights Go Down in Cairo: Cinema as Secular Ritual." *Visual Anthropology* 10: 413–22.

———. 2004. "Egyptian Cinema on Stage and Off." In *Off Stage/On Display: Intimacy and Ethnography in the Age of Public Culture*, edited by Andrew Shyrock, 69–98. Stanford, CA: Stanford University Press.

Arnold, Robert F. 1990. "Film Space/Audience Space: Notes Toward a Theory of Spectatorship." *Velvet Light Trap* 25 (Spring): 44–52.

Ashley, Kathleen. 2001. "Introduction: The Moving Subjects of Processional Performance." In *Moving Subjects: Processional Performance in the Middle Ages and the Renaissance*, edited by K. Ashley and W. Husten, 7–34. Amsterdam: Rodopi.

Athique, Adrian. 2009. "Leisure Capital in the New Economy: The Rapid Rise of the Multiplex in India. *Contemporary South Asia* 17 (2): 123–40.

Athique, Adrian, and Douglas Hill. 2011. *The Multiplex in India*. London: Routledge.

Austin, Bruce A. 1989. *Immediate Seating: A Look at Movie Audiences*. Belmont, CA: Wadsworth.

Awasthi, Suresh. 1989. " 'Theater of Roots': Encounter with Tradition." *Drama Review* 33 (4): 48–69.

Babb, Lawrence A. 1981. "Glancing: Visual Interaction in Hinduism." *Journal of Anthropological Research* 37 (4): 387–401.

Bakhtin, Mikhail. 1984. *Rabelais and His World*. Translated by Helene Iswolsky. Cambridge, MA: MIT Press.

Barber, Karin. 1997. "Preliminary Notes on the Audience in Africa." *Africa* 67 (3): 347–62.

Barnouw, Erik, and Subrahmanyam Krishnaswamy. (1963) 1980. *Indian Film*. New York: Oxford University Press.

Baskaran, Theodore S. 1981. *The Message Bearers: The Nationalist Politics and the Entertainment Media in South India, 1880–1945*. Madras: Cre-A.

Baumann, Carl-Friedrich. 1956. "Entwicklung und Anwerdung der Buhnenbeleuchtung seit der Mitte des 18 Jahrhundrets." PhD diss., University of Cologne.

Becker, Howard S. 1982. *Art Worlds*. Berkeley: University of California Press.

Becker, Howard S., Robert Faulkner, and Barbara Kirshenblatt-Gimblett. 2006. *Art from Start to Finish*. Chicago: University of Chicago Press.

Beeman, William O. 1993. "The Anthropology of Theater and Spectacle." *Annual Review of Anthropology* 22: 369–93.

Bestor, Theodore, 2004. *Tsukiji*. Berkeley: University of California Press.

Bhaktavatsala, M. 1997. "Romancing the Talkies." *Deccan Herald*. Friday, October, 17.

Bharucha, Rustom. 1994. On the Border of Fascism: Manufacture of Consent in Roja. *Economic and Political Weekly*, June 4, 1389–95.

Bhowmick, Someswar. 2009. *Cinema and Censorship: The Politics of Control in India*. New Delhi: Orient Blackswan.

Bird, Elizabeth. 1992. "Travels in Nowhere Land: Ethnography and the 'Impossible' Audience." *Critical Studies in Mass Communication* 9: 250–60.

Blumer, Herbert. (1933) 1970. *Movies and Conduct*. New York: Arno.

Booth, Gregory D. 1995. "Traditional Content and Narrative Structure in Hindi Commercial Cinema." *Asian Folklore Studies* 54: 169–90.

———. 2008. "Space, Sound, Auspiciousness, and Performance in North Indian Wedding Processions." In *South Asian Religion on Display: Religious Processions in South Asia and in the Diaspora*, edited by K. A. Jacobson, 63–76. London: Routledge.

———. 2009. *Behind the Curtain: Making Movies in Mumbai's Film Studios*. Oxford: Oxford University Press.

Bourdieu, Pierre. 1984. *Distinction: A Social Critique of the Judgment of Taste*. Translated by Richard Nice. Cambridge, MA: Harvard University Press.

Bose, Derek. 2006. *Brand Bollywood*. New Delhi: Sage.

Bottomore, Stephen. 1999. "The Panicking Audience? Early Cinema and the 'Train Effect.'" *Historical Journal of Film, Radio and Television* 19 (2): 177–216.

Boyle, Karen. 2009. "Attractions and Distractions: Mums, Babies and 'Early' Cinemagoing." *Participations* 6 (2): 260–83.

Brady, Neil F. 2002. "Lining Up for Star-Wars Tickets: Some Ruminations on Ethics and Economics Based on an Internet Study of Behavior in Queues." *Journal of Business Ethics* 38 (1/2): 157–65.

Breckenridge, Carol, ed. 1995. *Consuming Modernity: Public Culture in a South Asian World*. Minneapolis: University of Minnesota Press.

Brunsdon, Charlotte, and David Morley. 1978. *Everyday Television: Nationwide*. London: BFI.

Brunt, Rosalind. 1992. "Engaging with the Popular: Audiences for Mass Culture and What to Say About Them." In *Cultural Studies*, edited by Lawrence Grossberg, Cary Nelson, Paula A. Treichler, Linda Baughman, and John Macgregor Wise, 69–80. London: Routledge.

Callois, Roger. 1959. *Man and the Sacred*. Glencoe, IL: Free Press.

Caves, Richard E. 2000. *Creative Industries*. Cambridge, MA: Harvard University Press.

Certeau, Michel de. 1984. *The Practice of Everyday Life*. Berkeley: University of California Press.

Chakravarty, Sumita S. 1989. "National Identity and the Realist Aesthetic: Indian Cinema of the Fifties." *Quarterly Review of Film and Television* 11: 31–48.

———. 1993. *National Identity in Indian Popular Cinema, 1947–1987*. Austin: University of Texas Press.

Comolli, Jean-Louis. 1980. "Machines of the Visible." In *The Cinematic Apparatus*, edited by Teresa de Lauretis and Stephen Heath. New York: St. Martin's.

Consentino, Donald. 2004. "'My Heart Don't Stop': Haiti, the Carnival State." In *Carnival!*, edited by Barbara Mauldin, 93–120. Seattle: University of Washington Press.

Corbett, Kevin J. 1998. "Empty Seats: The Missing History of Movie-Watching." *Journal of Film and Video* 50 (4): 34–48.

Cruz, Jon, and Justin Lewis. 1994. *Viewing, Reading, Listening: Audiences and Cultural Reception*. San Francisco: Westview.

Curran, James. 1990. "The New Revisionism in Mass Communications Research: A Reappraisal." *European Journal of Communication* 5: 135–64.

Daniel, Valentine E. 1984. *Fluid Signs: Being a Person the Tamil Way*. Berkeley: University of California Press.

Das, Veena. 1980. "The Mythological Film and Its Framework of Meaning: An Analysis of Jai Santoshi Maa." *India International Centre Quarterly* 8 (1): 43–56.

Das Gupta, Chidananda. 1991. *The Painted Face: Studies in India's Popular Cinema*. New Delhi: Roli.

De, Aditi. 2008. *Multiple City, Writings on Bangalore*. New Delhi: Penguin.

Derne, Steve. 2000. *Movies, Masculinity and Modernity*. Westport, CT: Greenwood.

DeVault, Marjorie L. 2000. "Producing Family Time: Practices of Leisure Activity beyond the Home." *Qualitative Sociology* 23 (4): 485–503.

Dhareshwar, Vivek, and R. Srivatsan. 1996. "'Rowdy Sheeters': An Essay on Subalternity and Politics." *Subaltern Studies* 9: 201–31.

Diawara, Manthia. 1988. "Popular Culture and Oral Traditions in African Film." *Film Quarterly* 41: 6–14.

———. 1992. *African Cinema: Politics and Culture*. Bloomington: Indian University Press.

Dickey, Sara. 1993. *Cinema and the Urban Poor in South India*. Cambridge: Cambridge University Press.

———. 1995. "Consuming Utopia. Film Watching in Tamil Nadu." In *Consuming Modernity: Public Culture in a South Asian World*, edited by Carol A. Breckenridge, 131–56. Minneapolis: University of Minneapolis Press.

———. 1997. "Anthropology and Its Contribution to Studies of Mass Media." *International Social Science* 49 (3): 413–27.

———. 2000. "Permeable Homes: Domestic Service, Household Space, and the Vulnerability of Class Boundaries in Urban India." *American Ethnologist* 27 (2): 462–89.

———. 2006. Still "One Man in a Thousand." In *Living Pictures: Perspectives on the Film Poster in India*, edited by David Blamey and Robert E. D'Souza, 69–78. London: Open Editions.

Dissanayake, Wimal. 1997. "The Distinctiveness of Indian Cinema." In *Ananya: A Portrait of India*, edited by S. N. Sridhar and Nimal Mattoo,711–33. New York: Association of Indians in America.

Dissanayake, Wimal, and Malti Sahai, eds. 1992. *Sholay: A Cultural Reading*. New Delhi: Wiley Eastern.

Doane, Mary Ann. 1982. "Film and the Masquerade: Theorising the Female Spectator." *Screen* 23 (3/4): 74–87.

Douglas, Mary. 1966. *Purity and Danger: An Analysis of the Concepts of Pollution and Taboo*. London: Routledge.

Dudrah, Rajinder. 2006. *Bollywood: Sociology Goes to the Movies*. London: Sage.

Dunning, Eric, Patrick Murphy, and John Williams. 1986. Spectator Violence at Football Matches: Toward a Sociological Explanation. *British Journal of Sociology* 37 (2): 221–44.

Durkheim, Emile. (1912) 1995. *The Elementary Forms of Religious Life*. New York: Free Press.

Dwyer, Rachel. 2002. *Yash Chopra*. London: BFI.

Dwyer, Rachel, and Divia Patel. 2002. *Cinema India: The Visual Culture of Hindi Film*. London: Reaktion Books.

Edensor, Tim. 2000. "Walking in the British Countryside: Reflexivity, Embodied Practices and Ways to Escape." *Body and Society* 6 (3/4): 61–106.

Eleftheriosis, Dimitris. 2001. *Popular Cinemas of Europe: Studies of Texts, Contexts and Frameworks*. New York: Continuum.

Eliashberg, Jehoshua, Jedid-Jah Jonker, Mohanbir S. Sawhney, and Berend Wierenga. 2000. "MOVIEMOD: An Implementable Decision-Support System for Prerelease Market Evaluation of Motion Pictures." *Marketing Science* 19 (3): 226–43.

Eliashberg, Jehoshua, and Mohanbir S. Sawhney. 1994. "Modeling Goes to Hollywood: Predicting Individual Differences in Movie Enjoyment." *Management Science* 40 (9): 1151–73.

Elsaesser, Thomas. 1981. "Narrative Cinema and Audience-Oriented Aesthetics." In *Popular Television and Film*, edited by Tony Bennett, Susan Boyd-Bowman, Colin Mercer, and Janet Woollacott, 270–82. London: BFI.

Elsaesser, Thomas, and Adam Barker. 1990. *Early Cinema: Space, Frame, Narrative*, London: BFI.

Epstein, Edward J. 1998. "Multiplexities." *New Yorker*, July 13, pp. 34–37.

Evans, William. 1990. "The Interpretive Turn in Media Research: Innovation, Iteration, or Illusion?" *Critical Studies in Mass Communication* 7 (2): 147–68.

Faulkner, Robert R., and Andy B. Anderson. 1987. "Short Term Projects and Emergent Careers: Evidence from Hollywood." *American Journal of Sociology* 92 (4): 879–909.

Fiske, John. 1986. "Television, Polysemy and Popularity." *Critical Studies in Mass Communication* 7 (2): 147–68.

Fisher, Lawrence E. 1976. "Dropping Remarks and the Barbadian Audience." *American Ethnologist* 3 (2): 227–42.

Friedson, Elliot. 1952. "An Audience and Its Taste." PhD diss., University of Chicago.

———. 1953. "Communication Research and the Concept of the Mass." *American Sociological Review* 18 (3): 313–17.

———. 1954. "Consumption of Mass Media by Polish-American Children." *Quarterly Review of Film, Radio and Television* 9 (1): 92–101.

Fuller, Christopher J. 1992. *The Camphor Flame*. Princeton, NJ: Princeton University Press.

Fuller, Kathryn. 1990. "Boundaries of Participation: The Problem of Spectatorship and American Film Audiences, 1905–1930." *Film History* 20 (4): 75–86.

———. 1996. *At the Picture Show: Small-Town Audiences and the Creation of Movie Fan Culture*. Washington, DC: Smithsonian University Press.

Gabler, Neal. 1989. *An Empire of Their Own: How the Jews Invented Hollywood*. New York: Doubleday.

Gans, Herbert. 1999. *Popular Culture and High Culture: An Analysis and Evaluation of Taste*. New York: Basic Books.

Ganti, Tejaswini. 2004. *Bollywood: A Guidebook to Popular Hindi Cinema*. London: Routledge.

———. 2012. *Producing Bollywood*. Durham, NC: Duke University Press.

Gargi, Balwant. 1966. *Folk Theatre in India*. Seattle: University of Washington Press.

Geduld, Harry M., ed. 1971. *Focus on D. W. Griffith*. Englewood Cliffs, NJ: Prentice-Hall.

Geertz, Clifford. 1973. *The Interpretation of Cultures*. New York: Basic Books.

Geraghty, Christine. 2000. "Cinema as a Social Space: Understanding Cinema-Going in Britain, 1947–63." *Framework: The Journal of Cinema and Media*, 42. http://web.archive.org/web/20110122045222/http://www.frameworkonline.com/Issue42/42cg.html.

Ginsburg, Faye D. 2008. "Mass Media, Anthropology and Ethnography." In *The Sage Handbook of Film Studies*, edited by James Donald and Michael Renov, 216–25. London: Sage.

Gitlin, Todd. 2000. *Inside Primetime*. Berkeley: University of California Press.

Goffman, Erving. 1959. *The Presentation of Self in Everyday Life*. Garden City, NY: Doubleday.

———. 1963. *Behavior in Public Places*. New York: Free Press.

———. 1967. *Interaction Ritual*. New York: Pantheon Books.

———. 1974. *Frame Analysis*. Boston: Northeastern University Press.

Gokulsing, Moti K., and Wimal Dissanayake. 1998. *Indian Popular Cinema: A Narrative of Cultural Change*. London: Trentham Books.

Gomery, Douglas. 1982. "Movie Audiences, Urban Geography and the History of the American Film." *Velvet Light Trap* 19 (Spring): 23–29.

———. 1992. *Shared Pleasures: A History of Movie Presentation in the United States*. Madison: University of Wisconsin Press.

Goody, Jack. 1993. *The Culture of Flowers*. Cambridge: Cambridge University Press.

Gopalan, Lalitha. 2002. *Cinema of Interruptions*. London: BFI.

Gotham, Kevin Fox. 2005. "Theorizing Urban Spectacle: Festivals, Tourism and the Transformation of Urban Space." *City: Analysis of Urban Trends, Culture, Theory, Policy, Action* 9 (12): 225–46.

Grazian, David. 2008. *On the Make: The Hustle of Urban Nightlife*. Chicago: University of Chicago Press.

Grimaud, Emmanuel. 2004. Bollywood Film Studio: ou comment les films se font à Bombay. Paris: CNRS.

———. 2005. "Maps of Audiences: Bombay Films, the French Territory and the Making of an 'Oblique' Market." In *Globalizing India*, edited by Jackie Assayag and C. J. Fuller, 165–84. London: Anthem.

Grossberg, Lawrence. 1987. "The In-difference of Television." *Screen* 28 (2): 28–45.

Gunning, Tom. 1986. "The Cinema of Attraction: Early Film, Its Spectator and the Avant-Garde." *Wide Angle* 8 (3/4): 63–70.

———. 1989. "An Aesthetic of Astonishment: Early Film and the (In)credulous Spectator." *Art and Text* 34 (Spring): 31–45.

Guru, Gopal, and Sundar Sarukkai. 2012. *The Cracked Mirror. An Indian Debate on Experience and Theory*. New Delhi: Oxford University Press.

Hahn, Elizabeth. 1994. "The Tongan Tradition of Going to the Movies." *Visual Anthropology Review* 10: 103–11.

Hall, Stuart. 1973. *Encoding and Decoding in the Television Discourse*. Stencilled Paper No. 7. Birmingham: Centre for Contemporary Cultural Studies, University of Birmingham.

Handel, Leo. 1950. *Hollywood Looks at Its Audience*. Urbana: University of Illinois Press.

Hanich, Julian. 2010. *Cinematic Emotion in Horror Films and Thrillers*. London: Routledge.

Hannerz, Ulf. 1969. *Soulside: Inquiries into Ghetto Culture and Community*. New York: Columbia University Press.

———. 2004. *Foreign News: Exploring the World of Foreign Correspondents*. Chicago: University of Chicago Press.

———. 2010. Diversity Is Our Business. *American Anthropologist* 112 (4): 539–51.

Hansen, Miriam. 1991. *Babel and Babylon: Spectatorship in American Silent Film*. Cambridge, MA: Harvard University Press.

———. 1995. Early Cinema, Late Cinema: Permutations of the Public Sphere. In *Viewing Positions*, edited by Linda Williams, 134–52. New Brunswick, NJ: Rutgers University Press.

Hardgrave, Robert L. 1975. *When Stars Displace the Gods: The Folk Culture of Cinema in Tamil Nadu*. Arlington: Center for Asian Studies, University of Texas.

Hardgrave, Robert L., and Anthony C. Neidhart. 1975. "Film and Political Consciousness in Tamil Nadu." *Economic and Political Weekly* 10 (1/2): 27–35.

Hebdige, Dick. 1979. *Subculture: The Meaning of Style.* London: Methuen.

Hein, Norvin. 1959. "The Ram Lila." In *Traditional India: Structure and Change,* edited by M. Singer, 73–98. Philadelphia: American Folklore Society.

Heritage, John. 1984. *Garfinkel and Ethnomethodology.* Cambridge: Polity.

Hill, Annette. 1997. *Shocking Entertainment: Viewer Response to Violent Movies.* Luton: University of Luton Press.

Himpele, Jeffrey D. 1996. "Film Distribution as Media: Mapping Difference in the Bolivian Cinemascape." *Visual Anthropology Review* 12 (1): 47–66.

Hirsch, Paul M. 1972. "Processing Fads and Fashions: An Organizational Set Analysis of Cultural Industry Systems." *American Journal of Sociology* 77 (4): 639–59.

Hoek, Lotte. 2013. *Cut-Pieces: Celluloid Obscenity and Popular Cinema in Bangladesh.* New York: Columbia University Press.

Horkheimer, Max. 1941. "Art and Mass Culture." *Studies in Philosophy and Social Science* 9 (2): 290–304.

Hubbard, Phil. 2002. "Screen-Shifting: Consumption, 'Riskless Risks' and the Changing Geographies of Cinema." *Environment and Planning A* 34 (7): 1239–58.

———. 2003a. Fear and Loathing at the Multiplex: Everyday Anxiety in the Post-industrial City. *Capital and Class* 27 (2): 51–75.

———. 2003b. "A Good Night Out? Multiplex Cinemas as Sites of Embodied Leisure." *Leisure Studies* 22: 255–72.

Hughes, Everett C. 1971. "Good People and Dirty Work." In *The Sociological Eye,* 87–97. Chicago: Aldine-Atherton.

Hughes, Stephen P. 1996. "The Pre-Phalke Era in South India: Reflections on the Formation of Film Audiences in Madras." *South Indian Studies* 2: 161–204.

———. 1997. "Is There Anybody Out There?: Exhibition and the Formation of Silent Film Audiences in South India." PhD diss., University of Chicago.

———. 2000. "Policing Silent Film Exhibition in Colonial South India." In *Making Meaning in Indian Cinema,* edited by R. Vasudevan, 39–64. New Delhi: Oxford University Press.

———. 2003. "Pride of Place." *Seminar* 525: 1–9. http://www.india-seminar.com/2003/525/525%20stephen%20p.%20hughes.htm.

———. 2011. "Anthropology and the Problem of Audience Reception." In *Made to Be Seen: Perspectives on the History of Visual Anthropology,* edited by M. Banks and J. Ruby, 288–312. Chicago: University of Chicago Press.

Huizinga, Johan. 1955. *Homo Ludens: A Study of the Play-Element in Culture.* Boston: Beacon.

Inden, Ronald. 1999. "Transnational Class, Erotic Arcadia and Commercial Utopia in Hindi Films." In *Image Journeys: Audio-Visual Media and Cultural Change in India,* edited by Christiane Brosius and Melissa Butcher, 41–68. New Delhi: Sage.

Jacob, Preminda. 1998. "Media Spectacles: The Production and Reception of Tamil Cinema Advertisements." *Visual Anthropology* 11 (4): 287–322.

———. 2009. *Celluloid Deities: The Visual Culture of Cinema and Politics in South India.* Lanham, MD: Lexington Books.

Jancovich, Mark, Lucy Faire, and Sarah Stubbings. 2003. *The Place of the Audience: Cultural Geographies of Film Consumption*. London: BFI.

Jensen, Karl B., and K. E. Rosengren, 1990. "Five Traditions in Search of the Audience." *European Journal of Communication* 5: 207–38.

Johnson, James H. 1995. *Listening in Paris: A Cultural History*. Berkeley: University of California Press.

Jowett, Garth, and James Linton M. 1980. *Movies as Mass Communication*. Beverly Hills, CA: Sage.

Kabir, Nasreen M. 2001. *Bollywood: The Indian Cinema Story*. London: Channel 4 Books.

Kakar, Sudhir. 1980. "The Ties that Bind: Family Relationships in the Mythology of Hindi Cinema." *India International Centre Quarterly* 8 (1): 11–21.

Kalyan Raman, N. 1985. "The City and the World: Bangalore's Tangled Web." In *Beantown Boomtown*, edited by Jayanth Kodkani and R. Edwin Sudhir, 20–30, Delhi: Rupa.

Katz, Elihu, and Paul F. Lazarsfeld. 1955. *Personal Influence: The Part Played by People in the Flow of Mass Communications*. Glencoe, IL: Free Press.

Katz, Jack. 1988. *The Seductions of Crime*. New York: Basic Books.

———. 1996. "Families and Funny Mirrors: A Study of the Social Construction and Personal Embodiment of Humor." *American Journal of Sociology* 101 (5): 1194–237.

———. 1999. *How Emotions Work*. Chicago: University of Chicago Press.

Katz-Gerro, Tally. 1999. "Cultural Consumption and Social Stratification: Leisure Activities, Musical Tastes, and Social Location." *Sociological Perspectives* 42 (4): 627–46.

Kaviraj, Sudipta. 1997. "Filth and the Public Sphere: Concepts and Practice about Space in Calcutta." *Public Culture* 10 (1): 83–113.

Kazmi, Fareed. 1999. *The Politics of India's Conventional Cinema*. New Delhi: Sage.

Keil, Charles. 1966. *Urban Blues*. Chicago: University of Chicago Press.

Kelly, John R. 1975. "Leisure Decisions: Exploring Intrinsic and Role-Related Orientations." *Society and Leisure* 7: 45–61.

———. 1978. "Situational and Social Factors in Leisure Decisions." *Pacific Sociological Review* 21: 313–30.

Kesavan, Mukul. 1995. "Changing Pictures." *India Magazine of Her People and Culture*, October, 6–11.

Kirshenblatt-Gimblett, Barbara. 1998. *Destination Culture: Tourism, Museums, and Heritage*. Berkeley: University of California Press.

Klinger, Barbara. 1994. *Melodrama and Meaning: History, Culture, and the Films of Douglas Sirk*. Bloomington: Indiana University Press.

———. 1997. "Film History: Terminable and Interminable: Recovering the Past in Reception Studies. *Screen* 38 (2): 107–28.

Kohli-Khandekar, Vanita. 2006. *The Indian Media Business*. New Delhi: Sage.

Kratz, Corinne A. 1994. *Affecting Performance: Meaning, Movement and Experience in Okrek Women's Initiation*. Washington DC: Smithsonian Institution Press.

Kuhn, Annette. 2002. *An Everyday Magic: Cinema and Cultural Memory*. London: Tauris.

Larkin, Brian. 1997. "Indian Films and Nigerian Lovers: Media and the Creation of Parallel Modernities." *Africa* 67 (3): 406–38.

———. 1998. "Theaters of the Profane: Cinema and Colonialism." *Visual Anthropology Review*, 14 2: 46–62.

———. 2008. *Signal and Noise: Media, Infrastructure, and Urban Culture in Nigeria*. Durham, NC: Duke University Press.

Lecuyer, Hélène. 2013. "The Review of Creative Industries and Media." *INA Global*, November 26.

Levine, Lawrence W. 1988. *Highbrow, Lowbrow*. Cambridge, MA: Harvard University Press.

Liebes, Tamar, and Elihu Katz. 1990. *The Export of Meaning: Cross-cultural Readings of Dallas*. Oxford: Oxford University Press.

Lindlof, Thomas R. 1987. *Natural Audiences: Qualitative Research of Media Uses and Effects*. New York: Ablex.

———. 2012. "Media Audiences as Interpretive Communities." In *Communication Yearbook 11*, edited by J. A. Anderson, 81–107. New York: Routledge.

Liu, Yong. 2006. "Word of Mouth for Movies: Its Dynamics and Impact on Box Office Revenue." *Journal of Marketing* 70: 74–89.

Lofgren, Orvar. 2002. *On Holiday: A History of Vacationing*. Berkeley: University of California Press.

Lull, James. 1987. "*Critical Response*: Audience Texts and Contexts." *Critical Studies in Mass Communication* 4 (3): 318–22.

———, ed. 1988. *World Families Watch Television*. London: Sage.

———. 1990. *Inside Family Viewing*. London: Routledge.

Lutgendorf, Phillip. 1991. "Words Made Flesh: The Banaras Ram Lila as Epic Commentary." In *Boundaries of the Text: Epic Performances in South and Southeast Asia*, edited by Joyce Burkhalter-Flueckiger and Laurie Sears, 83–104. Ann Arbor: University of Michigan, Center for the Study of South and Southeast Asian Studies.

Lynch, Owen M. 1990. *Divine Passions: The Social Construction of Emotions in India*. Berkeley: University of California Press.

Madhava Prasad, M. 1998. *Ideology of the Hindi Film: A Historical Construction*. New Delhi: Oxford University Press.

Mankekar, Purnima. 1999. *Screening Culture, Viewing Politics*. Durham, NC: Duke University Press.

———. 2002. "National Texts and Gendered Lives: An Ethnography of Television Viewers in a North Indian City." In *The Anthropology of Media: A Reader*, edited by Kelly Askew and Richard Wilk, 299–322. London: Blackwell.

Mann, Leon. 1969. "Queue Culture: The Waiting Line as a Social System." *American Journal of Sociology* 75 (3): 340–53.

Marcus, George E. 1998. *Ethnography through Thick and Thin*. Princeton, NJ: Princeton University Press.

Masselos, Jim. 1991. "Appropriating Urban Space: Social Constructs of Bombay in the Time of the Raj." *South Asia* 14 (1): 33–63.

May, Lary. 1980. *Screening Out the Past: The Birth of Mass Culture and the Motion Picture Industry*. Chicago: University of Chicago Press.

Mayne, Judith. 1993. *Cinema and Spectatorship*. London: Routledge.

Mazzarella, William. 2013. *Censorium: Cinema and the Open Edge of Mass Publicity*. Durham, NC: Duke University Press.

McEachern, Charmaine. 1998. "A Mutual Interest? Ethnography in Anthropology and Cultural Studies." *Australian Journal of Anthropology* 9 (3): 251–64.

McQuail, Denis. 1997. *Audience Analysis*. London: Sage.

Metz, Christian. 1974. *Film Language: A Semiotics of the Cinema*. Translated by Michael Taylor. New York: New York University Press.

Miller, David, and Greg Philo. 2001. "The Active Audience and Wrong Turns in Media Studies." *Soundscapes* 4. http://www.icce.rug.nl/~soundscapes/VOLUME04/Active_audience .shtml.

Mishra, Pankaj. 1995. *Butter Chicken in Ludhiana: Travels in Small Town India*. New Delhi: Penguin Books India.

Mishra, Vijay. 2002. *Bollywood Cinema: Temples of Desire*. New York: Routledge.

Mittman, Barbara G. 1984. *Spectators on the Paris Stage in the Seventeenth and Eighteenth Centuries*. Ann Arbor, MI: UMI Research Press.

Moores, Shaun. 1993. *Interpreting Audiences: The Ethnography of Mass Consumption*. London: Sage.

Morley, David. 1980. *The Nationwide Audience: Structure and Decoding*. London: BFI.

———. 1986. *Family Television*. London: Comedia.

———. 1990. "Changing Paradigms in Audience Studies." In *Remote Control*, edited by Ellen Seiter et al., 16–43. London: Routledge.

———. 1992. "Towards an Ethnography of the Television Audience." In *Television, Audiences and Cultural Studies*, edited by David Morley, chap. 8, pp. 166–88. London: Routledge.

Morley, David, and Roger Silverstone. 1990. "Domestic Consumption." In *Media, Culture and Society* 12 (1): 31–56.

Moul, Charles C., and Steven M. Shugan. 2005. "Theatrical Release and the Launching of Motion Pictures." In *A Concise Handbook of Movie Industry Economics*, edited by C. C. Moul, 80–137. Cambridge: Cambridge University Press.

Mulvey, Laura. 1973. "Visual Pleasure and Narrative Cinema." *Screen* 16 (3): 6–18.

Musser, Charles. 1983. "The Nickelodeon Era Begins: Establishing the Framework for Hollywood's Mode of Representation." *Framework* 22/23 (Autumn): 4–11.

Nair, Janaki. 2005. *The Promise of the Metropolis*. New Delhi: Oxford University Press.

Nandy, Ashis. 1981. "The Popular Hindi Film: Ideology and First Principles." *India International Centre Quarterly* 8 (1): 89–96.

———. 1998. *The Secret Politics of Our Desires: Innocence, Culpability and Indian Popular Cinema*. New Delhi: Zed Books.

Narayan, K. 1993. How Native Is a "Native" Anthropologist? *American Anthropologist*, n.s., 95 (3): 671–86.

Nasaw, David. 1999. *Going Out: The Rise and Fall of Public Amusements*. Cambridge: Harvard University Press.

Niranjana, Tejaswini. 1994. Interrogating Whose Nation? Tourists and Terrorists in Roja. *Economic and Political Weekly*, January 15, 79–82.

Nisbett, Nicholas. 2009. *Growing Up in the Knowledge Society*. London: Routledge.

Ogihara, Junko. 1990. "The Exhibition of Films for Japanese Americans in Los Angeles during the Silent Film Era." *Film History* 4 (2): 81–87.

Ohmann, Richard. 1996. *Making and Selling Culture*. Hanover, NH: University Press of New England.

Okome, Oonokome, and Jonathan Haynes. 1995. *Cinema and Social Change in West Africa*. Jos, Nigeria: Nigerian Film Corporation.

Ortner, Sherry B. 2003. *New Jersey Dreaming*. Durham, NC: Duke University Press.

———. 2010. "Access: Reflections on Studying Up in Hollywood." *Ethnography* 11 (2): 211–33.

———. 2013. *Not Hollywood: Independent Film at the Twilight of the American Dream*. Durham, NC: Duke University Press.

Pandian, M. S. S. 1992. *The Image Trap*. New Delhi: Sage.

———. 1996. "Tamil Cultural Elites and Cinema." *Economic and Political Weekly*, April 13, 950–55.

Pani, Narendar, Tara Srinivas, and Vinod Vyasulu. 1985. "Impact of Colonialism on the Economic Structure of Indian Cities: Bangalore 1800–1900." In *Essays on Bangalore*, vol. 1, edited by Vinod Vyasulu and Amulya Reddy, 1–34. Bangalore: Karnataka State Council for Science and Technology.

Papp, Joseph, and Elizabeth Kirkland. 1988. *Shakespeare Alive*. New York: Bantam.

Paul, William. 1994. "The K-Mart Audience at the Mall Movies." *Film History* 6 (4): 487–501.

Pfleiderer, Beatrix, and Lothar Lutze. 1985. *The Hindi Film: Agent and Re-agent of Cultural Change*. New Delhi: Manohar.

Powdermaker, Hortense. 1962. "Going to the Movies." In *Copper Town: Changing Africa*, 254–71. New York: Harper and Row.

Press, Andrea. 1996. "Toward a Qualitative Methodology of Audience Study." In *The Audience and its Landscape*, edited by James Hay et al., 113–30. Oxford: Westview.

———. 1991. *Women Watching Television*. Philadelphia: University of Pennsylvania Press.

Punathambekar, Aswin. 2008. "'We're Online, not on the Streets': Indian Cinema, New Media, and Participatory Culture." In *Global Bollywood*, edited by Anandam P. Kavoori and Aswin Punathambekar, 282–99. New York: New York University Press.

Radway, Janice A. 1984. *Reading the Romance*. Chapel Hill: University of North Carolina Press.

———. 1988. "Reception Study: Ethnography and the Problems of Dispersed Audiences and Nomadic Subjects." *Cultural Studies* 2: 359–76.

Raghavendra, M. K. 2008. *Seduced by the Familiar: Narrative and Meaning in Indian Popular Cinema*. New Dehli: Oxford University Press.

Rai, Amit S. 2009. *Untimely Bollywood*. Durham, NC: Duke University Press.

Rajadhyaksha, Ashish. 1986. "Neo-Traditionalism: Film as Popular Art in India." *Framework* 32/33: 20–67.

———. 1993. "The Pre-Phalke Era: Conflict of Traditional Form and Modern Technology." In *Interrogating Modernity: Culture and Colonialism in India*, edited by Tejaswini Niranjana et al., 47–82. Delhi: Seagull.

———. 1994. "India's Silent Cinema: A 'Viewer's View.'" In *Light of Asia: Indian Silent Cinema, 1912–1934*. Pune: National Film Archive of India.

———. 2003. The Bollywoodization of Indian Cinema: Cultural Nationalism in a Global Arena. *Inter-Asia Cultural Studies* 4 (1): 25–39.

Rajadhyaksha, Ashish, and Paul Willemen. 1999. *The Encyclopedia of Indian Cinema*. New Delhi: Oxford University Press.

Ramachandran, T. M. 1985. *70 Years of Indian Cinema (1913–1983)*. Bombay: Cinema India-International.

Raman, A. 1994. *Bangalore-Mysore: A Disha Guide*. Bangalore: Sangam Books.

Reimer, Jeffrey M. 1977. "Varieties of Opportunistic Research." *Urban Life* 4 (5): 467–77.

Reisman, David, and Evelyn T. Reisman. 1952. "Movies and Audiences." *American Quarterly* 4 (3): 195–202.

Reisman, Karl. 1974. "Contrapuntal Conversations in an Antiguan Village." In *Explorations in the Ethnography of Speaking*, edited by Richard Bauman and J. Sherzer, 110–124. London: Cambridge University Press.

Rosenberg, Bernard, and David Manning White. 1957. *Mass Culture*. Glencoe, IL: Free Press.

Rosenzweig, Roy. 1983. *Eight Hours for What We Will: Workers and Leisure in an Industrial City, 1870–1920*. Cambridge: Cambridge University Press.

Schechner, Richard. 1993. *The Future of Ritual*. London: Routledge.

Schivelbusch, Wolfgang. 1988. *Disenchanted Night*. Berkeley: University of California Press.

Schutz, Alfred, 1962. *On Multiple Realities*. Vol. 1 of *Collected Papers*. The Hague: M. Nijhoff.

———. 1964. *Collected Papers*, vol. 2, 64–90. The Hague: M. Nijhoff.

Schwartz, Vanessa R. 1995. "Cinematic Spectatorship before the Apparatus: The Public Taste for Reality in Fin-de-Siecle Paris." In *Cinema and the Invention of Modern Life*, edited by Leo Charney and Vanessa R. Schwartz, 297–399. Berkeley: University of California, Press.

Seiter, Ellen, Hans Borchers, Gabriele Kreutzner, and Eva-Maria Warth. 1989. *Remote Control: Television, Audiences and Cultural Power*. London: Routledge.

Seizer, Susan. 2000. "Roadwork: Offstage with Special Drama Actresses in Tamilnadu, South India." *Cultural Anthropology* 5 (2): 217–59.

Sharma, Aparna. 2003. India's Experience with the Multiplex, *Seminar*, 525. Access through http://www.india-seminar.com/semframe.html.

Shively, JoEllen. 1992. "Cowboys and Indians: Perceptions of Western Films among American Indians and Anglos." *American Sociological Review* 7 (6): 725–34.

Silverstone, Roger. 1994. *Television and Everyday Life*. London: Routledge.

Simmel, Georg. 1949. "The Sociology of Sociability." *American Journal of Sociology* 55 (3): 245–61.

———. 1950. *The Sociology of Georg Simmel*. Translated by Kurt Wolff. Glencoe, IL: Free Press.

Singer, Ben. 1995. "Manhattan Nickelodeons: New Data on Audiences and Exhibitors." *Cinema Journal* 34 (3): 5–35.

Singer, Milton. 1959. *Traditional India: Structure and Change*. Philadelphia: American Folklore Society.

Sivathamby, Karthigesu. 1981. *The Tamil Film as a Medium of Political Communication*. Madras: New Century Book House.

Sklar, Robert. 1975. *Movie-Made America: A Social History of American Movies*. New York: Random House.

Slater, Don. 1997. *Consumer Culture and Modernity.* Cambridge: Polity.

Sobchack, Vivian. 1992. *The Address of the Eye: A Phenomenology of Film Experience.* Princeton, NJ: Princeton University Press.

———. 1999. "Toward a Phenomenology of Non-fictional Experience." In *Collecting Visible Evidence,* edited by M. Renov and J, Gaines, 241–54. Minneapolis: University of Minnesota Press.

Spitulnik, Debra. 1993. "Anthropology and the Mass Media." *Annual Review of Anthropology* 22: 293–315.

———. 2002. "Mobile Machines and Fluid Audiences: Rethinking Reception through Zambian Radio Culture." In *Media Worlds,* edited F. Ginsburg et al., 337–54. Berkeley: University of California Press.

Srinivas, Lakshmi. 1998. "Active Viewing: An Ethnography of the Cinematic Experience." *Visual Anthropology* 11 (4): 323–53.

———. 2002. "The Active Audience: Spectatorship, Social Relations and the Experience of Cinema in India." *Media Culture and Society* 24 (2): 155–73.

———. 2005. "Imaging the Audience." *South Asian Popular Culture* 3 (2): 101–16.

———. 2010a. "Cinema in the City: Tangible Forms, Transformations and the Punctuation of Everyday Life." *Visual Anthropology* 23 (1): 1–12.

———. 2010b. "Cinema Halls, Locality and Urban Life." *Ethnography* 11 (1): 189–205.

———. 2010c. "Ladies Queues, 'Roadside Romeos' and Balcony Seating: Ethnographic Observations on Women's Cinemagoing Experiences." *South Asian Popular Culture* (8) (3): 291–307.

———. 2013. "Active Audiences and the Experience of Cinema." In *Routledge Handbook of Indian Cinemas,* edited by Moti Gokulsing and Wimal Dissanayake, 377–90. London: Routledge.

Srinivas, M. N. 1966. *Social Change in Modern India.* Berkeley: University of California Press.

———. (1966) 2002. *Collected Essays.* New Delhi: Oxford University Press.

———. 1976. *The Remembered Village.* Berkeley: University of California Press.

Srinivas, Smiriti. 2001. *Landscapes of Urban Memory.* Minnesota: University of Minnesota Press.

Srinivas, S. V. 2000a. "Devotion and Defiance in Fan Activity." In *Making Meaning in Indian Cinema,* edited by Ravi Vasudevan ed., 297–317. New Delhi: Oxford University Press.

———. 2000b. "Is There a Public in the Cinema Hall?" *Framework* 42. http:www.sarai.net/research/media-city/resources/film-city-essays/sv_srinivas.pdf (no longer posted.)

———. 2003. "Hong Kong Action Film in the Indian B Circuit." *Inter-Asia Cultural Studies* 4 (1): 40–62.

———. 2009. *Megastar Chiranjeevi and Telugu Cinema after N.T. Rama Rao.* New Delhi: Oxford University Press.

Stacey, Jackie. 1994. *Star Gazing: Hollywood Cinema and Female Spectatorship.* London: Routledge.

Staiger, Janet. 1992. *Interpreting Films: Studies in Historical Reception of American Films.* Princeton, NJ: Princeton University Press.

———. 2000. *Perverse Spectators: The Practices of Film Reception.* New York: New York University Press.

Stam, Robert. 1989. *Subversive Pleasures: Bakhtin, Cultural Criticism, and Film.* Parallax: Revisions of Culture and Society. Baltimore: Johns Hopkins University Press.

Stoller, Paul. 1989. *The Taste of Ethnographic Things.* Philadelphia: University of Pennsylvania Press.

———. 1996. "Spaces, Places, and Fields: The Politics of West African Trading in New York City's Informal Economy." *American Anthropologist* 98 (4): 776–88.

Thissen, Judith. 1999. "Jewish Immigrant Audiences in New York City (1905–1914)." In *American Movie Audiences from the Turn of the Century to the Early Sound Era,* edited by M. Stokes and R. Maltby, 15–28. London: BFI.

Thomas, Rosie. 1985. Indian Cinema: Pleasures and Popularity. *Screen* 26 (3/4): 116–31.

———. 1995. Melodrama and the Negotiation of Morality in Mainstream Hindi Film. In *Consuming Modernity: Public Culture in a South Asian World,* edited by Carol Breckenridge, 157–81. Minnesota: University of Minnesota Press.

Thoraval, Yves. 2001. *The Cinemas of India.* Chennai: Macmillan India.

Traudt, Paul J., James A. Anderson, and Timothy P. Meyer. 1987. "Phenomenology, Empiricism and Media Experience." *Critical Studies in Mass Communication* 4 (3): 302–10.

Turner, Victor. 1982. *From Ritual to Theatre: The Human Seriousness of Play.* New York: Performing Arts Journal Publications.

Uberoi, Patricia. 2001. "Imagining the Family: An Ethnography of Viewing Hum Aapke Hain Kaun . . . !" In *Pleasure and the Nation,* edited by Rachel Dwyer and Christopher Pinney, 309–51. New Delhi: Oxford University Press.

Van der Veer, Peter. 1992. "Playing or Praying: A Sufi Saint's Day in Surat." *Journal of Asian Studies* 51 (3): 545–64.

Varma, Pavan K. 1998. *The Great Indian Middle Class.* New Delhi: Penguin Books.

Vasudev, Aruna, ed. 1995. *Frames of Mind: Reflections on Indian Cinema.* New Delhi: UBS.

Vasudevan, Ravi. 1990. "Indian Commercial Cinema." *Screen* 31 (4): 446–53.

———. 1991. "The Cultural Space of a Film Narrative: Interpreting Kismet (Bombay Talkies, 1943)." *Indian Economic and Social History Review* 28 (2): 171–85.

———. 1999. "Addressing the Spectator of a 'Third World' National Cinema: The Bombay 'Social' Film of the 1940s and 1950s." *Screen* 36 (4): 305–24.

———, ed. 2000. *Making Meaning in Indian Cinema.* New Delhi: Oxford University Press.

———. 2003. Cinema in Urban Space. *Seminar.* http://www.india-seminar.com/2003/525/525%20ravi%20vasudevan.htm.

Wacquant, Loic. 2004. *Body and Soul.* New York: Oxford University Press.

Waller, Gregory A. 1992. "Another Audience: Black Movie-going, 1907–16." *Cinema Journal* 31 (2): 3–25.

———. 1995. *Main Street Amusements: Movies and Commercial Entertainment in a Southern City, 1896–1930.* Washington DC: Smithsonian Institution Press.

West, Candace, and Don Zimmerman H. 1987. "Doing Gender." *Gender and Society* 1: 125–51.

Williams, Linda. 1995. *Viewing Positions: Ways of Seeing Film.* New Brunswick, NJ: Rutgers University Press.

Willis, Paul, 1980. "Notes on Method." In *Culture, Media, Language,* edited by Stuart Hall, Dorothy Hobson, Andrew Lowe, and Paul Willis, 88–95. London: Hutchinson.

Willis, Paul, and Mats Trondman. 2000. "Manifesto for Ethnography." *Ethnography* 1 (1): 5–16.

Wilson, John. 1980. Sociology of Leisure. *Annual Review of Sociology* 6: 21–40.

Wolff, Kurt. 1964. "Surrender and Community Study: The Study of Loma." In *Reflections on Community Studies*, edited by Arthur J. Vidich and Joseph Bensman, 233–63. New York: Wiley.

Zelnick, Strauss. 1996. "Twentieth Century Fox." In *Making and Selling Culture*, edited by Richard Ohmann, 19–33. Hanover, NH: University Press of New England.

INDEX

A (1998), 64, 125, 172–73
Aaptha Mitra (2004), 136
Aaptha Rakshaka (2010), 136, 197–98
Abhinay theater, 77, 81, 84, 103–4, *105*, 113–14, 121–22, 137
Abu-Lughod, Lila, 19
Achanak (1973), 83
active audience, 2–3, 159–88; in Bangalore, 6; in India, 3; live film experience associated with, 236; mainstream reception aesthetic complicated by, 9; in process of crafting film, 19, 24, 218; in questioning meaning and nature of film, 10; for studying reception in situ, 19; this study and works on, 20
actuality films, 227
adult films, 85, 131, 133
adventure, cinemagoing as, 146, 147, 148
advertising, 41, 42–43, 82, 86, 159
aesthetics: of active viewing, 3, 6, 19; audience, 17, 24, 27; carnival, 190, 217; changes in Indian cinema and, 235; conflicts of, 58, 181–82, 183, 268n102; decent films and, 51; devotional, 218; of documentary viewing, 168; of festival, 202–4, 231; of folk entertainment forms, 61; improvisational, 36; interactive, 161, 168; of live entertainment,

168; local, 190, 224, 231; of looking ahead, 176; participatory, 1, 3, 38, 162, 175, 224; popular, 52; reception, 6, 9, 17, 19, 166, 186–88; of repeat viewing, 174; of selective viewing, 165; of sightseeing, 167; social, 51, 160, 162, 168; versus the social, 130, 159; of spectatorship, 188; of street and marketplace, 170; varying forms of aesthetic engagement, 8, 13, 158; viewing, 164, 182; Western, 226
Agni Sakshi (1982), 165
Air Force One (1997), 120, 151, 161, 171, 176, 177–78, 180
Akasmika (1993), 83
Altman, Robert, 38
Amanush (1975), 83
America! America! (1995), 48, 77, 81, 185
Amruthavarshini (1996), 53
Andamans (1998), 106, 196, 217
Andhra Pradesh, 6, 8, 195, 223
Anjali (architect), 108, 134, 135, 156
Anne of the Thousand Days (1969), 79
Anthony (school administrator), 133, 139, 182
anticipatory viewing, 176–77
Appadurai, Arjun, 7
apparatus theory, 241n54

"mommy matinees," 158, 263n99; in movie routines, 150; reasons for preferring, 141; women buying their own tickets for, 133

Matthews, Chris, 225, 267n76

media audience research, 241n59

media effects research, 49

media studies, ethnographic turn in, 19. *See also* cinema studies

Megha Bantu Megha (1998), 48, 125, 159, 184

"Mehbooba" (song), 222

Menaka theater, *68*, 109, 136

Metz, Christian, 241n54

mezzanine, 116, 118

MGR. *See* Ramachandran, M. G. (MGR)

M. G. Road (Mahatma Gandhi Road): in the Cantonment, 66; as entertainment district, 68; location and deciding to attend cinema on, 74; movie theaters on, 67, 72, 77, 78–79, 84, 98, 142; Shivarajkumar unrecognized in, 92

middle class: alone at the cinema, 133; anglicized Cantonment lifestyle of, 5; Bangalore as, 6; and black-market tickets, 113; in Cantonment, 68, 69, 74; A class films for, 50; concern over loss of middle-class audience, 55; economic incentive for appealing to, 58; as expanding, 232; family movie outings, 151–53; fieldwork for this study, 27, 28; film preferences of, 65, 75–77; and first-day audiences, 193–94; on front benchers, 163; groups book seats together, 140; Hollywood film professionals as, 33–34; Indian filmmakers and, 34; "inside" spaces created in theaters by, 154–55; liberalization reforms and, 40; markers of, 64; movie treats among, 150–51; multiplexes associated with, 9, 91, 109, 158, 234, 258n53; narration of movie event as adventure for, 147; nonresident Indian audience compared with, 54; parking as concern of, 94; prejudice against the City in, 67; on raucous audiences, 183; seating preferences of, 113–14, 117, 118–21, 123, 125, 126, 127, 128; sophisticated fare preferred

by, 52; in theater condition debate, 89–90; theater prestige associated with, 82; ticket purchase negotiated by, 106–7; in ticket queues, 99, 100–101; ticket queues avoided by, 107, 108–9; as unaware of processions, 207; "using pull" to acquire tickets, 109, 111

mindscapes, 79–80, 92

minibalcony, 113, 114, 115, 118, 125

Minnasare (2010), 136, 150

Mittman, Barbara, 130–31, 171, 264n15

mobile phones (cellphones), 99, 139, 165

Mohan, Mr. (theater manager), 111

mood: audience in shaping of, 187; during intermission, 141; in movie outings, 136–38; of the new release, 190–94; play and, 162, 182; of repeat viewers, 174, 175

Morley, David, 243n97

movies. *See* cinema

movie talk, 26–27, 131, 171

movie theaters: as attraction, 15, 84; audiences negotiate exhibition setting, 94–129; in Bangalore, 5, 69–73, *71*, 85; on Brigade Road, 78, 85, 98, 151; in Cantonment, *70*, 72, 74, 79; chains, 228, 276n27; characteristics of early, 15, 226; charms to ward off evil eye, *46*, 203; concessions, 26, 94, 118, 142–43, 156, 256n3; crisis in infrastructure, 85–91, 254n74; dangers and discomforts of, 154; disappearance of old single-run theaters, 78; diversity of owners and managers, 34–35; film experience and conditions in, 86–91; films screened associated with theater conditions, 85; folklore surrounding particular, 83–84; in Gandhinagar, 66, 67, 103, 209; give off signs, 82; indoor gardens in, 84–85; "inside" spaces created in, 154–55; late arrivals, 121, 138, 171, 266n57; lavish picture palaces, 227; as less localized and individualized, 228; location and decision to attend, 74–75; lucky, 46–47, 81; in Majestic district, 66, 72, 79, 136, 137, 252n25; meaning of, 69–75; minimizing awareness of theater